DATE DUE

NO 27 '95			
DE 3 '97			
MY 8 '00			
JE 11 '03			
NO 3 '05			
NO 28 05			

DEMCO 38-296

Rethinking the Family

Prepared under the auspices of
The Institute for Research on Women and Gender
Stanford University

Rethinking the Family

Revised Edition

Some Feminist Questions

Edited by BARRIE THORNE
with MARILYN YALOM

NORTHEASTERN UNIVERSITY PRESS
BOSTON

Northeastern University Press

Library of Congress Cataloging-in-Publication Data

Rethinking the family : some feminist questions / edited by Barrie
 Thorne with Marilyn Yalom.—Rev. ed.
  p. cm.
 Includes bibliographical references and index.
  ISBN 1–55553–144–X (alk. paper)—ISBN 1–55553–145–8
(pbk. : alk. paper)
  1. Family—United States. 2. Feminism—United States.
I. Thorne, Barrie. II. Yalom, Marilyn.
 HQ536.R454 1992
 306.85'0973—dc20   92–20761

Designed by Lisa Diercks

Composed in Sabon by BookMasters, Ashland, Ohio.
Printed and bound by Edwards Brothers, Inc., Ann Arbor,
Michigan. The paper is Glatfelter Offset, an acid-free sheet.

MANUFACTURED IN THE UNITED STATES OF AMERICA
97 96 95 94 93 92   5 4 3 2 1

In memory of Shelly Rosaldo, our friend and colleague,

whose intellectual presence infuses this book

Contents

About the Authors

NANCY CHODOROW is Professor of Sociology at the University of California, Berkeley. She is the author of *The Reproduction of Mothering: Psychoanalysis and the Sociology of Gender* and *Feminism and Psychoanalytic Theory*. She is an Advanced Candidate at the San Francisco Psychoanalytic Institute and has a private practice in Berkeley.

JANE COLLIER is Professor of Anthropology at Stanford University. She has done research on conflict management among Maya Indians in Southern Mexico, and on family change among peasants in Southern Spain. Her most recent book is *Marriage and Inequality in Classless Societies*.

PATRICIA HILL COLLINS is Associate Professor in the Departments of Sociology and African-American Studies at the University of Cincinnati. She is the author of *Black Feminist Thought: Knowledge, Consciousness, and the Politics of Empowerment*, as well as many articles on gender, race, and ethnicity, and a coeditor, with Margaret Andersen, of *Race, Class and Gender*.

SUSAN CONTRATTO is a feminist psychologist in private practice in Ann Arbor, Michigan. She is also a Visiting Scholar in the Women's Studies Program at the University of Michigan, where she has taught in both Women's Studies and Psychology.

MICAELA DI LEONARDO is Associate Professor of Anthropology and Women's Studies and Fellow at the Center for Urban Affairs at Northwestern University. She has written *The Varieties of Ethnic Experience* and edited *Gender at the Crossroads of Knowledge: Feminist Anthropology in the Postmodern Era*. She is finishing *Exotics at Home*, essays on race, class, and gender in America.

WILLIAM GOODE has taught at Columbia University, where he was Giddings Professor of Sociology, and at Stanford University. He is currently associated with the Sociology Department of Harvard University. He has written extensively in the fields of work, family, religion, and sociological theory. His latest monograph is *World Changes in Divorce Patterns*.

LINDA GORDON is the Florence Kelley Professor of History at the University of Wisconsin. Her most recent publications include *Heroes of Their Own Lives: The Politics and History of Family Violence*, the second edition of *Woman's Body, Woman's Right: The History of Birth Control in America*, and *Women, the State, and Welfare*.

THOMAS LAQUEUR teaches history at the University of California, Berkeley. His most recent book is *Making Sex: Body and Gender from the Greeks to Freud*. He is currently working on a series of essays about fiction, commerce, desire, and sexuality in the eighteenth and early nineteenth centuries, and a study of the history of naming as a form of commemoration in the twentieth century.

RAYNA RAPP is Professor of Anthropology at the New School for Social Research. Currently completing a book on the social effects and cultural meaning of prenatal diagnosis, she has been active in the movement for women's studies, as well as the reproductive rights movement, for over twenty years.

MICHELLE ROSALDO was Associate Professor of Anthropology at Stanford University. Before her untimely death, she coedited *Woman, Culture, and Society*, with Louise Lamphere, and authored *Knowledge and Passion: Ilongot Notions of Self and Social Life*.

SARA RUDDICK is Professor of Philosophy and Feminist Studies at the Eugene Lang College of the New School for Social Research. She is the author of *Maternal Thinking: Toward a Politics of Peace*.

JUDITH STACEY is Professor of Sociology and Women's Studies at the University of California, Davis. She is the author of *Brave New Families: Stories of Domestic Upheaval in Late Twentieth Century America* and *Patriarchy and Socialist Revolution in China*, as well as numerous essays on family politics and feminism.

BARRIE THORNE is the Streisand Professor in the Program for the Study of Women and Men, and Professor of Sociology, at the University of Southern California. She coedited *Language, Gender, and Society* and is the author of a forthcoming book, *Gender Play: Girls and Boys in School.*

KATH WESTON is Assistant Professor of Anthropology at Arizona State University West in Phoenix. She is the author of *Families We Choose: Lesbians, Gays, Kinship* and a coeditor of "The Lesbian Issue," a special issue of the journal *Signs.* She is currently working on a collection of essays on gender theory entitled *Gender Rising.*

MARILYN YALOM is the Senior Scholar at the Institute for Research on Women and Gender at Stanford University. She was previously Professor of French at California State University, Hayward. She is the author of *Maternity, Mortality, and the Literature of Madness,* as well as numerous studies of French and American writers, and has edited several collections of essays in women's studies.

SYLVIA YANAGISAKO is Professor of Anthropology at Stanford University. In addition to numerous articles on kinship, gender, and ethnicity, her publications include *Transforming the Past: Kinship and Tradition among Japanese Americans* and *Gender and Kinship,* coedited with Jane Collier. She is currently writing a monograph on the transformation of family firms in northern Italy.

MAXINE BACA ZINN is Professor of Sociology and Senior Research Associate in the Julian Samora Research Institute at Michigan State University. She is a coauthor of *Diversity in American Families* and *In Conflict and Order: Understanding Society,* and a coeditor of *Women of Color in America* (forthcoming).

Preface to the Second Edition

When *Rethinking the Family* first appeared ten years ago, we did not suspect it would become a popular textbook and frequently cited reference work. We did not anticipate it would sell more than fifteen thousand copies in seven years, only to go out of print while it was still much in demand. We knew only that the essays represented vital feminist questions about the concept of "family" at a time when families were undergoing radical change.

Now, ten years later, we offer a new version of this book in the hope it will have the same success in the 1990s that it had in the 1980s. That hope is based on the knowledge that we have retained only those original essays that are still especially relevant, and added others that further illuminate the situation of American families from the perspective of a continuing feminist discourse.

The editors wish to thank Yelena Furman, an undergraduate student at Stanford University, for her volunteer assistance on this project. We also thank Lorraine Macchello and Dee Gustavson, staff members at the Institute for Research on Women and Gender, for their editorial and clerical help. We gratefully recall the original financial support from the Rockefeller Family Fund. Finally, we wish to thank William Frohlich, Director of the Northeastern University Press, for his encouragement, patience, and belief in the value of making this work once more available to concerned and thoughtful readers.

Barrie Thorne
*Department of Sociology
and Program for the Study of Women
and Men in Society,
University of
Southern California*

Marilyn Yalom
*Institute for Research
on Women and Gender,
Stanford University*

Rethinking the Family

1

Feminism and the Family: Two Decades of Thought

BARRIE THORNE

Over half of the articles on the front page of today's *Los Angeles Times* (22 January 1992) deal with family issues. One of them, headlined "Justices Agree to Review Abortion Restrictions," reports further limits on women's legal rights to abortion, while another notes that the Los Angeles School Board has approved the distribution of condoms, with some parents supporting and others opposing the policy. A third article describes a law in New Jersey that will end increases in welfare subsidies for each new child. And in the ambivalent patchwork of policies aimed at families living in poverty, another tells of a proposed increase in federal funding for the Head Start preschool program. Finally, there is medical news that people with heart disease who live alone are more vulnerable to subsequent heart attacks than those who live with others; the article reports that more people now live alone than ever before in U.S. history.

To some, the events compressed on this newspaper page offer further evidence that we are in the midst of a "family crisis." Those who claim that the family is in crisis cite as evidence the high divorce rate; the increase in single-parent families, which some see as a major cause of expanding welfare rolls; the increase in people living alone; the growing visibility of lesbian and gay couples; the rising employment rates of married women, especially mothers of young children; and a general undermining of parental authority. During the last two decades there have been calls for new federal policies to "strengthen" the family, while the New Right has played upon fears of family breakdown by using the term "profamily" to oppose policies ranging

I wish to thank Maxine Baca Zinn, Barbara Laslett, Judith Stacey, and Marilyn Yalom for helpful comments on an earlier draft of this essay.

from gay and lesbian rights to legal access to abortion and state help for women and children living in poverty.

Defenders of the family often locate feminists among those who would destroy the family; the conservative "profamily" movement is explicitly antifeminist. Critical analyses of the family, and efforts to change traditional family arrangements, *have* been central to the women's movement, although trends such as the high divorce rate and the increase in women's employment predated the feminist movement that emerged in the 1970s. Of all the issues raised by feminists, those that bear on the family—among them, demands for abortion rights, efforts to legitimate varied household and sexual arrangements, and challenges of men's authority and women's economic dependence and exclusive responsibility for nurturing—have been the most controversial.

We have designed this book to draw readers into two decades of feminist thinking about the family. Five of the essays, not including this updated overview, come from the original 1982 edition of *Rethinking the Family*. To encompass developments in the years since 1982, we have chosen another eight essays to reprint from other sources. The authors affirm the significance of feminist analysis and politics. Many also reflect upon the effects of feminism, as well as other forces like the New Right and economic restructuring, on processes of family change. The essays bring into sharp relief the nature and complexities of feminist analysis, as well as the relationship of feminist ideas and the women's movement to two decades of social change.

The authors come from the disciplines of anthropology, history, philosophy, psychology, and sociology. Each essay bears the stamp of its originating discipline, but the papers also draw upon and contribute to the cross-disciplinary ideas of feminism. Feminism, of course, is not all of a piece, and the authors' assumptions and preoccupations differ in interesting ways. But through the articles one can trace five themes that are central to feminist rethinking of the family:

1. Feminists have challenged the ideology of "the monolithic family," which has elevated the nuclear family with a breadwinner husband and a full-time wife and mother as the only legitimate family form. Feminists have sought to dislodge beliefs that any specific family arrangement is natural, biological, or "functional" in a timeless way.

2. Rather than starting with "the family" as a unit of analysis, feminists have focused upon underlying and encompassing structures of gender, generation, sexuality, and, increasingly, race and class. By taking gender as a basic category of analysis, understood in the context of other social divisions and lines of inequality, feminists have made important contributions to family theory.

3. Structures of gender, generation, race, and class result in widely varying experiences of family life, which are obscured by the glorification of the nuclear family, motherhood, and the family as a loving refuge. Feminists have voiced experiences that this ideology denies, including men's dominance and women's subordination within as well as outside families, varying experiences of motherhood, and the presence of inequitably distributed work, conflict, and sometimes violence within the "domestic haven." In the last decade feminists have increasingly attended to the supportive side of families, as well as structures of power and conflict and patterns of abuse, leading to a much more complex view.

4. Feminists have raised questions about family boundaries, showing that family isolation is in part illusory, since there are close and sometimes combustible connections between the internal life of families and the organization of paid work, state-organized welfare and legal systems, schools, day-care centers, and other institutions. By challenging traditional dichotomies between private and public, family and society, feminists have recentered social theory and brought hidden topics into view.

5. The public/private dichotomy is linked to an ambivalence embedded in feminism since the nineteenth century and strongly evident today. The ambivalence moves between values of individualism and equality—values that women have historically been denied and are now claiming—and values of nurturance and community, which are symbolically associated with women and the family. These latter values have been affirmed by some feminists as a basis for broader social change. The tension between individualism and community is basic to the politics of family change.

We have arranged the essays in a sequence that loosely follows these five themes. The papers by Jane Collier, Michelle Rosaldo, and Sylvia Yanagisako; Rayna Rapp; Maxine Beca Zinn; Judith Stacey; and Kath Weston all address the conventional ideology of The Family. They detail the conceptual limitations of this monolithic view, and they examine its effects on social policy and personal experience. Several of the authors also discuss economic, social, and political trends that have increasingly undermined that ideology. And they demonstrate the significance of gender, brought into close conjunction with race, ethnicity, social class, and sexual orientation, in the dynamics of families and households.

The next three essays pick up on hotly contested topics: the history of struggles for reproductive rights and the development of new reproductive technologies that stretch conventional assumptions of maternity and paternity. Linda Gordon, Thomas Laqueur, and Sara Ruddick raise intriguing questions about the gendered construction of phenomena often regarded as simply technological, like birth control, or as primarily biological, like the relative claims of women and men to children. They also reflect upon varied definitions and experiences of fatherhood and motherhood, a topic further expanded in the essay by Nancy Chodorow and Susan Contratto, on ideologies of motherhood; in Patricia Hill Collins's discussion of the mothering experiences of African-American women; and in Micaela di Leonardo's analysis of "women's work" in constructing ties among extended kin. In "Family Violence, Feminism, and Social Control," Linda Gordon provides a complex historical perspective on different forms of family violence, tracing fluid boundaries between families and external agents of social control, including the state. Finally, William Goode explores the dynamics of men's resistance to women's demands for equality.

Challenging the Ideology of the Monolithic Family

The language often used to refer to kinship, intimacy, and domestic sharing is monolithic: "The family" implies a firm, unchanging entity, always similar in shape and content. Feminists have long challenged this imagery, which is reified in functionalist theories of the family, for falsifying the actual variety of household forms and for perpetuating male dominance.[1] Elaborating this challenge, anthropologists Jane Collier, Michelle Rosaldo, and Sylvia Yanagisako argue that "the family" is a distorting ideological construct that "maps the function of 'nurturance' onto a collectivity of specific persons (presumably 'nuclear' relations) associated with specific spaces ('the home'), and specific affective bonds ('love')."[2] In contemporary parlance, "the family" often implies, in addition, a particular sexual division of labor: a breadwinner husband, freed for and identified with activities in a separate economic sphere, and a full-time wife and mother whose being is often equated with the family itself. In short, the modern nuclear family, with a particular sexual division of labor, has been writ large as The Family (in her essay, Stacey calls it "the modern family") and elevated as the most desirable and legitimate family form.

A number of critics have set out to demystify the ideology of the monolithic family.[3] But it is feminists, mostly in writings of the 1970s, who connected women's subordination to The Family as a specific household arrangement *and* as an ideology.[4] According to this argument, within households that resemble The Family in composition, insularity, and division of labor, women are excluded from gaining direct access to valued resources such as income, status-giving work, and political authority. They are economically dependent on their husbands; their unpaid work at home is often burdensome and devalued; and they do the work of mothering in relative isolation, to the detriment of both mother and child.

Furthermore, the ideology of The Family extends beyond families of that specific type to infuse general understandings of women's "proper place." Beliefs that most people live in nuclear families, that adult women usually have husbands to support them, and that motherhood is women's central vocation have been used to legitimate the subordination of women in the economy. Women's lower wages and their disadvantaged position in the labor force have been justified by the assumption that their paid work is secondary to that of men. The belief that women are uniquely suited for domestic service and nurturing has supported sex segregation in and of occupations and the confinement of women to generally low-paid jobs that resemble their wife-and-mother roles: clerical and service work, nursing, the care and teaching of the young, the production and selling of food and clothing. In short, the ideology of The Family has reinforced the economic exploitation of all women.

This line of analysis, emphasizing patterns of domination and constraint, shifted during the 1980s as feminists examined women's resistance to and negotiation of the structures that subordinate them. For example, Deniz Kandiyotti compares the "patriarchal bargains" that men and women have negotiated in different economic and cultural contexts. Within the patriarchal bargain of the traditional nuclear family, women seek men's economic support and protection in return for domestic services and subordination.[5] The feminist literature of the 1980s emphasizes both women's subordination *and* their active efforts to create viable lives within and outside families. This view of women as creating family life in active negotiation with men and children can be found in the essays by Stacey, Weston, Collins, di Leonardo, Gordon, and Goode.

There has been another notable shift over the past two decades of feminist writing about families. During the 1970s feminists were so intent on criticizing the prevalent ideology of The Family that they paid insufficient attention to other meanings and experiences of "family." Ironically, the very process of critique kept the monolithic family at center stage. Writings of African-American, Chicana and Latina, and Asian-American feminists have been especially insightful in revealing the white, middle-class assumptions embedded both in familial ideology and in much of the feminist critique.[6] Several essays in this book reflect feminists' growing awareness of diversity. Rapp reviews studies showing extensive social class, race, and ethnic variation in family and household experiences. Collins explains African-American conceptions of "family" that connect households and larger communities, link generations, and revolve around female kin. And Weston describes varied "families by choice" created by lesbians and gay men who have struggled with the deeply heterosexual assumptions of the ideology of The Family.

As both Maxine Baca Zinn and Rayna Rapp observe, people who live in poverty often lack the material resources to form autonomous households. Their households tend to be unstable, with networks of sharing, as well as dependence on the welfare system. The high rate of single-parent families among those living in poverty, who are disproportionately African-American and Hispanic, has entered into heated debates about social welfare policy. Baca Zinn shows dominant family ideology at work in the conservative argument that the single-parent family (seen as "family breakdown") is a major cause of poverty. As Baca Zinn argues, the problem of poverty lies not in family structure or in cultural deficiency, but in declining economic opportunities that devastate inner cities. Some proposals for changing the welfare system focus solely on the problem of African-American male unemployment, aiming to restore men as family providers.

These policies, rooted in a conventional understanding of family and gender arrangements, ignore the urgent training, employment, wage equity, and day-care needs of African-American women. The ideology of the monolithic family has been used to sustain racial-ethnic as well as gender oppression.

While the ideology of the monolithic family retains a deep hold on public policy and political debates, it has been increasingly undermined by trends of the past decade. Compare, for example, Rapp's portrait of working-class households, based on research done up to the mid-1970s, with Stacey's more recent research. Stacey began her ethnographic study expecting that working-class informants would uphold the ideal of the "modern" or traditional nuclear family. Instead she found a great deal of variation and fluidity in types of households and individual family trajectories, a pattern borne out by national statistics showing that in 1986 only 7 percent of households fit the pattern of breadwinning father, full-time mother, and at least one child under age eighteen. (To put that figure in perspective: nationally the most common household, nearly half of the total, now has an adult male and an adult female wage earner, with or without children; the next most common types of household are single-parent families and unmarried couples living together; then come individuals living alone.[7] Gay and lesbian couples, some with children, are increasingly visible, although census takers do not count them as a separate category.)

Households have *always* varied in composition, even in the 1950s and early 1960s, when the ideology of The Family was at its peak.[8] But there is more variation now than three decades ago because of economic shifts related to the steady rise in employment of women; high, although stabilized, rates of divorce; lower birth rates; longer life spans; and patterns of unemployment among both men and women. Furthermore, ideological challenges have led to increasing public debate about the notion of "family." Those challenges have come not only from feminists but also, as Weston discusses, from lesbians and gay men who have broadened definitions of "family" to include domestic partners of the same sex, as well as networks of friends. In addition, new reproductive technologies have led to debates about the legal meanings of "family," as discussed in the essays by Thomas Laqueur and by Sara Ruddick. Stacey observes that the family has become a "contested terrain," and Weston concludes that the family is not so much an institution, in the singular sense of that word, as a "contested concept."

Conservatives see these trends as signs of "family breakdown" at least partly because they idealize the family with a male wage earner and stay-at-home wife and children as the normal, most healthy household arrangement (conservative ideologues never acknowledge how few U.S. families actually fit their ideal). Feminists read other implications from the escalation of family change, observing that privatized nuclear families are not free from problems, and emphasizing the difficulties experienced by those living in households that do not match up to the monolithic family ideal.

For example, a fifth of the nation's children now live in poverty, the majority in female-headed households in a pattern related to women's disadvantaged position in the economy, the failure of many men to provide for the children they have fathered, and minimal state support for families with children.[9] A scarcity of publicly supported child-care facilities places a heavy burden on parents raising children alone and on two-earner families with young children. The poverty rate for elderly women, many of whom live by themselves, is nearly twice that for elderly men.[10] And as Weston discusses, the ideology of the monolithic family, equating homosexuality with "exile from kinship," stigmatizes intimate relationships among lesbians and gay men, who are denied job-related and tax benefits. Overall, the absence of national health insurance, housing allowances, and other state supports leaves U.S. households largely on their own. Responding to this disturbing range of problems, feminists have called for recognition of and support for diverse family arrangements in public policy and law, and in beliefs about legitimate choices concerning sexuality, reproduction, and domestic sharing.

Challenging Beliefs That the Family Is a Biological Given

The ideology of the monolithic family has been tenacious and difficult to demystify partly because, of all social institutions, it seems the most natural and biological, the most timeless and unchanging. Families deal with root biological events like birth, sickness, and death. They are places of sexuality, eating, sleeping, and of the thick and close forms of relatedness imaged by biological ("blood") ties of kinship. The rhythms of family life are organized more around bodily needs and the demands of children than are the time-governed rhythms of the workplace. Procreation and the raising of children, often seen as core family activities, seem inextricably linked with biology. And insofar as women are defined by their reproductive and mothering capacities, and embedded in the family, their situation too has been made to appear natural. Collier, Rosaldo, and Yanagisako note that this view, "uniting women and the family to an apparently unchanging set of biologically given needs," has infused traditional social theory.

Contemporary feminists have challenged beliefs that family arrangements are biological in any direct or immutable way; instead, they argue that families are socially and historically constructed. Feminists have emphasized the social organization of sexuality, intimacy, reproduction, motherhood, fatherhood, childhood, sexual divisions of labor, and the division of gender itself. Thomas Laqueur writes that "feminism has been the most powerful denaturalizing theoretical force in my intellectual firmament." His and several other essays in the book show the rich insights raised by feminist excavations of topics often thought to be primarily about the biological or "natural."

For example, in her first essay Linda Gordon traces changing feminist attitudes toward birth control as part of a long history of conflict over the social control of reproduction. For feminists, the issue of who should control reproduction, and how, has always been closely tied to efforts to improve the situation of women. In separate but linked essays, Thomas Laqueur and Sara Ruddick assess the extraordinary implications of new reproductive technologies as they shake the old assumption that the identity of a child's mother is obvious, while the identity of the father (who, after all, does not give birth) remains intrinsically open to question. The same child may now have three different mothers: one who donates the egg, another who nurtures the fetus in her womb and gives birth, and a mother who gives primary care after birth. Furthermore, recent technological developments make the tracing of biological paternity, through blood tests, far more certain than in the past. Not only do these rearrangements offer a striking example of the social altering of biology, but they also open up a series of questions about paternity and maternity, and about the relative claims of women and men, and of different women and men, to a given child. Sorting out these issues, as shown in the lively exchange between Ruddick and Laqueur, is by no means a straightforward matter. Beliefs, laws, politics, and feelings give cultural significance to biology.

Moving beneath and around "the Family" as a Unit of Analysis

If "the family" is a problematic concept, unraveled by variation and change as well as by criticisms of its ideological loading, how can we gain a theoretical grasp on experiences of kinship, intimacy, and domestic sharing—the three strands that weave, ambiguously, through the notion of "family"? In her essay Rapp suggests a useful distinction between "households," that is, residential units sharing resources, consumption, and housework, and "families," referring to ideologies and meanings of kinship and connection. Other essays in this book pick up this distinction, with some authors, such as Baca Zinn and Rapp, stressing concrete household realities, while others, such as Weston, emphasize symbolic meanings. Di Leonardo focuses on household-based activities, like dinners and holiday gatherings, that help sustain a larger sense of "family."

Feminists have found other ways of moving through this tangled thicket, starting with Juliet Mitchell, who urged in a pathbreaking analysis first published in 1966 that one should examine "not the family as an unanalyzed entity, but the separate structures which today compose it but which may tomorrow be decomposed into a new pattern." In Mitchell's framework, those underlying structures include production, reproduction, sexuality, and the socialization of children.[11] Others have moved beneath and around any particular notion of family by focusing on "social reproduction," that is, "the activities and attitudes, behaviors and emotions, responsibilities and relationships directly involved in the maintenance of life on a daily basis, and intergenerationally."[12] The activities of social reproduction—such as the provision of food, clothing, and shelter; care of children, the sick, and the elderly; and sexuality—are organized in widely varying ways, within and outside households and networks of kin. The state, market, and community are also involved. And all of this labor is centrally structured by gender.

Overall, feminists have pursued the analytic strategy of beginning not with a particular conception of family but rather with gender as a basic category of analysis. Feminists have rescued gender, and gender relations, from the realm of the taken-for-granted and made them problematic.[13] Far from being a fact of nature, gender is a complex social construction with multiple dimensions that bear on the dynamics of families and other institutions. At the individual level, dichotomous gender categories ("man-woman") and multiple forms of masculinity and femininity are central to processes of social placement and to the shaping of identity. The process of acquiring individual gender identity connects the dynamics of gender with the ongoing life of families, although gender identities, including varied styles of masculinity and femininity, are also learned and enacted in schools and in work sites.[14] Moving from the level of individual identity, gender is central to the social organization of households, work, schools, hospitals, the state, and other institutions. Gender divisions of labor and notions of "women's work" and "men's work" vary across cultures, although women typically sustain more responsibility than men for the tasks of social reproduction, including the forms of "caring work" discussed by Ruddick, Collins, and di Leonardo. Finally, gender takes shape through symbols and meanings, as shown, for example, in the varied conceptions of motherhood and fatherhood discussed by Laqueur, Ruddick, Chodorow and Contratto, and Collins.

Many of the essays in this volume point to a theme that preoccupied feminist theorists during the 1980s: the relationships between gender and other social categories. These include social class (emphasized by Rapp, Stacey, Baca Zinn, Collins, and Gordon); race and ethnicity (a focal point for Baca Zinn and Collins); age (in her essay on family violence, Gordon connects structures of gender and generation); and sexuality (discussed by Weston). This line of analysis concerns more than multiple and interacting differences; all of these social divisions are embedded in structures of power.

The Differentiation of Family Experiences

Because particular families and households take shape around structures of gender and age (inflected by other lines of difference like social class and ethnicity), women, men, girls, and boys do not have the same experiences.[15] This internal differentiation of family experiences has been distorted or denied by various conceptualizations that recur in writings on the family:

1. Some studies assume a harmony of interests among all family members. For example, demographers use terms like "family decision" and "family strategies" to refer to choices about limiting family size, a usage that obscures the history of conflict between women and men over reproductive control, as described in Gordon's first essay.[16]

2. Although they pay attention to the behavior of individuals within families, some studies do not consider the systematic relevance of gender and age. For example, "family violence" is sometimes portrayed as a series of individual assaults or else as a pathology of "family systems." These views ignore a crucial fact that Gordon closely examines in her second essay: violence runs along lines of power, with adult men and women abusing children, and men abusing women, much more than the reverse.

3. Nongendered language often masks specific gender assumptions. For instance, in *Haven in a Heartless World* Christopher Lasch usually means "father" when he writes "parent," and "son" when he writes "child."[17]

4. "Family" is sometimes tacitly equated with "mother," neglecting the presence of varied family members and their relations with one another, as in much of the traditional literature on families and mental illness.[18]

Feminists argue that the specifics of daily family living—the allocation of tasks; experiences of work and leisure; the giving and receiving of nurturance; conflicts and episodes of violence; and decisions about employment, moving, consumption, or family size—cannot be adequately understood without systematic attention to underlying structures of gender and age. Women's experiences of the family have, in particular, been buried by the use of overarching, homogeneous units of analysis such as "the household" and "the family"; by a tendency to equate women with family while men are allowed a separate and individualized status; and by the hegemony of male experience of families, as evidenced in Lasch's book and in much of the writing of Sigmund Freud and Max Horkheimer.[19] Three themes that infuse popular and academic portrayals of contemporary families have especially mystified women's varied experiences: ideologies of motherhood, the notion of the family as a domestic refuge, and an emphasis on love and consensus as the sole basis of family relations.

Motherhood as Ideology and as Varied Experience

At least since the eighteenth century motherhood has been glorified as women's chief vocation and central definition. The tie between mother and child has been exalted, and traits of nurturance and selflessness have been defined as the essence of the maternal, and hence, of the womanly. Nineteenth-century feminists, as Gordon explains in both of her essays, not only took for granted the definition of women as primarily child rearers but also drew on idealized images of motherhood as a basis for moral and family reform.

Contemporary feminists have challenged that ideology of motherhood, arguing that when motherhood is used as a mystique, "it becomes an instrument of oppression."[20] The women's movement has long worked to give women a choice of whether, and under what circumstances, to mother—hence, struggles for access to birth control and the right to abortion. Feminists have emphasized the right of all women, whether or not they are mothers, to engage in activities beyond motherhood—hence, efforts to bring women into an equal position in the labor force and to diminish their ideological encapsulation by the family. Feminists have demystified motherhood by documenting examples of unfavorable conditions of childbirth as it has been organized by the predominantly male medical profession and by challenging the division of labor that isolates mothers as full-time parents and separates fathers from children. Feminists have also pressed for extensive reorganization of arrangements of child care through proposals for equal male involvement, flexible work hours, parental leave from paid work, and policies and funding that would make high-quality day care more widely accessible.

In the late 1970s, as Nancy Chodorow and Susan Contratto observe in their essay, feminist discussions of motherhood began to turn from questions of choice and external conditions to attend more closely to women's experiences as mothers. Up to that time, the actual voices of mothers were missing in much of the writing on motherhood. The shift to an emphasis on experience is exemplified by Adrienne Rich's compelling book *Of Woman Born*, which made a key distinction between motherhood as an institution embedded in patriarchal ideology, and the complex and lived experiences of actual mothers. Drawing on her "private and sometimes painful experiences" as a mother, Rich invited other women to join in creating "a collective description of the world which will be truly ours."[21] Rich's book is an inspiring example of the feminist process of articulating women's experiences and transforming them into knowledge.[22]

Several of the essays in this book explore the disjuncture between maternal ideologies and experiences. Taken together, they reveal a process of critique that continues to add layers of understanding. In

"The Fantasy of the Perfect Mother," Chodorow and Contratto sketch a startling convergence between the assumptions some feminists (among them, Adrienne Rich, Shulamith Firestone, and Dorothy Dinnerstein) make about mothering and the assumptions of more conservative writers, like Selma Fraiberg. Both groups share an extreme larger-than-life picture of mothers as all-powerful, with an omnipotence embodied either in perfection or in destruction and death. Chodorow and Contratto trace the ideological roots of this picture and call for more realistic explorations of mothering, including more understanding that mothers have lives, needs, activities, and relationships apart from, interacting with, and sometimes contradicting the tasks of motherhood.

In "Black Women and Motherhood," a chapter reprinted from her book *Black Feminist Thought,* Patricia Hill Collins takes the process of critique a step further. She observes that analyses of African-American mothers have often come from white men like Daniel Moynihan, who have perpetuated the distorting view of female-headed households as a problem of "Black matriarchy," or from Black men who have glorified "the superstrong Black mother" and neglected the costs and difficulties of mothering for African-American women. Black women's experiences have also been denied by feminist views of motherhood that embed white, middle-class assumptions. For example, the feminist writings that Chodorow and Contratto discuss say nothing about "controlling images" that African-American women must continually confront, such as the mammy, the matriarch, and the welfare mother. Furthermore, in emphasizing the privatization of mothering, white feminists have ignored historically high rates of employment among Black mothers, as well as networks of kin and community that share the daily tasks of caring for children. African Americans have condensed experiences of shared mothering into a language of "bloodmothers," "othermothers," and "community othermothers," who are often activists on behalf of children. A definition of motherhood is also a definition of childhood, and Collins insightfully observes that these collective practices of mothering challenge the pervasive view of children as private property. Refusing a simplified portrayal of African-American mothers, Collins discusses their contradictory feelings of exploitation and of empowerment.

The experiences of lesbian mothers challenge another piece of ideology inscribed in both conventional and feminist thought: the assumption that procreation is inextricably linked to heterosexuality (from that perspective, "lesbian mother" is an oxymoron). Lesbians, and gay men, have struggled for the right to procreate and raise children. This struggle has legal dimensions, as in the court cases Laqueur describes, and it is anchored in the building of communities, networks of support, and the broadened "families we choose" that are the focus of Weston's discussion.[23]

Constructions of motherhood are closely tied to those of fatherhood, a topic that has received increasing attention in the 1980s. In their debate about definitions of fatherhood and motherhood, Laqueur and Ruddick discuss the relative import of public authority, formal concepts of inheritance and descent, economic providing, affective connections, and the everyday labor of child rearing. While some fathers are spending more time caring for children now than in the past, national census data show that from 1960 to 1980 there was an overall decline in the average number of years men spent in households living with children.[24] The frequent absence of men from the care of children weighs into the exchange between Laqueur and Ruddick, as well as in essays by Stacey, Baca Zinn, and Collins. As Stacey has observed, it is odd that in their nostalgic writings on family decline, conservatives indict women for abandoning domesticity, since ample evidence shows that even as they enter paid employment, it is women who continue to bear responsibility for care of the children and the elderly, and for sustaining kin ties. If there is a family crisis, Stacey concludes, "it is a male family crisis."[25]

Feminists have called for the reconstruction of fatherhood, as well as motherhood, but they see different possibilities in the future. Ruddick hopes for a world where men will also "mother" or share the primary care of children. But Barbara Katz Rothman, who shares Ruddick's feminist hopes, highlights a countertrend she finds disturbing. By using new reproductive technologies and paid child-care workers, affluent women can behave like traditional "fathers," appropriating the labor of other women to do the daily work of child care and even to physically bear children.[26]

A Domestic Refuge for Whom? The Rediscovery of Housework

Romanticized conceptions of motherhood reinforce an image of the family as a refuge, a "haven in a heartless world." Talcott Parsons tapped into that view when he argued that the historical process of industrialization had stripped the family of its productive functions, leaving it, and especially wives and mothers, to specialize in socializing children and providing "socioemotional" support to family members.[27]

Alert to varied experiences within the same family, feminists have asked, for whom is the home a refuge or a nurturant haven? For the vast majority of women, the home is a place of considerable work, even when they are employed full-time out of the home. Researchers have found that women work in and out of the home an average of fifteen hours more than men each week, which adds up to an extra month of twenty-four-hour days a year. Calling this women's "second shift," Arlie Hochschild observes that there is a "leisure gap" between the majority of women and men at home just as there is a wage gap in the workplace.[28] From the earliest years of the contemporary women's movement feminists have cited these patterns with a sense of injustice, arguing that a "politics of housework," fraught with male privilege, places an unfair burden on women and should be changed.[29]

The women's movement helped establish housework as an important topic for research as well as political action. Feminist scholars have traced historical shifts in the array of tasks lumped together under the rubric of "housework," as well as variation and continuity in the allocation of tasks to different family members.[30] Terms like *housework* and, more broadly, *domestic labor* or *reproductive labor* encompass multiple and sometimes contradictory activities, such as the work of procreation and birthing discussed by Ruddick and by Laqueur; the complex activities of caring for children; and tasks like cleaning, cooking, laundering, and marketing.

In the early 1970s feminists mostly examined housework as exploited labor that maintains and reinforces the wage labor force, to the benefit of both capitalists and men (Rapp reviews this argument in her essay). That approach sees women primarily as victims whose lives are determined by external forces; it neglects their resistance to oppressive structures, as well as the more creative and supportive dimensions of family life. In the past decade, as part of the turn to examining women's varied experiences, feminists have paid closer attention to the positive as well as negative sides of domestic work.

This more complicated view is evident in a growing literature on women's "caring work,"[31] including Micaela di Leonardo's essay on "kinwork." Drawing on a study of Italian-American families in California, di Leonardo observes that through activities like visiting, writing letters, telephoning, sending cards, and organizing holiday gatherings, women helped sustain a larger sense of "family," reaching across households. Pursuing similar themes, Marjorie DeVault used open-ended interviews to probe women's experiences of "feeding and provisioning" both as concrete and sometimes exploited labor, and as a means of building a collective sense of "family."[32] This more complicated perspective also appears in Collins's discussion of African-American women's mixed experiences of satisfaction and loss in their lives as mothers.

The notion of "caring work" has gained widespread usage because it alludes to the contradictory and sometimes poignant mix of labor that is often burdensome and inequitably distributed, with experiences of caring and love. Feminist scholars have studied the "caring work" of mothers, teachers, social workers, community activists, day-care workers, and those, paid and unpaid, who care for the elderly and the disabled.[33] "Caring work" connects households with hospitals, nursing homes, day-care centers, and schools. When done for pay, it is usually devalued; when unpaid, it is often taken for granted.

The literature on domestic labor pursues a troubling question: Given women's rapid entry into the paid labor force, why haven't more men, in parallel fashion, increased their contributions to housework and child care? Why do so many women work a fatiguing "second shift"? While women make up over 44 percent of the paid labor force, they remain in a secondary position, and their continuing economic, legal, and political subordination outside of households affects their ability to claim full equality within.[34] Housework, in fact, often symbolizes subordination. When done for pay, domestic labor is one of the least desirable forms of work; and within organizations, housework chores, like KP in the army or making coffee and cleaning up in offices, are done by the lowest-status workers, promoting deference and discipline.[35] But housework also has other meanings. Many women and men see the doing of housework as what women "properly" or "naturally" do; through cooking, keeping the house clean, and engaging in caring work, women affirm their "gendered relation to the work and to the world."[36] On the other hand, doing housework detracts from some men's notions of masculinity. The link between housework and gender, as a division of labor filled with contradictory meanings, has proven to be extremely complex.

The Tangle of Love and Domination in Family Relations

The idealized vision of the family as a domestic haven includes an emphasis on consensus as the basis of family relationships. Much of the sociological literature from the 1950s and early 1960s portrayed contemporary marriage as an arrangement of love between equals, or near equals, using terms like "the companionate marriage," "egalitarian marriage," and "the symmetrical family." The emphasis on love has also infused conventional portrayals of relationships between parents and children.

In the 1970s feminists joined other critics of the family in putting forth a more conflictual portrayal of relations between wives and husbands, parents and children.[37] Instead of love and companionship, they emphasized patterns of inequality and conflict. Shulamith Firestone helped initiate this shift of vision, arguing that love is "the pivot of women's oppression today" because love between women and men is "complicated, corrupted, or obstructed by an unequal balance of power."[38] (Unlike many subsequent feminist theorists, Firestone attended to the subordination of children as well as women.) Firestone, like other radical feminists, used the concept of *patriarchy*, denoting family relationships as the core of domination by gender and age. However, *patriarchy*, which refers to the rule of the father over his wife and children, is a term that most aptly describes men's authority in societies where the household is the unit of production and fathers control the labor of wives and children. That structure has been undermined by capitalism and by the modern state, which are not, by and large, based on relations of kinship. As Linda Gordon observes in her second essay, over the last century male supremacy has been "modernized." Men continue to exert power and authority within families, although women's entry into wage work and patterns of male unemployment tend to undermine men's domestic privileges.[39]

The power of men over women is still evident in the inequitable distribution of housework and child care, in patterns of communication between husbands and wives,[40] in processes of decision-making,[41] and, in extreme form, in patterns of physical and sexual abuse. William Goode argued two decades ago that the power of husbands over wives, and of parents over children, is ultimately backed by force.[42] The least powerful members of families—women and children—are the most likely to be victims of domestic violence. In her essay on family violence, Linda Gordon documents these patterns with historical data. But she argues against depicting women simply as victims in the past or in the present. Women have actively resisted male dominance, and—a fact she urges other feminists to acknowledge more fully—women also perpetrate violence; for example, they are responsible for about half of all physical abuse of children. (Sexual abuse of children is much more skewed by gender; about 95 percent of reported cases of incest involve a male perpetrator, such as a father, stepfather, grandfather, or uncle, and a girl as victim.)[43]

Gordon describes working-class women as active strategists maneuvering within the constraints of male and class dominance. Her essay exemplifies the more complex understanding of gender relations that has consolidated in feminist thought over the past decade. This understanding encompasses the tension between oppressive structures and the actions of people who resist and change them.[44] In the last decade, feminists have also paid closer attention to the supportive side of families, especially in resistance against class and race domination. The history of Chicana, Asian-American, and African-American families shows that they have been simultaneously oppressive to women and a source of support for women, men, and children joining together to survive harsh conditions.[45] Feminists are reaching for insight into families as contradictory sites both of domination and of cooperation and solidarity.

Issues of gender and power are central to William Goode's concluding essay on "why men resist" women's demands for equality. Goode observes that like whites or those of dominant social classes, men often "are not aware of how much the social structure yields advantages for them," and they "view small losses of deference, or advantages, or opportunities as large threats." The structural position of men differs from that of groups that dominate on the basis of class or race. Men and women who live in heterosexual family arrangements develop mutual caring and shared stakes, in contrast with class and race groups, who are more spatially, materially, and emotionally separated from one another. Goode observes that men's dominance over women, especially within the family, is entwined with intimacy and mutual dependence. That paradox, that tangle of love and domination, is a recurring theme throughout this volume.

The Question of Family Boundaries

At least since the nineteenth century, social theorists have viewed the family as a private and distinctive sphere, set apart from the public world. Feminists have challenged that view, arguing that the division between "public" and "private" is deeply ideological.[46] By starting with women's experiences and with structures of gender rather than with a view of The Family as a bounded and distinctive unit, feminists have raised fruitful questions about ongoing relationships between families and paid employment, the market, schools, political activism, and the state.

Several of the essays discuss the integration of households into larger economic and social structures. For example, Baca Zinn and Stacey discuss the effects of the shift to a service-based, low-wage economy on the organization and dynamics of U.S. households. And in her discussion of African-American "othermothers," Collins relates processes of mothering to community and political activism. In addition, a growing body of research, previously mentioned, links gender structures in paid employment with patterns of domestic labor. Scholars have explored the ways in which paid domestic labor mixes market and household relations and involves exploitation between women of different classes and races.[47] They have also studied the consequences of different types of work, such as shift work or work involving travel, for the gender arrangements of households; the activities of some wives in constructing their husbands' careers; and the work-family experiences of women who are raising children on their own.[48]

Boundaries between households and other institutions sometimes dissolve as "work transfers" (a concept developed by Nona Glazer) alter women's and men's domestic activities.[49] For example, when grocery stores and gas stations moved to self-service in order to lower their costs, consumers were forced to do tasks previously done by paid clerks. Hospitals now release patients much earlier than they have in the past, presuming that there is someone at home (usually a woman) to continue the nursing care. In short, unpaid household activities are more central to market and state labor processes than one might think.

Historians have demonstrated that the opposition between "the family" and "the state" was established only with the consolidation of market capitalism in the early nineteenth century. State policies helped establish the family, with a gendered division of labor, as a private economic unit.[50] Structures of gender, as well as those of race and class, have always linked families and the social welfare system, as discussed in the essays by Gordon on family violence and by Baca Zinn on poverty. Families and households are also affected by laws governing divorce, child custody, sexuality, marital rape, and domestic violence. There are close and ongoing connections between families and the state.[51]

The Ambivalence between Nurturance and Individualism, and the Politics of Social Change

Feminist thinking about families continually returns to questions of social change. As Renate Bridenthal has observed, feminists "opened a whole new vista by asking, *not what do women do for the family* (an older question), *but what does the family do for women?* What does it do *to* women?"[52] Feminists have claimed women's right to break from their embeddedness in the family and to seek full individualism and equality in all institutions. They have advocated women's reproductive self-determination and more sharing of child care and household tasks as ways of fostering gender equality and justice, and providing more autonomy for women.

This emphasis on equality and individualism has long been in tension with another feminist approach that Gordon, in her first essay, calls "the refusal to accept merely integration of female individuals into a competition whose rules we did not define and do not endorse. There is, in fact, a tradition of feminist criticism of capitalism itself, representing it as the opposite of the nurturing values of motherhood." This tradition goes back to "social housekeeping" feminists in the late nineteenth century, who saw themselves as bringing maternal nurturance into the larger world as they worked for social reform. Contemporary "difference" feminists like Sara Ruddick, who argues that maternal activity promotes distinctive qualities of thought that can be used to transform public institutions, and Carol Gilligan, who articulates women's "different voice" of relationality, also affirm values of nurturance and community as an alternative and challenge to dominant social values.[53]

These two strands of feminist thought, one emphasizing individualism and equality, and the other stressing difference and community, are often presented as alternatives. This binary framing relates to a deep symbolic opposition between the market, seen as impersonal and contractual, and the family, representing nurture and support. In their essay Collier, Rosaldo, and Yanagisako criticize that symbolic opposition for distorting reality. In a similar vien, Joan Scott has argued that we should question and transcend the opposition between "equality" and "difference."[54] Many feminists uphold a vision of social change that encompasses both individualism and community, equality and difference. As Gordon writes in her first essay, the task of feminism is to defend the positive gains of individualism and liberal feminism, "while transcending the capitalist-competitive aspects of individualism with a vision of loving, egalitarian communities."

The conservative "defense of the family" also vacillates between values of individualism and family-based nurturance. Unlike feminists, however, conservatives turn to the family as a retreat from, rather than a potential challenge of, the "heartless" world of the market. Beneath the New Right's concern about the future of the family lies concern about the fate of care giving and nurturance, about values and needs denied and undermined by the fragmentation and impersonality fostered by capitalism.[55] Rather than challenge capitalist and patriarchal arrangements in the public sphere, however, defenders of the family retreat to an idealized family with the nurturant mother as its symbolic core. They demand that the family, and women, make up for everything the indifferent and hostile outer world refuses to do.[56]

The family that conservatives defend is an idealized, middle-class, patriarchal family. Feminists have shown the many drawbacks of that family ideal, and its largely ideological nature is becoming ever more apparent in the present period of widely varying and fluid family forms. This variation is the result of demographic, economic, and social change, not of moral decline. Nostalgia for the fading nuclear family will not solve serious problems like the poverty of women and children living in female-headed households or the shortage of quality day care. As Arlene Skolnick has written, "if we care about children, we need to focus less on the form of the families they live in and more on ways of supporting their well-being in all kinds of families."[57]

From a visionary feminist perspective, this period of rapid social change opens up dramatically new possibilities. As Judith Stacey concludes in her book *Brave New Families,* "In the postmodern period, a truly democratic gender and kinship order, one that does not favor male authority, heterosexuality, a particular division of labor, or a singular household or parenting arrangement, becomes thinkable for the first time in history."[58] There is strong resistance to that vision because it threatens vested class, race, and gender interests, as well as deeply held notions of social order. But it is a vision that I believe we should hold steadily in view.

Feminists are seeking a realistic and complex understanding of families as part of a larger program of social change. Our attention to the supportive and nurturant, as well as the oppressive, sides of families is not just an ambivalence; it points to a series of contradictions with which we are struggling in an effort to create a better society. This struggle necessarily moves beyond families to encompass as well the organization of paid work, state policies, laws, the health care system, the schools. The fragmentation and isolation that some call a "family crisis" is, in fact, a social crisis of much larger proportions whose solution will require changing the whole of social, economic, and political life.

Notes

1. Functionalist theorists argued that the nuclear family is more or less inevitable. For example, the anthropologist Bronislaw Malinowski claimed that the nuclear family is a universal human institution because it functions to fulfill the human need of nurturing children. In their essay in this volume, Collier, Rosaldo, and Yanagisako thoroughly undermine his argument. Talcott Parsons, an influential sociologist, argued that a division between "the expressive role" of wife and mother and the "instrumental" role of the male provider is functional in advanced industrial societies (see Talcott Parsons and Robert F. Bales, *Family, Socialization, and Interaction Process* [New York: Free Press, 1955]).

Feminist criticisms of Parsons go back at least to *The Feminine Mystique* (New York: Norton, 1963), in which Betty Friedan argued that the "functionalist freeze" made women's confinement to domesticity and subordination seem inevitable. Feminists have deepened this critique by showing that the reduction of gender divisions to a language of roles ("the male role," "the female role," "gender roles") obscures realities of power and conflict and provides, at best, a shallow understanding of complex dynamics of gender. See Helena Lopata and Barrie Thorne, "On the Term 'Sex Roles,' " *Signs* 3 (1978): 638–51, and R. W. Connell, *Gender and Power* (Stanford, Calif.: Stanford University Press, 1987). For a review of feminist criticisms of mainstream family theories, including functionalism, role theory, exchange theory, and general systems theory, see Marie Osmond and Barrie Thorne, "Feminist Theories: The Social Construction of Gender in Families and Society," in *Sourcebook of Family Theories and Methods*, ed. Pauline Boss, William Doherty, Ralph LaRossa, Walter Schumm, and Suzanne Steinmetz (New York: Plenum, 1992).

2. Collier, Rosaldo, and Yanagisako subtitle their paper (which was written for the original 1982 edition of this book) "New Anthropological Views." A decade later these views are not so new; a flourishing literature reexamines constructions of gender and kinship, including Jane Fishburne Collier and Sylvia Junko Yanagisako, eds., *Gender and Kinship: Essays toward a Unified Analysis* (Stanford, Calif.: Stanford University Press, 1987).

The essays in this book by Collier, Rosaldo, and Yanagisako; Weston; and Stacey reflect the growing influence of postmodern frameworks (emphasizing the hidden assumptions of dominant beliefs and the construction of varied discourses) on feminist writing about families. For a further taste of this theoretical and empirical approach to families, see Faye Ginsburg and Anna Lowenhaupt Tsing, eds., *Uncertain Terms: Negotiating Gender in American Culture* (Boston: Beacon Press, 1990). For entrée into feminist debates about the epistemology and politics of postmodern theories, see Linda J. Nicholson, ed., *Feminism/ Postmodernism* (New York: Routledge, 1990).

3. For example, Mark Poster, *Critical Theory of the Family* (New York: Seabury Press, 1978); D. H. J. Morgan, *Social Theory and the Family* (Boston: Routledge & Kegan Paul, 1975); and Arlene S. Skolnick and Jerome H. Skolnick, eds., *Family in Transition* (Boston: Little, Brown, 1971, and subsequent editions).

4. This line of argument can be found, in more complexity, in Juliet Mitchell, "Women: The Longest Revolution," *New Left Review* 40 (November–December 1966): 11–37; Jessie Bernard, *The Future of Marriage* (New York: Bantam Books, 1973); Heidi Hartmann, "Capitalism, Patriarchy, and Job Segregation by Sex," *Signs* 1, no. 3, pt. 2 (Spring 1976): 137–70; and Michèle Barrett and Mary McIntosh, *The Anti-Social Family* (London: Verso, 1982).

5. Deniz Kandiyotti, "Bargaining with Patriarchy," *Gender & Society* 2 (1988): 274–90.

6. See, for example, Bonnie Thornton Dill, "Our Mother's Grief: Racial Ethnic Women and the Maintenance of Families," *Journal of Family History* 13 (1988): 415–31; Evelyn Nakano Glenn, "Gender and the Family," in *Handbook of Sex and Gender*, ed. Beth Hess and Myra Marx Ferree (Beverly Hills, Calif.: Sage, 1987), 348–80; Maxine Baca Zinn, "Family, Feminism, and Race in America," *Gender & Society* 4 (1990): 68–82.

7. Sanford M. Dornbusch and Myra H. Strober, eds., *Feminism, Children, and the New Families* (New York: Guilford Press, 1988).

8. For an accessible historical overview of family change, including recent political controversies, see Arlene Skolnick, *Embattled Paradise: The American Family in an Age of Uncertainty* (New York: Basic Books, 1991).

9. Sheila Kamerman, "Women, Children and Poverty: Public Policies and Female-Headed Families in Industrialized Countries," *Signs* 10 (1984): 249–72.

10. U.S. Department of Labor, *Employment and Earnings, July 1987* (Washington, D.C.: Government Printing Office, 1987).

11. Mitchell, "Women: The Longest Revolution."

12. Barbara Laslett and Johanna Brenner, "Gender and Social Reproduction: Historical Perspectives," *Annual Review of Sociology* 15 (1989): 381–404.

13. Gayle Rubin developed a pioneering theory of "the sex/gender system" in "The Traffic in Women: Notes on the 'Political Economy' of Sex," in *Toward an Anthropology of Women*, ed. Rayna Rapp Reiter (New York: Monthly Review Press, 1975), 157–210. Also see Jane Flax, "Postmodernism and Gender Relations in Feminist Theory," *Signs* 12 (1987): 621–43; Sandra Harding, *The Science Question in Feminism* (Ithaca, N.Y.: Cornell University Press, 1986); Joan Scott, *Gender and the Politics of History* (New York: Columbia University Press, 1988); and Connell, *Gender and Power.*

14. In *The Reproduction of Mothering* (Berkeley and Los Angeles: University of California Press, 1978), Nancy Chodorow connects the theorizing of families with the theorizing of gender. Connections of individual gender to the dynamics of schools and occupations are discussed in Connell, *Gender and Power,* and in Joan Acker, "Hierarchies, Jobs, Bodies: A Theory of Gendered Organizations" *Gender & Society* 4 (1990): 139–58.

15. In her essay, Weston observes that lesbian and gay families are not structured through gender hierarchy. Nonetheless, gendered meanings enter into their construction, and those with children are organized around the hierarchy of generation.

16. This criticism of the language used by demographers can be found in Ellen Ross, "Examining Family History: Women and Family," *Feminist Studies* 5 (Spring 1979): 188. Along similar lines, Susan Moller Okin criticizes recent theories of justice for assuming an undifferentiated notion of the family and thereby ignoring unequal gender relations (*Gender, Justice, and the Family* [New York: Basic Books, 1989]).

17. Christopher Lasch, *Haven in a Heartless World: The Family Besieged* (New York: Basic Books, 1977).

18. This point is developed in David Spiegel, "Mothering, Fathering, and Mental Illness," in *Rethinking the Family: Some Feminist Questions*, ed. Barrie Thorne with Marilyn Yalom, 1st ed. (New York: Longman, 1982), 95–110.

19. For example, Sigmund Freud, *Dora: An Analysis of a Case of Hysteria*, ed. Philip Rieff (New York: Collier Books, 1963), and Max Horkheimer, "Authority and the Family," in *Critical Theory*, English ed. (New York: Herder & Herder, 1972).

20. Mitchell, "Women: The Longest Revolution," 28.

21. Adrienne Rich, *Of Woman Born: Motherhood as Experience and Institution* (New York: Bantam Books, 1977), xviii.

22. For perceptive discussions of this process, see Bettina Aptheker, *Tapestries of Life: Women's Work, Women's Consciousness, and the Meaning of Daily Experience* (Amherst: University of Massachusetts Press, 1989); Audre Lorde, *Sister Outsider* (Trumansburg, N.Y.: The Crossing Press, 1984); and Dorothy E. Smith, *The Everyday World as Problematic: A Feminist Sociology* (Boston: Northeastern University Press, 1987).

23. We have reprinted the concluding chapter of Kath Weston's book *Families We Choose: Lesbians, Gays, Kinship* (New York: Columbia University Press, 1991), a study drawing on eighty in-depth interviews with lesbians and gay men living in the San Francisco Bay area. An earlier chapter discusses the parenting experiences of lesbians and gay men.

24. Frank J. Furstenberg, Jr., "Good Dads–Bad Dads: Two Faces of Fatherhood," in *The Changing American Family and Public Policy*, ed. Andrew J. Cherlin (Washington, D.C.: Urban Institute Press, 1988), 193–218.

25. Judith Stacey, *Brave New Families: Stories of Domestic Upheaval in Late Twentieth-Century America* (New York: Basic Books, 1990), 268–69.

26. Barbara Katz Rothman, "Women as Fathers: Motherhood and Child Care under a Modified Patriarchy," *Gender & Society* 3 (1989): 89–104.

27. Talcott Parsons, *Social Structure and Personality* (New York: Free Press, 1970). The subtitle of this section, "The Rediscovery of Housework," alludes to home economists' recognition, since the turn of the century, that women do much more than provide socioemotional support within households. Their research on housework, spanning many decades, has been a crucial resource for recent feminist scholars.

28. Arlie Hochschild with Anne Machung, *The Second Shift: Working Parents and the Revolution at Home* (New York: Viking Press, 1989). See also the reviews of research on housework in Myra Marx Ferree, "Beyond Separate Spheres: Feminism and Family Research," *Journal of Marriage and the Family* 52 (1990): 866–84; Glenn, "Gender and the Family," 348–80; and Linda Thompson and Alexis J. Walker, "Gender in Families: Women and Men in Marriage, Work, and Parenthood," *Journal of Marriage and the Family* 51 (1989): 845–71.

29. An early, influential article was Pat Mainardi, "The Politics of Housework," in *Sisterhood is Powerful*, ed. Robin Morgan (New York: Vintage Books, 1970), 447–55.

30. For example, see Susan Strasser, *Never Done: A History of American Housework* (New York: Pantheon Books, 1982) and the review in Ferree, "Beyond Separate Spheres."

31. For reviews, see Arlene Kaplan Daniels, "Invisible Work," *Social Problems* 34 (1987): 403–15, and Emily Abel and Margaret K. Nelson, eds., *Circles of Care: Work and Identity in Women's Lives* (Albany: State University of New York Press, 1990). The concept of "caring" is developed in Nel Noddings, *Caring: A Feminine Approach to Ethics and Moral Education* (Berkeley and Los Angeles: University of California Press, 1984).

32. Marjorie L. DeVault, *Feeding the Family: The Social Organization of Caring as Gendered Work* (Chicago: University of Chicago Press, 1991).

33. See ibid.; Abel and Nelson, eds., *Circles of Care;* and Rannveig Trastadottir, "Mothers Who Care: Gender, Disability, and Family Life," *Journal of Family Issues* 12 (1991): 211–28.

34. For information on the relative position of women and men in the U.S. paid labor force, see Barbara Reskin and Patricia Roos, *Job Queues, Gender Queues* (Philadelphia: Temple University Press, 1990). The complex question of why men don't do more housework is discussed in Ferree, "Beyond Separate Spheres"; Hochschild, *The Second Shift;* and Thompson and Walker, "Gender in Families."

35. Ferree, "Beyond Separate Spheres."

36. Sarah Fenstermaker Berk, *The Gender Factory: The Apportionment of Work in American Households* (New York: Plenum, 1985), 204; see also DeVault, *Feeding the Family.*

37. Lasch, *Haven in a Heartless World,* discusses sociological writings on the family dating back to the 1920s that do take account of conflict (e.g., the work of Willard Waller in the 1930s). Freud also was alert to family conflict, as were Horkheimer, Laing, and other family theorists. I do not claim that recent feminists discovered that families are scenes of conflict and domination, but rather that they have emphasized that side of family life. Freud and Laing stressed the domination of parents over children, while feminists have been more sensitive to the domination and conflict built into gender relations.

38. Shulamith Firestone, *The Dialectic of Sex* (New York: Morrow, 1970), 130. For a recent discussion of ideologies of family love and what they obscure, see Marcia Millman, *Warm Hearts and Cold Cash: The Intimate Dynamics of Families and Money* (New York: Free Press, 1991).

39. Alice Kessler-Harris and Karen Brodkin Sacks, "The Demise of Domesticity in America," in *Women, Households, and the Economy*, ed. Lourdes Benería and Catharine R. Stimpson (New Brunswick, N.J.: Rutgers University Press, 1987), 65–84.

40. Pamela Fishman ("Interaction: The Work Women Do," *Social Problems* 25 [1978]: 397–406) discovered vivid patterns of male control and female deference in conversations of three heterosexual couples at home. She analyzed fifty-two hours of taped conversations and found that men controlled which conversational topics were pursued, while women did much more of the "interaction work" of asking questions and providing verbal support. In a related, more recent study of seven white married couples, Victoria Leto DeFrancisco found that women did more conversational work, yet were more likely to be silenced by their husbands ("The Sounds of Silence: How Men Silence Women in Marital Relations," *Discourse & Society* 2 [1991]: 413–23). The "deferential dialectic" between wives and husbands is analyzed in Colin Bell and Howard Newby, "Husbands and Wives: The Dynamics of the Deferential Dialectic," in *Dependence and Exploitation in Work and Marriage*, ed. Diana Leonard Barker and Sheila Allen (New York: Longman, 1976), 152–68.

41. For a review of research on marital power, illuminated from a feminist perspective, see Osmond and Thorne, "Feminist Theories." The dynamics of marital power may be extremely complex, as shown by Aafke Komter in "Hidden Power in Marriage," *Gender & Society* 3 (1989): 187–216, a study of lower- and upper-middle-class married couples. Komter usefully distinguishes "manifest power" (visible outcomes of decisions and conflicts); "latent power" (wives may not express their desires because they anticipate negative reactions from their husbands); and "invisible power" (perceptual biases in everyday family living; for example, husbands may overestimate their contribution to domestic labor and underestimate the contribution of their wives). Many of the couples in Komter's study affirmed a commitment to egalitarian marriage, but manifest, latent, and invisible power operated in favor of husbands.

42. William J. Goode, "Force and Violence in the Family," *Journal of Marriage and the Family* 33 (1971): 624–36.

43. Diana Russell, *The Secret Trauma: Incest in the Lives of Girls and Women* (New York: Basic Books, 1986). Gordon highlights a theme that feminists have tended to neglect: the gendered experiences of children in families and other institutions, and the intersection of age-based inequality with inequality based on gender. For a discussion of the neglect of children in feminist thought, see Barrie Thorne, "Re-visioning Women and Social Change: Where Are the Children?" *Gender & Society* 1 (1987): 85–109.

44. The dual view of women both as victims of male domination and as active agents has been central to feminist debates about sexuality. Some feminists emphasize men's control of women's sexuality, ideologically and through coercion and violence; others have argued that an emphasis on violence should not eclipse attention to women's experiences of sexual pleasure. See Ann Snitow, Christine Stansell, and Sharon Thompson, eds., *Powers of Desire: The Politics of Sexuality* (New York: Monthly Review Press, 1983), and Carole Vance, ed., *Pleasure and Danger: Exploring Female Sexuality* (Boston: Routledge & Kegan Paul, 1984).

45. Glenn, "Gender and the Family," and idem, *Issei, Nisei, War Bride: Three Generations of Japanese-American Women in Domestic Service* (Philadelphia: Temple University Press, 1986).

46. See Laslett and Brenner, "Gender and Social Reproduction"; Linda Nicholson, *Gender and History: The Limits of Social Theory in the Age of the Family* (New York: Columbia University Press, 1986); and Osmond and Thorne, "Feminist Theories."

47. Glenn, *Issei, Nissei, War Bride;* Judith Rollins, *Between Women: Domestics and Their Employees* (Philadelphia: Temple University Press, 1985).

48. See Naomi Gersel and Harriet Engel Gross, eds., *Families and Work* (Philadelphia: Temple University Press, 1987), and the reviews of literature in Ferree, "Beyond Separate Spheres," and Laslett and Brenner, "Gender and Social Reproduction."

49. Nona Y. Glazer, "Servants to Capital: Unpaid Domestic Work and Paid Work," *Review of Radical Political Economics* 6 (1984): 61–87.

50. Eli Zaretsky, "The Place of the Family in the Origins of the Welfare State," in *Rethinking the Family,* ed. Thorne with Yalom, 1st ed., 188–224.

51. For discussions of the centrality of gender to the organization of the state, see R. W. Connell, "The State in Sexual Politics: Theory and Appraisal," *Theory and Society* 19 (1991): 507–44; Irene Diamond, ed., *Families, Politics, and Public Policy: A Feminist Dialogue on Women and the State* (New York: Longman, 1983); and Linda Gordon, ed., *Women, the State, and Welfare* (Madison: University of Wisconsin Press, 1990).

52. Renate Bridenthal, "The Family: The View from a Room of Her Own," in *Rethinking the Family,* ed. Thorne with Yalom, 1st ed., 231–32.

53. Sara Ruddick, *Maternal Thinking* (Boston: Beacon Press, 1989); Carol Gilligan, *In a Different Voice: Psychological Theory and Women's Development* (Cambridge, Mass.: Harvard University Press, 1982).

54. Joan Scott, "Deconstructing Equality-Versus-Difference; or, The Uses of Poststructuralist Theory for Feminism," *Feminist Studies* 14 (1988): 33–50. Also see Ann Snitow, "A Gender Diary," in *Conflicts in Feminism,* ed. Marianne Hirsch and Evelyn Fox Keller (New York: Routledge, 1990), 8–43.

55. Linda Gordon and Allen Hunter, "Sex, Family, and the New Right: Anti-Feminism as a Political Force," *Radical America* 11 and 12, nos. 7 and 1 (combined issue, 1978): 9–26.

56. Barbara Ehrenreich and Deirdre English, *For Her Own Good: One Hundred and Fifty Years of the Experts' Advice to Women* (New York: Doubleday/Anchor, 1979); Susan Cohen and Mary Fainsod Katzenstein, "The War over the Family is Not over the Family," in *Feminism, Children, and the New Families,* ed. Sanford M. Dornbusch and Myra H. Srober (New York: Guilford Press, 1988), 25–46.

57. Skolnick, *Embattled Paradise,* 212.

58. Stacey, *Brave New Families,* 258.

2

Is There a Family?
New Anthropological Views

Jane Collier, Michelle Z. Rosaldo, Sylvia Yanagisako

This essay poses a rhetorical question in order to argue that most of our talk about families is clouded by unexplored notions of what families "really" are like. It is probably the case, universally, that people expect to have special connections with their genealogically closest relations. But a knowledge of genealogy does not in itself promote understanding of what these special ties are about. The real importance of The Family in contemporary social life and belief has blinded us to its dynamics. Confusing ideal with reality, we fail to appreciate the deep significance of what are, cross-culturally, various ideologies of intimate relationship, and at the same time we fail to reckon with the complex human bonds and experiences all too comfortably sheltered by a faith in the "natural" source of a "nurture" we think is found in the home.

This essay is divided into three parts. The first examines what social scientists mean by The Family. It focuses on the work of Bronislaw Malinowski, the anthropologist who first convinced social scientists that The Family was a universal human institution. The second part also has social scientists as its focus, but it examines works by the nineteenth-century thinkers Malinowski refuted, for if—as we shall argue—Malinowski was wrong in viewing The Family as a universal human institution, it becomes important to explore the work of theorists who did not make Malinowski's mistakes. The final section then draws on the correct insights of nineteenth-century theorists to sketch some implications of viewing The Family, not as a concrete institution designed to fulfill universal human needs, but as an ideological construct associated with the modern state.

This essay appeared in the first edition of *Rethinking the Family.*

Malinowski's Concept of the Family

In 1913 Bronislaw Malinowski published a book called *The Family among the Australian Aborigines,*[1] in which he laid to rest earlier debates about whether all human societies had families. During the nineteenth century, proponents of social evolution argued that primitives were sexually promiscuous and therefore incapable of having families because children would not recognize their fathers.[2] Malinowski refuted this notion by showing that Australian aborigines, who were widely believed to practice "primitive promiscuity," not only had rules regulating who might have intercourse with whom during sexual orgies but also differentiated between legal marriages and casual unions. Malinowski thus "proved" that Australian aborigines had marriage, and so proved that aboriginal children had fathers, because each child's mother had but a single recognized husband.

Malinowski's book did not simply add data to one side of an ongoing debate. It ended the debate altogether, for by distinguishing coitus from conjugal relationships, Malinowski separated questions of sexual behavior from questions of the family's universal existence. Evidence of sexual promiscuity was henceforth irrelevant for deciding whether families existed. Moreover, Malinowski argued that the conjugal relationship, and therefore The Family, had to be universal because it fulfilled a universal human need. As he wrote in a posthumously published book:

> The human infant needs parental protection for a much longer period than does the young of even the highest anthropoid apes. Hence, no culture could endure in which the act of reproduction, that is, mating, pregnancy, and childbirth, was not linked up with the fact of legally-founded parenthood, that is, a relationship in which the father and mother have to look after the children for a long period, and, in turn, derive certain benefits from the care and trouble taken.[3]

In proving the existence of families among Australian aborigines, Malinowski described three features of families that he believed flowed from The Family's universal function of nurturing children. First, he argued that families had to have clear boundaries, for if families were to perform the vital function of nurturing young children, insiders had to be distinguishable from outsiders so that everyone could know which adults were responsible for the care of which children. Malinowski thus argued that families formed bounded social units, and to prove that Australian families formed such units, he demonstrated that aboriginal parents and children recognized one another. Each aboriginal woman had a single husband, even if some husbands had more than one wife and even if husbands occasionally allowed wives to sleep with other men during tribal ceremonies. Malinowski thus proved that each aboriginal child had a recognized mother and father, even if both parents occasionally engaged in sexual relations with outsiders.

Second, Malinowski argued that families had to have a place where family members could be together and where the daily tasks associated with child rearing could be performed. He demonstrated, for example, that aboriginal parents and their immature children shared a single fire—a home and hearth where children were fed and nurtured—even though, among nomadic aborigines, the fire might be kindled in a different location each night.

Finally, Malinowski argued that family members felt affection for one another—that parents who invested long years in caring for children were rewarded by their own and their children's affections for one another. Malinowski felt that long and intimate association among family members fostered close emotional ties, particularly between parents and children, but also between spouses. Aboriginal parents and their children, for example, could be expected to feel the same emotions for one another as did English parents and children, and as proof of this point, Malinowski recounted touching stories of the efforts made by aboriginal parents to recover children lost during conflicts with other aborigines or with white settlers and efforts made by the stolen aboriginal children to find their lost parents.

Malinowski's book on Australian aborigines thus gave social scientists a concept of The Family that consisted of a universal function, the nurturance of young children, mapped onto (1) a bounded set of people who recognized one another and who were distinguishable from other like groups; (2) a definite physical space, a hearth and home; and (3) a particular set of emotions, family love. This concept of The Family as an institution for nurturing young children has been enduring, probably because nurturing children is thought to be the primary function of families in modern industrial societies. The flaw in Malinowski's argument is the flaw common to all functionalist arguments: because a social institution is observed to perform a necessary function does not mean either that the function would not be performed if the institution did not exist or that the function is responsible for the existence of the institution.

Later anthropologists have challenged Malinowski's idea that families always include fathers, but, ironically, they have kept all the other aspects of his definition. For example, later anthropologists have argued that the basic social unit is not the nuclear family including father but the unit composed of a mother and her children: "Whether or not a mate becomes attached to the mother on some more or less permanent basis is a variable matter."[4] In removing father from the family, however, later anthropologists have nevertheless retained Malinowski's concept of The Family as a functional unit, and so have retained all the features Malinowski took such pains to demonstrate. In the writings of modern anthropologists, the mother-child unit is described as performing the universally necessary function of nurturing young children. A mother and her children form a bounded group, distinguishable from other units of mothers and their children. A mother and her children share a place, a home and hearth. And, finally, a mother and her children share deep emotional bonds based on their prolonged and intimate contact.

Modern anthropologists may have removed father from The Family, but they did not modify the basic social science concept of The Family in which the function of child rearing is mapped onto a bounded set of people who share a place and who "love" one another. Yet it is exactly this concept of The Family that we, as feminist anthropologists, have found so difficult to apply. Although the biological facts of reproduction, when combined with a sufficiently elastic definition of marriage, make it possible for us, as social scientists, to find both mother-child units and Malinowski's conjugal-pairs-plus-children units in every human society, it is not at all clear that such Families necessarily exhibit the associated features Malinowski "proved" and modern anthropologists echo.

An outside observer, for example, may be able to delimit family boundaries in any and all societies by identifying the children of one woman and that woman's associated mate, but natives may not be interested in making such distinctions. In other words, natives may not be concerned to distinguish family members from outsiders, as

Malinowski imagined natives should be when he argued that units of parents and children have to have clear boundaries in order for child-rearing responsibilities to be assigned efficiently. Many languages, for example, have no word to identify the unit of parents and children that English speakers call a "family." Among the Zinacantecos of southern Mexico, the basic social unit is identified as a "house," which may include from one to twenty people.[5] Zinacantecos have no difficulty talking about an individual's parents, children, or spouse, but Zinacantecos do not have a single word that identifies the unit of parents and children in such a way as to cut it off from other like units. In Zinacanteco society, the boundary between "houses" is linguistically marked, while the boundary between "family" units is not.

Just as some languages lack words for identifying units of parents and children, so some "families" lack places. Immature children in every society have to be fed and cared for, but parents and children do not necessarily eat and sleep together as a family in one place. Among the Mundurucu of tropical South America, for example, the men of a village traditionally lived in a men's house together with all the village boys over the age of thirteen; women lived with other women and young children in two or three houses grouped around the men's house.[6] In Mundurucu society, men and women ate and slept apart. Men ate in the men's house, sharing food the women had cooked and delivered to them; women ate with other women and children in their own houses. Married couples also slept apart, meeting only for sexual intercourse.

Finally, people around the world do not necessarily expect family members to "love" one another. People may expect husbands, wives, parents, and children to have strong feelings about one another, but they do not necessarily expect prolonged and intimate contact to breed the loving sentiments Malinowski imagined as universally rewarding parents for the care they invested in children. The mother-daughter relationship, for example, is not always pictured as warm and loving. In modern Zambia, girls are not expected to discuss personal problems with, or seek advice from, their mothers. Rather, Zambian girls are expected to seek out some older female relative to serve as confidante.[7] Similarly, among the Cheyenne Indians who lived on the American Great Plains during the last century, a mother was expected to have strained relations with her daughters.[8] Mothers are described as continually admonishing their daughters, leading the latter to seek affection from their fathers' sisters.

Of course, anthropologists have recognized that people everywhere do not share our deep faith in the loving, self-sacrificing mother, but in matters of family and motherhood, anthropologists, like all social scientists, have relied more on faith than evidence in constructing theoretical accounts. Because we *believe* mothers to be loving, anthropologists have proposed, for example, that a general explanation of the fact that men marry mother's brothers' daughters more frequently than they marry father's sisters' daughters is that men naturally seek affection (i.e., wives) where they have found affection in the past (i.e., from mothers and their kin).[9]

Looking Backward

The Malinowskian view of The Family as a universal institution—which maps the "function" of "nurturance" onto a collectivity of specific persons (presumably "nuclear" relations) associated with specific spaces ("the home") and specific affective bonds ("love")—corresponds, as we have seen, to that assumed by most contemporary writers on the subject. But a consideration of available ethnographic evidence suggests that the received view is a good deal more problematic than a naive observer might think. If Families in Malinowski's sense are *not* universal, then we must begin to ask about the biases that, in the past, have led us to misconstrue the ethnographic record. The issues here are too complex for thorough explication in this essay, but if we are to better understand the nature of "the family" in the present, it seems worthwhile to explore the question, first, of why so many social thinkers continue to believe in Capital-Letter Families as universal institutions, and second, whether anthropological tradition offers any alternatives to a "necessary and natural" view of what our families are. Only then will we be in a position to suggest "new anthropological views" on the family today.

Our positive critique begins by moving backward. In the next few pages, we suggest that tentative answers to both questions posed above lie in the nineteenth-century intellectual trends that thinkers like Malinowski were at pains to reject. During the second half of the nineteenth century, a number of social and intellectual developments—among them, the evolutionary researches of Charles Darwin, the rise of "urban problems" in fast-growing cities, and the accumulation of data on non-Western peoples by missionaries and agents of the colonial states—contributed to what most of us would now recognize as the beginnings of modern social science. Alternately excited and perplexed by changes in a rapidly industrializing world, thinkers as diverse as socialist Frederick Engels[10] and bourgeois apologist Herbert Spencer[11]—to say nothing of a host of mythographers, historians of religion, and even feminists—attempted to identify the distinctive problems and potentials of their contemporary society by constructing *evolutionary* accounts of "how it all began." At base, a sense of "progress" gave direction to their thought, whether, like Spencer, they believed "man" had advanced from the love of violence to a more civilized love of peace or, like Engels, that humanity had moved from primitive promiscuity and incest toward monogamy and "individual sex love." Proud of their position in the modern world, some of these writers claimed that rules of force had been transcended by new rules of law,[12] while others thought that feminine "mysticism" in the past had been supplanted by a higher male "morality."[13]

At the same time, and whatever else they thought of capitalist social life (some of them criticized, but none wholly abhorred it), these writers also shared a sense of moral emptiness and a fear of instability and loss. Experience argued forcefully to them that moral order in their time did not rest on the unshakable hierarchy—from God to King to Father in the home—enjoyed by Europeans in the past.[14] Thus, whereas Malinowski's functionalism led him to stress the underlying continuities in all human social forms, his nineteenth-century predecessors were concerned to understand the facts and forces that set their experiential world apart. They were interested in comparative and, more narrowly, evolutionary accounts because their lives were torn between celebration and fear of change. For them, the family was important not because it had at all times been the same but because it was at once the moral precondition for, the triumph of, and the victim of developing capitalist society. Without the family and female spheres, thinkers like John Ruskin feared we would fall victim to a market that destroys real human bonds.[15] Then again, while men like Engels could decry the impact of the market on familial life and love, he joined with more conservative counterparts to insist that our contemporary familial forms benefited from the individualist morality of modern life and reached to moral and romantic heights unknown before.

Given this purpose and the limited data with which they had to work, it is hardly surprising that the vast majority of what these nineteenth-century writers said is easily dismissed today. They argued that in simpler days such things as incest were the norm; they thought that women ruled in "matriarchal" and peace-loving states or, alternatively, that brute force determined the primitive right and wrong. None of these visions of a more natural, more feminine, more sexy, or more violent primitive world squares with contemporary evidence about what, in technological and organizational terms, might be reckoned relatively "primitive" or "simple" social forms. We would suggest, however, that whatever their mistakes, these nineteenth-century thinkers *can* help us rethink the family today, at least in part because we are (unfortunately) their heirs, in the area of prejudice, and partly because their concern to characterize difference and change gave rise to insights much more promising than their functionalist critics may have thought.

To begin, although nineteenth-century evolutionary theorists did not believe The Family to be universal, the roots of modern assumptions can be seen in their belief that women are, and have at all times been, defined by nurturant, connective, and reproductive roles that *do not change* through time. Most nineteenth-century thinkers imaged social development as a process of differentiation from a relatively confused (and thus incestuous) and indiscriminate female-oriented state to one in which men fight, destroy their "natural" social bonds, and then forge public and political ties to create a human "order." For some, it seemed reasonable to assume that women dominated as matriarchs in the undifferentiated early state, but even those theorists believed that women everywhere were "mothers" first, defined by "nurturant" concerns and thus excluded from the business of competition, cooperation, social ordering, and social change propelled and dominated by their male counterparts. And so, while nineteenth-century writers differed in their evaluations of such things as "women's status," they all believed that female reproductive roles made women different from and complementary to men and guaranteed both the relative passivity of women in human history and the relative continuity of "feminine" domains and functions in human societies. Social change consisted in the acts of men, who left their mothers behind in shrinking homes. And women's nurturant sphere was recognized as a complementary and necessary corrective to the more competitive pursuits of men, not because those thinkers recognized women as political actors who influence the world, but because they feared the unchecked and morally questionable growth of a male-dominated capitalist market.

For nineteenth-century evolutionists, women were associated, in short, with an unchanging biological role and a romanticized community of the past, while men were imaged as the agents of all social process. And though contemporary thinkers have been ready to dismiss manifold aspects of their now-dated school of thought, on this point we remain, perhaps unwittingly, their heirs. Victorian assumptions about gender and the relationship between competitive male markets and peace-loving female homes were not abandoned in later functionalist schools of thought at least in part because pervasive sexist biases make it easy to forget that women, like men, are important actors in *all* social worlds. Even more, the functionalists, themselves concerned to understand all human social forms in terms of biological "needs," turned out to strengthen earlier beliefs associating action, change, and interest with the deeds of men because they thought of kinship in terms of biologically given ties, of "families" as units geared to reproductive needs, and finally, of women as mere "reproducers" whose contribution to society was essentially defined by the requirements of their homes.

If most modern social scientists have inherited Victorian biases that tend ultimately to support a view uniting women and The Family to an apparently unchanging set of biologically given needs, we have at the same time failed to reckon with the one small area in which Victorian evolutionists were right. They understood, as we do not today, that families—like religions, economies, governments, or courts of law—are *not* unchanging but the product of various social forms, that the relationships of spouses and parents to their young are apt to be different things in different social orders. More particularly, although nineteenth-century writers had primitive society all wrong, they were correct in insisting that *family* in the modern sense—a unit bounded, biologically as well as legally defined, associated with property, self-sufficiency, with affect and a space "inside" the home—is something that emerges not in Stone Age caves but in complex state-governed social forms. Tribal peoples may speak readily of lineages, households, and clans, but—as we have seen—they rarely have a word denoting Family as a particular and limited group of kin; they rarely worry about differences between legitimate and illegitimate heirs or find themselves concerned (as we so often are today) that what children or parents do reflects on their family's public image and self-esteem. Political influence in tribal groups in fact consists in adding children to one's home and, far from distinguishing Smith from Jones, encouraging one's neighbors to join one's household as if kin. By contrast, modern bounded Families try to keep their neighbors out. Clearly their character, ideology, and functions are not given for all times. Instead, to borrow the Victorian phrase, The Family is a "moral" unit, a way of organizing and thinking about human relationships in a world in which the domestic is perceived to be in opposition to a politics shaped outside the home, and in which individuals find themselves dependent on a set of relatively noncontingent ties in order to survive the dictates of an impersonal market and external political order.

In short, what the Victorians recognized and we have tended to forget is, first, that human social life has varied in its "moral"— we might say its "cultural" or "ideological"—forms, and so it takes more than making babies to make Families. And having seen The Family as something more than a response to omnipresent, biologically given needs, they realized too that Families do not everywhere exist; rather, the Family (thought to be universal by most social scientists today) is a moral and ideological unit that appears, not universally, but in particular social orders. The Family as we know it is not a "natural" group created by the claims of "blood" but a sphere of human relationships shaped by a state that recognizes Families as units that hold property, provide for care and welfare, and attend particularly to the young—a sphere conceptualized as a realm of love and intimacy *in opposition* to the more "impersonal" norms that dominate modern economies and politics. One can, in nonstate social forms, find groups of genealogically related people who interact daily and share material resources, but the contents of their daily ties, the ways they think about their bonds and their conception of the relationship between immediate "familial" links and other kinds of sociality, are apt to be different from the ideas and feelings we think rightfully belong to families we know. Stated otherwise, because our notions of The Family are rooted in a contrast between "public" and "private" spheres, we will not find that Families like ours exist in a society where public and political life is radically different from our own.

Victorian thinkers rightly understood the link between the bounded modern Family and the modern state, although they thought the two related by a necessary teleology of moral progress. Our point resembles theirs not in the *explanations* we would seek but in our feeling that if we, today, are interested in change, we must begin to probe and understand change in the families of the past. Here the Victorians, not the functionalists, are our rightful guides, because the former recognized that *all* human social ties have "cultural" or "moral" shapes and, more specifically, that the particular "morality" of contemporary familial forms is rooted in a set of processes that link our intimate experiences and bonds to public politics.

Toward a Rethinking

Our perspective on families therefore compels us to listen carefully to what the natives in other societies say about their relationships with genealogically close kin. The same is true of the natives in our own society. Our understanding of families in contemporary American society can be only as rich as our understanding of what The Family represents symbolically to Americans. A complete cultural analysis of The Family as an American ideological construct, of course, is beyond the scope of this essay. But we can indicate some of the directions such an analysis would take and how it would deepen our knowledge of American families.

One of the central notions in the modern American construct of The Family is that of nurturance. When antifeminists attack the Equal Rights Amendment, for example, much of their rhetoric plays on the anticipated loss of the nurturant, intimate bonds we associate with The Family. Likewise, when prolife forces decry abortion, they cast it as the ultimate denial of nurturance. In a sense, these arguments are variations of a functionalist view that weds families to specific functions. The logic of the argument is that because people need nurturance, and people get nurtured in The Family, then people need The Family. Yet if we adopt the perspective that The Family is an ideological unit rather than merely a functional unit, we are encouraged to subject this syllogism to closer scrutiny. We can ask, first, What do people mean by nurturance? Obviously, they mean more than mere nourishment—that is, the provision of food, clothing, and shelter required for biological survival. What is evoked by the work *nurturance* is a certain kind of relationship: a relationship that entails affection and love, that is based on cooperation as opposed to competition, that is enduring rather than temporary, that is noncontingent rather than contingent upon performance, and that is governed by feeling and morality instead of law and contract.

The reason we have stated these attributes of The Family in terms of oppositions is because in a symbolic system the meanings of concepts are often best illuminated by explicating their opposites. Hence, to understand our American construct of The Family, we first have to map the larger system of constructs of which it is only a part. When we undertake such an analysis of The Family in our society, we discover that what gives shape to much of our conception of The Family is its symbolic opposition to work and business, in other words, to the market relations of capitalism. For it is in the market, where we sell our labor and negotiate contract relations of business, that we associate with competitive, temporary, contingent relations that must be buttressed by law and legal sanctions.

The symbolic opposition between The Family and market relations renders our strong attachment to The Family understandable, but it also discloses the particularity of our construct of The Family. We can hardly be speaking of a universal notion of The Family shared by people everywhere and for all time, because people everywhere and for all time have not participated in market relations out of which they have constructed a contrastive notion of the family.

The realization that our idea of The Family is part of a set of symbolic oppositions through which we interpret our experience in a particular society compels us to ask to what extent this set of oppositions reflects real relations between people and to what extent it also shapes them. We do not adhere to a model of culture in which ideology is isolated from people's experience. On the other hand, neither do we construe the connection between people's constructs and people's experience to be a simple one of epiphenomenal reflection. Rather, we are interested in understanding how people come to summarize their experience in folk constructs that gloss over the diversity, complexity, and contradictions in their relationships. If, for example, we consider the second premise of the aforementioned syllogism—the idea that people get "nurtured" in families—we can ask how people reconcile this premise with the fact that relationships in families are not always this simple or altruistic. We need not resort to the evidence offered by social historians (e.g., Philippe Ariès[16] and Lawrence Stone[17]) of the harsh treatment and neglect of children and spouses in the history of the Western family, for we need only read our local newspaper to learn of similar abuses among contemporary families. And we can point to other studies, such as Michael Young and Peter Willmott's *Family and Kinship in East London*,[18] that reveal how people often find more intimacy and emotional support in relationships with individuals and groups outside The Family than they do in their relationships with family members.

The point is not that our ancestors or our contemporaries have been uniformly mean and nonnurturant to family members but that we have all been both nice and mean, both generous and ungenerous, to them. In like manner, our actions toward family members are not always motivated by selfless altruism but are also motivated by instrumental self-interest. What is significant is that, despite the fact that our complex relationships are the result of complex motivations, we ideologize relations within The Family as nurturant while casting relationships outside The Family—particularly in the sphere of work and business—as just the opposite.

We must be wary of oversimplifying matters by explaining away those disparities between our notion of the nurturant Family and our real actions toward family members as the predictable failing of imperfect beings. For there is more here than the mere disjunction of the ideal and the real. The American construct of The Family, after all, is complex enough to comprise some key contradictions. The Family is seen as representing not only the antithesis of the market relations of capitalism; it is also sacralized in our minds as the last stronghold against The State, as the symbolic refuge from the intrusions of a public domain that constantly threatens our sense of privacy and self-determination. Consequently, we can hardly be surprised to find that the punishments imposed on people who commit physical violence are lighter when their victims are their own family members.[19] Indeed, the American sense of the privacy of the things that go on inside families is so strong that a smaller percentage of homicides involving family members are prosecuted than those involving strangers.[20] We are faced with the irony that in our society the place where nurturance and noncontingent affection are supposed to be located is simultaneously the place where violence is most tolerated.

There are other dilemmas about The Family that an examination of its ideological nature can help us better understand. For example, the hypothesis that in England and the United States marriages among lower-income ("working-class") groups are characterized by a greater degree of "conjugal role segregation" than are marriages among middle-income groups has generated considerable confusion. Since Elizabeth Bott observed that working-class couples in her study of London families exhibited more "segregated" conjugal roles than "middle-class" couples, who tended toward more "joint" conjugal roles,[21] researchers have come forth with a range of diverse and confusing findings. On the one hand, some researchers have found that working-class couples indeed report more segregated conjugal role relationships—in other words, clearly differentiated male and female tasks, as well as interests and activities—than do middle-class couples.[22] Other researchers, however, have raised critical methodological questions about how one goes about defining a joint activity and hence measuring the degree of "jointness" in a conjugal relationship.[23] Platt's finding that couples who reported "jointness" in one activity were not particularly likely to report "jointness" in another activity is significant because it demonstrates that "jointness" is not a general characteristic of a relationship that manifests itself uniformly over a range of domains. Couples carry out some activities and tasks together or do them separately but equally; they also have other activities in which they do not both participate. The measurement of the "jointness" of conjugal relationships becomes even more problematic when we recognize that what one individual or couple may label a "joint activity," another individual or couple may consider a "separate activity." In Bott's study, for example, some couples felt that all activities carried out by husband and wife in each other's presence were

> similar in kind regardless of whether the activities were complementary (e.g. sexual intercourse, though no one talked about this directly in the home interview), independent (e.g. husband repairing book while the wife read or knitted), or shared (e.g. washing up together, entertaining friends, going to the pictures together). It was

not even necessary that husband and wife should actually be together. As long as they were both at home it was felt that their activities partook of some special, shared, family quality.[24]

In other words, the distinction Bott drew among "joint," "differentiated," and "autonomic" (independent) relationships summarized the way people thought and felt about their activities rather than what they were observed to actually do. Again, it is not simply that there is a disjunction between what people say they do and what they in fact do. The more cogent point is that the meaning people attach to action, whether they view it as coordinated and therefore shared or in some other way, is an integral component of that action and cannot be divorced from it in our analysis. When we compare the conjugal relationships of middle-income and low-income people, or any of the family relationships among different class, age, ethnic, and regional sectors of American society, we must recognize that our comparisons rest on differences and similarities in ideological and moral meanings as well as on differences and similarities in action.

Finally, the awareness that The Family is not a concrete "thing" that fulfills concrete "needs" but an ideological construct with moral implications can lead to a more refined analysis of historical change in the American or Western family than has devolved upon us from our functionalist ancestors. The functionalist view of industrialization, urbanization, and family change depicts The Family as responding to alterations in economic and social conditions in rather mechanistic ways. As production gets removed from the family's domain, there is less need for strict rules and clear authority structures in the family to accomplish productive work. At the same time, individuals who now must work for wages in impersonal settings need a haven where they can obtain emotional support and gratification. Hence, The Family becomes more concerned with "expressive" functions, and what emerges is the modern "companionate family." In short, in the functionalist narrative The Family and its constituent members "adapt" to fulfill functional requirements created for it by the industrialization of production. Once we begin to view The Family as an ideological unit and pay due respect to it as a moral statement, however, we can begin to unravel the more complex, dialectical process through which family relationships and The Family as a construct were mutually transformed. We can examine, for one, the ways in which people and state institutions acted, rather than merely re-acted, to assign certain functions to groupings of kin by making them legally responsible for these functions. We can investigate the manner in which the increasing limitations placed on agents of the community and the state with regard to negotiating the relationships between family members enhanced the independence of The Family. We can begin to understand the consequences of social reforms and wage policies for the age and sex inequalities in families. And we can elucidate the interplay between these social changes and the cultural transformations that assigned new meanings and modified old ones to make The Family what we think it to be today.

Ultimately, this sort of rethinking will lead to a questioning of the somewhat contradictory modern views that families are things we need (the more "impersonal" the public world, the more we need them) and at the same time that loving families are disappearing. In a variety of ways, individuals today *do* look to families for a "love" that money cannot buy and find; our contemporary world makes "love" more fragile than most of us hope and "nurturance" more self-interested than we believe.[25] But what we fail to recognize is that familial nurturance and the social forces that turn our ideal families into mere fleeting dreams are *equally* creations of the world we know *today*. Rather than think of the ideal family as a world we lost (or, like the Victorians, as a world just recently achieved), it is important for us to recognize that while families symbolize deep and salient modern themes, contemporary families are unlikely to fulfill our equally modern nurturant needs.

We probably have no cause to fear (or hope) that The Family will dissolve. What we can begin to ask is what we *want* our families to do. Then, distinguishing our hopes from what we have, we can begin to analyze the social forces that enhance or undermine the realization of the kinds of human bonds we need.

Notes

1. Bronislaw Malinowski, *The Family among the Australian Aborigines* (London: University of London Press, 1913).

2. Lewis Henry Morgan, *Ancient Society* (New York: Holt, 1877).

3. Bronislaw Malinowski, *A Scientific Theory of Culture* (Chapel Hill: University of North Carolina Press, 1944), 99.

4. Robin Fox, *Kinship and Marriage* (London: Penguin Books, 1967), 39.

5. Evon Z. Vogt, *Zinacantan: A Maya Community in the Highlands of Chiapas* (Cambridge, Mass.: Harvard University Press, 1969).

6. Yolanda Murphy and Robert Murphy, *Women of the Forest* (New York: Columbia University Press, 1974).

7. Ilsa Schuster, *New Women of Lusaka* (Palo Alto, Calif.: Mayfield, 1979).

8. E. Adamson Hoebel, *The Cheyennes: Indians of the Great Plains* (New York: Holt, Rinehart & Winston, 1978).

9. George C. Homans and David M. Schneider, *Marriage, Authority, and Final Causes* (Glencoe, Ill.: Free Press, 1955).

10. Frederick Engels, *The Origin of the Family, Private Property and the State*, in *Karl Marx and Frederick Engels: Selected Works*, vol. 2 (Moscow: Foreign Language Publishing House, 1955).

11. Herbert Spencer, *The Principles of Sociology*, vol. 1, *Domestic Institutions* (New York: Appleton, 1973).

12. John Stuart Mill, *The Subjection of Women* (London: Longmans, Green, Reader & Dyer, 1869).

13. J. J. Bachofen, *Das Mutterrecht* (Stuttgart, 1861).

14. Elizabeth Fee, "The Sexual Politics of Victorian Social Anthropology," in *Clio's Banner Raised*, ed. M. Hartman and L. Banner (New York: Harper & Row, 1974).

15. John Ruskin, "Of Queen's Gardens," in *Sesame and Lilies* (London: J. M. Dent, 1907).

16. Philippe Ariès, *Centuries of Childhood*, trans. Robert Baldick (New York: Vintage Books, 1962).

17. Lawrence Stone, *The Family, Sex, and Marriage in England, 1500–1800* (London: Weidenfeld & Nicholson, 1977).

18. Michael Young and Peter Willmott, *Family and Kinship in East London* (London: Routledge & Kegan Paul, 1957).

19. Henry P. Lundsgaarde, *Murder in Space City: A Cultural Analysis of Houston Homicide Patterns* (New York: Oxford University Press, 1977).

20. Ibid.

21. Elizabeth Bott, *Family and Social Network: Roles, Norms, and External Relationships in Ordinary Urban Families* (London: Tavistock, 1957).

22. Herbert J. Gans, *The Urban Villagers* (New York: Free Press, 1962); C. Rosser and C. Harris, *The Family and Social Change* (London: Routledge & Kegan Paul, 1965).

23. John Platt, "Some Problems in Measuring the Jointness of Conjugal Role-Relationships," *Sociology* 3 (1969): 287–97; Christopher Turner, "Conjugal Roles and Social Networks: A Re-examination of an Hypothesis," *Human Relations* 20 (1967): 121–30;

and Morris Zelditch, Jr., "Family, Marriage and Kinship," in *A Handbook of Modern Sociology,* ed. R. E. L. Faris (Chicago: Rand McNally, 1964), 680–707.

24. Bott, *Family and Social Network,* p. 240.

25. See the following essay in this volume, Rayna Rapp's "Family and Class in Contemporary America: Notes toward an Understanding of Ideology."

3

Family and Class in Contemporary America: Notes toward an Understanding of Ideology

RAYNA RAPP

This essay is grounded in two contexts, one political and one academic. The political context is that of the women's movement, in which a debate seems always to be raging concerning the future of the family. Many of us have been to an archetypical meeting in which someone stands up and asserts that the nuclear family ought to be abolished because it is degrading and constraining to women. Usually, someone else (often representing a Third World position) follows on her heels, pointing out that the attack on the family represents a white middle-class position and that other women need their families for support and survival. Evidently both speakers are, in some senses, right. And just as evidently they aren't talking about the same families. We need to explore those different notions of family if we are to heal an important split in our movement. To do so, we must take seriously the things women say about their experiences in their families, especially as they vary by class.

The second context out of which this essay grows is the academic study of the contemporary American family. Over the last few years, in reading eclectically in sociology, demography, urban planning, and policy literature, I've been trying to sort out what is known (or not

The University of Michigan's Women Studies Program called this paper into being, gave it a first airing, and contributed a stimulating set of discussions. Subsequent presentation of these ideas at the New School for Social Research, the URPE Spring conference on Public Policy, and the Anthropology Department of the University of Northern Colorado provided invaluable feedback. I especially want to thank Jill Cherneff, Ingelore Fritsch, Susan Harding, Mike Hooper, Janet Siskind, Deborah Jay Stearns, Batya Weinbaum, and Marilyn Young for their comments. The women of Marxist-Feminist Group II posed the questions that led me to write this paper; they supplied, as always, the supportive context within which the meaning of my work has been discussed. Above all, Gayle Rubin deserves my thanks for her general intellectual aid, and the specific editorial work she did in turning my primary process into a set of written ideas, originally published in a special issue of the *University of Michigan Papers in Woman's Studies* and subsequently published in *Science and Society* 42 (1978): 278–300 and the first edition of *Rethinking the Family*. Reprinted by permission of the author and *Science and Society*.

known) about women's experiences in their families. Here, too, a debate is raging over the future of the family. On the one hand, there is a tremendous alarmism that presages the end of the family—recent books have included titles such as *The Fractured Family;* journals on family coordination and counseling, and courses at every level from high school through graduate studies speak of the family in crisis. On the other hand, *Here to Stay* (to name but one title) and a spate of studies reanalyzing the divorce rates reassure us that the American family is simply changing, but not disappearing. This debate seems to mystify the subject it claims to clarify.[1] This is not surprising, since the family is a topic that is ideologically charged. In order to get some understanding of the importance of ideology in analyses of the family, there are two fields to which we ought to turn for perspective. One is the recent work that has been done on the history of the family.[2] A great many innovative studies reveal similar issues in historical perspective; for as long as modern records have been kept concerning families, it seems that people have been speculating on the future of the institution. The last decade of social history should caution us to moderate our alarmism. At the least, we have learned that all societies contain a multiplicity of family forms whose structural arrangements respond to complex conditions.

The second field that adds perspective to the issue is anthropology, which studies the family and kinship systems both at home and abroad. Anthropology reminds us that we are *all* participant observers when we study the American family. It has been pointed out that our understandings often get in the way and more often express the ideology and norms of our culture than an analysis. This word of warning leads me to examine not only what differing groups of people *say* about their families but also what they actually *do* in their families. It also leads me to examine the ways in which I think the concept of family itself is ideological in social science.

The archetypical political debaters arguing over the meaning of the family aren't talking about the same families. Neither are the social scientists. We need to make a distinction between families and households, and to examine their relation to one another. The entities in which people actually live are not families but households (as any census taker, demographer, or fieldworking anthropologist will tell you). Households are the empirically measurable units within which people pool resources and perform certain tasks. Jack Goody analyzes them as units of production, reproduction, and consumption.[3] They are residential units within which personnel and resources get distributed and connected. Households may vary in their membership composition and in their relation to resource allocation, especially in a system such as our own. That is, they vary systematically in their ability to hook into, accumulate, and transmit wealth, wages, or welfare. This seems a simple unit to define.

Families, on the other hand, are a bit more slippery. In English we tend to gloss "family" to mean household. But analytically, the concept means something else. For all classes of Americans, the word has at least two levels of meaning.[4] One is normative: husbands, wives, and children are a set of relatives who should live together (that is, the nuclear family). The other meaning includes a more extended network of kin relations that people may activate selectively. That is, the American family includes the narrower and broader webs of kin ties that are "the nuclear family" and all relations by blood and marriage. The concept of family is presumed in America to carry a heavy load of affect. We say "blood is thicker than water," "till death do us part," "you can choose your friends, but not your relatives," and so on. What I will argue in this essay is that the concept of family also carries a heavy load of ideology.

The reason for this is that the family is the normative, correct way in which people get recruited into households. It is through families that people enter into productive, reproductive, and consumption relations. The two genders enter them differently. Families organize households, and it is within families that people experience the absence or presence, the sharing or withholding, of basic poolable resources. "Family" (as a normative concept in our culture) reflects those material relations; it also distorts them. As such, the concept of family is a socially necessary illusion that simultaneously expresses and masks recruitment to relations of production, reproduction, and consumption—relations that condition different kinds of household resource bases in different class sectors. Our notions of family absorb the conflicts, contradictions, and tensions actually generated by those material, class-structured relations that households hold to resources in advanced capitalism. "Family," as we understand (and misunderstand) the term, is conditioned by the exigencies of household formation and serves as a shock absorber to keep households functioning. People are recruited and kept in households by families in all classes, yet the families they have (or don't have) are not all the same.

Having asserted that households and families vary by class, we now need to consider that third concept, class. If ever a concept carried a heavy weight of ideology, it is the concept of class in American social science. We have a huge and muddled literature that attempts to reconcile objective and subjective criteria, to sort people into lowers, uppers, and middles, to argue about the relation of consciousness to material reality.[5] I will say only the following: "Social class" is a shorthand for a process, not a thing. That process is the one by which different social relations to the means of production are inherited and reproduced under capitalism. As the concept is developed by Karl Marx, the process of capital accumulation generates and constantly deepens relations between two categories of people: those who are both available and forced to work for wages because they own no means of production, and those who control those means of production. The concept of class expresses a historical process of expanding capital. In the process, categories of people get swept up at different times and places and deposited into different relations to the means of production and to one another. People then get labeled blue collar or white collar; they may experience their social existence as mediated by ethnicity or the overwhelming legacy of slavery and racism. Yet all these categories must be viewed in the light of the historic process of capitalist accumulation in the United States. To a large extent, what are actually being accumulated are changing categories of proletarians. Class formation and composition is always in flux; what gets accumulated in it are relationships. Under advanced capitalism, there are shifting frontiers that separate poverty, stable wage earning, affluent salaries, and inherited wealth. The frontiers may be crossed by individuals, and in either direction. That is, both upward and downward mobility are real processes. The point is, "class" isn't a static place that individuals inhabit. It is a process determined by the relationships set up in capital accumulation.

Returning to the initial distinction between family and household, I want to explore how these two vary among differing class sectors in contemporary America and to draw a composite picture of the households formed around material relations by class, and of the families that organize those households. I will argue that those families mean different things by class, and by genders as well, because classes and genders stand in differing material relations to one another. I'll further argue that their meanings are highly ideological.

I'd like to begin with a review and interpretation of the studies done on the working-class family. Studies span the postwar decades from the late 1940s to the present. They are regionally diverse and report on both cities and suburbs. The data provided by researchers such as Bennett Berger, Herbert J. Gans, Mirra Komarovsky, Joseph Howell, Lillian Rubin, and others reveal a composite portrait.[6] The most salient characteristic of household organization in the working class is dependency on hourly wages. Stable working-class households participate in relations of production, reproduction, and consumption by sending out their labor power in exchange for wages. "Sending out" is important: there is a radical split between household and workplace, yet the resources upon which the household depends come from participation in production outside of itself. How much labor power a working-class household needs to send out is determined by many things: the cost of reproducing (or maintaining) the household, the work careers and earning trajectories of individual members, and the domestic cycle (that is, the relations between the genders and the generations, which specify when and if wives and adolescent children are available to work outside the home). Harry Braverman estimates that the average working-class household now sends out 1.7 full-time equivalent workers.[7] That figure tells us that a high percentage of married women and teenaged children are contributing their wages to the household. In many ways, the work patterns for nineteenth-century European capitalism described by Louise Tilly and Joan Scott[8] still leave their mark on the contemporary American working-class household; it is not only male heads of households upon whom survival depends.

What the working class sends out in exchange for basic resources is labor power. Labor power is the only commodity without which there can be no capitalism. It is also the only commodity for which the working class controls its own means of production.[9] Control over the production of labor power undoubtedly affected women's experiences historically, as it does today.[10] In the early stages of industrialization, it appears that working-class households literally produced a lot of babies (future labor power) as their strategy for dealing with a market economy.[11] Now workers produce fewer children, but the work of caring for them (social reproduction) is still a major process that goes on in the household. Households are the basic units in which labor power is reproduced and maintained. This takes place in a location radically removed from the workplace. Such relations therefore appear as autonomous from capital, but of course they are not; without wages, households are hard to form and keep functioning; without the production of a disciplined labor force, factories cannot produce and profit.

The work that gets done in households (primarily by women) is not simply about babies. Housework itself has recently been rediscovered as work, and its contribution to arenas beyond the household is clear.[12] At the least, housework cuts the reproduction costs of wage workers. Imagine if all those meals had to be bought at restaurants, those clothes cleaned at laundry rates, those beds made by hotel employees! Housework is also what women do in exchange for access to resources that are bought by their husband's wages. As such, it is a coin of exchange between men and women. As housework is wageless, it keeps its workers dependent on others for access to commodities bought with wages. It makes them extremely vulnerable to the work conditions of their men. When women work (as increasingly they do), their primary definition as houseworker contributes to the problems they encounter in entering the paid labor force. They are available for part-time (or full-time) work in the lowest-paid sectors of the labor market, in jobs that leave them less economically secure than men. Participation in the "sexregated" labor market then reinforces dependency upon the earnings of other household members and the continued importance of women's domestic labor.[13]

Of course, these rather abstract notions of "household participation" in the labor market or in housework are experienced concretely by family members. Working-class families are normatively nuclear. They are formed via marriage, which links men and women "for love" and not "for money."[14] This relation is of course both real and a socially necessary illusion. As such, it is central to the ideology of the family. The cultural distinction between love and money corresponds to the distinction between private family life in the home and work life outside the home. The two are experienced as opposite; in fact they are interpenetrating. The seeming autonomy to exchange love at home expresses something ideological about the relation between home and work: one must work for the sake of the family, and having a family is the "payoff" for leading a good life. Founding a family is what people do for personal gratification, for love, and for autonomy. The working-class family literature is full of life histories in which young women saw "love" as a way to get out of their own, often difficult families. Rubin's interviews, for example, are full of teenaged girls who said, "When I grow up, I'll marry for love, and it will be better than my parents' marriage." You may marry for love, but what you mainly get is babies. Forty to 60 percent of teenaged pregnancies are conceived premaritally, and approximately 50 percent of working-class women marry in their teen years.[15] It's a common experience to go from being someone's child to having someone's child in under a year. This is not exactly a situation that leads to autonomy.

For men, the situation is complementary. As one of the young working-class men in Rubin's study puts it:

> I had to work from the time I was thirteen and turn over most of my pay to my mother to help pay the bills. By the time I was nineteen, I had been working for all those years and I didn't have anything— not a thing. I used to think a lot about how when I got married, I would finally get to keep my money for myself. I guess that sounds a little crazy when I think about it now because I have to support the wife and kids. I don't know *what* I was thinking about, but I never thought about that then.[16]

What you get from the romance of love and marriage is in fact not simply a family but a household, and that's quite another matter. Romance is implicated in gender identity and ideology. We are all aware of the cultural distinction made between the sexual identity of a good and a bad girl; a good girl is one who accumulates her sexual resources for later investment. Autonomy means escaping your childhood family to become an adult with your own nuclear family. For young men, the identity process includes the cultural role of wild boy—one who "sows some wild oats," hangs out on street corners, perhaps gets in trouble with the police, and drinks.[17] Ideally, the good girl domesticates the wild boy; she gives him love, and he settles down and goes out to work. Autonomy means becoming an adult with your own nuclear family as an escape. But of course, autonomy is illusive. The family is classically seen as an escape from production, but in fact it is what sends people into relations of production, for they need to work to support their families. The meaning of production is simultaneously denied and experienced through family relations; working-class wives say of a good husband that he works steadily, provides for the kids, and never harms anyone in the family. The complementary statement is uttered by working-class husbands, who define a good wife as one who keeps the kids under control when he comes home from a hard day's work, and who runs the household well.[18] To exchange love is also to underwrite both the necessity and the ability to keep on working. *This* is the heritage that working-class families pass on, in lieu of property, to their children.

The family expresses ideology in another sense as well—the distinction between norms and realities. The norms concerning families are that people should be loving and sharing within them and that they should be protective. The reality is too often otherwise, as the recent rising consciousness of domestic violence indicates. Even without domestic violence, there are more commonplace stresses to which families are often subjected. Rubin found in her study that 40 percent of the adults she interviewed had an alcoholic parent.[19] Fifty percent had experienced parental desertion or divorce in their childhoods. National statistics confirm these figures.[20] About half the adults in her study had seriously destabilizing experiences within their families. The tension generated by relations to resource base can often tear households apart. Under these conditions, to label the working-class personality "authoritarian" seems a cruel hoax. When the household is working, it expresses work discipline.

Ideology is expressed in gender role in families in another sense as well. Throughout the urban kinship literature, across classes and ethnic groups, the work of reproducing families is in part undertaken by larger kinship groups (the family in the broader sense of relatives). Family networks in this larger sense are women-centered and tend to be serviced by women. There exists a large literature on women-centered kinship networks in which it is usually assumed that women minister to kinship because they minister to families in general. Sylvia Yanagisako suggests that there is also a symbolic level to the kinship work that women do; ideologically, women are assigned to "inside, home, private" domains, while men are seen to represent the outside world.[21] Nuclear families are under cultural constraints to appear as autonomous and private. Yet they are never as private in reality as such values might indicate. The ideal autonomy of an independent

nuclear family is constantly being contradicted by the realities of social need, in which resources must be pooled, borrowed, shared. It is
women who bridge the gap between what a household's resources really are and what a family's position is supposed to be. Women exchange babysitting, share meals, lend small amounts of money. When
a married child is out of work, his (or her) nuclear family turns to the
mother and often moves in for a while. The working-class family literature is filled with examples of such pooling.[22] To the extent that
women "represent" the family, they facilitate the pooling needed at
various points in the domestic cycle. Men maintain, at least symbolically, the autonomy of their families. Pooling is a norm in family behavior, but it's a hard norm to live with, to either meet or ignore. To
comply with the demands of the extended family completely is to lose
control over material and emotional resources; to refuse is very dangerous, as people know they will need one another. The tightrope act
that ensues is well characterized in the classic mother-in-law story,
which usually concerns a young wife and her husband's mother. The
two women must figure out a way to share the small services, the material benefits, and the emotional satisfactions one man brings to
them both in their separate roles of mother and wife. The autonomy
of the younger woman is often compromised by the elder's needs; the
authority of the mother is sometimes undermined by the demands of
the wife. Women must constantly test, strain, and repair the fibers of
their kinship networks.

Such women-centered networks are implicated in a process that
has not yet been discussed. We have spoken of production and reproduction as they affect the working-class household and family. We
ought briefly to mention consumption as well. As a household function, consumption includes turning an amount of wages into commodities so that labor power may be reproduced. This is often
women's work. And work it really is. Batya Weinbaum and Amy
Bridges tell us that the centralization and rationalization of services
and industry under advanced capitalism may be most efficient from
the point of view of capital, but it leaves a lot of unrewarding, technical work to be done by women shopping in supermarkets, paying
bills, and dealing with huge bureaucracies.[23] Women experience the
pay packet in terms of the use values it will buy. Yet their consumption work is done in the world of exchange value. They mediate the
tension between use and exchange, as exemplified in the classic tales

concerning domestic quarrels over money in which the man blames the woman for not making his paycheck stretch far enough. In stable working-class neighborhoods, the consumption work is in part done by women united by family ties who exchange services, recipes, sales information, and general life-style skills. Kinship networks are part of "community control" for women. As Nancy Seifer notes, working-class women become involved in political issues that threaten the stability of their neighborhoods.[24] Perhaps one reason is that their neighborhoods are the locus of extended families within which both work needs and emotional needs are so often met.

When everyone submits to the conditions described here "for the sake of the family," we see the pattern that Howell labels settled living.[25] Its opposite, in his words, is hard living, a family life-style that includes a lot of domestic instability, alcohol, and rootlessness. I want to stress that I am here departing from a "culture of poverty" approach. The value of a label like "hard living" is that it stresses a continuum made up of many attributes. It is composed of many processes with which the working class has a lot of experience. Given the national statistics on alcoholism, desertion, divorce, premarital pregnancy, and the like, everyone's family has included such experiences, either in its own domestic cycle or in the wider family network.[26] Everyone had a wild brother, or was a bad girl, or had an uncle who drank too much or cousins who got divorced. In each of such cases, everyone experienced the pooling of resources (or the lack of pooling) as families attempted to cope with difficult, destabilizing situations. In a sense, the hard livers keep the settled livers more settled: The consequences of leaving the normative path are well known and are not appealing. This, too, is part of the working-class heritage. In studies by Seifer, Howell, and Rubin, young women express their hopes of leaving a difficult family situation by finding the right man to marry. They therefore marry young, with little formal education, possibly about to become parents, and the cycle begins again.

Of course, hard living is most consistently associated with poverty in the urban family literature. For essentially political reasons, Black poverty has more frequently been the subject of social science analysis than has white poverty, but the pattern is found across races. African Americans have survived under extremely difficult conditions; many of their household and family patterns have evolved to deal with their specific history, while others are shared with Americans of similar class and regional backgrounds. The problems of household formation under poverty conditions are not unique to any group of people; some of the specific, resilient solutions to those problems may be. Because we know far more about Black families in poverty than we do about whites, I'll draw a composite picture of households and families using studies that are primarily Black.[27] Even when talking about very poor people, analysts such as Elliot Liebow, Ulf Hannerz, Charles Valentine, and Carol B. Stack note that there are multiple household types, based on domestic cycles and the relative ability to draw on resources. Hannerz, for example, divides his Black sample into four categories.[28] Mainstreamers live in stable households composed of husband, wife, and children. The adults are employed and either own their own homes or aspire to do so. Their households don't look very different from the rest of the working class. Swingers (Hannerz's second type) are younger, single persons who may be on their way into mainstream life, or they may be tending toward street families (type three), whose households are headed by women. This type is most important for our study. The fourth category is composed of street men who are peer-oriented and predominantly hardcore unemployed or underemployed. They are similar to the men of *Tally's Corner.*[29] While Hannerz and Liebow both give us a wealth of information about what men are doing, they don't analyze their domestic arrangements in detail. Carol Stack, who did her fieldwork from the perspective of female-centered households, most clearly analyzes household formation of the very poor. She presents us with domestic networks: extremely flexible and fluctuating groups of people committed to resource pooling, to sharing, to mutual aid, who move in and out from under one another's roofs.[30]

Given the state of the job market, welfare legislation, and segregated slum housing, households are unstable. These are people essentially living below socially necessary reproduction costs. They therefore reproduce themselves by spreading out the aid and the risks involved in daily life. For the disproportionally high numbers who are prevented from obtaining steady employment, being part of what Marx called the floating surplus population is a perilous endeavor. What this means in human terms is not only that the poor pay more (as David Caplowitz tells us)[31] but that the poor share more as well. Stack's monograph contains richly textured descriptions of the way that food, furniture, clothing, appliances, kids, and money make the rounds between individuals and households. She subtitles one chapter "What Goes Round Comes Round" and describes the velocity with which pooling takes place. People try to give what they can and take what they need. Meeting consumption requirements is hard work under these conditions, and domestic networks get the task done. The pleasures and pressures of such survival networks are predominantly organized around the notion of family.

Meyer Fortes tells us that "domestic groups are the workshops of social reproduction."[32] Whatever else they do, the families that organize domestic networks are responsible for children. As Joyce Ladner and Stack remind us, poverty, low levels of formal education, and early age for first pregnancy are highly correlated; a lot of young girls have children while they are not fully adults.[33] Under these circumstances, at least among Black families, there is a tremendous sharing of the children themselves. On the whole, these are not kids who grow up in "isolated nuclear families." Stack, for example, found that 20 percent of the Aid to Families with Dependent Children (AFDC) children in her study were being raised in a household other than that which contained the biological mother. In the vast majority of cases, the household was related through the biological mother's family. Organizing kinship networks so that children are cared for is a primary function of families. Men, too, often contribute to child rearing. Like women, they share out bits and pieces of whatever they have. While some men make no contribution, others may be simultaneously contributing to sisters and to a mother and aunt, as well as to wives or lovers. They may sleep in one household, but take groceries, money, and affection to several others.[34] Both Stack and Ladner analyze the importance of a father's recognition of his children, by which act he links the baby to his own kinship network. It is family in the broader sense of the term that organizes social reproduction.

Family may be a conscious construction of its participants. Liebow, Stack, Ladner, and others describe fictive kinship, by which friends are turned into family. Since family is supposed to be more reliable than friendship, "going for brothers," "for sisters," "for cousins," increases the commitment of a relationship, and makes people ideally more responsible for one another. Fictive kinship is a serious relationship. Stack (who is white) describes her own experience with Ruby, a Black woman with whom she "went for sisters." When Ruby's child was seriously ill, Stack became deeply involved in the crisis. When the baby was admitted to the hospital, she and Ruby rushed over for visiting hours. They were stopped by a nurse, who insisted that only the immediate family could enter. Ruby responded, "Caroline here is my sister, and nothing's stopping her from visiting this baby." And they entered, unchallenged. Ruby was correct; under the circumstances, white Caroline was her sister.[35]

Liebow notes that fictive kinship increases the intensity of relationships to the point where they occasionally explode: the demands of brothers and sisters for constant emotional and material aid may lead to situations that shatter the bonds. Fictive kinship is a prime example of family-as-ideology. In this process, reality is inverted. "Everybody" gets a continuous family, even though the strains and mobility associated with poverty may conspire to keep biological families apart. The idiom of kinship brings people together despite centrifugal circumstances.

It is important not to romanticize this pattern. It has enormous benefits, but is participants also pay high costs. One of the most obvious costs is leveling: Resources must be available for all and none may get ahead. Variations in the chance for survival are smoothed out in domestic networks via sharing. Stack tells the story of a central couple, Calvin and Magnolia, who unexpectedly inherit a sum of money. While the money might have enabled them to ensure their own security, it is gone within a few months. It disappears into the network to pay off bills, buy clothing for children, allow people to eat better.[36] Similar stories are told by Hannerz, Liebow, and Howell. No one gets ahead because individual upward mobility can be bought only at the price of cutting off the very people who have contributed to one's survival. Upward mobility becomes a terribly scarring experience under these circumstances. To get out, a person must stop sharing, which is unfamilial, unfriendly, and quite dangerous. It also requires exceptional circumstances. Gans speaks of the pain that working-class children face if they attempt to use school as a means to achieve mobility, for they run into the danger of being cut off from their peer group.[37] The chance for mobility may occur only once or twice in a lifetime—for example, at specific moments in a school career or in marriage. People rarely get the occasion, and when they do, to grasp it may simply be too costly. The pressures to stay in a supportive and constraining network and to level out differences may be immense. They contribute to the instability of marriage and the normative nuclear family, for the old networks compete with the new unit for precious resources.

The family as an ideological construction is extremely important to poor people. Many studies show that the poor don't aspire to less "stable families," if that term is understood as nuclear families. They are simply much more realistic about their life chances. Ties to family, including fictive family, are the lifelines that simultaneously hold together and sustain individuals. My guess is that among the poor, families do not exhibit the radical split between "private, at home" and "public, at work" found in families of the stable working class. Neither work relations nor household relations are as continuous or as distinct. What *is* continuous is the sharing of reproduction costs throughout a network whose resources are known to all. There can be no privatization when survival may depend on rapid circulation of limited resources. In this process, women don't "represent" kinship to the outside world. They become the nodal points in family nets that span whatever control very poor people have over domestic and resource-getting arrangements. Families are what make the huge gap between norm and reality survivable.

It is particularly ironic that the ideology of family, so important to poor people, is used by ruling-class ideologues to blame the poor for their own condition. In a society in which *all* Americans subscribe to some version of the normative nuclear family, it is cruelty to attack "the Black family" as pathological. Mainstream culture, seeing the family as " what you work for" (and what works for you), uses "family language" to stigmatize those who are structurally prevented from accumulating stable resources. The very poor have used their families to cement and patch tenuous relations to survival; out of their belief in "family" they have invented networks capable of making next-to-nothing go a long way.[38] In response, they are told that their notion of family is inadequate. It isn't their notion of family that is deficient, but the relationship between household and productive resources.

If we now return to the political debate that opened this essay, I believe we can see that there are two different concepts of family at work. To achieve a normative family is something many categories of Americans are prevented from doing because of the ways that their households plug into tenuous resource bases. And when normative families are achieved, it is at substantial and differential costs to both men and women.

Having considered the meaning of family and household among class sectors with regular or unstable relations to wages, we should now consider those sectors for whom resource bases are more affluent. Analyzing the family and household life of the middle class is a tricky business. The term *middle class* is ambiguous; a majority of Americans identify themselves as part of it whenever they answer questionnaires, and the category obviously carries positive connotations. Historically, we take the notion from the Marxian definition of the petty bourgeoisie: that category of people who own small amounts of productive resources and have control over their working conditions in ways that proletarians do not. The term signifies a state in proletarianization in which small-scale entrepreneurs, tradesfolk, artisans, and professionals essentially stand outside the wage-labor/capital relation. That stage is virtually over: there are ever fewer small-scale proprietors or artisans working on their own account in post–World War II America. We now use the term to refer to a different sector—employees in corporate management, government and organizational bureaucrats of various kinds, and professionals, many of whom work directly or indirectly for big business, the state, and semipublic institutions. On the whole, this "new middle class" is dependent on wages; as such, it bears the mark of proletarianization. Yet the group lives at a level that is quite different from the wage levels of workers.[39] Such a category is obviously hard to define; like all class sectors, it must be historically situated, for the middle class of early twentieth-century America differs markedly from that of our own times. To understand what *middle class* means for the different groups, we need to know not only their present status but also the ethnic and regional variations in class structure within which their families entered America.

In a sense, the middle class is a highly ideological construction that pervades American culture; it is, among other things, the perspective from which mainstream social scientists approach the experiences of all the other sectors they attempt to analyze. To analyze the middle class's household formations and family patterns, we have to examine not only the data available on all the people who claim to be middle class but also explore the biases inherent in much of social science. This is a task beyond the scope of the present essay. Instead, I merely suggest a few tentative ideas as notes toward future research.

Households among the middle class are obviously based on a stable resource base that allows for some amount of luxury and discretionary spending. When exceptional economic resources are called for, nonfamilial institutions usually are available in the form of better medical coverage, expense accounts, pension plans, credit at banks, and so on. Such households may maintain their economic stability at the cost of geographical instability; male career choices may move households around like pieces on a chessboard. When far from family support networks, such households may get transitional aid from professional moving specialists, or institutions like the Welcome Wagon.[40] Middle-class households probably are able to rely on commodity forms rather than kinship processes to ease both economic and geographic transitions.

The families that organize such households are commonly thought to be characterized by egalitarian marriages.[41] Rubin comments that "egalitarian marriage" may be a biased gloss for a communication pattern in which the husband's career is in part reflected in the presentation of his wife.[42] To entertain intelligently, and instill the proper educational and social values in the children, women may need to know more about the male world. They represent the private credentials of family to the public world of their men at work. If this is the case, then "instrumental communication" might be a more appropriate term.

I am not prepared at this point to offer an analysis of middle-class kinship patterns, but I have a few hunches to present:

1. At this level, kinship probably shifts from the lateral toward the lineal. That is, resources (material and economic) are invested lineally, between parents, children, and grandchildren, and not dispersed into larger networks, as happens with working-class and poor families. Such a pattern would of course vary with geographical mobility, and possibly with ethnicity. There is usually a greater investment across generations, and a careful accumulation within them. This kind of pattern can be seen, for example, in the sums invested in children's educations, setting up professional practices, wedding gifts (in which major devolvement of property may occur), and so forth.

2. Perhaps friendship, rather than kinship, is the nexus within which the middle class invests its psychic and "familial" energies. Friendship allows for a great deal of affective support and exchange but usually does not include major resource pooling. It is a relation consistent with resource accumulation rather than dispersal. If the poor convert friendship into kinship to equalize pooling, it seems to

me that the middle class does the converse: It reduces kinship exchanges and replaces them with friendship, which protects them from pooling and leveling.[43]

There is one last sector of the American class system whose household and family patterns would be interesting to examine—the upper class, sometimes identified as the ruling class or the very rich. Once again, I limit myself to a few tentative observations. As one sociologist (either naive or sardonic) commented, "We know so little about the very wealthy because they don't answer our questionnaires." Indeed! They fund them rather than answer them. The few studies we do have (by authors such as G. William Domhoff, Cleveland Amory, E. Digby Baltzell, Thorstein Veblen) are highly suggestive. The upper class, they tell us, seems to hang together as a cultural phenomenon. Its members defend their own interests corporately and have tremendous ideological importance.

We know very little about the household structure of the very rich. They are described as having multiple households that are recomposed seasonally and filled with service workers rather than exclusively with kin and friends.[44] While there is a general tendency toward "conspicuous consumption," we have no basic information on the relation of their resource bases to domestic arrangements.

When we turn to the family structure of the very rich, some interesting bits and pieces emerge (which may possibly be out of date). Families are described as extremely lineal and concerned with who they are rather than what they do. People have access to one another through their control of neighborhoods, schools, universities, clubs, churches, and ritual events. They are ancestor-oriented and conscious of the boundaries that separate the "best" families from all others. Families are obviously the units within which wealth is accumulated and transmitted. Yet the link between wealth and class is not so simple; some of the "best" families lose fortunes but remain in the upper class. Mobility is also possible. According to Baltzell, under certain circumstances it is possible for nonmembers to enter the class via educational and work-related contacts.[45] What emerges from the literature is a sketch of a group that is perhaps the only face-to-face subculture that America contains.

Women serve as gatekeepers of many of the institutions of the very rich.[46] They launch children, serve as board members at private schools, run clubs, and facilitate marriage pools through events like debuts and charity balls. Men also preside over exclusive clubs and schools, but different ones. The upper class appears to live in a world that is very sex-segregated. Domhoff mentions several other functions that very rich women fulfill. These include (1) setting social and cultural standards and (2) softening the rough edges of capitalism by doing charity and cultural work. While he trivializes the cultural standards that women set to things like dress and high art, I think he has alerted us to something more important. In the upper class, women "represent" the family to the outside world. But here, it is an outside world that is in many senses created by their own class (in the form of high cultural institutions, education, social welfare, and charity). Their public presence is an inversion of reality; they appear as wives and mothers, but it is not really their family roles but their class roles that dictate those appearances. To the extent that "everyone else" either has a wife/mother or is a wife/mother, upper-class women are available to be perceived as something both true and false. What they can do because of their families (and, ultimately, for their families) is utterly, radically different from what other women who "represent" their families can do. Yet what everyone sees is their womanness as family members rather than class members. They influence our cultural notions of what feminine and familial behavior should be. They simultaneously become symbols of domesticity and public service to which others may aspire. The very tiny percentage of very wealthy women who live in a sex-segregated world and have no need to work are thus perceived as benevolent and admirable by a much larger group of women whose relation to sex role segregation and work is not nearly so benign. "Everybody" can yearn for a family in which sex role segregation is valued; nobody else can have a family in which it is valued as highly as theirs. In upper-class families, at least as they present themselves to "the public," we see a systematic confusion of cultural values with the values of family fortunes. We have here an excellent illustration of how the ideas of the ruling class become part of the ruling ideas of society.

At each level of American society, households vary systematically as to resource base and their ability to tap wealth, wages, and welfare. Households are organized by families (which means relatives both distant and close, imaginary and real). Families both reflect and distort the material relations within which households may *appear* isolated from the arenas in which production takes place. But, in fact, their families are formed to generate and deepen relations to those work processes that underwrite their illusion of autonomy. Women's experience with "the family" varies systematically by class because class expresses the material and social relations upon which their household bases rest. We need to explore their transformatory potential as well as the constraints that differential family patterns provide.

Women have structurally been put in the position of representing the contradictions between autonomy and dependence, between love and money, in the relations of families to capitalism. The ideological role that women have played needs to be demystified as we struggle toward a future in which consumption and reproduction will not be determined by capitalist production, in which households will not have access to such uneven resource bases, and in which women will neither symbolically nor in their real relations be forced to bridge the gap between affective norms and contradictory realities under the name of love. To liberate the notion of voluntary relations that the normative family is supposed to represent, we have to stop paying workers off in a coin called love.

Notes

1. The demographic concerns are clearly outlined in Mary Jo Bane, *Here to Stay: American Families in the Twentieth Century* (New York: Basic Books, 1976); historical issues of rapid change are briefly reviewed in Lois Decker O'Neill, "The Changing Family," *Wilson Quarterly,* Winter 1977; the political issues and public policy concerns are presented with polemical flair in Michael Novak, "The Family Out of Favor," *Harper's,* April 1976.

2. Overviews of the history of the family literature may be found in Elizabeth H. Pleck, "Two Worlds in One: Work and Family," *Journal of Social History* 1 (December 1976): 178–95; Christopher Lasch, "The Family and History," *New York Review of Books* 22 (1975–76): 18–20; and Louise Tilly and Joan Scott, *Women, Work, and Family* (New York: Routledge, 1978). They all stress the complex relation between political-economic and ideological change that both condition and are conditioned by family patterns.

3. Jack Goody, "The Evolution of the Family," in *Household and Family in Past Time,* ed. Peter Laslett and Richard Wall (Cambridge: Cambridge University Press, 1972).

4. Ibid. Also see David M. Schneider and Raymond T. Smith, *Class Differences and Sex Roles in American Kinship and Family Structure* (Englewood Cliffs, N.J.: Prentice-Hall, 1973).

5. There is a vast literature on this subject. Its mainstream interpretations in relation to family research are reviewed in Luther B. Otto, "Class and Status in Family Research," *Journal of Marriage and the Family* 37 (1975): 315–32. Marxist perspectives are presented

in Charles H. Anderson, *The Political Economy of Social Class* (Englewood Cliffs, N.J.: Prentice-Hall, 1974); idem, *Toward a New Sociology,* rev. ed. (Homewood, Ill.: Dorsey Press, 1974); Alfred Szymanski, "Trends in the American Class Structure," *Socialist Revolution,* no. 10 (July–August 1972); and Harry Braverman, *Labor and Monopoly Capital: The Degradation of Work in the Twentieth Century* (New York: Monthly Review Press, 1974).

6. This composite is drawn from the works of Bennett Berger, *Working Class Suburb: A Study of Auto Workers in Suburbia* (Berkeley and Los Angeles: University of California Press, 1968); Herbert J. Gans, *The Urban Villagers* (New York: Free Press, 1962), idem, *The Levittowners* (New York: Columbia University Press, 1967); Louise Kapp Howe, ed., *The White Majority: Between Poverty and Affluence* (New York: Random House, 1970); Joseph Howell, *Hard Living on Clay Street: Portraits of Blue Collar Families* (New York: Waveland Press, 1973); Mirra Komarovsky with Jane H. Philips, *Blue-Collar Marriage* (New York: Summit Books, 1986); Lillian Rubin, *Worlds of Pain: Life in the Working-Class Family* (New York: Basic Books, 1976); Joseph A. Ryan, ed., *White Ethnics: Life in Working Class America* (Englewood Cliffs, N.J.: Prentice-Hall, 1973); Nancy Seifer, *Absent from the Majority: Working Class Women in America,* Middle America Pamphlet Series, National Project on Ethnic America (American Jewish Committee, 1973), idem, *Nobody Speaks for Me: Self-Portraits of American Working Class Women* (New York: Simon & Schuster, 1976); Arthur B. Shostak, *Blue-Collar Life* (New York: Random House, 1969); Richard Sennett and Jonathan Cobb, *The Hidden Injuries of Class* (New York: Knopf, 1972); Patricia Cayo Sexton and Brendan Sexton, *Blue Collars and Hard Hats: The Working Class and the Future of American Politics* (New York: Random House, 1971); and Studs Terkel, *Working* (New York: Ballantine, 1972).

7. Braverman, *Labor and Monopoly Capital.*

8. Louise Tilly and Joan Scott, "Women's Work in Nineteenth Century Europe," *Comparative Studies in Society and History* 17 (1975): 36–64.

9. See Ira Gernstein, "Domestic Work and Capitalism," *Radical America* 7 (1973): 101–30.

10. Linda Gordon, *Women's Body, Women's Right: A Social History of Birth Control in America* (New York: Viking Press, 1976).

11. Louise Tilly, "Reproduction, Production, and the Family among Textile Workers in Roubaix, France" (Paper presented at the Conference on Social History, February 1977).

12. The economic value of housework has been the subject of vigorous debate in Marxist literature in recent years. The debate was begun with the publication of Mariarosa Dalla Costa, "Women and the Subversion of the Community," *Radical America* 6 (1972): 67–102, and continued by Wally Secombe, "The Housewife and Her Labour under Capitalism," *New Left Review* 83 (1974): 3–24; Jean Gardiner, "Women's Domestic Labour," *New Left Review* 89 (1975): 47–71; Lise Vogel, "The Earthly Family," *Radical America* 7 (1973): 9–50; Gerstein, "Domestic Work and Capitalism"; and others. See also Heidi I. Hartmann, "Capitalism and Women's Work in the Home, 1900–1930" (Ph.D. diss., Yale University, 1974), and Joann Vanek, "Time Spent in Housework," *Scientific American,* November 1974, 116–20, for American case historical materials, and Nona Glazer-Malbin, "Review Essay: Housework," *Signs* 1 (1975): 905–22, for a review of the field.

13. For historical, sociological, and political-economic analyses of women's economic position in the labor market, see the special issue of *Signs,* ed. Barbara B. Reagan and Martha

Blaxall, "Women and the Workplace," 1, no. 3, pt. 2 (1976). See also U.S. Bureau of the Census, *Statistical Abstract of the U.S.*, 1974, for statistical data on demography and work-force participation rates of women.

14. Schneider and Smith, *Class Differences and Sex Roles in American Kinship and Family Structure*, chap. 5.

15. Rubin, *Worlds of Pain*, chap. 4.

16. Ibid., 56–57.

17. See ibid.; also Shostak, *Blue Collar Life*, and Howell, *Hard Living on Clay Street*.

18. See Rubin, *Worlds of Pain*; Shostak, *Blue Collar Life*; Sennett and Cobb, *The Hidden Injuries of Class*; and Terkel, *Working*.

19. Rubin, *Worlds of Pain*.

20. U.S. Bureau of the Census, *Statistical Abstract of the U.S.*, 1974, 221–22.

21. Sylvia Junko Yanagisako, "Women-Centered Kin Networks in Urban, Bilateral Kinship," *American Ethnologist* 4 (1977): 207–26.

22. This literature is reviewed in ibid. Further instances are found in the sources listed in note 6. The pattern is given much attention in Michael Young and Peter Wilmott, *Family and Kinship in East London* (London: Routledge & Kegan Paul, 1957); and in Elizabeth Bott, *Family and Social Network: Roles, Norms, and External Relationships* (New York: Free Press, 1971).

23. Batya Weinbaum and Amy Bridges, "The Other Side of the Paycheck: Monopoly Capital and the Structure of Consumption," *Monthly Review* 28 (1976): 88–103.

24. Seifer, *Absent from the Majority*, and idem, *Nobody Speaks For Me*.

25. Howell, *Hard Living on Clay Street*.

26. Throughout her work, Rubin is especially sensitive to this issue and provides an excellent discussion of individual life cycles in relation to domestic cycles. She explains why the labeling issue is such a critical one (*Worlds of Pain*, 223, note 5).

27. Howell's *Hard Living on Clay Street* provides important and sensitive insights into the domestic lives of poor and working white families, collected in the style of Oscar Lewis. Composite black family studies include Ulf Hannerz, *Soulside: Inquiries into Ghetto Culture and Community* (New York: Columbia University Press, 1969); Joyce Ladner, *Tomorrow's Tomorrow: The Black Woman* (Garden City, N.Y.: Doubleday, 1971); Elliot Liebow, *Tally's Corner: A Study of Negro Street Corner Men* (Boston: Little, Brown, 1967); Lee Rainwater, *Behind Ghetto Walls: Black Families in a Federal Slum* (Chicago: Aldine De Gruyter, 1970); John H. Scanzoni, *The Black Family in Modern Society* (Boston: Allyn & Bacon, 1971); Carol B. Stack, *All Our Kin: Strategies for Survival in a Black Community* (New York: Harper & Row, 1974); and Charles Valentine, *Culture and Poverty: Critique and Counter-Proposals* (Chicago: University of Chicago Press, 1968), and idem, "Black Studies and Anthropology: Scholarly and Political Interests in Afro-American Culture," *McCaleb Module in Anthropology*, no. 15.

28. Hannerz, *Soulside*.

29. Liebow, *Tally's Corner*.

30. Stack, *All Our Kin*.

31. David Caplovitz, *The Poor Pay More: Consumer Practices of Low-Income Families* (New York: Free Press, 1967).

32. Meyer Fortes, "Introduction," in *The Developmental Cycle in Domestic Groups*, ed. Jack Goody (Cambridge: Cambridge University Press, 1972).

33. Ladner, *Tomorrow's Tomorrow*; Stack, *All Our Kin*.

34. See especially Stack, *All Our Kin*, chap. 7.

35. Ibid., 21.

36. Ibid., 105–7.

37. Gans, *The Urban Villagers*.

38. It is easier to make this point given the consciousness-raising works of Alex Haley, *Roots* (Garden City, N.Y.: Doubleday, 1976); and Herbert Gutman, *The Black Family in Slavery and Freedom, 1750–1925* (New York: Random House, 1976). They point out— in popular and scholarly language respectively—the historical depth and importance of this pattern.

39. Braverman, *Labor and Monopoly Capital*, chap. 18.

40. Vance Packard, "Mobility: Restless America," *Mainliner Magazine*, May 1977.

41. Schneider and Smith, *Class Differences and Sex Roles in American Kinship and Family Structure*, chap. 4.

42. Rubin, *Worlds of Pain*.

43. I know of no substantial work describing the uses of friendship versus kinship in the middle class.

44. William Hoffman, *David: Report on a Rockefeller* (Secaucus, N.J., 1971); E. Digby Baltzell, *Philadelphia Gentlemen: The Making of a National Upper Class* (New York: Transaction, 1958).

45. Baltzell, *Philadelphia Gentlemen*.

46. G. William Domhoff, *The Higher Circles: The Governing Class in America* (New York: Random House, 1970).

4

Family, Race, and Poverty in the Eighties

M A X I N E B A C A Z I N N

The 1960s civil rights movement overturned segregation laws, opened voting booths, created new job opportunities, and brought hope to Black Americans. As long as it could be said that conditions were improving, Black family structure and life-style remained private matters. The promises of the 1960s faded, however, as the income gap between whites and Blacks widened. Since the middle 1970s, the Black underclass has expanded rather than contracted, and along with this expansion has emerged a public debate about the Black family. Two distinct models of the underclass now prevail—one that is cultural and one that is structural. Both of them focus on issues of family structure and poverty.

The Cultural Deficiency Model

The 1980s ushered in a revival of old ideas about poverty, race, and family. Many theories and opinions about the urban underclass rest on the culture-of-poverty debate of the 1960s. In brief, proponents of the culture-of-poverty thesis contend that the poor have a different way of life than the rest of society and that these cultural differences explain continued poverty. Within the current national discussion are three distinct approaches that form the latest wave of deficiency theories.

The first approach—culture as villain—places the cause of the swelling underclass in a value system characterized by low aspirations, excessive masculinity, and the acceptance of female-headed families as a way of life.

This essay first appeared in *Signs: Journal of Women in Culture and Society* (1989) 14, no. 4.

The second approach—family as villain—assigns the cause of the growing underclass to the structure of the family. While unemployment is often addressed, this argument always returns to the causal connections between poverty and the disintegration of traditional family structure.

The third approach—welfare as villain—treats welfare and anti-poverty programs as the cause of illegitimate births, female-headed families, and low motivation to work. In short, welfare transfer payments to the poor create disincentives to work and incentives to have children out of wedlock—a self-defeating trap of poverty.

Culture as Villain

Public discussions of urban poverty have made the "disintegrating" Black family the force most responsible for the growth of the under-class. This category, by definition poor, is overwhelmingly Black and disproportionately composed of female-headed households. The members are perceived as different from striving, upwardly mobile whites. The rising number of people in the underclass has provided the catalyst for reporters' and scholars' attention to this disadvan-taged category. The typical interpretation given by these social com-mentators is that the underclass is permanent, being locked in by its own unique but maladaptive culture. This thinking, though flawed, provides the popular rationale for treating the poor as the problem.

The logic of the culture-of-poverty argument is that poor people have distinctive values, aspirations, and psychological characteristics that inhibit their achievement and produce behavioral deficiencies likely to keep them poor not only within generations but also across generations, through socialization of the young.[1] In this argument, poverty is more a function of thought processes than of physical environment.[2] As a result of this logic, current discussions of ghetto poverty, family structure, welfare, unemployment, and out-of-wedlock births connect these conditions in ways similar to the 1965 Moyni-han Report.[3] Because Daniel P. Moynihan maintained that the patho-logical problem within Black ghettos was the deterioration of the Negro family, his report became the generative example of blaming the victim.[4] Furthermore, Moynihan dismissed racism as a salient force in the perpetuation of poverty by arguing that the tangle of pa-thology was "capable of perpetuating itself without assistance from the white world."[5]

The reaction of scholars to Moynihan's cultural-deficiency model was swift and extensive, although not as well publicized as the model itself. Research in the 1960s and 1970s by Andrew Billingsley, Robert Hill, Herbert Gutman, Joyce Ladner, Elliot Leibow, and Carol Stack, to name a few, documented the many strengths of Black families, strengths that allowed them to survive slavery, the enclosures of the South, and the depression of the North.[6] Such work revealed that many patterns of family life were not created by a deficient culture but were instead "a rational adaptational response to conditions of deprivation."[7]

A rapidly growing literature in the 1980s documents the disproportionate representation of Black female-headed families in poverty. Yet, recent studies on Black female-headed families are largely unconcerned with questions of adaptation. Rather, they study the strong association between female-headed families and poverty, the effects of family disorganization on children, the demographic and socioeconomic factors that are correlated with single-parent status, and the connection between the economic status of men and the rise in Black female-headed families.[8] While most of these studies do not advance a social-pathology explanation, they do signal a regressive shift in analytic focus. Many well-meaning academics who intend to call attention to the dangerously high level of poverty in Black female-headed households have begun to emphasize the family structure and the Black ghetto way of life as contributors to the perpetuation of the underclass.

The popular press, on the other hand, openly and enthusiastically embraced the Moynihan thesis both in its original version and in Moynihan's restatement of the thesis in his book *Family and Nation*.[9] Here Moynihan repeats his assertion that poverty and family structure are associated, but now he contends that the association holds for Blacks and whites alike. This modification does not critique his earlier assumptions; indeed, it validates them. A profoundly disturbing example of this is revealed in a widely publicized 1986 television documentary, CBS Reports' "The Vanishing Family."[10] According to this refurbished version of the old Moynihan Report, a breakdown in family values has allowed Black men to renounce their traditional breadwinner role, leaving Black women to bear the economic responsibility for children.[11] The argument that the Black community is devastating itself fits neatly with the resurgent conservatism that is manifested among Black and white intellectuals and policymakers.

Another contemporary example of the use of the culture of poverty is Nicholas Lemann's two-part 1986 *Atlantic* article about the Black underclass in Chicago.[12] According to Lemann, family structure is the most visible manifestation of Black America's bifurcation into a middle class that has escaped the ghetto and an underclass that is irrevocably trapped in the ghetto. He explains the rapid growth of the underclass in the 1970s by pointing to two mass migrations of Black Americans. The first was from the rural South to the urban North and numbered in the millions during the 1940s, 1950s, and 1960s; the second, a migration out of the ghettos by members of the Black working and middle classes, who had been freed from housing discrimination by the civil rights movement. As a result of the exodus, the indices of disorganization in the urban ghettos of the North (crime, illegitimate births) have risen, and the underclass has flourished.[13] Loose attitudes toward marriage, high illegitimacy rates, and family disintegration are said to be a heritage of the rural South. In Lemann's words, they represent the power of culture to produce poverty:

> The argument is anthropological, not economic; it emphasizes the power over people's behavior that culture, as opposed to economic incentives, can have. Ascribing a society's condition in part to the culture that prevails there seems benign when the society under discussion is England or California. But as a way of thinking about black ghettos it has become unpopular. Twenty years ago ghettos were often said to have a self-generating, destructive culture of poverty (the term has an impeccable source, the anthropologist Oscar Lewis). But then the left equated cultural discussions of the ghetto with accusing poor blacks of being in a bad situation that was of their own making. . . . The left succeeded in limiting the terms of the debate to purely economic ones, and today the right also discusses the ghetto in terms of economic "incentives to fail," provided by the welfare system. . . . In the ghettos, though, it appears that the distinctive culture is now the greatest barrier to progress by the black underclass, rather than either unemployment or welfare.[14]

Lemann's essay, his "misreading of left economic analysis, and cultural anthropology itself,"[15] might be dismissed if it were atypical in the debate about the culture of poverty and the underclass. Unfortunately, it shares with other studies the problems of working "with neither the benefit of a well-articulated theory about the impact of personality and motivation on behavior nor adequate data from a representative sample of the low-income population."[16]

The idea that poverty is caused by psychological factors and that poverty is passed on from one generation to the next has been called into question by the University of Michigan's Panel Study of Income Dynamics (PSID), a large-scale data collection project conceived, in part, to test many of the assumptions about the psychological and demographic aspects of poverty. This study has gathered annual information from a representative sample of the U.S. population. Two striking discoveries contradict the stereotypes stemming from the culture-of-poverty argument. The first is the high turnover of individual families in poverty and the second is the finding that motivation cannot be linked to poverty. Each year the number of people below the poverty line remains about the same, but the poor in one year are not necessarily the poor in the following year. "Blacks from welfare dependent families were no more likely to become welfare dependent than similar Blacks from families who had never received welfare. Further, measures of parental sense of efficacy, future orientation, and achievement motivation had no effects on welfare dependency for either group."[17] This research has found no evidence that highly motivated people are more successful at escaping from poverty than those with lower scores on tests.[18] Thus, cultural deficiency is an inappropriate model for explaining the underclass.

The Family as Villain

A central notion within culture-of-poverty arguments is that family disintegration is the source and sustaining feature of poverty. Today, nearly six out of ten Black children are born out of wedlock, compared to roughly three out of ten in 1970. In the twenty-five-to-thirty-four-year age bracket, today the probability of separation and divorce for Black women is twice that of white women. The result is a high probability that an individual Black woman and her children will live alone. The so-called deviant mother-only family, common among Blacks, is a product of "the feminization of poverty," a shorthand reference to women living alone and being disproportionately represented among the poor. The attention given to increased marital breakups, to births to unmarried women, and to the household patterns that accompany those changes would suggest that the bulk of contemporary poverty is a family-structure phenomenon. Common knowledge—whether true or not—has it that family-structure changes cause most poverty, or changes in family structure have led to current poverty rates that are much higher than they would have been if family composition had remained stable.[19]

Despite the growing concentration of poverty among Black female-headed households in the past two decades, there is reason to question the conventional thinking. Research by Mary Jo Bane finds that changes in family structure have less causal influence on poverty than is commonly thought.[20] Assumptions about the correlation and association between poverty and family breakdown avoid harder questions about the character and direction of causal relations between the two phenomena.[21] Bane's longitudinal research on household composition and poverty suggests that much poverty, especially among Blacks, is the result of already poor two-parent households that break up, producing poor female-headed households. This differs from the event transition to poverty that is more common for whites: "Three-quarters of whites who were poor in the first year after moving into a female-headed or single person household became poor simultaneously with the transition; in contrast, of the blacks who were poor after the transition, about two-thirds had also been poor before. Reshuffled poverty as opposed to event-caused poverty for blacks challenges the assumption that changes in family structure have created ghetto poverty. This underscores the importance of considering the ways in which race produces different paths to poverty."[22]

A two-parent family is no guarantee against poverty for racial minorities. Analyzing data from the PSID, Martha Hill concluded that the long-term income of Black children in two-parent families throughout the decade was even lower than the long-term income of non-Black children who spent most of the decade in mother-only families: "Thus, increasing the proportion of Black children growing up in two-parent families would not by itself eliminate very much of the racial gap in the economic well-being of children; changes in the economic circumstances of the parents are needed most to bring the economic status of Black children up to the higher status of non-Black children."[23]

Further studies are required if we are to understand the ways in which poverty, family structure, and race are related.

Welfare as Villain

An important variant of the family-structure and deficient-culture explanations, one especially popular among political conservatives, is
the argument that welfare causes poverty. This explanation proposes
that welfare undermines incentives to work and causes families to
break up by allowing Black women to have babies and encouraging
Black men to escape family responsibilities. This position has been
widely publicized by Charles Murray's influential book *Losing
Ground*.[24] According to Murray, liberal welfare policies squelch
work incentives and thus are the major cause of the breakup of the
Black family. In effect, increased Aid to Families with Dependent
Children (AFDC) benefits make it desirable to forgo marriage and
live on the dole.

Research has refuted this explanation for the changes in the structure of families in the underclass. Numerous studies have shown that
variations in welfare across time and in different states have not produced systematic variation in family structure.[25] Research conducted
at the University of Wisconsin's Institute for Research on Poverty
found that poverty increased after the late 1960s due to a weakening
economy through the 1970s. No support was found for Murray's assertion that spending growth did more harm than good for Blacks
because it increased the percentage of families headed by women.
Trends in welfare spending increased between 1960 and 1972, and
declined between 1970 and 1984; yet there were no reversals in
family-composition trends during this period. The percentage of
those households headed by women increased steadily from 10.7 percent to 20.8 percent between 1968 and 1983.[26]

Further evidence against the "welfare dependency" motivation for
the dramatic rise in the proportion of Black families headed by females is provided by William Darity and Samuel Meyers. Using statistical causality tests, they found no short-term effects of variations
in welfare payments on female headship in Black families.[27]

Other research draws similar conclusions about the impact of welfare policies on family structure. Using a variety of tests, David Ellwood and Lawrence Summers dispute the adverse effects of AFDC.[28]
They highlight two facts that raise questions about the role of welfare
policies in producing female-headed households. First, the real value
of welfare payments has declined since the early 1970s, while family
dissolution has continued to rise. Family-structure changes do not

mirror benefit-level changes. Second, variations in benefit levels across states do not lead to corresponding variations in divorce rates or numbers of children in single-parent families. Their comparison of groups collecting AFDC with groups that were not found that the effects of welfare benefits on family structures were small.[29] In sum, the systematic research on welfare and family structure indicates that AFDC has far less effect on changes in family structure than has been assumed.

Opportunity Structures in Decline

A very different view of the underclass has emerged alongside the popularized cultural-deficiency model. This view is rooted in a substantial body of theory and research. Focusing on the opportunity structure of society, these concrete studies reveal that culture is not responsible for the underclass.

Within the structural framework there are three distinct strands. The first deals with transformations of the economy and the labor force that affect Americans in general and Blacks and Hispanics in particular. The second is the transformation of marriage and family life among minorities. The third is the changing class composition of inner cities and their increasing isolation of residents from mainstream social institutions.

All three are informed by new research that examines the macrostructural forces that shape family trends and demographic patterns that expand the analysis to include Hispanics.

Employment

Massive economic changes since the end of World War II are causing the social marginalization of Black people throughout the United States. The shift from an economy based on the manufacture of goods to one based on information and services has redistributed work in global, national, and local economies. While these major economic shifts affect all workers, they have more serious consequences for Blacks than whites, a condition that scholars call "structural racism."[30] Major economic trends and patterns, even those that appear race neutral, have significant racial implications. Blacks and other minorities are profoundly affected by (1) the decline of industrial manufacturing sectors and the growth of service sectors of the economy, and (2) shifts in the geographical location of jobs from central cities to the suburbs and from the traditional manufacturing cities (the rustbelt) to the sunbelt and to other countries.

In their classic work *The Deindustrialization of America*, Barry Bluestone and Bennett Harrison revealed that "minorities tend to be concentrated in industries that have borne the brunt of recent closing. This is particularly true in the automobile, steel, and rubber industries."[31] In a follow-up study, Bluestone, Harrison, and Lucy Gorham have shown that people of Color, particularly Black men, are more likely than whites to lose their jobs due to the restructuring of the U.S. economy and that young Black men are especially hard hit.[32] Further evidence of the consequences of economic transformation for minority males is provided by Richard Hill and Cynthia Negrey.[33] They studied deindustrialization in the Great Lakes region and found that the race-gender group that was hardest hit by the industrial slump was Black male production workers. Fully 50 percent of this group in five Great Lakes cities studied lost their jobs in durable-goods manufacturing between 1979 and 1984. They found that Black male production workers also suffered the greatest rate of job loss in the region and in the nation as a whole.

The decline of manufacturing jobs has altered the cities' roles as opportunity ladders for the disadvantaged. Since the start of World War II, well-playing blue-collar jobs in manufacturing have been a main avenue of job security and mobility for Blacks and Hispanics. Movement into higher-level blue-collar jobs was one of the most important components of Black occupational advancement in the 1970s. The current restructuring of industries creates the threat of downward mobility for middle-class minorities.[34]

Rather than offering opportunities to minorities, the cities have become centers of poverty. Large concentrations of Blacks and Hispanics are trapped in cities in which the urban employment base is shifting. Today inner cities are shifting away from being centers of production and distribution of physical goods toward being centers of administration, information, exchange, trade, finance, and government service. Conversely, these changes in local employment structures have been accompanied by a shift in the demographic composition of large central cities away from European white to predominantly Black and Hispanic, with rising unemployment. The transfer of jobs away from central cities to the suburbs has created a residential job opportunity mismatch that literally leaves minorities behind in the inner city. Without adequate training or credentials, they are relegated to low-paying, nonadvancing exploitative service work or they are unemployed. Thus, Blacks have become, for the most part, superfluous people in cities that once provided them with opportunities.

The composition and size of cities' overall employment bases have also changed. During the past two decades most older, larger cities have experienced substantial job growth in occupations associated with knowledge-intensive service industries. However, job growth in these high-skill, predominantly white-collar industries has not compensated for employment declines in manufacturing, wholesale trade, and other predominantly blue-collar industries that once constituted the economic backbone of Black urban employment.[35]

While cities once sustained large numbers of less skilled persons, today's service industries typically have high educational requisites for entry. Knowledge and information jobs in the central cities are virtually closed to minorities given the required technological education and skill level. Commuting between central cities and outlying areas is increasingly common; white-collar workers commute daily from their suburban residences to the central business districts while streams of inner-city residents are commuting to their blue-collar jobs in outlying nodes.[36]

An additional structural impediment inner-city minorities face is their increased distance from current sources of blue-collar and other entry-level jobs. Because the industries that provide these jobs have moved to the suburbs and nonmetropolitan peripheries, racial discrimination and inadequate incomes of inner-city minorities now have the additional impact of preventing many from moving out of the inner city in order to maintain their access to traditional sources of employment. The dispersed nature of job growth makes public transportation from inner-city neighborhoods impractical, requiring virtually all city residents who work in peripheral areas to commute by personally owned automobiles. The severity of this mismatch is documented by John Kasarda: "More than one half of the minority households in Philadelphia and Boston are without a means of personal transportation. New York City's proportions are even higher with only three of ten black or Hispanic households having a vehicle available."[37]

This economic restructuring is characterized by an overall pattern of uneven development. Manufacturing industries have declined in the North and Midwest while new growth industries, such as computers and communications equipment, are locating in the southern and southwestern part of the nation. This regional shift has produced some gains for Blacks in the South, where Black poverty rates have declined. Given the large minority populations in the sunbelt, it is conceivable that industrial restructuring could offset the economic threats to racial equality. However, the sunbelt expansion has been based largely on low-wage, labor-intensive enterprises that use large numbers of underpaid minority workers, and a decline in the northern industrial sector continues to leave large numbers of Blacks and Hispanics without work.

Marriage

The connection between declining Black employment opportunities (especially male joblessness) and the explosive growth of Black families headed by single women is the basis of William J. Wilson's analysis of the underclass. Several recent studies conducted by Wilson and his colleagues at the University of Chicago have established this link.[38] Wilson and Kathryn Neckerman have documented the relationship between increased male joblessness and female-headed households. By devising an indicator called "the index of marriageable males," they reveal a long-term decline in the proportion of Black men, and particularly young Black men, who are in a position to support a family. Their indicators include mortality and incarceration rates, as well as labor-force participation rates, and they reveal that the proportion of Black men in unstable economic situations is much higher than indicated in current unemployment figures.[39]

Wilson's analysis treats marriage as an opportunity structure that no longer exists for large numbers of Black people. Consider, for example, why the majority of pregnant Black teenagers do not marry. In 1960, 42 percent of Black teenagers who had babies were unmarried; by 1970 the rate jumped to 63 percent and by 1983 it was 89 percent.[40] According to Wilson, the increase is tied directly to the changing labor-market status of young Black males. He cites the well-established relationship between joblessness and marital instability in support of his argument that "pregnant teenagers are more likely to marry if their boyfriends are working."[41] Out-of-wedlock births are sometimes encouraged by families and absorbed into the kinship system because marrying the suspected father would mean adding someone who was unemployed to the family's financial burden.[42] Adaptation to structural conditions leaves Black women disproportionately separated, divorced, and solely responsible for their children. The mother-only family structure is thus the consequence, not the cause, of poverty.

Community

These changes in employment and marriage patterns have been accompanied by changes in the social fabric of cities. "The Kerner Report Twenty Years Later," a conference of the 1988 Commission on the Cities, highlighted the growing isolation of Blacks and Hispanics.[43] Not only is inner-city poverty worse and more persistent than it was twenty years ago, but ghettos and barrios have become isolated and deteriorating societies with their own economies and with increasingly isolated social institutions, including schools, families, businesses, churches, and hospitals. According to Wilson, this profound social transformation is reflected not only in the high rates of joblessness, crime, and poverty but also in a changing socioeconomic class structure. As Black middle-class professionals left the central city, so too did working-class Blacks. Wilson uses the term "concentration effects" to capture the experiences of low-income families who now make up the majority of those who live in inner cities. The most disadvantaged families are disproportionately concentrated in the sections of the inner city that are plagued by joblessness, lawlessness, and a general milieu of desperation. Without working-class or middle-class role models, these families have little in common with mainstream society.[44]

The departure of the Black working and middle classes means more than a loss of role models, however. As David Ellwood has observed, the flight of Black professionals has meant the loss of connections and networks. If successfully employed persons do not live nearby, then the informal methods of finding a job, by which one worker tells someone else of an opening and recommends her or him to the employer, are lost.[45] Concentration and isolation describe the processes that systematically entrench a lack of opportunities in inner cities. Individuals and families are thus left to acquire life's necessities though they are far removed from the channels of social opportunity.

The Changing Demography of Race and Poverty

Hispanic poverty, virtually ignored for nearly a quarter of a century, has recently captured the attention of the media and scholars alike. Recent demographic and economic patterns have made "the flow of Hispanics to urban America among the most significant changes occurring in the 1980s."[46]

As the Hispanic presence in the United States has increased in the last decade, Hispanic poverty rates have risen alarmingly. Between 1979 and 1985 the percentage of Latinos who were poor grew from 21.8 percent to 29.0 percent. Nationwide, the poverty rate for all Hispanics was 27.3 percent in 1986. By comparison, the white poverty rate in 1986 was 11 percent; the Black poverty rate was 31.1 percent.[47] Not only have Hispanic poverty rates risen alarmingly, but like Black poverty, Hispanic poverty has become increasingly concentrated in inner cities. Hispanics fall well behind the general population on all measures of social and economic well-being: jobs, income, educational attainment, housing, and health care. Poverty among Hispanics has become so persistent that, if current patterns continue, Hispanics will emerge in the 1990s as the nation's poorest racial-ethnic group.[48] Hispanic poverty has thus become a trend to watch in national discussions of urban poverty and the underclass.

While Hispanics are emerging as the poorest minority group, poverty rates and other socioeconomic indictors vary widely among Hispanic groups. Among Puerto Ricans, 39.9 percent of the population lived below the poverty level in 1986. For Mexicans, 28.4 percent were living in poverty in 1986. For Cubans and Central and South Americans, the poverty rate was much lower: 18.7 percent.[49] Such diversity has led scholars to question the usefulness of this racial-ethnic category that includes all people of Latin American descent.[50] Nevertheless, the labels Hispanic or Latino are useful in general terms in describing the changing racial composition of poverty populations. In spite of the great diversity among Hispanic nationalities, they face common obstacles to becoming incorporated into the economic mainstream of society.

Researchers are debating whether trends of rising Hispanic poverty are irreversible and if those trends point to a permanent underclass among Hispanics. Do macrostructural shifts in the economy and the labor force have the same effects on Blacks and Latinos? According to Joan W. Moore, national economic changes do affect Latinos, but they affect subgroups of Latinos in different ways:

> The movement of jobs and investments out of Rustbelt cities has left many Puerto Ricans living in a bleak ghetto economy. This same movement has had a different effect on Mexican Americans living in the Southwest. As in the North, many factories with job ladders have disappeared. Most of the newer Sunbelt industries offer either high paying jobs for which few Hispanics are trained or low paying ones that provide few opportunities for advancement. Those industries that depend on immigrant labor (such as clothing manufacturing in Los Angeles) often seriously exploit their workers, so the benefits to Hispanics in the Southwest of this influx of industries and investments are mixed. Another subgroup, Cubans in Miami, work and live in an enclave economy that appears to be unaffected by this shift in the national economy.[51]

Because shifts in the subregional economies seem more important to Hispanics than changes in the national economy, Moore is cautious about applying William Wilson's analysis of how the underclass is created.

Opportunity structures have not declined in a uniform manner for Latinos. Yet Hispanic poverty, welfare dependence, and unemployment rates are greatest in regions that have been transformed by macrostructural economic changes. In some cities, Puerto Rican poverty and unemployment rates are steadily converging with, and in some cases exceeding, the rates of Blacks. In 1986, 40 percent of Puerto Ricans in the United States lived below the poverty level and 70 percent of Puerto Rican children lived in poverty.[52]

Family structure is also affected by economic dislocation. Among Latinos, the incidence of female-headed households is highest for Puerto Ricans—43.3 percent—compared to 19.2 percent for Mexicans, 17.7 for Cubans, and 25.5 percent for Central and South Americans.[53] The association between national economic shifts and high rates of social dislocation among Hispanics provides further evidence for the structural argument that economic conditions rather than culture create distinctive forms of racial poverty.

Family, Poverty, and Gender

The structural model described above advances our understanding of poverty and minority families beyond the limitations of the cultural model. It directs attention away from psychological and cultural issues and toward social structures that allocate economic and social rewards. It has generated a substantial body of research and findings that challenge culture-of-poverty arguments.

On matters of gender, however, the structural model would benefit from discussion, criticism, and rethinking. This is not to deny the structural model's value in linking poverty to external economic conditions but, rather, to question the model's assumptions about gender and family structure and to point to the need for gender as a specific analytic category.

Although several key aspects of the structural model distinguish it from the cultural model, both models are remarkably close in their thinking about gender. Patricia Hill Collins exposes the gender ideologies that underlie cultural explanations of racial inferiority.[54] Those same ideologies about women and men, about their place in the family and their relationship to the public institutions of the larger society, reappear, albeit in modified ways, in the structural model.

Collins shows how assumptions about racial deficiency rest on cultural notions about unfit men and women. In contrast, the structural approach focuses on the social circumstances produced by economic change. It therefore avoids drawing caricatures of men who spurn work and unmarried women who persist in having children. Yet both models find differences between mainstream gender roles and those of the underclass. Indeed, some of the most striking and important findings of the structural approach focus on this difference. Clearly, the reasons for the difference lie in the differing economic and social opportunities of the two groups, yet the structural model assumes that the traditional family is a key solution for eliminating racial poverty. Although the reasons given for the erosion of the traditional family are very different, both models rest on normative definitions of women's and men's roles. Two examples reveal how the structural perspective is locked into traditional concepts of the family and women's and men's places within it.

Wilson identifies male joblessness and the resulting shortage of marriageable males as the conditions responsible for the proliferation of female-headed households. His vision of a soluttion is a restoration of marital opportunities and the restoration of family structures in which men provide for their families by working in the labor force and women have children who can then be assured of the economic opportunities afforded by two-parent families. He offers no alternative concept of the family, no discussion of lesbian families or other arrangements that differ from the standard male-female married pair. Instead of exploring how women's opportunities and earning capacities outside of marriage are affected by macrostructural economic transformations, instead of calling "for pay equity, universal day care and other initiatives to buttress women's capacities for living independently in the world . . . Wilson goes in exactly the opposite direction."[55]

Ellwood's comprehensive analysis of American family poverty and welfare, *Poor Support: Poverty in the American Family,* contains a discussion that says a great deal about how women, men, and family roles are viewed by authoritative scholars working within the structural tradition. Looking at the work of adults in two-parent families, Ellwood finds that all families must fulfill two roles—a nurturing/child-rearing role and a provider role—and that in two-parent families these responsibilities are divided along traditional gender lines. Therefore, Ellwood raises the question "Do we want single mothers to behave like husbands or like wives? Those who argue that single mothers ought to support their families through their own efforts are implicitly asking that they behave like husbands."[56] While Ellwood's discussion is meant to illustrate that single mothers experience difficulty in having to fulfill the dual roles of provider and nurturer, it confuses the matter by reverting to a gendered division of labor in which women nurture and men provide. By presenting family responsibilities as those of "husbands" and "wives," even well-meaning illustrations reproduce the ideology they seek to challenge.

Structural approaches have failed to articulate gender as an analytic category even though the conditions uncovered in contemporary research on the urban underclass are closely intertwined with gender. In fact, the problems of male joblessness and female-headed households form themselves around gender. Although these conditions are the result of economic transformations, they change gender relations as they change the marital, family, and labor arrangements of women and men. Furthermore, the economic disenfranchisement of large numbers of Black men, what Clyde Franklin calls "the institutional decimation of Black men,"[57] is a gender phenomenon of enormous magnitude. It affects the meanings and definitions of masculinity for Black men, and it reinforces the public patriarchy that controls Black women through their increased dependence on welfare. Such gender issues are vital. They reveal that where people of Color "end up" in the social order has as much to do with the economic restructuring of gender as with the economic restructuring of class and race.

The new structural analyses of the underclass reveal that the conditions in which Black and Hispanic women and men live are extremely vulnerable to economic change. In this way, such analyses move beyond "feminization of poverty" explanations that ignore class and race differences among women and ignore poverty among minority men.[58] Yet many structural analyses fail to consider the interplay of gender-based assumptions with structural racism. Just as the "feminization of poverty" approach has tended to neglect the way in which race produces different routes to poverty, structural discussions of the underclass pay far too little attention to how gender produces different routes to poverty for Black and Hispanic women and men. Many social forces are at work in the current erosion of family life among Black and Hispanic people. Careful attention to the interlocking systems of class, race, and gender is imperative if we are to understand and solve the problems resulting from economic transformation.

Notes

1. Mary Corcoran, Greg J. Duncan, Gerald Gurin, and Patricia Gurin, "Myth and Reality: The Causes and Persistence of Poverty," *Journal of Policy Analysis and Management* 4, no. 4 (1985): 516–36.

2. Mary Corcoran, Greg J. Duncan, and Martha S. Hill, "The Economic Fortunes of Women and Children: Lessons from the Panel Study of Income Dynamics," *Signs* 10, no. 2 (Winter 1984): 232–48.

3. Daniel P. Moynihan, "The Negro Family: The Case for National Action," in *The Moynihan Report and the Politics of Controversy*, ed. L. Rainwater and W. L. Yancy (Cambridge, Mass.: MIT Press, 1967), 39–132.

4. Margaret Cerullo and Marla Erlien, "Beyond the 'Normal Family': A Cultural Critique of Women's Poverty," in *For Crying Out Loud*, ed. Rochelle Lefkowitz and Ann Withorn (New York: Pilgrim Press, 1986), 246–60.

5. Moynihan, "The Negro Family," 47.

6. Leith Mullings, "Anthropological Perspectives on the Afro-American Family," *American Journal of Social Psychiatry* 6, no. 1 (Winter 1986): 11–16; see the following revisionist works on the Black family: Andrew Billingsley, *Black Families in White America* (Englewood Cliffs, N.J.: Prentice-Hall, 1968); Robert Hill, *The Strengths of Black Families* (New York: Emerson-Hall, 1972); Herbert Gutman, *The Black Family in Slavery and Freedom, 1750–1925* (New York: Random House, 1976); Joyce Ladner, *Tomorrow's Tomorrow: The Black Woman* (Garden City, N.Y.: Doubleday, 1971); Elliot Leibow, *Tally's Corner: A Study of Negro Street Corner Men* (Boston: Little, Brown, 1967); Carol B. Stack, *All Our Kin: Strategies for Survival in a Black Community* (New York: Harper & Row, 1974).

7. William J. Wilson and Robert Aponte, "Urban Poverty," *Annual Review of Sociology* 11 (1985): 231–58, esp. 241.

8. For a review of recent studies, see ibid.

9. Daniel Patrick Moynihan, *Family and Nation* (San Diego: Harcourt, Brace, Jovanovich, 1986).

10. "The Vanishing Family: Crisis in Black America," narrated by Bill Moyers, Columbia Broadcasting System (CBS) Special Report, January 1986.

11. "Hard Times for Black America," *Dollars and Sense*, no. 115 (April 1986): 5–7.

12. Nicholas Lemann, "The Origins of the Underclass: Part 1," *Atlantic*, June 1986, 31–55, and "The Origins of the Underclass: Part 2," *Atlantic*, July 1986, 54–68.

13. Lemann, "Part 1," 35.

14. Ibid.

15. Jim Sleeper, "Overcoming 'Underclass': More Jobs Are Still the Key," *In These Times*, 11–24 June 1986, 16.

16. Corcoran et al., "Myth and Reality," 517.

17. Martha S. Hill and Michael Ponza, "Poverty and Welfare Dependence across Generations," *Economic Outlook U.S.A.*, Summer 1983, 61–64, esp. 64.

18. Anne Rueter, "Myths of Poverty," *Research News* 35, nos. 7–9 (July–September 1984): 18–19.

19. Mary Jo Bane, "Household Composition and Poverty," in *Fighting Poverty*, ed. Sheldon H. Danziger and Daniel H. Weinberg (Cambridge, Mass.: Harvard University Press, 1986), 209–31.

20. Ibid.

21. Betsy Dworkin, "40% of the Poor Are Children," *New York Times Book Review*, 2 March 1986, 9.

22. Bane, "Household Composition," 277.

23. Martha Hill, "Trends in the Economic Situation of U.S. Families and Children, 1970–1980," in *American Families and the Economy*, ed. Richard R. Nelson and Felicity Skidmore (Washington, D.C.: National Academy Press, 1983), 9–53, esp. 38.

24. Charles Murray, *Losing Ground* (New York: Basic Books, 1984).

25. David T. Ellwood, *Poor Support: Poverty in the American Family* (New York: Basic Books, 1988).

26. Sheldon Danziger and Peter Gottschalk, "The Poverty of *Losing Ground*," *Challenge* 28 (May–June 1985): 32–38.

27. William A. Darity and Samuel L. Meyers, "Does Welfare Dependency Cause Female Headship? The Case of the Black Family," *Journal of Marriage and the Family* 46, no. 4 (November 1984): 765–79.

28. David T. Ellwood and Lawrence H. Summers, "Poverty in America: Is Welfare the Answer or the Problem?" in *Fighting Poverty*, ed. Danziger and Weinberg, 78–105.

29. Ibid., 96.

30. "The Costs of Being Black," *Research News* 38, nos. 11–12 (November–December 1987): 8–10.

31. Barry Bluestone and Bennett Harrison, *The Deindustrialization of America* (New York: Basic Books, 1982), 54.

32. Barry Bluestone, Bennett Harrison, and Lucy Gorham, "Storm Clouds on the Horizon: Labor Market Crisis and Industrial Policy," 68, as cited in "Hard Times for Black America."

33. Richard Child Hill and Cynthia Negrey, "Deindustrialization and Racial Minorities in the Great Lakes Region, U.S.A.," in *The Reshaping of America: Social Consequences of the Changing Economy*, ed. D. Stanley Eitzen and Maxine Baca Zinn (Englewood Cliffs, N.J.: Prentice-Hall, 1989), 168–77.

34. Elliot Currie and Jerome H. Skolnick, *America's Problems: Social Issues and Public Policy* (Boston: Little, Brown, 1984), 82.

35. John D. Kasarda, "Caught in a Web of Change," *Society* 21 (November–December 1983): 41–47.

36. Ibid., 45–47.

37. John D. Kasarda, "Urban Change and Minority Opportunities," in *The New Urban Reality*, ed. Paul E. Peterson (Washington, D.C.: Brookings Institution, 1985), 33–68, esp. 55.

38. William J. Wilson with Kathryn Neckerman, "Poverty and Family Structure: The Widening Gap between Evidence and Public Policy Issues," in *The Truly Disadvantaged* (Chicago: University of Chicago Press, 1987), 63–92.

39. Ibid.

40. Jerelyn Eddings, "Children Having Children," *Baltimore Sun*, 2 March 1986, 71.

41. As quoted in ibid.

42. Noel A. Cazenave, "Alternate Intimacy, Marriage, and Family Lifestyles among Low-Income Black Americans," *Alternative Lifestyles* 3, no. 4 (November 1980): 425–44.

43. "The Kerner Report Updated," Report of the 1988 Commission on the Cities (Racine, Wis., 1 March 1988).

44. Wilson, *The Truly Disadvantaged*, 62.

45. Ellwood, *Poor Support*, 204.

46. Paul E. Peterson, "Introduction: Technology, Race, and Urban Policy," in *The New Urban Reality*, ed. Peterson, 1–35, esp. 22.

47. Jennifer Juarez Robles, "Hispanics Emerging as Nation's Poorest Minority Group," *Chicago Reporter* 17, no. 6 (June 1988): 1–3.

48. Ibid., 2–3.

49. Ibid., 3.

50. Alejandro Portes and Cynthia Truelove, "Making Sense of Diversity: Recent Research on Hispanic Minorities in the United States," *Annual Review of Sociology* 13 (1987): 359–85.

51. Joan W. Moore, "An Assessment of Hispanic Poverty: Does a Hispanic Underclass Exist?" *Tomás Rivera Center Report* 2, no. 1 (Fall 1988): 8–9.

52. Robles, "Hispanics," 3.

53. U.S. Bureau of the Census, *Current Population Reports*, ser. P-20, nos. 416, 422 (Washington, D.C.: Government Printing Office, March 1987).

54. Patricia Hill Collins, "A Comparison of Two Works on Black Family Life," *Signs* 14 (1989): 874–84.

55. Adolph Reed, Jr., "The Liberal Technocrat," *Nation*, 6 February 1988, 167–70.

56. Ellwood, *Poor Support*, 133.

57. Clyde W. Franklin II, "Surviving the Institutional Decimation of Black Males: Causes, Consequences, and Intervention," in *The Making of Masculinities*, ed. Harry Brod (Winchester, Mass.: Allen & Unwin, 1987), 155–69, esp. 155.

58. See Maxine Baca Zinn, "Minority Families in Crisis: The Public Discussion," Working Paper no. 6 (Memphis, Tenn.: Memphis State University, Center for Research on Women, 1987), for an extended critique of the culture-of-poverty model.

5

Backward toward the Postmodern Family: Reflections on Gender, Kinship, and Class in the Silicon Valley

JUDITH STACEY

The extended family is in our lives again. This should make all the people happy who were complaining back in the sixties and seventies that the reason family life was so hard, especially on mothers, was that the nuclear family had replaced the extended family.... Your basic extended family today includes your ex-husband or -wife, your ex's new mate, your new mate, possibly your new mate's ex, and any new mate that your new mate's ex has acquired. It consists entirely of people who are not related by blood, many of whom can't stand each other. This return of the extended family reminds me of the favorite saying of my friend's extremely pessimistic mother: Be careful what you wish for, you might get it.
—Delia Ephron, *Funny Sauce*

In the summer of 1986 I attended a wedding ceremony in a small Christian pentecostal church in the Silicon Valley. The service celebrated the same "traditional" family patterns and values that two years earlier had inspired a "profamily" movement to assist Ronald Reagan's landslide reelection to the presidency of the United States. At the same time, however, the pastor's rhetoric displayed substantial sympathy with feminist criticisms of patriarchal marriage. "A ring is not a shackle, and marriage is not a relationship of domination," he instructed the groom. Moreover, complex patterns of divorce, remarriage, and stepkinship linked the members of the wedding party and their guests, which bore far greater resemblance to the New Age

This essay first appeared in *America at Century's End,* ed. Alan Wolfe (Berkeley and Los Angeles: University of California Press, 1991). Copyright 1991 by the Regents of the University of California. It summarizes and excerpts from my ethnographic book *Brave New Families: Stories of Domestic Upheaval in Late Twentieth-Century America* (New York: Basic Books, 1990). For constructive responses to an earlier draft, I am grateful to Alan Wolfe, Aihwa Ong, Ruth Rosen, Evelyn Fox Keller, and Naomi Schneider.

extended family satirized by Delia Ephron than they did to the image of "traditional" family life which arouses the nostalgic fantasies that are so widespread among religious and other social critics of contemporary family practices.

In the final decades before the twenty-first century, passionate contests over changing family life in the United States have polarized vast numbers of citizens. Outside the Supreme Court of the United States, righteous, placard-carrying right-to-lifers square off against feminists and civil libertarians demonstrating their anguish over the steady dismantling of women's reproductive freedom. On the same day in July 1989 when New York's highest court expanded the legal definition of a family to extend rent control protection to gay couples, a coalition of conservative clergymen in San Francisco blocked implementation of their city's new "domestic partners" ordinance. "It is the totality of the relationship," proclaimed the New York judge, "as evidenced by the dedication, caring and self-sacrifice of the parties which should, in the final analysis, control" the definition of family.[1] But this concept of family is anathema to "profamily" activists. Declaring that the attempt by the San Francisco Board of Supervisors to grant legal status to unmarried heterosexual and homosexual couples "arbitrarily redefined the time-honored and hallowed nature of the family," the clergymen's petition was signed by sufficient citizens to force the ordinance into a referendum battle.[2] When the reckoning came in November 1989, the electorate of the city many consider to be the national capital of family change had narrowly defeated the domestic-partners law.

Betraying a good deal of conceptual and historical confusion, most popular, as well as many scholarly, assessments of family change anxiously and misguidedly debate whether "the family" will survive the twentieth century at all.[3] Anxieties like these are far from new. "For at least 150 years," the historian Linda Gordon writes, "there have been periods of fear that 'the family'—meaning a popular image of what families were supposed to be like, by no means a correct recollection of any actual 'traditional' family—was in decline; and these fears have tended to escalate in periods of social stress."[4] The actual subject of this recurring, fretful discourse is a historically specific form and concept of family life, one that most historians identify as the "modern" family. No doubt, many of us who write and teach about American family life have not abetted public understanding of family change with our counterintuitive use of the concept, the "modern" family. The "modern" family of sociological theory and historical convention designates a family form no longer prevalent in the United States—an intact nuclear household unit composed of a male breadwinner, his full-time homemaker wife, and their dependent children—precisely the form of family life that many mistake for an ancient, essential, and now-endangered institution.

The past three decades of postindustrial social transformations in the United States have rung the historic curtain on the "modern" family regime. In 1950, three-fifths of American households contained male breadwinners and full-time female homemakers, whether children were present or not.[5] By 1986, in contrast, more than three-fifths of married women with children under the age of eighteen were in the labor force, and only 7 percent of households conformed to the "modern" pattern of breadwinning father, homemaking mother, and one to four children under the age of eighteen.[6] By the middle of the 1970s, moreover, divorce outstripped death as the source of marital dissolutions, generating in its wake a complex array of family arrangements caricatured by Delia Ephron in the epigraph.[7] The diversity of contemporary gender and kinship relationships undermines Tolstoy's famous contrast between happy and unhappy families: now even happy families are not all alike.[8] No longer is there a single culturally dominant family pattern, like the modern one, to which the majority of Americans conform and most of the rest aspire. Instead, Americans today have crafted a multiplicity of family and household arrangements, which we inhabit uneasily and reconstitute frequently in response to changing personal and occupational circumstances.

Recombinant Family Life

We are living, I believe, through a tumultuous and contested period of family history, a period *after* the modern family order, but before what we cannot foretell. Precisely because it is not possible to characterize with a coherent descriptive term the competing sets of family cultures that coexist at present, I identify this family regime as postmodern. I do this, despite my reservations about employing such a fashionable and elusive cultural concept, to signal the contested, ambivalent, and undecided character of contemporary gender and kinship arrangements.

"What is the post-modern?" Clive Dilnot asks rhetorically in the title of a detailed discussion of literature on postmodern culture, and his answers apply readily to the domain of present family conditions in the United States.[9] The postmodern, Dilnot maintains, "is first, an uncertainty, an insecurity, a doubt." Most of the "post-" words provoke uneasiness, because they imply simultaneously "both the end, or at least the radical transformation of, a familiar pattern of activity or group of ideas" and the emergence of "new fields of cultural activity whose contours are still unclear and whose meanings and implications . . . cannot yet be fathomed." The postmodern, moreover, is "characterized by the process of the linking up of areas and the crossing of the boundaries of what are conventionally considered to be disparate realms of practice."[10]

Like postmodern culture, contemporary U.S. family arrangements are diverse, fluid, and unresolved. *The* postmodern family is not a new model of family life equivalent to that of the modern family, not the next stage in an orderly progression of family history, but the stage in that history when the belief in a logical progression of stages breaks down.[11] Rupturing the teleology of modernization narratives that depict an evolutionary history of the family and incorporating both experimental and nostalgic elements, "the" postmodern family lurches forward and backward into an uncertain future.

Family Revolutions and Vanguard Classes

Two centuries ago leading white, middle-class families in the newly united American states spearheaded a family revolution that gradually replaced the diversity and fluidity of the premodern domestic order with a more uniform and hegemonic modern family system.[12] But "modern family" was an oxymoronic label for this peculiar institution, which dispensed modernity to white, middle-class men only by withholding it from women. The former could enter the public sphere as breadwinners and citizens because their wives were confined to the newly privatized family realm. Ruled by an increasingly absent patriarchal landlord, the modern, middle-class family, a woman's domain, soon was sentimentalized as "traditional."

It took most of the subsequent two centuries for substantial numbers of white working-class men to achieve the rudimentary economic passbook to "modern" family life—a male family wage.[13] By the time they had done so, however, a second family revolution was well underway. Once again, white middle-class families appeared to be in the vanguard. This time women were claiming the benefits and burdens of modernity, a status we could achieve only at the expense of the "modern" family itself. Reviving a long-dormant feminist movement, frustrated middle-class homemakers and their more militant daughters subjected modern domesticity to a sustained critique, at times with little sensitivity to the effects our anti–modern family ideology might have on women for whom full-time domesticity had rarely been feasible. Thus, feminist family reform came to be regarded widely as a white middle-class agenda, and white working-class families its most resistant adversaries.

I shared these presumptions before conducting fieldwork among families in Santa Clara County, California, the "Silicon Valley," radically altered my understanding of the class basis of the postmodern family revolution. Once a bucolic agribusiness orchard region, during the 1960s and 1970s this county became the global headquarters of the electronics industry, the world's vanguard postindustrial region. While economic restructuring commanded global attention, most outside observers overlooked concurrent gender and family changes that preoccupied many residents. During the late 1970s, before the conservative shift in the national political climate made feminism seem a derogatory term, local public officials proudly described San Jose, the county seat, as a feminist capital. The city elected a feminist mayor and in 1974 hosted the statewide convention of the National Organization for Women. Santa Clara County soon became one of the few counties in the nation to elect a female majority to its board of supervisors. And in 1981 high levels of feminist activism made San Jose the site of the nation's first successful strike for a comparable-worth standard of pay for city employees.[14]

During its postindustrial makeover, the Silicon Valley also became a vanguard region for family change, a region whose family and household data represent an exaggeration of national trends. For example, while the national divorce rate doubled after 1960, in Santa Clara County it nearly tripled, "nonfamily households" and single-parent households grew faster than in the nation as a whole, and abortion rates were one and one-half times the national figures.[15] The high marriage casualty rate among workaholic engineers was dubbed "the silicon syndrome,"[16] and many residents shared the alarmist view of the fate of family life in their locale captured in the opening lines of an article in a local university magazine:

"There is an endangered species in Silicon Valley, one so precious that when it disappears Silicon Valley will die with it. This endangered species is the family. And sometimes it seems as if every institution in this valley—political, corporate, and social—is hellbent on driving it into extinction."[17]

The coincidence of epochal changes in occupational, gender, and family patterns make the Silicon Valley a propitious site for exploring ways in which "ordinary" working people have been remaking their families in the wake of postindustrial and feminist challenges. The Silicon Valley is by no means a typical or "representative" U.S. location, but precisely because national postindustrial work and family transformations were more condensed, rapid, and exaggerated there than elsewhere, they are easier to perceive. Most of the popular and scholarly literature about white working-class people, on the other hand, portrays them as the most traditional, as the last bastion, that is, of the modern family. Relatively privileged members of the white working class especially are widely regarded as the bulwark of the Reagan revolution and the constituency least sympathetic to feminism and family reforms. Those whose hold on the accoutrements of the American Dream is so recent and tenuous, it is thought, have the strongest incentives to defend it.[18]

For nearly three years, therefore, between the summer of 1984 and the spring of 1987, I conducted a commuter fieldwork study of two extended kin networks composed primarily of white working people who had resided in Santa Clara County throughout the period of its startling transformation. My research among them convinced me that white middle-class families are less the innovators than the propagandists and principal beneficiaries of contemporary family change. To illustrate the innovative and courageous character of family reconstitution among pink- and blue-collar people, I present radically condensed stories from my book-length ethnographic treatment of their lives.[19]

Remaking Family Life in the Silicon Valley

Two challenges to my class and gender prejudices provoked my turn to ethnographic research and my selection of the two kin groups who became its focus. Pamela Gama,* an administrator of social services

*I employ pseudonyms and change identifying details when describing participants in my study.

for women at a Silicon Valley antipoverty agency when I met her in July 1984, provided the first of these when she challenged my secular feminist preconceptions by "coming out" to me as a recent born-again Christian convert. Pamela was the forty-seven-year-old bride at the Christian wedding ceremony I attended two years later. There she exchanged vows with her second husband, Albert Gama, a construction worker, with whom she had previously cohabited. Pamela's first marriage in 1960 to Don Franklin, the father of her three children, had lasted fifteen years, spanning the headiest days of Silicon Valley development and the period of Don's successful rise from a telephone repairman to an electronics packaging engineer.

In contrast, Dotty Lewison, my central contact in the second kin network I came to study, secured that status by challenging my class prejudices. The physical appearance and appurtenances of the worn and modest Lewison abode, Dotty's polyester attire and bawdy speech, her husband's heavily tattooed body, and the demographic and occupational details of her family's history that Dotty supplied satisfied all of my stereotypic notions of an authentic working-class family. But the history of feminist activism Dotty recounted proudly, as she unpacked a newly purchased Bible, demonstrated the serious limitations of my tacit understandings. When I met Dotty in October 1984, she was the veteran of an intact and reformed marriage of thirty years' duration to her disabled husband, Lou, formerly an electronics maintenance mechanic and supervisor, and, I would later learn, a wife and child abuser.

Pamela and Dotty, like several of their friends whom I came to know during my study, were members of Betty Friedan's "feminine mystique" generation, but not of her social class. Unlike the more affluent members of Friedan's intended audience, Pam and Dotty were "beneficiaries" of the late, ephemeral achievement of a male family wage and homeownership won by privileged sectors of the working class. This was a Pyrrhic victory, as it turned out, that had allowed this population a brief period of access to the modern family system just as it was decomposing. Pam and Dotty, like most white women of their generation, were young when they married in the 1950s and early 1960s. They entered their first marriages with conventional "Parsonsian" gender expectations about family and work roles. For a significant period of time they and their husbands conformed, as best they could, to the then culturally prescribed pattern of instrumental male breadwinner and expressive female homemaker.

Assuming primary responsibility for rearing the children they began to bear immediately after marriage, Pam and Dotty supported their husbands' successful efforts to progress from working-class to middle- and upper-middle-class careers in the electronics industry. Their experiences with the modern family, however, were always more tenuous, less pure, than those women to whom, and for whom, Betty Friedan spoke.

Insecurities and inadequacies of their husbands' earnings made itinerant labor force participation by Dotty and Pam both necessary and resented by their husbands before feminism made female employment a badge of pride. Dotty alternated frequent childbearing with multiple forays into the labor force in a wide array of low-wage jobs. In fact, Dotty assembled semiconductors before her husband, Lou, entered the electronics industry, but she did not perceive or desire significant opportunities for her own occupational mobility at that point. Pamela's husband began his career ascent earlier than Dotty's, but Pamela still found his earnings insufficient, and his spending habits too profligate, to balance the household budget. To make the ends of their beyond-their-means, middle-class life-style meet without undermining her husband's pride, Pam shared child care and a clandestine housecleaning occupation with her African-American neighbor and friend, Lorraine. Thus Pam and Dotty did not manage to suffer the full effects of the "problem without a name" until feminism had begun to name it, and in terms both women found compelling.

In the early 1970s, while their workaholic husbands were increasingly absent from their families, Pam and Dotty joined friends taking reentry courses in local community colleges. There they encountered feminism, and their lives and their modern families were never to be the same. Feminism provided an analysis and rhetoric for their discontent, and it helped each develop the self-esteem she needed to exit or reform her unhappy modern marriage. Both women left their husbands, became welfare mothers, and experimented with the single life. Pam divorced, pursued a college degree, and developed a social service career. Dotty, with lesser educational credentials and employment options, took her husband back, but on her own terms, after his disabling heart attack (and after a lover left her). Disabled Lou ceased his physical abuse and performed most of the housework, while Dotty had control over her time, some of which she devoted to feminist activism in antibattering work.

By the time I met Pamela and Dotty a decade later, at a time when my own feminist-inspired joint household of the prior eight years was failing, national and local feminist ardor had cooled. Pam was then a recent convert to born-again Christianity, receiving Christian marriage counseling to buttress and enhance her second marriage, to Al, a construction worker. Certainly her actions represented a retreat from feminist family ideology, but, as Pamela gradually taught me, and as Susan Gerard and I have elaborated elsewhere, a far less dramatic retreat than I at first imagined.[20] Like other women active in the contemporary evangelical Christian revival, Pam was making creative use of its surprisingly flexible patriarchal ideology to reform her husband in her own image. She judged it "not so bad a deal" to cede Al nominal family headship in exchange for substantive improvements in his conjugal behavior. Indeed, few contemporary feminists would find fault with the Christian marital principles that Al identified to me as his goals: "I just hope that we can come closer together and be more honest with each other. Try to use God as a guideline. The goals are more openness, a closer relationship, be more loving both verbally and physically, have more concern for the other person's feelings." Nor did Pamela's conversion return her to a modern family pattern. Instead she collaborated with her first husband's live-in, Jewish lover, Shirley Moskowitz, to build a remarkably harmonious and inclusive divorce-extended kin network whose constituent households swapped resources, labor, and lodgers in response to shifting family circumstances and needs.

Dotty Lewison was also no longer a political activist when we met in 1984. Instead she was supplementing Lou's disability pension with part-time paid work in a small insurance office and pursuing spiritual exploration more overtly postmodern in form than Pam's in a metaphysical Christian church. During the course of my fieldwork, however, an overwhelming series of tragedies claimed the lives of Dotty's husband and two of the Lewisons' five adult children. Dotty successfully contested her negligent son-in-law for custody of her four motherless grandchildren. Struggling to support them, she formed a matrilocal joint household with her occupationally successful child, Kristina, an electronics drafter-designer and a single mother of one child. While Dotty and Pamela both had moved "partway back" from feminist fervor, at the same time both had migrated ever further away from the (no longer) modern family.

Between them, Pamela and Dotty had eight children—five daughters and three sons—children of modern families disrupted by postindustrial developments and feminist challenges. All were in their twenties when I met them in 1984 and 1985, members of the quintessential postfeminist generation. Although all five daughters distanced themselves from feminist identity and ideology, all too had semiconsciously incorporated feminist principles into their gender and kin expectations and practices. They took for granted, and at times eschewed, the gains in women's work opportunities, sexual autonomy, and male participation in child rearing and domestic work for which feminists of their mothers' generation had struggled. Ignorant or disdainful of the political efforts feminists expended to secure such gains, they were preoccupied instead with coping with the expanded opportunities and burdens women now encounter. They came of age in a period in which a successful woman was expected to combine marriage to a communicative, egalitarian man with motherhood and an engaging, rewarding career. All but one of these daughters of successful white working-class fathers absorbed these postfeminist expectations, the firstborns most fully. Yet none has found such a pattern attainable. Only Pam's younger daughter, Katie, the original source of the evangelical conversions in her own marriage and her mother's, explicitly rejected such a vision. At fourteen, Katie had joined the Christian revival, where, I believe, she found an effective refuge from the disruptions of parental divorce and adolescent drug culture that threatened her more rebellious siblings. Ironically, however, Katie's total involvement in a pentecostal ministry led her to practice the most alternative family arrangement of all. Katie, with her husband and young children, has lived "in community" in various joint households (occasionally interracial households) whose accordion structures and shared child rearing, ministry labors, and expenses have enabled her to achieve an exceptional degree of sociospatial integration of her family, work, and spiritual life.

At the outset of my fieldwork, none of Pam's or Dotty's daughters inhabited a modern family. Over the next few years, however, discouraging experiences with the work available to them led three to retreat from the world of paid work and to attempt a modified version of the modern family strategy their mothers had practiced earlier. All demanded, and two received, substantially greater male involvement in child care and domestic work than had their mothers (or mine) in the prefeminist past. Only one, however, had reasonable prospects of succeeding in her "modern" gender strategy, and these she secured through unacknowledged benefits feminism helped her to enjoy. Dotty's second daughter, Polly, had left the Silicon Valley when the electronics company she worked for opened a branch in a state with lower labor and housing costs. Legalized abortion and liberalized sexual norms for women allowed Polly to experiment sexually and defer marriage and childbearing until she was able to negotiate a marriage whose domestic labor arrangements represented a distinct improvement over that of the prefeminist modern family.

I have less to say, and less confidence in what I do have to say, about postmodern family strategies among the men in Pam's and Dotty's kin groups. Despite my concerted efforts to study gender relationally by defining my study in gender-inclusive terms, the men in the families I studied remained comparatively marginal to my research. In part, this imbalance is an unavoidable outcome for any one individual who attempts to study gender in a gendered world. Being a women inhibited my access to, and likely my empathy with, as full a range of male family experience as that which I enjoyed among their female kin. Still, the relative marginality of men in my research is not due simply to methodological deficiencies. It also accurately reflects their more marginal participation in contemporary family life. Most of the men in Pam's and Dotty's networks narrated gender and kinship stories that were relatively inarticulate and undeveloped, I believe, because they had less experience, investment, or interest in the work of sustaining kin ties.[21]

While economic pressures have always encouraged expansionary kin work among working-class women, these have often weakened men's family ties. Men's muted family voices in my study whisper of a masculinity crisis among blue-collar men. As working-class men's access to breadwinner status recedes, so too does confidence in their masculinity.[22] The decline of the family wage and the escalation of women's involvement in paid work seems to generate profound ambivalence about the eroding breadwinner ethic. Pam's and Dotty's male kin appeared uncertain whether a man who provides sole support to his family is a hero or a chump. Two avoided domestic commitments entirely, while several embraced these wholeheartedly. Two vacillated between romantic engagements and the unencumbered single life. Too many of the men I met expressed their masculinity in antisocial, self-destructive, and violent forms.

Women strive, meanwhile, as they always have, to buttress and reform their male kin. Responding to the extraordinary diffusion of feminist ideology as well as to sheer overwork, working-class women, like middle-class women, have struggled to transfer some of their domestic burdens to men. My fieldwork leads me to believe that they have achieved more success in the daily trenches than much of the research on the "politics of housework" yet indicates, more success, I suspect, than have most middle-class women.[23] While only a few of the women in my study expected, or desired, men to perform an equal share of housework and child care, none were willing to exempt men from domestic labor. Almost all of the men I observed or heard about routinely performed domestic tasks that my own blue-collar father and his friends never deigned to contemplate. Some did so with reluctance and resentment, but most did so willingly. Although the division of household labor remains profoundly inequitable, I am convinced that a major gender norm has shifted here.[24]

Farewell to Archie Bunker

If this essay serves no other purpose, I hope it will shatter the image of the white working class as the last repository of old-fashioned, "modern" American family life. The postmodern family arrangements I found among blue-collar people in the Silicon Valley are at least as diverse and innovative as those found within the middle class. Pundits of postmodern family arrangements, like Delia Ephron, satirize the hostility and competition of the contemporary divorce-extended family. But working women like Pamela and Dotty have found ways to transform divorce from a rupture into a kinship resource, and they are not unique. A recent study of "ex-familia" among middle-class divorced couples and their parents in the suburbs of San Francisco found one-third sustaining kinship ties with former spouses and their relatives.[25] It seems likely that cooperative, ex-familial relationships are even more prevalent among lower-income groups, where divorce rates are higher and where women have far greater experience with, and need for, sustaining cooperative kin ties.[26]

Certainly, the dismantling of welfare state protections and the reprivatizing policies of the Reagan-Bush era have given such women renewed incentives to continue their traditions of active, expansionary kin work. The accordion households and kin ties crafted by Dotty Lewison, by Katie's Christian ministry, and by Pam and Shirley draw more on the "domestic network" traditions of poor, urban African Americans described by Carol Stack and on the matrifocal strategies of poor and working-class whites than they do on family reform innovations by the white middle class.[27] Ironically, sociologists are now identifying as a new middle-class "social problem" those "crowded," rather than empty, nests filled with "incompletely launched young adults," long familiar to the less privileged, like the Lewisons.[28] Postindustrial conditions have reversed the supply-side, "trickle-down" trajectory of family change predicted by modernization theorists. The diversity and complexity of postmodern family patterns rivals that characteristic of premodern kinship forms.[29]

One glimpses the ironies of class and gender history here. For decades industrial unions struggled heroically for a socially recognized male breadwinner wage that would allow the working class to participate in the modern gender order. Those struggles, however, contributed to the cheapening of female labor that helped gradually to undermine the regime of the modern family.[30] Then escalating consumption standards, the expansion of mass collegiate coeducation, and the persistence of high divorce rates gave more and more women ample cause to invest a portion of their identities in the "instrumental" sphere of paid labor.[31] Thus middle-class women began to abandon their confinement in the modern family just as working-class women were approaching its access ramps. The former did so, however, only after the wives of working-class men had pioneered the twentieth-century revolution in women's paid work. Entering employment in midlife during the catastrophic 1930s, participating in defense industries in the 1940s, and raising their family incomes to middle-class standards by returning to the labor force rapidly after child rearing in the 1950s, wives of working-class men quietly modeled and normalized the postmodern family standard of employment for married mothers. Whereas in 1950 the less a man earned, the more likely his wife was employed, by 1968 wives of middle-income men were the most likely to be in the labor force.[32]

African-American women and white working-class women have been the genuine postmodern family pioneers, even though they also suffer most from its most negative effects. Long denied the mixed benefits that the modern family order offered middle-class women, less privileged women quietly forged alternative models of femininity to that of full-time domesticity and mother-intensive child rearing. Struggling creatively, often heroically, to sustain oppressed families and to escape the most oppressive ones, they drew on "traditional," premodern kinship resources and crafted untraditional ones, creating in the process the postmodern family.

Rising divorce and cohabitation rates, working mothers, two-earner households, single and unwed parenthood, and matrilineal extended- and fictive-kin support networks appeared earlier and more extensively among poor and working-class people.[33] Economic pressures, more than political principles, governed these departures from domesticity, but working women soon found additional reasons to appreciate paid employment.[34] Eventually white middle-class women, sated and even sickened by our modern family privileges,[35] began to emulate, elaborate, and celebrate many of these alternative family practices. How ironic and unfortunate it seems, therefore, that feminism's anti–modern family ideology should then offend many women from the social groups whose gender and kinship strategies helped to foster it.

If, as my research suggests, postindustrial transformations encouraged modern working-class families to reorganize and diversify themselves even more than middle-class families, it seems time to inter the very concept of "*the* working-class family." This deeply androcentric and class-biased construct distorts the history and current reality of wage-working people's intimate relationships. Popular images of working-class family life, like the Archie Bunker family, rest upon the iconography of unionized, blue-collar, male, industrial breadwinners and the history of their lengthy struggle for the family wage. But the male family wage was a late and ephemeral achievement of only the most fortunate sections of the modern industrial working class. It is doubtful that most working-class men ever secured its patriarchal domestic privileges.

Postmodern conditions expose the gendered character of this social-class category, and they render it atavistic. As feminists have argued, only by disregarding women's labor and learning was it ever plausible to designate a family unit as working class.[36] In an era when most married mothers are employed, when women perform most "working-class" jobs,[37] when most productive labor is unorganized and fails to pay a family wage, when marriage links are tenuous and transitory, and when more single women than married homemakers are rearing children, conventional notions of a normative working-class family fracture into incoherence. The life circumstances and mobility patterns of the members of Pamela's kin set and of the Lewisons, for example, are so diverse and fluid that no single social-class category can adequately describe any of the family units among them.

If the white working-class family stereotype is inaccurate, it is also consequential. Stereotypes are moral (alas, more often, immoral) stories people tell to organize the complexity of social experience. Narrating members of the working class as profamily reactionaries suppresses the diversity and the innovative character of a great deal of working-class kin relationships. A plot with socially divisive and conservative political effects, the Archie Bunker stereotype may have helped to contain feminism by estranging middle-class from working-class women. Barbara Ehrenreich argues that caricatures that portray the working class as racist and reactionary are recent, self-serving inventions of middle-class professionals eager "to seek legitimation for their own more conservative impulses."[38] In the early 1970s, ignoring rising labor militancy as well as racial, ethnic, and gender diversity among working-class people, the media effectively imaged them as the new conservative bedrock of "middle America." "All in the Family," the early 1970s television sitcom series that immortalized racist, chauvinist, working-class hero-buffoon Archie Bunker, can best be read, Ehrenreich suggests, as "the longest-running Polish joke," a projection of middle-class bad faith.[39] Yet if this bad faith served professional middle-class interests, it did so at the expense of feminism. The inverse logic of class prejudice construed the constituency of that enormously popular social movement as exclusively middle class. By convincing middle-class feminists of our isolation, perhaps the last laugh of that "Polish joke" was on us. Even Ehrenreich, who sensitively debunks the Bunker myth, labels "startling" the findings of a 1986 Gallup poll that "56 percent of American women considered themselves to be 'feminists,' and the degree of feminist identification was, if anything, slightly higher as one descended the socioeconomic scale."[40] Feminists must be attuned to the polyphony of family stories authored by working-class as well as middle-class people if we are ever to transform poll data like these into effective political alliances.

While my ethnographic research demonstrates the demise of "*the working-class family*," in no way does it document the emergence of the classless society once anticipated by postindustrial theorists.[41] On the contrary, recent studies of postindustrial occupation and income distribution indicate that the middle classes are shrinking and the economic circumstances of Americans polarizing.[42] African Americans have borne the most devastating impact of economic restructuring and the subsequent decline of industrial and unionized occupations.[43] But formerly privileged white working-class men—those, like Pam's two husbands and Lou Lewison, who achieved access to the American Dream in the 1960s and 1970s—now find their gains threatened and not easy to pass on to their children.

While high-wage blue-collar jobs decline, the window of postindustrial opportunity that admitted undereducated men and women, like Lou and Kristina Lewison and Don Franklin, to middle-class status, is slamming shut. "During the 1980s, the educated got richer and the uneducated got poorer. And it looks like more of the same in the 1990s," declared a recent summary of occupational statistics from the U.S. Census Bureau and the Labor Department.[44] Young white families earned 20 percent less in 1986 than did comparable families in 1979, and their homeownership prospects plummeted.[45] Real earnings for young men between the ages of twenty and twenty-four dropped by 26 percent between 1973 and 1986, while the military route to upward mobility that many of their fathers traveled constricted.[46] In the 1950s men like Lou Lewison, equipped with Veterans Administration loans, could buy homes with token down payments and budget only 14 percent of their monthly wages for housing costs. By 1984, however, carrying a median-priced home would cost would-be first-time homeowners—those men's children—44 percent of an average male's monthly earnings.[47] Few could manage this, and in 1986 the U.S. government reported "the first sustained drop in home ownership since the modern collection of data began in 1940."[48]

Postindustrial shifts have reduced blue-collar job opportunities for the undereducated sons of working-class fathers I interviewed. And technological developments like computer-aided design have escalated the entry criteria and reduced the ranks of those middle-level occupations that recently employed uncredentialed young people like Kristina Lewison and Pam's oldest child, Lanny.[49] Thus the proportion of American families in the middle-income range fell from 46 percent in 1970 to 39 percent in 1985. Two earners in a household now are necessary just to keep from losing ground.[50] Data like these led social analysts to anxiously track "the disappearing middle class," a phrase that, Barbara Ehrenreich now believes, "in some ways missed the point. It was the blue-collar working class that was 'disappearing,' at least from the middle range of comfort."[51]

Postindustrial restructuring has had contradictory effects on the employment opportunities of former working-class women. Driven by declines in real family income, by desires for social achievement and independence, and by an awareness that committed male breadwinners are in scarce supply, such women have flocked to expanding jobs in service, clerical, and new industrial occupations. These provide the means of family subsidy or self-support and self-respect gained by many women, like Pam and Dotty, but few enjoy earnings or prospects equivalent to those of their former husbands or fathers. Recent economic restructuring has replaced white male workers with women and minority men, but at lesser-paid, more vulnerable jobs.[52]

Whose Family Crisis?

This massive reordering of work, class, and gender relationships during the past several decades is what has turned family life into a contested terrain. It seems ironic, therefore, to observe that at the very same time that women were becoming the new proletariat, the postmodern family, even more than the modern family it is replacing, is proving to be a woman-tended domain. To be sure, there is some empirical basis for the enlightened father imagery celebrated by films like *Kramer vs. Kramer*. Indeed, my fieldwork corroborates emerging evidence that the determined efforts by many working women and feminists to reintegrate men into family life have not been entirely without effect. There are data, for example, indicating that increasing numbers of men would sacrifice occupational gains in order to have more time with their families, just as there are data documenting actual increases in male involvement in child care.[53] The excessive media attention that the faintest signs of new paternity enjoy, however, may be a symptom of the deeper, far less comforting reality it so effectively obscures. We are experiencing, as Andrew Cherlin aptly puts it, "the feminization of kinship."[54] Demographers report a drastic decline in the average number of years that men live in households with young children.[55] Few of the women who assume responsibility for their children in 90 percent of divorce cases in the U.S. today had to wage a custody battle for the privilege.[56] We hear few proposals for a "daddy track." And few of the adults providing care to sick and elderly relatives are male.[57] Yet ironically, most of the alarmist, nostalgic literature about contemporary family decline impugns women's abandonment of domesticity, the flip side of our tardy entry into modernity. Rarely do the anxious public outcries over the destructive effects on families of working mothers, high divorce rates, institutionalized child care, or sexual liberalization scrutinize the family behaviors of men.[58] Anguished voices, emanating from all bands on the political spectrum, lament state and market interventions that are weakening "the family."[59] But whose family bonds are fraying? Women have amply demonstrated our continuing commitment to sustaining kin ties. If there is a family crisis, it is a male family crisis.

The crisis cannot be resolved by reviving the modern family system. While nostalgia for an idealized world of "Ozzie and Harriet" and Archie Bunker families abounds, little evidence suggests that most Americans genuinely wish to return to the gender order those families symbolize. On the contrary, the vast majority, like the people in my study, are actively remaking family life. Indeed, a 1989 survey conducted by the *New York Times* found more than two-thirds of women, including a substantial majority of even those living in "traditional"—that is to say, "modern"—households, as well as a majority of men, agreeing that "the United States continues to need a strong women's movement to push for changes that benefit women."[60] Yet many seem reluctant to own their family preferences. They cling, like Shirley Moskowitz, to images of themselves as "back from the old days," while venturing ambivalently, but courageously, into the new.[61]

Responding to new economic and social insecurities as well as to feminism, higher percentages of families in almost all income groups have adopted a multiple-earner strategy.[62] Thus, the household form that has come closer than any other to replacing the modern family with a new cultural and statistical norm consists of a two-earner, heterosexual married couple with children.[63] It is not likely, however, that any single household type will soon achieve the measure of normalcy that the modern family long enjoyed. Indeed, the postmodern success of the voluntary principle of the modern family system precludes this, assuring a fluid, recombinant familial culture. The routinization of divorce and remarriage generates a diversity of family patterns even greater than was characteristic of the premodern period, when death prevented family stability or household homogeneity. Even cautious demographers judge the new family diversity to be "an intrinsic feature . . . rather than a temporary aberration" of contemporary family life.[64]

"The family" is *not* "here to stay." Nor should we wish it were. An ideological concept that imposes mythical homogeneity on the diverse means by which people organize their intimate relationships, "the family" distorts and devalues this rich variety of kinship stories. And along with the class, racial, and heterosexual prejudices it promulgates, this sentimental fictional plot authorizes gender hierarchy. Because the postmodern family crisis ruptures this seamless modern family script, it provides a democratic opportunity. Efforts to expand and redefine the definition of family by feminists and gay liberation activists, and by many minority rights organizations, are responses to this opportunity, seeking to extend social legitimacy and institutional support for the diverse patterns of intimacy that Americans have already forged.

If feminist identity threatens many and seems out of fashion, struggles to reconstitute gender and kinship on a just and democratic basis are more popular than ever.[65] If only a minority of citizens are willing to grant family legitimacy to gay domestic partners, an overwhelming majority subscribe to the postmodern definition of a family by which the New York Supreme Court validated a gay man's right to retain his deceased lover's apartment. "By a ratio of 3-to-1," people surveyed in a Yale University study defined the family as "a group of people who love and care for each other." And while a majority of those surveyed gave negative ratings to the quality of American family life in general, 71 percent declared themselves "at least very satisfied" with their own family lives.[66]

I find an element of bad faith in popular lament over family decline. Family nostalgia deflects criticism from the social sources of most "personal troubles." Supply-side economics, governmental deregulation, and the right-wing assault on social welfare programs have intensified the destabilizing effects of recent occupational upheavals on flagging modern families and emergent postmodern ones alike. Indeed, the ability to provide financial security was the chief family concern of most surveyed in the Yale study. If the postmodern family crisis represents a democratic opportunity, contemporary economic and political conditions enable only a minority to realize its tantalizing potential.

The discrepant data reported in the Yale study indicate how reluctant most Americans are to fully own the genuine ambivalence we feel about family and social change. Yet ambivalence, as Alan Wolfe suggests, is an underappreciated but responsible moral stance, and one well-suited for democratic citizenship: "Given the paradoxes of modernity, there is little wrong, and perhaps a great deal right, with being ambivalent—especially when there is so much to be ambivalent about."[67]

Certainly, as my experiences among Pamela's and Dotty's kin and my own have taught me, there are good grounds for ambivalence about contemporary postmodern family conditions. Nor do I imagine that even a successful feminist family revolution could eliminate all family distress. At best, it would foster a social order that could invert Tolstoy's aphorism by granting happy families the freedom to differ, and even to suffer. Truly postfeminist families, however, would suffer only the "common unhappiness" endemic to intimate humane relationships; they would be liberated from the "hysterical misery" generated by social injustice.[68] No nostalgic movement to restore the modern family can offer as much. For better and/or worse, the postmodern family revolution is here to stay.

Notes

1. Writing the majority opinion in the New York ruling, Judge Vito Titone elaborated four judicial criteria for determining what constitutes a family: (1) "exclusivity and longevity of a relationship"; (2) the "level of emotional and financial commitment"; (3) how a couple has "conducted their everyday lives and held themselves out to society"; and (4) the "reliance placed upon one another for daily family services." Philip S. Gutis, "Court Widens Family Definition," *New York Times,* 7 July 1989, A1, A13.

2. Kathy Bodovitz, "Referendum Petitions Block S.F. Domestic Partners Law," *San Francisco Chronicle,* 7 July 1989, A1, A20, and Don Lattin, "How Religious Groups Stopped Partners Law," *San Francisco Chronicle,* 10 July 1989, A1, A20.

3. For pessimistic assessments of family decline, see Christopher Lasch, *Haven in a Heartless World: The Family Besieged* (New York: Basic Books, 1977); Kingsley Davis, "The Meaning and Significance of Marriage in Contemporary Society," in *Contemporary Marriage: Comparative Perspectives on a Changing Institution,* ed. Kingsley Davis and Amyra Grossbard-Schectman (New York: Russell Sage Foundation, 1985); and Peter Berger and Brigette Berger, *The War over the Family* (Garden City, N.Y.: Anchor Books, 1983). For optimistic appraisals of "the family," see Mary Jo Bane, *Here to Stay: American Families in the Twentieth Century* (New York: Basic Books, 1976); Theodore Caplow, Howard Bahr, Bruce Chadwick, Reuben Hill, and Margaret Holmes Williamson, *Middletown Families: Fifty Years of Change and Continuity* (Toronto: Bantam Books, 1983); and Randall Collins, *Sociology of Marriage and the Family: Gender, Love, and Property* (Chicago: Nelson-Hall, 1985). More centrist, but still somewhat anxious evaluations of the state of "the family" include Alan Wolfe, *Whose Keeper? Social Science and Moral Obligation* (Berkeley and Los Angeles: University of California Press, 1989); Robert Bellah, Richard Madsen, William M. Sullivan, Ann Swidler, and Steven M. Tipton, *Habits of the Heart* (Berkeley and Los Angeles: University of California Press, 1985); and Andrew Cherlin, "Marriage, Divorce, Remarriage: From the 1950s to the 1980s" (Paper presented at the annual meeting of the American Sociological Association, San Francisco, 11 August 1989).

4. Linda Gordon, *Heroes of Their Own Lives,* (New York: Viking Press, 1988), 3.

5. Kathleen Gerson, *Hard Choices: How Women Decide about Work, Career, and Motherhood* (Berkeley and Los Angeles: University of California Press, 1985), 237.

6. Andrew Cherlin, ed., *The Changing American Family and Public Policy* (Washington, D.C.: Urban Institute Press, 1988), 5, and Susan Householder Van Horn, *Women, Work, and Fertility, 1900–1986* (New York: New York University Press, 1988), 152. Of course, far more than 7 percent of American families pass through a life cycle stage in which they practice the "modern" pattern, but the sharp contrast in the demographic snapshots of the two periods reflects the steady decline in both the duration of that stage and the proportion of Americans who experience it at all.

7. For data and analyses on the steady rise of divorce rates, see Carl Degler, *At Odds: Women and the Family in America from the Revolution to the Present* (Oxford: Oxford University Press, 1980), 165–177; Kingsley Davis, "Wives and Work: A Theory of the Sex-Role Revolution and Its Consequences," in *Feminism, Children, and the New Families,* ed. Sanford Dornbusch and Myra Strober (New York: Guilford Press, 1985); Lawrence Stone, "The Road to Polygamy," *New York Review of Books* 36, no. 3 (2 March 1989): 12–15; and Sar Levitan, Richard Belous, and Frank Gallo, *What's Happening to the American Family? Tensions, Hopes, Realities,* rev. ed. (Baltimore: John Hopkins University Press, 1988). The first "modern" American divorce case, which included "alienation of affection" as one of its complaints, occurred in 1776 (Sara M. Evans, *Born for Liberty: A History of Women in America* [New York: Free Press, 1989], 42).

8. The memorable opening line of Leo Tolstoy's *Anna Karenina:* "All happy families are like one another; each unhappy family is unhappy in its own way" (trans. David Magarshack [New York: New American Library, 1961]).

9. Clive Dilnot, "What is the Post-Modern?" *Art History* 9, no.2 (June 1986): 245–63.

10. Ibid., 245, 249.

11. The postmodern condition emerges, Jean-François Lyotard argues, when legitimation through grand historical narratives has broken down. See *The Postmodern Condition: A*

Report on Knowledge, trans. Geoff Bennington and Brian Massumi (Manchester: Manchester University Press, 1984). I sidestep here the debate over whether the postmodern represents a clear break with the modern, or, as Nancy Scheper-Hughes has argued (during a conference on "Anthropology and Modernity" held at the University of California, Berkeley, in April 1989), is simply "capitalism on speed." Frances E. Mascia-Lees, Patricia Sharpe, and Colleen Ballerino Cohen, in "The Postmodernist Turn in Anthropology: Cautions from a Feminist Perspective," *Signs* 15, no.1 (Autumn 1989): 7–33, discuss feminist concerns that the rejection of grand narratives coincides with new attempts by women and other subordinated groups to write their own. For additional useful discussions of feminism, modernism, and postmodernism, see Janet Wolff, *Feminine Sentences: Essays on Women and Culture* (Berkeley and Los Angeles: University of California Press, 1990).

12. The frequency and irregularity of mortality in the premodern period and the economic interdependence of women and men fostered high remarriage rates and the complex kinship relationships remarriages generate. There were also significant regional differences in premodern family patterns. For excellent overviews of the diversity of premodern family patterns, see Stephanie Coontz, *The Social Origins of Private Life: A History of American Families, 1600–1900* (London: Verso, 1988), and Steven Mintz and Susan Kellogg, *Domestic Revolutions: A Social History of American Family Life* (New York: Free Press, 1988).

13. Alice Kessler-Harris and Karen Sacks doubt that a majority of working-class men ever earned a family wage. See "The Demise of Domesticity," in *Women, Households, and the Economy,* ed. Lourdes Beneria and Catharine R. Stimpson (New Brunswick, N.J.: Rutgers University Press, 1987).

14. Janet Flammang, "Female Officials in the Feminist Capital: The Case of Santa Clara County," *Western Political Quarterly* 38, no. 1 (March 1985): 94–118; idem, "Women Made a Difference: Comparable Worth in San Jose," in *The Women's Movements of the United States and Western Europe,* ed. Ira Katznelson and Carole Mueller (Philadelphia: Temple University Press, 1987), 290–309; Linda Blum, *Re-evaluating Women's Work: The Significance of the Comparable Worth Movement* (Berkeley and Los Angeles: University of California Press, 1991). Ironically, the San Jose comparable-worth strike was called when the feminist mayor and the city council, on which women held the majority of seats, failed to meet the city employees' demand to proceed on a proposed job study prerequisite to evaluating pay equity.

15. For data on divorce rates and household composition for Santa Clara County in comparison with California and the United States as a whole, see U.S. Department of Commerce, Bureau of the Census, *Census of Population* for 1960, 1970, and 1980. During the 1970s the county recorded 660 abortions for every 1,000 live births, compared with a statewide average of 489.5 and a ratio of less than 400 for the nation. See U.S. Department of Commerce, Bureau of the Census, *Statistical Abstract of the United States, 1981.*

16. Jean Holland, *The Silicon Syndrome: A Survival Handbook for Couples* (Palo Alto, Calif.: Coastlight Press, 1983).

17. Michael S. Malone, "Family in Crisis," *Santa Clara Magazine,* Spring 1989, 15.

18. For literature describing working-class families as favoring "traditional" gender arrangements, see Mirra Komarovsky with Jane H. Philips, *Blue-Collar Marriage* (New York: Summit Books, 1986); Lillian Rubin, *Worlds of Pain: Life in the Working-Class Family* (New York: Basic Books, 1976); Van Horn, *Women, Work and Fertility;* Caplow et al., *Middletown Families;* and Robert Coles and Jane Hallowell Coles, *Women of Crisis:*

Lives of Struggle and Hope (New York: Delacorte Press, 1978). Barbara Ehrenreich argues that the media constructed this stereotype of the blue-collar working class after it briefly "discovered" that class in 1969 (see *Fear of Falling: The Inner Life of the Middle Class* [New York: Pantheon Books, 1989]). I return to this issue below.

19. Judith Stacey, *Brave New Families: Stories of Domestic Upheaval in Late Twentieth-Century America* (New York: Basic Books, 1990).

20. Judith Stacey and Susan Elizabeth Gerard, " 'We Are Not Doormats': The Influence of Feminism on Contemporary Evangelicalism in The United States," in *Uncertain Terms: Negotiating Gender in American Culture*, ed. Faye Ginsburg and Anna Tsing (Boston: Beacon Press, 1990).

21. There is a great deal of empirical and theoretical support for this view, from feminist psychoanalytic analyses of mothering to time-budget studies of the domestic division of labor. For a direct discussion of women and "the work of kinship," see Micaela di Leonardo, *The Varieties of Ethnic Experience: Kinship, Class, and Gender among California Italian-Americans* (Ithaca, N.Y.: Cornell University Press, 1984), 194–205. For an in-depth treatment of domestic labor, see Arlie Hochschild with Anne Machung, *The Second Shift: Working Parents and the Revolution at Home* (New York: Viking Press, 1989).

22. For fuller discussion of this masculinity crisis see Kathleen Gerson, "Coping with Commitment: Dilemmas and Conflicts of Family Life," in *America at Century's End*, ed. Alan Wolfe (Berkeley and Los Angeles: University of California Press, 1991), and Lynne Segal, *Slow Motion: Changing Masculinities, Changing Men* (London: Virago, 1990).

23. Lynne Segal arrives at a similar conclusion (see ibid., chap. 2). Patricia Zavella's research on the division of household labor among "Hispano" couples provides additional support for this view. See her "Sunbelt Hispanics on the Line" (paper presented at History and Theory Conference, University of California, Irvine, April 1989). A more comprehensive treatment of these issues among Anglo and Hispanic households will appear in Louise Lamphere, Felipe Gonzales, Patricia Zavella, and Peter Evans, "Working Mothers and Sunbelt Industrialization," a book-length manuscript in progress.

24. Segal's summary of research on changes in the domestic division of labor supports this view (see *Slow Motion*, chap. 2). And while Arlie Hochschild's recent study of domestic labor emphasizes men's resistance to assuming a fair share of the burden, it also demonstrates that this has become a widely contested issue (see Hochschild with Machung, *The Second Shift*).

25. Colleen Leahy Johnson, *Ex-Familia: Grandparents, Parents, and Children Adjust to Divorce* (New Brunswick, N.J.: Rutgers University Press, 1988).

26. On extended, cooperative kin ties among the poor, see Michael Young and Peter Willmott, *Family and Kinship in East London* (Middlesex, England: Penguin Books, 1962); David M. Schneider and Raymond T. Smith, *Class Differences and Sex Roles in American Kinship and Family Structure* (Englewood Cliffs, N.J.: Prentice-Hall, 1973); Carol B. Stack, *All Our Kin: Strategies for Survival in a Black Community* (New York: Harper & Row, 1974). David Halle, *America's Working Man* (Chicago: University of Chicago Press, 1984), 279, takes as a premise the existence of extensive kin ties among blue-collar workers.

27. Stack, *All Our Kin*, and Young and Willmott, *Family and Kinship*.

28. Allan Schnaiberg and Sheldon Goldenberg, "From Empty Nest to Crowded Nest: The Dynamics of Incompletely-Lauched Young Adults," *Social Problems* 36, no.3 (June 1989): 251–69.

29. On premodern family patterns, see Coontz, *Social Origins of Private Life*, and Mintz and Kellogg, *Domestic Revolutions*.

30. Martha May, "Bread before Roses: American Workingmen, Labor Unions, and the Family Wage," in *Women, Work, and Protest: A Century of U.S. Women's Labor History*, ed. Ruth Milkman (Boston: Routledge & Kegan Paul, 1985), argues that the demand for a family wage was primarily a class-based demand made by labor unions on behalf of working-class men and their wives in the nineteenth century, but it was achieved in the twentieth century through a cross-class gender alliance between capitalists and unionized men. This analysis helps to resolve a theoretical and political debate among feminist and socialist labor historians concerning the class and gender character of the family wage struggle. Heidi Hartmann, "Capitalism, Patriarchy, and Job Segregation by Sex," in *Capitalist Patriarchy and the Case for Socialist-Feminism*, ed. Zillah Eisenstein (New York: Monthly Review Press, 1979), criticizes the sexist character of the struggle, while Jane Humphries, "The Working-Class Family, Women's Liberation and Class Struggle: The Case of Nineteenth-Century British History," *Review of Radical Political Economics* 9 (Fall 1977): 25–41, defends the struggle as a form of class and family resistance.

31. After a sharp postwar spurt, divorce rates stabilized only temporarily during the 1950s, and above prewar levels (Levitan et al., *What's Happening to the American Family?*, 27). The proportion of women entering college climbed slowly throughout the 1950s, before escalating sharply since the mid-1960s: in 1950, 12 percent of women ages twenty-four to twenty-nine had completed one year of college; that figure rose to 22 percent in 1965 and reached 43 percent by 1984 (Steven D. McLaughlin et al., *The Changing Lives of American Women* [Chapel Hill: University of North Carolina Press, 1988], 33–34). Van Horn, *Women, Work, and Fertility*, 194, makes the interesting and provocative argument that a disjuncture between the limited kinds of jobs available to women and the increasing numbers of educated women seeking jobs during the 1960s helped to regenerate feminism. For additional discussions of the rise of working wives, see Davis, "Wives and Work"; Gerson, *Hard Choices*; Degler, *At Odds*, chap. 17; Elaine Tyler May, *Homeward Bound: American Families in the Cold War Era* (New York: Basic Books, 1988); and Evans, *Born for Liberty*, chap. 11.

32. See Evans, *Born for Liberty*, 253–54; Van Horn, *Women, Work, and Fertility*, chap. 12; and Kessler-Harris and Sacks, "Demise of Domesticity."

33. Larry Bumpass and James Sweet, *Preliminary Evidence on Cohabitation*, NSFH Working Paper no. 2 (Madison: Center for Demography and Ecology, University of Wisconsin, September 1988), report higher education rates among those with high school education than among those with college education, and higher divorce rates among those who cohabit before marriage. For differential divorce rates by income and race, see also Van Horn, *Women, Work, and Fertility;* Levitan et al., *What's Happening to the American Family?;* and Henry A. Walker, "Black-White Differences in Marriage and Family Patterns," in *Feminism, Children, and the New Families*, ed. Dornbusch and Strober. A classic ethnography of matrilineal support systems among working-class people is Young and Wilmott, *Family and Kinship in East London;* see also Schneider and Smith, *Class Differences and Sex Roles*. Stack, *All Our Kin*, is the classic ethnographic portrayal of matrifocal cooperative kin networks among poor African Americans. Gordon, *Heroes of Their Own Lives*, however, cautions against the tendency to exaggerate and romanticize the existence of extended kinship support systems among the very poor.

34. For data and discussions of noneconomic motives for paid employment among blue-collar women, see Mary Lindenstein Walshok, "Occupational Values and Family Roles,"

in *Working Women and Families,* ed. Karen Wolk Feinstein (Beverly Hills, Calif.: Sage, 1979); Gerson, *Hard Choices;* and Kessler-Harris and Sacks, "Demise of Domesticity." Even Komarovsky's early, classic study *Blue-Collar Marriage* discusses the growth of noneconomic motives for employment among the wives of blue-collar men.

35. See Jessie Bernard, *The Future of Marriage* (New York: Bantam Books, 1973), 53, for her famous pronouncement that being a housewife makes many women sick.

36. For example, Barbara Ehrenreich suggests that "the working class, from the moment of its discovery" by the professional middle class in 1969, "was conceived in masculine terms" (*Fear of Falling,* 108). See also Joan Acker, "Women and Social Stratification: A Case of Intellectual Sexism," *American Journal of Sociology* 78, no. 4 (1973): 936–45.

37. This was one of the understated findings of a study that attempted to operationalize Marxist categories of class. See Eric Olin Wright, Cynthia Costello, David Hacker and Joey Sprague, "The American Class Structure," *American Sociological Review* 47, no. 6 (1982): 709–26.

38. Ehrenreich, *Fear of Falling,* 101.

39. Ibid., 115.

40. Ibid., 223. In December 1989 *Time* magazine ran a cover story on the future of feminism that drew quick, angry rebuttals from many feminists, a response I find out of proportion to the substance or the data in the story. A survey of one thousand women conducted in 1989 by Yankelovich Clancy Shulman for *Time*/CNN found a smaller proportion of the women sampled, 33 percent, choosing to identify themselves as "feminists." However, 77 percent of the women surveyed claimed that the women's movement has made life better, 94 percent said the movement helped women become more independent, and 82 percent said it was still improving the lives of American women. Addressing a perceived discrepancy among these numbers, Claudia Wallis, the story's author, opined that "in many ways, feminism is a victim of its own resounding achievements" ("Onward, Women!" *Time,* 4 December 1989, 80–89, esp. 82).

41. For example, Daniel Bell, *The End of Ideology: On the Exhaustion of Political Ideas in the Fifties* (New York: Free Press, 1962), and Seymour Martin Lipset, *Political Man* (Garden City, N.Y.: Doubleday, 1963).

42. Employing conservative measurement techniques designed to understate the extent of income loss, a recent study of changes in family income found that 40 percent of American families lost income since 1979, and another 20 percent maintained stable incomes only because employment of wives compensated for falling wages of husbands (Stephen Rose and David Fasenfest, *Family Incomes in the 1980s: New Pressure on Wives, Husbands, and Young Adults,* Working Paper no. 103 [Washington, D.C.: Economic Policy Institute, November 1988]). See also Katherine S. Newman, *Falling from Grace: The Experience of Downward Mobility in the American Middle Class* (New York: Free Press, 1988); Bennett Harrison and Barry Bluestone, *The Great U-Turn* (New York: Basic Books, 1988); Sara Kuhn and Barry Bluestone, "Economic Restructuring and Female Labor: The Impact of Industrial Change on Women," in *Women, Households, and the Economy,* ed. Beneria and Stimpson; Joan Smith, "Marginalized Labor Forces during the Reagan Recovery" (paper presented to Society for the Study of Social Problems, Berkeley, California, August 1989); Ehrenreich, *Fear of Falling;* and Wolfe, *Whose Keeper?* Moreover, measures of income inequality grossly understate the extent of economic inequality in this society. A recent study of the distribution of wealth commissioned by the U.S. Census Bureau surveyed assets as well as income and found much graver disparities. For example, the median net worth of

the top 1 percent of American households was twenty-two times greater than the median net worth of the remaining 99 percent (David R. Francis, "Study Finds Steep Inequality in Wealth," *San Francisco Chronicle*, 30 March 1990, A19).

43. William J. Wilson, *The Truly Disadvantaged: The Inner City, the Underclass, and Public Policy* (Chicago: University of Chicago Press, 1987), and Smith, "Marginalized Labor Forces." One consequence of this is an increasing divergence in the family patterns of whites and African Americans as marriage rates, in particular, plummet among the latter (see Cherlin, "Marriage, Divorce, Remarriage," 17–18). Francis, "Study Finds Steep Inequality in Wealth," reports that the median net worth of whites is 11.7 times that of African Americans.

44. Vlae Kershner, "The Payoff for Educated Workers," *San Francisco Chronicle*, 26 December 1989, A2.

45. Smith, "Marginalized Labor Forces," 1. See also *The Forgotten Half: Pathways to Success for America's Youth and Young Families* (Washington, D.C.: William T. Grant Foundation Commission on Work, Family and Citizenship, November 1988).

46. Smith, "Marginalized Labor Forces," 1; Levitan et al., *What's Happening to the American Family?*, 117. Rose and Fasenfast report a 17 percent decline in absolute earnings between 1979 and 1986 for men with high school educational levels or less (*Family Incomes in the 1980s*, 11). Kershner reports that workers with five or more years of college gained 11 percent income between 1980 and 1987, while workers with high school diplomas broke even, and those with less education lost at least 5 percent of their earnings ("Payoff for Educated Workers"); see also *The Forgotten Half* and Harrison and Bluestone, *Great U-Turn*. As the size of the standing army has decreased, military recruiters can be much more selective. For example, the U.S. Army now takes very few recruits who do not have a high school diploma. The sudden collapse of the Cold War is likely to exaggerate this trend.

47. Ehrenreich, *Fear of Falling*, 205.

48. Quoted in Wolfe, *Whose Keeper?*, p. 65.

49. Eric Olin Wright and Bill Martin, "The Transformation of the American Class Structure, 1960–1980," *American Journal of Sociology* 93, no. 1 (1987): 1–29; Kuhn and Bluestone, "Economic Restructuring and Female Labor"; and Kershner, "Payoff for Educated Workers."

50. Ehrenreich, *Fear of Falling*, 202, and Rose and Fasenfest, "Family Incomes in the 1980s," 8. The gap between single-parent and married-couple households is even more dramatic when assets are surveyed. A recent Census Bureau study found the net financial assets of married couple households to be nine times greater than those headed by nonmarried people (Francis, "Study Finds Steep Inequality in Wealth").

51. Ehrenreich, *Fear of Falling*, 206. For supportive data see Wright and Martin, "Transformation of Class Structure."

52. Smith, "Marginalized Labor"; Kuhn and Bluestone, "Economic Restructuring and Female Labor"; and Kessler-Harris and Sacks, "Demise of Domesticity."

53. The controversial *Time* cover story on the future of feminism, for example, reports a 1989 survey by Robert Half International in which 56 percent of men polled said they would forfeit one-fourth of their salaries "to have more family or personal time," and 45 percent "said they would probably refuse a promotion that involved sacrificing hours with

their family." See Zavella, "Sun Belt Hispanics on the Line," for a discussion of the active participation in child care and housework by Hispanic husbands of women who are "mainstay providers" for their households. See also Gerson, "Coping with Commitment," and Segal, *Slow Motion*, chaps. 2 and 10, for fuller discussions of men's changing family lives.

54. Cherlin, "Marriage, Divorce, Remarriage," 17.

55. Between 1960 and 1980 a 43 percent decline occurred among men between the ages of twenty and forty-nine (research by Eggebeen and Uhlenberg reported in Frank J. Furstenberg, Jr., "Good Dads–Bad Dads: Two Faces of Fatherhood," in *The Changing American Family*, ed. Cherlin, 201). Furstenberg offers an intelligent, historically situated analysis of the contradictory evidence on contemporary fatherhood.

56. The 90 percent datum is reported in Andrew Cherlin's introductory essay to *The Changing American Family*, 8. See also, Nancy D. Polikoff, "Gender and Child-Custody Determinations: Exploding the Myths," in *Families, Politics, and Public Policy: A Feminist Dialogue on Women and the State*, ed. Irene Diamond (New York: Longman, 1983), for a careful refutation of the widespread view that women retain an unfair advantage over men in child custody decisions by divorce courts.

57. Emily Abel, "Adult Daughters and Care for the Elderly," *Feminist Studies* 12, no.3 (Fall 1986): 479–97.

58. Particularly histrionic, but not unique, is the rhetoric in the promotional letter I received in 1990 for a new journal, *The Family in America*, which promises to cover such issues as "Vanishing Moms" and "Day Care: Thalidomide of the 90's."

59. See, for example, Lasch, *Haven in a Heartless World*; Davis, "The Meaning and Significance of Marriage in Contemporary Society"; and Berger and Berger, *The War over the Family*. Recently, Alan Wolfe attempted in *Whose Keeper?* to formulate a centrist position in the debate over contemporary family change that would resist nostalgia for patriarchal family forms while recognizing the destructive effects of state and market intrusions on "the family." He too worries about women's increasing involvement in the market and neglects to question men's inadequate involvement in domesticity.

60. Lisa Belkin, "Bars to Equality of Sexes Seen as Eroding, Slowly," *New York Times*, 20 August 1989, A1, A16. The *Time*/CNN survey data found even greater support for the women's movement: 77 percent said the movement made life better; only 8 percent claimed it had made things worse; and 82 percent said it was still improving the lives of American women (Wallis, "Onward, Women!," 82). Similarly, Furstenberg reports a variety of surveys indicating steady increases in preferences for more egalitarian marriages ("Good Dads–Bad Dads," 207–8).

61. Zavella, "Sunbelt Hispanics on the Line," finds a similar discrepancy between "traditionalist" ideology and reformist practice among Chicanas who serve as primary wage earners in their households.

62. According to Joan Smith, low-income African Americans provide the sole exception to this generalization because the majority contain only one possible wage earner ("Marginalized Labor Forces," 1). For additional data, see Myra Strober, "Two-Earner Families," in *Feminism, Children, and the New Families*, ed. Dornbusch and Strober.

63. According to Myra Strober, in 1985, 42 percent of households were of this type (ibid., 161). However, U.S. Census Bureau data for 1988 report that only 27 percent of all house-

holds included two parents living with children (quoted in Philip S. Gutis, "What Makes a Family? Traditional Limits Are Challenged," *New York Times*, 31 August 1989, B1).

64. Larry Bumpass and Teresa Castro, *Trends in Marital Disruption*, Working Paper 87–20 (Madison: Center for Demography and Ecology, University of Wisconsin, June 1987), 28.

65. As one of the journalists reporting the results of the *New York Times* survey reported above concluded, "Despite much talk about the decline of feminism and the women's movement, American women very much want a movement working on their behalf as they try to win equal treatment in the workplace and to balance the demands of work and family" (E. J. Dionne, Jr., "Struggle for Work and Family Fueling Women's Movement," *New York Times*, 22 August 1989, A1, A14). The *Time*/CNN survey data cited in note 40 provide strong support for this claim, as do survey data reported by Furstenberg, for example: "From 1974 to 1985, women significantly increased (from 46 to 57 percent) their preference for a marriage in which husband and wife shared responsibility for work, household duties, and child care more equitably" ("Good Dads–Bad Dads," 208).

66. Study by Albert Solnit quoted in "Most Regard Family Highly," *New York Times*, 10 October 1989, A18. Andrew Cherlin also reports increasing marital satisfaction rates despite popular concerns over family decline ("Economic Interdependence and Family Ties" [paper presented at meeting of American Sociological Association, San Francisco, 9 September 1982]).

67. Wolfe, *Whose Keeper?*, 211.

68. Freud's famous goal for psychoanalysis was to convert "hysterical misery into common unhappiness" (Sigmund Freud with Joseph Breuer, *Studies in Hysteria* [1895], in *Complete Works*, vol. 2, ed. and trans. James Strachey [London: Hogarth Press, 1954], 305).

For every way in which families we choose seem to depart from hegemonic understandings of kinship, however, there is another way in which the two appear to be cut from the same cloth. Certainly discourse on gay families reworks meanings and symbols that already enjoy wide currency wherever people in the United States think about, argue about, and practice kinship. Even within the relation that opposes straight to gay families, the "same" elements of blood and choice surface on both sides of the contrast between these "different" categories of kin. Chosen families incorporate the physiological contributions to procreation of gay men who donate sperm and lesbians who bear children, while biological family encompasses the elements of selectivity implicit in counting someone as a close relative or severing kinship ties. At best, gay families and other family forms can be classified as simultaneously like and unlike. Just as the looking-glass language of sameness and difference obscures the complexities of relationships between lovers, so it provides a reductionist view of the relationship between gay families and more conventional interpretations of kinship.

Assimilation or Transformation?

In the absence of close attention to history and context, there is the constant temptation for a person to view phenomena new to her experience as a reflection, extension, or imitation of something she thinks she already knows. Imagine you come across two women dressed as bride and groom, tossing rice over the heads of a crowd of onlookers. Would you consider them essentially the same as a heterosexual couple who had just been married? Different from a straight couple because both are women? Within the relationship, are they "like" based upon a common gender identity? Are they different from each other, and from the majority of lesbians, in their practice of butch/fem? What significance would you attribute to the inversion of throwing rice at the crowd, when the custom at weddings in the United States is for onlookers to throw rice toward the newlyweds? Perhaps you would revise your earlier conclusions if you learned that these women, dressed as bride and groom, were not stepping out of a chapel but rather riding a motorcycle down Market Street in San Francisco's annual Gay Pride Parade. After discovering more about its context, the scene immediately lends itself to reinterpretation. You might well find yourself searching for evidence of parodic intention and noticing the appreciative laughter of bystanders as the couple drives by.

Consider, then, the way most discussions of gay families have evaluated the political significance of laying claim to kinship as either inherently assimilationist or inherently progressive, without respect to social or historical context. Though less hotly contested than in former years, debate continues as to whether or not the struggle to relocate lesbians and gay men within the domain of kinship will, in the long run, move gay people in a conservative direction. Some gay commentators have argued that chosen families represent an impossible bid for respectability, a misguided attempt to become just like the happily, heterosexually married Joneses who live down the street. Was this the goal of gay liberation, they ask: to deflect charges of deviancy by becoming the proud possessors of the very institution no upstanding citizen can do without? On the other side of the issue, advocates praise chosen families for leading to a decisive break with genealogically calculated relations. Those who fear assimilation into a predominantly heterosexual society tend to identify "the family" solely with procreation and heterosexuality, while those who believe that gay kinship offers an authentic alternative often accept at face value ideologies that depict chosen families as independent of all social constraint.

Since the gay movement of the 1970s, certain activists have contended that having no family should constitute a point of pride for gay people, or at least remain a distinguishing feature of being lesbian or gay. To quote Dennis Altman, a gay proponent of the "straight is to gay as family is to no family" thesis: "The homosexual represents the most clear-cut rejection of the nuclear family that exists, and hence is persecuted because of the need to maintain the hegemony of that concept."[1] In 1978 Michael Lynch reported some gay men looking down on gay fathers for having failed to escape "the family."[2] E. M. Ettore has argued that lesbian and gay identity, in and of itself, denies the primacy of family.[3] In place of family ties, Guy Hocquenghem has encouraged gay people to elaborate friendship networks, which he portrays as a more democratic form than kinship and a welcome alternative to Freud's derivation of significant relationships from filiation.[4] In this view, kinship itself becomes a symbol of assimilation and marks the boundary between heterosexual and gay identity.[5] Why speak of lovers, friends, or even children as kin? "We" (gay men and lesbians) should develop "our" own terminology to describe "our" (presumably distinct) experiences, rather than adopting "their" (heterosexual) language and institutions. In a twist whose irony has yet to be fully appreciated, activists organizing against the same New Right that accuses homosexuals of being antifamily ended up condemning gay people for trafficking in kinship.

"We know how myths work: through the impoverishment of history," Hortense Spillers has written.[6] In the Bay Area many who argued against gay families interpreted kinship in a strictly procreative sense, taking it as a biogenetic given. By treating family as always and everywhere the same entity, they generally overlooked the context-dependent meanings that have given life to the concept and allowed it to become an object of contention. Gay families emerged in the context of historical developments that made coming out to relatives a possibility contemplated by most self-identified lesbians and gay men. Also related to the timing and content of this discourse was a legacy of building nonerotic solidarities among gay people, followed by a period of community building and the subsequent deliberation of differences that brought the concept of a unified gay community into disrepute. The very complexity of this history demonstrates that the appearance of families we choose during the 1980s represented something more than a knee-jerk reaction to the "profamily" politics of the New Right during the same decade. To formulate a critique of gay families in the abstract is to ignore the very circumstances that brought lesbians and gay men to the place of claiming and constructing kinship ties.

More useful than rhetorical attacks on a monolith called "the family" are ethnographically and historically grounded accounts that ask what families mean to people who say they have or want them. A basic insight to emerge from feminist examinations of kinship has been that the meanings carried by "family" can and will differ according to individual circumstances, identities, and intention to persuade.[7] In the words of Kenneth Burke, "When you have a 'Rome' term to which all roads lead, you thereby have as many different variants of the motive as there are roads."[8] Because family is not some static institution but a cultural category that can represent assimilation *or* challenge (again, in context), there can be no definitive answer to the debate on assimilationism. Rather than representing a crystallized

variation of some mythically mainstream form of kinship, gay families simply present one element in a broader discourse on family
whose meanings are continuously elaborated in everyday situations
of conflict and risk, from holidays and custody disputes to disclosures
of lesbian or gay identity.

Significantly, lesbians and gay men have not abandoned the distinction between heterosexual and gay identity in the course of refusing
to accept continued exile from kinship. Relocating the straight/gay
boundary *within* the mediating domain of kinship made it possible
for the establishment of a gay family to signify not assimilation but
(like coming out) a "point of exit" from heterosexuality.[9] Yet it is
also entirely possible for some people to talk about gay families with
the expectation that this new category will allow them to fit more
comfortably into a predominantly heterosexual society. Others, with
an interest in developing new forms of families, may portray their
chosen families strictly as social experiment. A lesbian can choose
to bear a child in the hope of gaining acceptance from "society"
and straight relatives, or she can embark on the same course with
a sense of daring and radical innovation, knowing that children
tend to be "protected" from lesbians and gay men in the United
States. For someone who associates kinship very closely with racial
or cultural identity, the threat of assimilation might lie not in embracing the notion of gay families but in claiming membership in a lesbian
or gay "community" where whites maintain hegemony. Politics do
not inhere in the term *family* per se, but in its deployment in particular contexts.

All this is not to say that discourse on gay families lacks a radical
potential. The notion of choice, for example, is very much an indi-
vidualistic formulation, elevated in discourse on gay kinship to the
level of a principle organizing a certain type of family. In the United
States people often tend to image social organization as the additive
end product of a series of voluntary choices: individuals create groups
(like families) which in turn create society.[10] Yet gay families can also
structure lived experiences that mitigate the utopianism that is always
a danger in adopting any concept so closely tied to individualism.
Many lesbian mothers, for example, spoke about their peers without
children as though the latter had been deluded by the ideologies of
freedom and creativity that inform chosen families. Jeanne Riley con-
trasted her own experience as the mother of two young children with

the idealism of friends who had heard about "choosing children" but lacked personal experience as parents.

> Last night, [my best friend] calls me and she says, "Let's talk." I said, "I can't. I have my two kids, and I have a little boy over here visiting. So I have three kids, I really can't. I have to feed them dinner." So she says, "Well, I'm just home alone." So I said, "Well, I'm here. Why don't you come over?" She said, "With three kids?" It's real clear that no matter how much your friends love you, if they don't want to be around kids, they're no longer your friends. They resent and chafe at the fact that they have to incorporate the family into their social environment. There's not that spontaneity. "Let's go watch whales." (laughter) You kidding?

It is ironic that parenting, one of the phenomena within gay families most frequently taken as a sign of accommodation to "the traditional," should also become a place where people can come to realize that social conditions impose limits on ostensibly unrestricted choice.

There is also a radical potential associated with the one sense in which gay men and lesbians consistently concern themselves with "reproduction" in forming their own families. If "society" wants to define us as nonreproductive beings in the physical sense, some asked, why should we "reproduce" social arrangements that further the status quo? This double-edged usage of reproduction lends itself to a social critique that extends beyond gender and sexual identity to issues such as class that lie beyond the arena of concerns customarily attributed to gay people.

Having always assumed that he would marry, Stephen Richter said he had had to reevaluate everything after coming out made him realize that his life would not be "like" his parents'. People whose parents had pursued managerial or professional careers sometimes formulated a class critique by invoking images of a suburban home with its picket fence, signifiers of the complacent bourgeois life they attributed to their straight families. If he had not come out, Andy Wentworth insisted,

> I would have just followed the same path that I was expected to, that everybody else did, that society says you should. And it's very easy to just continue the same traditions over and over again, get the

same white picket fence that your grandparents have and your children will have after you. Where as soon as I realized I was gay, I said, hey, I've got a totally different situation going on here. My parents' expectations are now meaningless. Society's expectations are now meaningless. I have to build my own life. So that gave me more inner strength and durability and ability to be creative and in control of my environment.

Individuals from working-class backgrounds tended to experience coming out somewhat differently from Stephen and Andy. If they had determined to live openly as lesbians or gay men, they often perceived this not so much as declining to copy their parents' lives, but as departing from their parents' dream of upward mobility. Believing that heterosexism and antigay discrimination might render that dream unattainable, they saw themselves failing to reproduce not their parents' situation but rather their parents' ambitions. In the process, they sometimes began to question the value of those ambitions.

Viewed through the timeless sort of chronology that reproduction represents, a family can be pictured as an endless chain in which each individual replicates, exceeds, or fails to attain what "your grandparents have and your children will have after you." Gay families, in contrast, have not incorporated the chronological succession implicit in the Anglo-European notion of genealogical descent. Although chosen families can incorporate biological symbolism through childbearing and adoption, the children raised in gay families are not expected to go on to become gay or to form gay families of their own. Following the principle of choice, the kind of families these children establish should depend on their own sexual identities, and whether they establish families at all should be left to their discretion. By substituting images of creation and selection for the logic of reproduction and succession, discourse on gay families can—and does—remind people of their power to alter the circumstances into which they were born.

Common Ground

Gay families not only dispute exclusively procreative interpretations of kinship, but introduce a new basis for rendering heterosexuality and lesbian or gay identity commensurable. Put simply, two things that are commensurable are capable of being compared. In the context of the symbolic contrast between straight and gay families, kinship effectively bridges the opposition of straight versus gay by providing a third term capable of relating each to the other. Because commensurability reserves the distinctive identities of its contrasting terms in the course of establishing this common ground, it is not to be confused with the notion of likeness that informs an identity politics. In the case of gay families, the opposition between biological and chosen families reaffirms the straight/gay boundary even as the vocabulary of kinship links categories of beings hitherto isolated by the species difference often attributed to homosexuality.

To view gay identity as a species difference is to regard gay people as beings so separate, so different in kind, that many heterosexuals believe they do not know and have never met a lesbian or gay man.[11] To make such an assertion with certitude implies a belief that the difference gay identity makes is so significant it should be immediately detectable. Stereotyping that reduces gay men and lesbians to sexual beings only reinforces this perception of utter otherness. But "in real life, and usually in good novels and films, individuals are not defined only by their sexuality. Each has a history, and his or her eroticism is involved in a certain situation."[12] Being a lesbian "is more than somebody I sleep with," protested Charlyne Harris. "I mean, that's just like saying to a straight woman that a man, is that a big part of your life?" By countering any tendency to view gay people as what one lesbian dubbed "a walking sex act," a discourse on gay families that encompasses nonerotic as well as erotic ties invites heterosexuals to abandon the standpoint of the voyeur in favor of searching for areas of shared experience that join the straight self to the lesbian or gay other.

Despite their overt allegiance to values of autonomy and individualism, people in the United States tend to conceive commonality through a notion of humanity, and species membership through kinship more than other sorts of social bonds. Former soldiers interviewed by Studs Terkel described how, during World War II, they found it relatively simple to shoot at a nameless, faceless enemy.[13] In their narratives it is not the name of a captured solider on identification papers, or even a glimpse of the eyes, mouths, and faces of fallen enemy troops, that shocks combatants into recognition of a shared humanity. Instead, recognition and regret come with the discovery of a letter in a dead soldier's pocket written by sister or sweetheart, or from stumbling across kin gathered around the picture of a boy in soldier's uniform at a residence in the war zone. The enduring image that organizes these stories of wartime, recounted nearly half a century later, is a transformation of "the enemy" into a person—someone "just like me"—at the very moment of learning about relatives he cared for and who cared for him in return.

The concept of humanity as a unified species is deeply rooted in the procreative bias of a culture that dissociates gay men and lesbians from family by defining them as nonprocreative beings. Thus the notion of a species difference that divides gay from straight resonates with the strategic location of gay people outside the domain of kinship. Viewed against the backdrop of species difference, a seemingly matter-of-fact situation such as walking into the building that two gay lovers call home can evoke a startled recognition reminiscent of the emotion felt by Terkel's veterans when enemy soldiers assumed human form in the context of familial relations. In his coming-out narrative, Stephen Richter described one of his initial encounters with another gay person:

> The first time I was in a home where two men were living . . . I went off to the baths and I met a man there who had a lover and he introduced me, had me to dinner with he and his friend. And it was a very normal-looking house. I looked around and there was a sofa, and tables, and lamps. And I thought, "Isn't it amazing that two gay men can have a house that looks just like anybody else's house!" That was a fascination for me.

Situated in relation to symbols like home that carry kinship (as well as gender, class, and ethnicity), gay men and lesbians suddenly appear as social creatures rather than as self-absorbed and sex-obsessed caricatures of what a person might be. That "gay people have furniture!" look says worlds about just how incommensurable essentialized notions of identity can become, and what it can take to bring them back into relation with one another.

By advancing a claim to kinship, discourse on gay families bears the potential to break apart what Michel Foucault has called the "frozen countenance of the perversions" without discarding lesbian or gay identity in the process.[14] Alfred Kinsey long ago depicted homosexuality and heterosexuality as aspects along a single continuum of human sexuality.[15] Evelyn Hooker's finding that psychiatrists could not sort homosexuals from heterosexuals on the basis of psychological tests was considered revolutionary in its time.[16] Alan Bell and Martin Weinberg painstakingly documented the tremendous diversity among gay men and lesbians in order to argue that relatively little separates gays from straights.[17] Yet such studies have had a negligible impact on the continued objectification of gay men and lesbians by those who write "Kill Queers" on alley walls, or those who place a lower value on gay lives by failing to approve adequate funding for AIDS programs.

I am not arguing here that gay people are "just like" heterosexuals, or even that because Alfred Kinsey once placed the two along a sexual continuum that a continuum offers the best way to imagine their relationship. As a cultural category now linked to gay identity, kinship opens up new possibilities for relating gay to straight that shift discussion away from the tired rhetoric of sameness and difference. In discourse on gay families, straight remains opposed to gay, the two identities distinct but rendered commensurable through the vocabulary of kinship that conveys a common humanity to most people in the United States. The product of this discourse need not be a humanism that, like metaphor, dissolves difference into a larger whole. When lesbians and gay men can present themselves as fully social persons capable of laying claims to families, their distinctive sexual identities need no longer sharply segregate them as members of a species unto itself.

The Big Picture

After exposing the often oppressive ways in which families construct age and gender and organize inequitable divisions of labor, feminists have often been highly critical of "the family." In their works on kinship, they have warned of the twin dangers of ignoring power relations within families, and examining familial relations in isolation from relations of power in society at large. Michèle Barrett and Mary McIntosh have called for "the total eradication of familial ideology," while Susan Harding has asked feminists to set about the task of "creating kinship without families."[18]

Without doubt many travesties have been perpetrated in the name of family, including attempts to bar gay people from homes and workplaces across the United States. Because gay families are not structured through hierarchically ordered categories of relationship, however, they do not systematically produce gendered divisions of labor or relations stratified by age and gender. Such stratification is not incompatible with chosen families and, in particular instances, hierarchies can emerge within them, especially when children are involved. But neither is hierarchy essential to the constitution of gay families, which are often composed primarily of relationships with peers. Rather than being organized through marriage and child rearing, most chosen families are characterized by fluid boundaries, eclectic composition, and relatively little symbolic differentiation between erotic and nonerotic ties. Where kinship terminology has developed in association with gay families, it has not been particularly marked by gender ("lover" and "biological [or nonbiological] parent" offer two cases in point).

Families we choose interpose face-to-face relationships between what Bonnie Zimmerman has called the "isolating structure" of identity and a more holistic, but exclusive, vision of a unified community.[19] Does embracing gay families then mean abandoning all hope of resurrecting a notion of gay and/or lesbian community? Lesbian and gay activists have traveled a long road since the time when community seemed to some "the place we feel at home—a radical kinship in the making."[20] By the late 1980s even white activists situated in the most privileged of circumstances had realized that not all lesbians and gay men have participated in this "we," just as not everyone felt at home in what once passed for an encompassing community. To some activists who have spent hours negotiating their way through the politics of identity and difference, the unresolved problem seems to be how to create "a new sense of political community which gives up the desire for the kind of home where the suppression of positive differences underwrites familial identity."[21]

I have suggested that discourse on gay families offers one response to the differences and divisions encountered in the search for the holy grail of community, though probably not the one sought by those feminists who have devoted a considerable amount of energy to analyzing the drawbacks of familialism. In the Bay Area, families we choose were not constructed solely by people willing to pay any price to create a zone of comfort or a retreat from the weariness attendant upon years of political activism. People tended to describe their chosen families in terms that were as much about sustenance as safety.

Gay families have created a cultural space in which people can love but also fight, without expecting their chosen kin to walk away, much less go off to organize a faction. These families are not opposed to collectivism, nor are they inherently privatizing; on the contrary, they have proved capable of integrating relationships that cross household lines, exchanges of material and emotional assistance, co-parenting arrangements, and support for persons with AIDS. Although families we choose do not offer a substitute for political organizing, neither do they pose an inherent threat to political action or collective initiatives.

This is an idealized portrait, of course. There are problems raised by identity politics that gay families may well never address. Following the individualized logic of choice, many people have a tendency to create ties primarily with people they perceive to be "like" them, using one criterion or another to gauge similarity. In that case, difference once again disappears below the personal and political horizon. At the same time, however, families we choose offer novel possibilities for healing some of the rifts and wounds left over from a painful decade of learning to deal in difference. By this point it should be evident that family can mean very different things from person to person and situation to situation. During the 1980s some women of color labeled the feminist critique of "the family" as a *white* feminist critique that took as its point of departure the nuclear family ideal of the white "middle class."[22] Speaking about Black feminists in 1983, Barbara Smith explained, "Unlike some white feminists who have questioned, and at times rightfully rejected, the white patriarchal family, we want very much to retain our blood connections without sacrificing ourselves to rigid and demeaning sex roles."[23] The same year, Cherríe Moraga had written: "Being Chicana and having family are synonymous for me."[24] For some people of color who felt marginal to "gay community"—partly due to experiences of racism in gay contexts, but also because they associated claiming a lesbian or gay identity with exile from kinship—discourse on gay families offered an opportunity to bring ethnicity and gay identity into a relationship of integration rather than constant tension. Such a reconciliation of identities is by no means predetermined, however; some lesbians and gay men of color find it difficult to accept the authenticity of gay families and link their rejection of the concept of chosen kin to a particular racial or ethnic identification.

At this point it remains unclear how the emerging discourse on gay families will unfold, or in what directions lesbians and gay men will pursue the political implications of families organized by choice. Rayna Rapp has noted that in a period when kinship has become highly politicized, lesbians and gay men have been somewhat less successful than others in making their bid for recognition of so-called alternative family forms.[25] In the landmark *Bowers v. Hardwick* decision that upheld Georgia's sodomy law and convicted one man for having consensual sex with another in the privacy of his own home, Justice White, in formulating the opinion of the Court, justified its finding that most areas of family law were inapplicable to the case by concluding, "No connection between family, marriage, or procreation on the one hand and homosexual activity on the other has been demonstrated."[26]

One measure of the challenge gay families pose to the status quo is to ask whether basic changes in the social, economic, and political order would be required to grant gay families legitimacy and legal recognition, or whether chosen families could be accommodated by simply extending certain "rights" to lesbians and gay men and treating them as members of another minority group. From insurance companies to the courts, major institutions in the United States will find it easier to validate domestic partnerships, custody rights for lesbian and gay parents, and the right to jointly adopt children, than to recognize gay families that span several households or families that include friends.

Because the relationship of lovers, like marriage, brings together two individuals united by the symbolism of sex and love, many in the United States have drawn analogies between this bond and more customary affinal arrangements. Relatives and judges alike perceive the option of treating gay or lesbian lovers as they would a childless heterosexual couple: as an exceptional relationship in a procreative world. Likewise, they have the option of treating lesbian or gay coparents as though only the gender of individual parents has changed, while everything else about the social conditions in which child rearing occurs remains unaffected. Due to this sort of reasoning by analogy from heterosexual relations, coming out seems to make a much clearer statement about kinship when a person has a partner or is the nonbiological coparent to a child. Without either of these ties, many gay people have reported finding it difficult to demonstrate the importance of friendship as kinship or to convince heterosexuals that lesbian and gay identity involves anything other than sex.

Pressure is building even now to take the path of least resistance. In the years to come it will be important that gay men and lesbians not become so concerned about gaining recognition for their families that they settle for whatever sort of recognition it seems possible to get. For lesbian and gay organizations that take up the issues raised by discourse on gay families, the future will bring difficult questions about where to devote limited resources. Should they work toward the legalization of same-sex partnerships, following Sweden's example?[27] Does marriage have political implications that families per se do not? If gay people begin to pursue marriage, joint adoptions, and custody rights to the exclusion of seeking kinship status for some categories of friendship, it seems likely that gay families will develop in ways largely congruent with socioeconomic and power relations in the larger society. This accommodationist thrust is already apparent in the requirements for shared residence or cohabitation for a specified period of time that are built in to most domestic partner legislation.[28] Following the logic of chosen families, an individual should be able to pick any one person as a partner—domestic or otherwise—and designate that person as the recipient of insurance or other employment benefits, even when that choice entails crossing household boundaries.

If legal recognition is achieved for some aspects of gay families at the expense of others, it could have the effect of privileging certain forms of family while delegitimating others by contrast. The most likely scenario would involve narrowing the definition of gay families to incorporate only couples and parents with children, abandoning attempts to achieve any corresponding recognition for families of friends. Legal recognition for friends, or at least measures that would eliminate any automatic elevation of blood ties over ties of friendship, must also assume its place on lesbian and gay political agendas. Relatives calculated by blood should not be able to break a properly executed will that leaves possessions to a relative calculated by choice—whether that chosen relative be friend or lover—simply because the former can lay claim to a genealogical connection to the deceased.[29] In the widest political and economic arenas, taking advantage of the transformative potential of discourse on gay families—for it is only a potential—will require great care and attention to cultural context in framing legislation, laying the basis for court cases, and selecting particular kinship-related practices to challenge as exclusionary.

Reengineering Biogenetics

Change and continuity are more closely related than many people tend to think. No search is more fruitless than the one that seeks revolutionary forms of social relations that remain "uncontaminated" by existing social conditions. Not surprisingly, then, discourse on gay families transfigures the exclusively procreative interpretations of kinship with which it takes issue in such a way that it remains of them but no longer completely contained within them.

By implicitly identifying family with procreation, the equation "straight is to gay as family is to no family" concedes the entire domain of kinship to heterosexuality. Only when displaced onto one side of the relation that opposes straight to gay families does procreatively organized kinship become marked as "biological family" and qualified as one subset of a larger kinship universe. Although this transformation does not challenge the interpretation of biology as a "natural fact," it represents a truly significant departure from more conventional construction of kinship in that it displaces biology onto a particular type of family identified with heterosexuality. Some gay men and lesbians in the Bay Area had chosen to create families and some had not, some had become parents and some had not, but almost all associated their sexual identities with a release from any sort of procreative imperative. In this sense the radical potential of a discourse on gay families is not limited to contesting the species difference of homosexuality, the "reproduction" of class relations, or even the individualism implicit in notions of choice.

In the absence of a notion of genealogy, David Schneider has argued, kinship would cease to have meaning as a cultural domain: "Robbed of its grounding in biology, kinship is nothing."[30] After examining discourse on gay families, however, it would seem more accurate to say that, robbed of its *relation* to biology, kinship is nothing. Families we choose are defined through contrast with biological or blood family, making biology a key feature of the opposing term that conditions the meanings of gay kinship. To put it another way, biological family and chosen families are mutually constituted categories related through a principle of determinism that opposes free will to biogenetic givens. Through this relationship biology remains implicated in the concept of a family that can be chosen. On the one hand, discourse on gay families refutes any claim by procreation to be the privileged, precultural foundation for all conceivable forms of kinship. On the other hand, by retaining biology on one side of the symbolic opposition between straight and gay families, this same discourse removes procreation from center stage without dissolving kinship into the whole of social relations.

Lesbians and gay men have defined their own families not so much by analogy as by contrast, however overdrawn the opposition between gay and straight families might sometimes become as individuals argue for the distinctiveness of "their" type of family. Defined through their difference, blood family and chosen families assume equivalent status as they move away from the dualism of real versus ideal and authentic versus derivative concealed within the concept of fictive kinship. Through the fear and sometimes the experience of being disowned or rejected after coming out to blood relatives, many lesbians and gay men come to question not so much the "naturalness" of a biological tie, but rather the assumption that shared biogenetic substance in itself confers kinship. This heightened awareness of the selectivity incorporated into genealogical modes of calculating relationship has shaped the constitution of gay families as families we choose, and allowed gay people to argue that their chosen families represent something more than a second-best imitation of blood ties.

Nevertheless, isn't there a danger that by subjecting kinship to choice, the concept of family will lose its significance? A similar sort of dilution has occurred with the concept of community: people now speak blithely of "the community of artists," "the sports community," and even "the straight community." With respect to family, some tendency in this direction also exists. Of late, any assemblage of persons within a household, from halfway houses for people recovering from addiction to retirement homes sheltering hundreds, may be billed as a site for the development of familial relationships. Where discourse on gay families differs from these cases is in its emergence from a specific history of categorical exclusion from participation in kinship relations, an exclusion associated with claiming a lesbian or gay identity. A second characteristic that sets this discourse apart is its application of the term "family" to face-to-face ties that already carry deep attachment and commitment in the absence of any corresponding recognition from society at large.

Descriptively speaking, the categories of gay kinship might better be labeled families we struggle to create, struggle to choose, struggle to legitimate, and—in the case of blood or adoptive family—struggle to keep. Among gay men and lesbians, there is the pervasive sense that, as Diane Kunin put it, "gay people really have to work to make family." In a sense, people of all sexual identities "work" to make kinship. The Victorian depiction of family as a domestic retreat from the working world disguises a variety of labors, from housework and child rearing to the more intangible emotional work believed necessary to sustain relationships.[31] Yet gay men and lesbians encounter added dimensions that complicate the practice of constructing kin ties: parenting children in a heterosexist society, maintaining erotic relationships without viewing them through the one-dimensional lens of a gendered sameness, risking kin ties in coming out to straight relatives, interweaving peer relationships in multiples of three or four or seven, consistently asserting the importance of relationships that lack social status or even a vocabulary to describe them. Always in the background are strictly procreative interpretations of kinship, relative to which the opposition between biological and chosen families has taken shape. Too often in the foreground are opponents, well meaning or otherwise, who reduce gay families to a metaphorical rendition of more conventional kinship arrangements, treating them as pretended family relations that will never quite measure up to a heterosexual standard.

When cast in narrative form, the shift from the identification of gayness with the renunciation of kinship (no family) to a correspondence between gay identity and a particular type of family (families we choose) presents a kind of collective coming-out story: a tale of lesbians and gay men moving out of isolation and into kinship. By the 1980s, when gay people came out to relatives by blood or adoption, they often were hoping not only to maintain and strengthen those biologically calculated bonds but also to gain recognition for ties to lovers and other chosen relatives who could not be located on any biogenetic grid. If disclosure led to the pain of rejection, they were able to remind themselves that blood ties no longer exhausted the options open to them within the domain of kinship.

Like most stories, however, this one adopts a particular point of view. Without careful attention to the context from which gay kinship has emerged, an observer could easily overlook the rich history of friendships, erotic connections, community building, and other modalities of lesbian and gay solidarity that have preceded the contemporary discourse on families we choose. In a sense, gay people have come full circle. According to John D'Emilio, a key precondition for the historical appearance of a gay or lesbian identity was the possibility of establishing a life *outside* "the family" once the expansion of commodity production under capitalism offered wage work to individuals in return for their formally "free" labor.[32] By the end of the twentieth century, many lesbians and gay men were busy establishing families of their own.

Any attempt to evaluate the political implications of a particular discourse must take into account Michel Foucault's contention that power feeds upon resistance, and knowledge upon its apparent negation.[33] Inversions that protest a given dominance, like the opposition of liberation to repression or antifamily to profamily, remain trapped within terms that frame the act of resistance as a protest *against* a given representation or paradigm. Significantly, chosen families do not directly oppose genealogical modes of reckoning kinship. Instead, they undercut procreation's status as a master term imagined to provide the template for all possible kinship relations. In displacing rather than disallowing biogenetic symbolism, discourse on gay families moves obliquely toward the future, responding to hegemonic forms of kinship not with a defensive countermove but by deftly stepping aside to evade the paradigmatic blow.

Notes

1. Dennis Altman, *Coming Out in the Seventies* (Sidney: Wild & Woolley, 1979), 47.

2. Michael Lynch, "Forgotten Fathers," in *Flaunting It!: A Decade of Gay Journalism from the Body Politic,* ed. Ed Jackson and Stan Persky (Vancouver: New Star Books, 1982), 55–63.

3. E. M. Ettore, *Lesbians, Women, and Society* (Boston: Routledge & Kegan Paul, 1980), 20.

4. Guy Hocquenghem, *Homosexual Desire* (London: Alison & Busby, 1978).

5. That view is in contrast to most structural-functionalist studies of immigrant populations, which tend to take renunciation of "traditional" kinship structures as a sign of acculturation.

6. Hortense J. Spillers, "Interstices: A Small Drama of Words," in *Pleasure and Danger: Exploring Female Sexuality,* ed. Carole S. Vance (Boston: Routledge & Kegan Paul, 1984), 185.

7. See Jane Collier, Michelle Z. Rosaldo, and Sylvia Yanagisako's essay in this volume.

8. Kenneth Burke, *A Grammar of Motives* (New York: Prentice-Hall, 1945), 105.

9. Karla Jay, "Coming Out as Process," in *Our Right to Love: A Lesbian Resource Book*, ed. Ginny Vida (Englewood Cliffs, N.J.: Prentice-Hall, 1978), 28.

10. Hervé Varenne, *Americans Together: Structured Diversity in a Midwestern Town* (New York: Teachers College Press, 1977).

11. Amber Hollibaugh, "Sexuality and the State: The Defeat of the Briggs Initiative and Beyond," *Socialist Review* 9, no. 3 (1979): 55–72.

12. Simone de Beauvoir, *Brigitte Bardot and the Lolita Syndrome* (New York: Arno Press, 1972), 26.

13. Studs Terkel, *"The Good War": An Oral History of World War Two* (New York: Ballantine Books, 1984).

14. Michel Foucault, *The History of Sexuality,* vol. 1 (New York: Vintage Books, 1978), 48.

15. Alfred C. Kinsey, Wardell B. Pomeroy, and Clyde E. Martin, *Sexual Behavior in the Human Male* (Philadelphia: W. B. Saunders, 1948).

16. Evelyn Hooker, "The Homosexual Community," in *Sexual Deviance,* ed. John H. Gagnon and William Simon (New York: Harper & Row, 1967), 167–84.

17. Allan P. Bell and Martin S. Weinberg, *Homosexualities: A Study of Diversity among Men and Women* (New York: Simon & Schuster, 1978).

18. Michèle Barrett and Mary McIntosh, *The Anti-Social Family* (London: Verso/NLB, 1982), and Susan Harding, "Feminist Reform Movements: Recent Feminism and Its Opposition," *Feminist Studies* 7, no. 1 (1981): 73. See also Lynch, "Forgotten Fathers"; Rosalind Coward, *Patriarchal Precedents: Sexuality and Social Relations* (Boston: Routledge & Kegan Paul, 1983); Gillian Dalley, *Ideologies of Caring: Rethinking Community and Collectivism* (London: Macmillan, 1988); Jane Flax, "The Family in Contemporary Feminist Thought: A Critical Review," in *The Family in Political Thought,* ed. Jean Bethke Elshtain (Amherst: University of Massachusetts Press, 1982), 223–53; Linda J. Nicholson, *Gender and History: The Limits of Social Theory in the Age of the Family* (New York: Columbia University Press, 1986); Rayna Rapp, "Toward a Nuclear Freeze? The Gender Politics of Euro-American Kinship Analysis," in *Gender and Kinship: Essays toward a Unified Analysis,* ed. Jane Fishburne Collier and Sylvia Junko Yanagisako (Stanford, Calif.: Stanford University Press, 1987), 119–31; Gayle Rubin, "The Traffic in Women: Notes on the 'Political Economy' of Sex," in *Toward an Anthropology of Women,* ed. Rayna R. Reiter (New York: Monthly Review Press, 1975), 157–210; Barrie Thorne with Marilyn Yalom, eds., *Rethinking the Family: Some Feminist Questions* (1st ed., New York: Longman, 1982); Carole S. Vance, "Gender Systems, Ideology, and Sex Research," in *Powers of Desire: The Politics of Sexuality,* ed. Ann Snitow, Christine Stansell, and Sharon Thompson (New York: Monthly Review Press, 1983), 371–84; and Jean Elshtain, "Feminism, Family, and Community," *Dissent* 29, no. 4 (1982): 442–49.

19. Bonnie Zimmerman, "The Politics of Transliteration: Lesbian Personal Narratives," in *The Lesbian Issue: Essays from "Signs,"* ed. Estelle B. Freedman, Barbara C. Gelpi, Susan L. Johnson, and Kathleen M. Weston (Chicago: University of Chicago Press, 1985), 27–42.

20. Jacquelyn N. Zita, "Historical Amnesia and the Lesbian Continuum," *Signs* 7, no. 1 (1981): 175.

21. Biddy Martin and Chandra Talpade Mohanty, "Feminist Politics: What's Home Got to Do with It?" in *Feminist Studies/Critical Studies*, ed. Teresa de Lauretis (Bloomington: Indiana University Press, 1986), 204–5.

22. Gloria I. Joseph and Jill Lewis, *Common Differences: Conflicts in Black and White Feminist Perspectives* (Garden City, N.Y.: Anchor/Doubleday, 1981).

23. Barbara Smith, ed., *Home Girls: A Black Feminist Anthology* (New York: Kitchen Table/Women of Color Press, 1983), 1.

24. Cherríe Moraga, *Loving in the War Years* (Boston: South End Press, 1983), 54.

25. Rapp, "Toward a Nuclear Freeze?"

26. Bowers v. Hardwick, 106 Supreme Court (1986), 2841.

27. Paula L. Ettelbrick, "Since When Is Marriage a Path to Liberation?," *Out/Look* 2, no. 9 (1989); and Thomas B. Stoddard, "Why Gay People Should Seek the Right to Marry," in *Out/Look* 2, no. 9 (1989).

28. Richard Green, "Domestic Partner Benefits: A Status Report to the ACLU" (Washington, D.C.: Lesbian and Gay Rights Project, American Civil Liberties Union, 1987).

29. Ettore, *Lesbians, Women, and Society*, 20.

30. David Schneider, *A Critique of the Study of Kinship* (Ann Arbor: University of Michigan Press, 1984), 112.

31. See Collier, Rosaldo, and Yanagisako's essay in this volume.

32. John D'Emilio, "Capitalism and Gay Identity," in *Powers of Desire*, ed. Snitow, Stansell, and Thompson, 100–113, and Stephen D. Murray, *Social Theory, Homosexual Realities* (New York: Gai Saber, 1984), 27. See also Hocquenghem, *Homosexual Desire*.

33. Foucault, *History of Sexuality*, vol. 1, and Teresa de Lauretis, "Displacing Hegemonic Discourses: Reflections on Feminist Theory in the 1980's," in *Inscriptions* 3, no. 4 (1988): 127–41. De Lauretis agrees that taking a position counter to something imputes the existence of a unified subject whose coherence is not achievable in practice. De Lauretis's point would also apply to the allegedly solidary collectivity known as "lesbians and gay men."

7

Why Nineteenth-Century Feminists Did Not Support "Birth Control" and Twentieth-Century Feminists Do: Feminism, Reproduction, and the Family

LINDA GORDON

The question of changes in feminist attitudes toward reproductive control has been understandably neglected in the face of today's beleaguered but relatively unified feminist position in support of women's reproductive rights. Still, changes in the feminist position over time and conflicts within the feminist tradition are important. This historical overview provides some insights into the contemporary controversy over reproductive rights and the more inclusive controversy over the family norms our society should have.

In this essay I narrate a complex historical story very briefly,[1] offering only the minimum of information required to answer the title question in a rudimentary way. In addition, the narrative sheds light on several related issues: (1) the relation between technology and social change, as exemplified in the development of birth control technology; (2) the poverty of generalizations about the family that do not specifically focus on the sex/gender system;[2] (3) certain political and ideological contradictions within the feminist tradition; and (4) some sources of the revival of the right wing, particularly the Moral Majority, in the United States.

No existing social theory, religious or materialist, has satisfactorily explained why and how societies regulate reproduction as they do. This lack of explanation is even more odd when one bears in mind that all societies regulate reproduction, and there are many differences among these sets of social rules.

This essay appeared in the first edition of *Rethinking the Family*.

One reason for the absence of satisfactory theorizing is that human reproduction involves a relation between two sexes and therefore two genders. No social theory prior to modern feminism tried to use gender as a fundamental category of social analysis. To some extent, this blind spot has been reinforced in the last century, despite the existence of feminist theory as a new vision. In the nineteenth century, Marxism began to remove the blinders and examine the material origins and perpetuation of male supremacy; more recently, the dominant Marxism became vulgarized into a productionist determinism that once again ignored the gender system.

The popularity of technological explanations, and technological determinism, further reinforced the blinders. By technological determinism I mean the view that inventions, the product of human inventiveness, shape basic social alternatives. In the field of birth control this view has constructed the following picture: once there were no effective means of birth control, and therefore the birthrate was controlled only by natural variables such as women's health and physiological fertility, or people's sexual drive; the development of contraception in this century has revolutionized the birthrate, family size, and women's life options. These changes, of course, were conditioned by other technological advances that reduced mortality rates.[3] This technological explanation is wrong, however. Technological changes have been influential, but in themselves they do not provide an explanation for the history and continuity of the birth control controversy.

Neither will so-called family history explanations, which usually employ the assumptions of "modernization theory." This approach to birth control argues that urbanization and industrialization created an economic preference for smaller families along with a character structure more secular and more oriented to pleasure.[4] Ignoring class and sexual conflicts within these "modernizing" societies, the modernization theorists cannot explain the controversy about reproductive control.

And this controversy badly needs explanation. The abortion struggle today is in part an updated version of a birth control struggle at least 150 years old. No issue of women's liberation has ever been as hotly contested; no conflict in industrial society, with the exception of the social relations of labor itself, has been as bitter; and there may be no social issue that is more passionately debated.

Let me introduce a brief historical summary. Between earliest recorded history, and even as far back as some prehistoric archeological evidence, until the 1870s, there were no significant technological advances in birth control whatever. All the basic forms of birth control—abortions, douches, condoms, and devices to cover the cervix—are ancient. The social regulation of the use of these techniques changed in various historical eras and places in the context of power relations and economic needs. By and large, birth control was uncontroversial and widely practiced in preagricultural societies; by contrast, in peasant societies large families were an asset, continuing high infant mortality necessitated many pregnancies, and birth control was suppressed.

Let us proceed now to the early nineteenth-century United States. At that time there were two developments: (1) a falling birthrate and an increased use of birth control, and (2) the first political movements for reproductive control. At this time, urbanization and industrialization began to create living conditions in which large families were no longer economical. In 1810 the birthrate in the United States started to fall and has been falling ever since. In the early nineteenth century, in a society with a strong element of prudery, it was difficult to get evidence of private use of contraception, and at first puzzled observers thought that there was a physiological decline in fertility! But by the 1840s new evidence appeared: a rise in abortions.[5] The demand for birth control had outstripped the availability of contraceptive techniques. Moreover, the average abortion client was no longer a single girl in trouble but a married woman who already had children.

Also from the 1840s there appeared the first American birth control movement within the women's rights movement, in the form of a demand for "voluntary motherhood." The meaning of that phrase should be evident. It had no antimotherhood implications; in fact, Voluntary Motherhood advocates argued that willing mothers would be better mothers.

In their line of argument we can see that motherhood had broader connotations for them than for us today. A century ago, feminists and nonfeminists alike assumed (at least I have found no exception) that women were naturally those who should not only give birth to children but should also do primary child raising, as well as perform the nurturing functions for the whole society: maintaining friendship networks, cultural institutions, and rituals; creating beautiful environments; and nurturing husbands, relatives, and other women. Their feminism manipulated the cult of domesticity, translating it into what was later called "social housekeeping," spreading the virtues of an idealized home throughout the society.[6] Thus, in the nineteenth century the overall demand for women's rights was frequently couched in terms of a greater respect for motherhood.

Voluntary Motherhood was a campaign exclusively focused on women. It must be distinguished from two other, separate streams in the historical movement for contraception. The first was neo-Malthusianism, or population control, a plan to ameliorate social problems by reducing the size of populations on a large scale. This ideology says nothing about women's rights; a satisfactory solution in an overcrowded country might be to sterilize half the women and let the other half have all the children they wanted. Neo-Malthusianism came late to the United States because in this country underpopulation, not overpopulation, was the dominant fear until World War II.

The second movement, eugenics, was really a subcategory of neo-Malthusianism, an effort to apply population control differentially and thus to reduce the size of certain unwanted human "types." Eugenical thought originally was primarily directed at the elimination of idiocy, criminality, and drunkenness, on the misguided theory that such undesirable qualities were hereditary. After the Civil War, however, with social stratification deepening, eugenics took on a different orientation. The upper-class WASP elite of the industrial North became increasingly aware of its own small-family pattern, in contrast to the continuing large-family preferences of immigrants and the rural poor. From as early as the 1860s the fear of so-called race suicide emerged. In that phrase, race was used ambiguously: to equate the "human race" with WASPs. Out of fears of a loss of political (and social and economic) dominance to an expanding population of "inferiors" grew a plan for reestablishing social stability through differential breeding: the superior should have more children, the inferior fewer. (In the twentieth century Blacks and the welfare poor replaced immigrants and sharecroppers as the primary targets of eugenical policies. But that is getting ahead of our story.)

By the end of the century, then, there were three separate reproductive control movements—Voluntary Motherhood, population control, and eugenics. All three were to some extent responses to the fact that birth control *was* being widely used. And all three to some extent required better reproductive control techniques. Yet on another, crucial dimension there was a sharp difference among them: the eugenists and population controllers supported the legalization of contraception, but the Voluntary Motherhood advocates opposed it. For birth control, they proposed abstinence—either periodic, based on an incorrect rhythm method, or long-term, allowing for intercourse only when a conception was desired. Their position was the more odd since they were the ones most blamed for the rise in birth control use. Antifeminists of the mid-nineteenth century, just as today, charged feminism with destroying motherhood and the family and encouraging sexual licentiousness. In a way, their opponents were (and are) right, and the feminists wrong. Despite their denials, the feminists, by raising women's self-respect and aspirations, did lend implicit support to birth control use.

Furthermore, the backlash was able, in the nineteenth century, to ride its antifeminist rhetoric to several important victories. First, a physicians' campaign to outlaw abortion got most states to legislate against it for the first time; before this, abortion in the early months was legal. Second, in the mid-nineteenth century the Catholic church also banned abortion for the first time, having previously accepted it in the early months. Third, in 1873 the Comstock law, named after a notorious prude who was postmaster general, made it a federal crime to send obscene material through the mails, and listed birth control as an obscene subject. Most opponents of birth control at this time did not distinguish contraception from abortion; they called it all murder and immorality. Nevertheless, the repression did not work. Then, as now, birth control use continued to rise and the birthrate continued to fall.

It bears repeating that this struggle took place *with no new technological inventions*. The only nineteenth-century contribution to birth control technology—the vulcanization of rubber, which permitted the manufacturing of better condoms and diaphragms—had no impact in this country until this century. What, then, caused the decline in the birthrate, the rise of pro–birth control movements, and the backlash against birth control?

In the late nineteenth century a debate raged about this question. One side blamed feminism, arguing that women, stirred up by licentious propaganda, were rejecting their duties to society and seeking selfish gratification. The other side blamed the industrial economy, showing that children were no longer respectful nor economically profitable toward their parents. In fact, these two explanations were both correct and were fundamentally the same. Feminism was a response to the industrial economy that had robbed women of their traditional productive labor and turned them—at least those of the prosperous classes, who were most likely to become feminists—into unpaid, disrespected housekeepers. Feminism was also, ideologically, a response to the liberal individualism that was once the revolutionary credo of the bourgeoisie and later became the justifying ideology of capitalism. The convergence between feminism and a new economic setup can be seen further in the fact that decisions about birth control and family size have in the main not been controversial within families; new class aspirations shared by husbands and wives included new views of the place of women as well as of family size. The birthrate drop started first among the professional and managerial strata, who cared most about educating their children well (which is expensive), and who contributed most feminists to the movement. From here the small-family tendency moved both upward to the capitalist class and downward to the working class, just as women's rights ideas moved both up and down from their middle-class origins. The biggest differential in family size was not primarily class, defined in a static way, but urbanization. By and large, migrants, both foreigners and southern Blacks, coming from peasant societies, slowly relinquished their large-family preferences, settled for fewer children, and adopted positive attitudes toward birth control.

Why, then, did nineteenth-century feminists cling so hard to such a backward position as their condemnation of contraception? (And they were tenacious. As late as the 1920s, feminists of the earlier generations were lined up against Margaret Sanger and other birth control pioneers.) There are two reasons I want to advance. The first is that they wanted Voluntary Motherhood not as a single-issue reform but as part of a broad movement for the empowerment of women, and some possible reforms within the spectrum of women's needs contradicted each other, creating a double bind for the feminists. A second reason lies in a great intellectual and cultural ambivalence within feminism: it represented both the highest development of liberal individualism and also a critique of liberal individualism. Let me discuss these reasons briefly.

The Voluntary Motherhood advocates, as I have said, were part of a general women's rights movement; they were also working for suffrage, property rights, employment opportunities, and some of the more daring for divorce rights. Their concern for all the needs of women, even to some extent their attempt to grasp the larger problems of working-class women, led them to recognize a number of contradictions. First, they realized that while women needed freedom from excessive childbearing, they also needed the respect and self-respect motherhood brought. By and large, motherhood then was the only challenging, dignified, and rewarding work that women could get (it still is, for the majority of women). Second, they understood that while women needed freedom from pregnancy, they also needed freedom from male sexual tyranny, especially in a society that had almost completely suppressed accurate information about female sexuality and replaced it with information and attitudes so false as to virtually guarantee that women would not enjoy sex. Abstinence as a form of birth control may well have been the solution that made most sense in the particular historical circumstance. Abstinence helped women strengthen their ability to say no to their husbands' sexual demands, for example, while contraception and abortion would have weakened it. Nineteenth-century feminists have often been considered prudish, and indeed they were reluctant, for example, to name the sexual parts of the body; but they were not reluctant to speak of marital rape, which traditionalists found even more shocking. A few feminists even began discussing the possibility of forms of sexual contact other than intercourse as a means of nonprocreative sex, thus opening a challenge to phallic sexual norms that was continued a century later. In other words, some women had figured out that it was not sex they disliked so much as the particular sexual activity they had experienced.

The Voluntary Motherhood advocates faced a second set of contradictions in their ambivalent attitude toward individualism. The essence of their feminism was their anger at the suppression of the capabilities and aspirations of individual women. They envisaged a public sphere of adults equal in rights, though unequal in native abilities, each individual guaranteed maximum opportunity for self-development. At the same time they were firmly committed to the family. They did not challenge gender, or even "sex roles." They did not challenge heterosexual marriage based on a firm sexual division of labor (man the chief breadwinner, woman the mother in that expanded sense described above), even though this family form condemned women to remaining primarily out of the public sphere. Many of them could see the problems with this arrangement, but all of them felt sure that the family was an absolutely essential institution for the maintenance of civilization. At moments, some of their rhetoric suggests that they glimpsed the possibility of the further individualization and atomization of people the wage labor system could bring, and they feared it. Fear of that individualism reverberates in many socialists and among feminists today; a world in which self-improvement, competition, and isolation dominate human energies is not appealing. Indeed, what civilization meant to nineteenth-century feminists was the tempering of the individual struggle for survival by greater social values and aspirations that, they believed, women supported through their nurturing role in the division of labor. And yet their very movement was increasing the number of women who joined that atomized world of the labor market. Their historic compromise must be seen sympathetically in that context: they argued that more respect for women should be used to reinforce motherhood, to give it more freedom, respect, and self-respect. Hence their reluctance to accept a form of birth control that could exempt women from motherhood.

Feminists changed their minds about contraception in the early twentieth century. Again, no new techniques affected them; rather, after they changed their minds, they took the initiative in finding the technology they needed. Two leaders, Emma Goldman and Margaret Sanger, separately traveled to Europe, where rubber diaphragms were being prescribed in labor and trade union–funded health clinics. The women personally imported these devices into the United States. In America, as in Europe, these new pro–birth control feminists were mainly in and around the Socialist party. It is logical, I think, that socialist feminists were the first to take a pro-contraception position. Concerned as they were with the working class, they realized the consequences and hardships of a massive employment of women; attempting as they were to build a working-class movement, they saw the weakness of a movement in which women were politically immobilized by sexism and exclusive responsibilities for large families;

having rejected religion and viewing traditional morality as a form of social control beneficial to the capitalist class, they saw liberating possibilities in a freer sexual life.

All along, feminists had been responding to family change and trying to direct and even initiate it. The trajectory of change that formed the primary experience of most nineteenth-century feminists was a decline of patriarchy[7] that produced increased independence for grown children without enhancing very much the autonomy of women (with one exception, educated single women). In that context it was reasonable for women to cling to their work as mothers as the basis for their social status and desired political power. By the early twentieth century, the further development of industrial capitalism had begun to allow a vision of greater independence for women. Not only prosperous women but also working-class women in the World War I era were experiencing the effects of public education, mass employment of women, the transformation of virtually the entire male population into a wage labor force, and extensive commodity production replacing most household production. These changes created both negative and positive consequences for women. Negatively, the separation of productive from reproductive labor, in the context of a capitalist culture, demeaned the social status of motherhood. Positively, the devaluing of domestic work allowed a vision of a public role for women, in work and politics, that for the first time in the history of feminism made women want equality. (Early feminists did not dream of full equality between the sexes.) And equality for women absolutely required reproductive self-control.

When socialist feminists first adopted pro—birth control positions in the early twentieth century, nonfeminist socialists had divided reactions. The majority of the U.S. Socialist party, for example, believed that, at best, birth control was a dangerous distraction from the class struggle. Some responded even more negatively, out of a traditional anti-neo-Malthusian appraisal that the major purpose of reproductive control was to reduce the numbers and hence the strength of the working class. Some Socialists, however, supported the birth control movement, if weakly, because they believed it could reduce women's domestic burdens and free them for greater political activity in support of their class interests.

By contrast, Black radicals in the United States in the 1910s tended to support birth control far more frequently. They saw it as a tool for the self-determination of Black Americans. In the 1920s and afterward, however, birth control was increasingly absorbed into programs aimed not at self-determination but at social control by the elite. Eugenics became a dominant motif in the effort to legalize contraception and sterilization, and even birth controllers from the socialist-feminist tradition, such as Margaret Sanger, made accommodations with the eugenists. These policies cost the birth controllers most of their Black support—and many of their white radical supporters as well.

Sanger and other spokespeople used racist rhetoric, urging reduction of the birthrates of the "undesirables"; private birth control clinics in the 1910s and 1920s experimented with evaluating the eugenic worth of their clients and advising them on the desirability of their reproductive intentions. The first publicly funded birth control clinics appeared in the South in the 1930s, sold to southern state public health services on the grounds that they would lower the Black birthrate. Throughout the country during the Great Depression, birth control was touted as a means of lowering welfare costs. In these developments were premonitions of the involuntary and coercive sterilizations performed today. (A 1979 study shows that 70 percent of hospitals fail to comply with sterilization guidelines set by the Department of Health, Education, and Welfare.)[8]

Thus the cry of genocide that began to be raised against reproductive control campaigns in the 1930s, and continues today, is not wrong. It is only too simple. It arises from at least three sources. First, the tensions between white feminism and Black liberation movements that arose in the struggle over the Fourteenth Amendment underlie this problem and have virtually blotted out the contribution of Black feminists (not only today but historically). So convoluted are these tensions that antiabortionists have manipulated the fear of genocide in a racist way—suggesting, for example, that Black and working-class women do not need or want reproductive self-determination, that they are satisfied with their status, that aspirations for independence and prestige exist only among privileged white women.[9]

Second, beyond this general distrust is the actual racism of the white-dominated women's movement, which was clearly manifested in the birth control movement as much by socialist as by liberal feminists. Its pattern resembled that of the white-dominated labor movement. Elizabeth Cady Stanton's appeal for giving the vote to educated women in preference to ignorant men is of a piece with trade unionists' denunciation of Blacks as scabs even as they excluded them from their unions.

Third, and most pertinent, is the dominance of the relatively conservative population control and eugenics programs over the feminist birth control program. Planned Parenthood's use of small-family ideology and its international emphasis on sterilization rather than safe and controllable contraception have far overshadowed its feminist program for women's self-determination. Most Americans do not distinguish between birth control as a program of individual rights and population control as social policy. Moreover, many scholars continue this ideological confusion and fail to make this essential analytic distinction. The tendency to fetishize reproductive control technology, as if the diaphragm or the pill, rather than the social relations that promote their use, were the news, further legitimates this analytic mush.

The distinctions started to reappear in the 1960s with the emergence of abortion as the key reproductive control issue. In the early twentieth century most feminists did not support abortion for several reasons: reluctance to take on too much of a backlash at once; their own conviction that sex belonged primarily in marriage, where contraceptive use was more likely to be systematic and where an unplanned child was not usually the total disaster it might be for an unmarried woman; and the fact that most poor women still had no access to decent medical care. The contemporary drive for abortion rights was a response to several factors that developed gradually in the 1920–60 period. First, there was a great increase in teenage sexual activity without contraceptive use—in other words, it was not technology that increased sexual activity but the behavior that increased the demand. Second, there was a great increase in the number of families absolutely dependent on two incomes and an increase in women-headed families, thus making it no longer possible for mothers to stay home with an unplanned baby; this spurred the demand for abortion among married women for whom contraception had failed. The third and perhaps more surprising factor behind the movement for abortion rights was the relative underdevelopment of contraception. In this factor we see yet another flaw in the technological-determinist explanation of birth control. Far from being an area of great progress, the field of contraception today lags far behind our need for it. Women must still do almost all the contracepting, and they are forced to choose among unwieldy, dangerous, or irreversible methods.

The changes in the dominant feminist positions about birth control should now be clearer. For feminists, the issue of reproductive control is a part of an overall calculus of how to improve women's situation. The birth control campaign of the late 1960s and 1970s was not a single-issue reform campaign, such as that of the population controllers and eugenists who had dominated in the 1920s through 1950s. Feminists always have to balance the gains and losses from contraception and abortion against the other problems women face, such as unequal employment opportunity, unequal wealth, unequal education, and unequal domestic responsibilities. Thus a position appropriate to one historical era was not appropriate in another when the balance of women's needs and possibilities had changed.

Contemporary feminist positions about birth control are still ambivalent. Within the reproductive rights rubric, groups have primarily emphasized single issues: abortion, sterilization abuse, vaginal self-examination. Few have addressed the issues of sex and motherhood overall, and their contemporary meanings for women of different classes. These two questions, about the proper role of sex and motherhood in women's lives, are publicly asked now mainly by the New Right, because of the "crisis" in the family. This crisis of the family is not new—indeed, it was the foundation of the rise of feminism, the crack in the social structure that made feminism possible. It is hardly a criticism of contemporary feminism that it has not been able to produce a definitive program for liberated sex and parenthood—these failings are part of what propels the women's movement, just as they propel the new right-wing antifeminist movement. Still, it is important to call attention to the centrality of the family crisis to contemporary politics and to the need for further development of feminist theory about sex, reproduction, and the family.

In thinking about the family, contemporary feminism, like feminism a century ago, contains an ambivalence between individualism and its critique. The individualism has reached a much higher development with the challenge to gender definitions. Few modern feminists would argue that women are innately suited to domestic activity and unsuited to public activity. The rejection of gender is an ultimate commitment to the right of all individuals to develop to their highest potential. Unfortunately, the most visible heroines of such struggles immediately suggest some of the problems with this uncritical individualism; for example, a new image of the liberated woman, complete with briefcase, career, sex partners, and silk blouse, but absolutely without nurturing responsibilities. Of course, this liberated woman is primarily a creature of the capitalist economy, not feminism. Moreover, she is a creature of the media, for there are few such women in reality. But parts of the feminist movement identify with this ideal. Those parts of the movement have deemphasized the other side of the feminist tradition: the critique of the man-made society, the refusal to accept merely integration of female individuals into a competition whose rules we did not define and do not endorse. There is, in fact, a tradition of feminist criticism of capitalism itself, representing it as the opposite of the nurturing values of motherhood.[10] Without weakening our support of the rights of individual women to seek achievement, it is important to keep both sides of this ambivalence in view. Feminists have conducted a close scrutiny of the family in the last years and have seen how oppressive it can be for women. But undermining the family has costs, for women as well as men, in the form of isolation and the further deterioration of child raising, general unhappiness, social distrust, and solipsism; and sensitivity to these problems is also part of the feminist heritage.

The feminist critique of individualism should give us some insight into the opposition. What are the abortion opponents afraid of? I do not think it is the loss of fetuses, for most. For example, I doubt there would have been such a big backlash had the legalization of abortion occurred under the auspices of the population controllers rather than in the context of a powerful women's liberation movement. The abortion opponents today, like those of a hundred years ago, are afraid of a loss of mothering, in the symbolic sense.[11] They fear a completely individualized society with all services based on cash nexus relationships, without the influence of nurturing women counteracting the completely egoistic principles of the economy, and without any forms in which children can learn about lasting human commitments to other people. Many feminists have the same fears. The overlap is minimal, of course. Most abortion opponents are right-wingers, involved in a deeply antidemocratic, anti–civil libertarian, violent, and sexist philosophy. Still, their fear of unchecked individualism is not without substance.

The problem is to develop a feminist program and philosophy that defends individual rights and also builds constructive bonds between individuals. This raises anew the question of the family. The truth is that feminism has undermined the family as it once existed faster than it has been able to substitute more egalitarian communities. This is not a criticism of the women's movement. Perhaps families held together by domination, fear, violence, squelched talents, and resignation should not survive. Furthermore, the women's movement has already done a great deal toward building supportive institutions that prefigure a better society: day-care centers, shelters, women's centers, communes, gay bars and bars where women feel comfortable, publications, women's studies programs, and health clinics. The movement has done even more in creating a new consciousness that pervades the entire culture. There has been a veritable explosion of feminist cultural work, a new definition of what is political and of what is a social problem, a new concept—sexism—that is widely understood. Even the mass media reflect a new respect for relations between women; a strong lesbian liberation movement has arisen; and, perhaps one of the best indices of the status of women in the whole society, a more respectful attitude toward single women has developed.

These very successes have created problems. Clearly the successes created a backlash. More complicated, the successes in consciousness changing outstripped successes in community and institution building. The nuclear, male-dominated family remains for the vast majority the only experience of permanent, noninstrumental personal commitments. Within the family, motherhood still is—and may forever be—one of the most challenging and rewarding emotional and work experiences people can have. The feminist reproductive rights movement faces the task of finding a program that equally defends women's individual rights to freedom, including sexual freedom, *and* the dignity of women's need and capacity for nurturance and being nurtured, with or without biological motherhood. This is but the application to one issue—reproduction—of the general task of feminism: to defend all the gains of bourgeois individualism and liberal feminism while transcending the capitalist-competitive aspects of individualism with a vision of loving, egalitarian communities.

Notes

1. I have told this story more fully in my book *Woman's Body, Woman's Right: A Social History of Birth Control in America* (New York: Viking Penguin, 1977). In the interpretation offered here, I am indebted to ideas garnered in my discussions with many feminist scholars, and particularly the work of Ellen Dubois and Allen Hunter.

2. The phrase "sex-gender system" was first used by Gayle Rubin in her essay "The Traffic in Women," in *Toward an Anthropology of Women,* ed. Rayna R. Reiter (New York:

Monthly Review, 1975), and I am indebted to her theoretical conception. What I mean in using the phrase here, and elsewhere in this essay, is that sexual differences, which are biological, are everywhere in human society accompanied by socially constructed concepts of feminine and masculine gender. Gender includes the sexual division of labor, personality attributes, self-conception. Gender is much deeper than the popular sociological concept "sex roles," but is nevertheless culturally, not biologically, determined. An example of the difference is that female pregnancy and childbirth are biologically determined, while feeding and mothering are assigned to women by social regulation. (In this context it is worth noting that sex is a biological dichotomy only loosely and that there are many exceptions—infertile men and women, people whose chromosomal and anatomical construction is neither exclusively male nor female, among others.)

3. My characterization of the technological-determinist view of birth control history is a composite picture and therefore schematic and slightly exaggerated. Some recent examples of such an interpretation can be found in James Reed's *From Private Vice to Public Virtue* (New York: Basic Books, 1978).

4. An example of this use of modernization theory is Edward Shorter's *The Making of the Modern Family* (New York: Basic, Books, 1975).

5. See Gordon, *Woman's Body, Woman's Right*, chap. 3. For corroboration in a more recent historical study, see James Mohr's *Abortion in America* (New York: Oxford University Press, 1978), chaps. 2 and 3.

6. This view of feminism was offered by the nineteenth-century suffragists themselves; it can be found argued well in several general surveys of the women's rights movement, including Aileen Kraditor's *Ideas of the Woman Suffrage Movement* (New York: Columbia University Press, 1965).

7. Today many feminists use the term *patriarchy* as a general synonym for male supremacy; in that sense it would be questionable to assert that patriarchy had declined. I use *patriarchy* in a specific historical sense: referring to a system of family production in which the male head of the family (hence patriarchy, meaning rule of the father) controls the wealth and labor power of all family members. In a patriarchal system, for example, unmarried and childless men lacked the power of fathers since they often lacked labor power; by comparison, it would be hard to argue that today unmarried or childless men were weaker than fathers. The development of industrial production (incidentally, in its "socialist" as well as capitalist varieties) tended to weaken patriarchy by providing opportunities for economic and social independence for children and women. Thus, notice that patriarchy is a system of generational as well as gender relations.

8. R. Bogue and D. W. Sigelman, *Continuing Violations of Federal Sterilization Guidelines by Teaching Hospitals in 1979*, Sterilization Report no. 3 (Washington, D.C.: Public Citizen Health Research Group, 1979), as summarized in *Family Planning Perspectives* 11, no. 6 (November–December 1979): 366–67.

9. For example, Elizabeth Moore, in *In These Times*, 28 February 1979.

10. These ideas are argued more fully and supported in my "Individualism and the Critique of Individualism in the History of Feminist Theory" (paper given at the Simone de Beauvoir Commemorative Conference, 1979).

11. See Linda Gordon and Allen Hunter, "Sex, Family, and the New Right: Anti-feminism as a Political Force," *Radical America*, November 1977–February 1978; reprinted as a pamphlet by the New England Free Press. Throughout this paper I am indebted to Hunter's work on the New Right.

8

The Facts of Fatherhood

THOMAS W. LAQUEUR

This essay puts forward a labor theory of parenthood in which emotional work counts. I want to say at the onset, however, that it is not intended as a nuanced, balanced academic account of fatherhood or its vicissitudes. I write it in a grumpy, polemical mood.

In the first place I am annoyed that we lack a history of fatherhood, a silence which I regard as a sign of a more systemic pathology in our understanding of what being a man and being a father entail. There has unfortunately been no movement comparable to modern feminism to spur the study of men. Or conversely, history has been written almost exclusively as the history of men and therefore man-as-father has been subsumed under the history of a pervasive patriarchy—the history of inheritance and legitimate descent, the history of public authority and its transmission over generations. Fatherhood, insofar as it has been thought about at all, has been regarded as a backwater of the dominant history of public power. The sources, of course, support this view. Fathers before the eighteenth century appear in prescriptive texts about the family largely in their public roles, as heads of families or clans, as governors of the "little commonwealth," of the state within the state.

The rule of the patriarchy waned, but historians have not studied the cultural consequences for fathers of its recession. Instead, they have largely adopted the perspective of nineteenth-century ideologues: men belong to the public sphere of the marketplace and women to the private sphere of the family. A vast prescriptive literature explains how to be a good mother: essentially how to exercise proper moral influence and display appropriate affections in the home, duties that in earlier centuries would have fallen to the father.

This essay first appeared in *Conflicts in Feminism*, ed. Marianne Hirsch and Evelyn Fox Keller (New York: Routledge, 1990).

But there is little in the era of "separate spheres" on how to be the new public man in private. A rich and poignant source material on the affective relationship between fathers and children in the nineteenth century—Gladstone's account of watching for days by the bedside of his dying daughter, for example—speaks to the power of emotional bonds, but historians have largely ignored it. They have instead taken some Victorians at their word and written the father out of the family except as a parody of the domestic autocrat or as the representative of all those forces that stood in the way of the equality of the sexes.

Second, I write in the wake of Baby M and am annoyed with the neoessentialism it has spawned. Baby M was the case of the decade in my circles, a "representative anecdote" for ancient but ageless questions in the late twentieth century. Like most people, I saw some right on both sides and had little sympathy for the marketplace in babies that brought them together. On the one hand Mary Beth Whitehead this . . . ; on the other William Stern that . . . The baby broker who arranged the deal was manifestly an unsavory character, the twentieth-century avatar of the sweatshop owners who in ages past profited unconscionably from the flesh of women. It was difficult not to subscribe to the doctrine that the baby's best interests must come first and it was by no means consistently clear where these lay. Each day brought new emotional tugs as the narrative unfolded on the front pages of every paper.

I was surprised that, for so many people, this transaction between a working-class woman and a professional man (a biochemist) became an epic prism through which the evils of capitalism and class society were refracted. It did not seem newsworthy to me that the poor sold their bodies or that the rich exploited their willingness to do so. What else would they sell? Malthus had pointed out almost two centuries ago that those who labored physically gave of their flesh and in the long run earned just enough to maintain and replenish it. So had Marx, who also identified women as the agents of social re-production.

Admittedly, the contract entered into by Whitehead and Stern was stripped of all shreds of decency and aesthetic mystification, flatfootedly revealing the deal for what it was—not a womb rental but a baby sale. This is why the New Jersey Supreme Court ruled it unenforceable. Every account that one reads of the surrogate baby broker's operations, with its well-dressed couples sitting in little cubicles interviewing long lines of well-dressed but hopeful, spiffed-up women seeking work as surrogates, conjures up distasteful reminders of depression labor exchanges, starlet casting couches, or academic hiring fairs. But there surely are no new horrors in this case. Basically the Baby M narratives are modern versions of the industrial novel and allied genres in which factory labor is portrayed as wage slavery; in which children's tiny thin fingers are metamorphosed into the pin wire they hour after hour produce; in which paupers, whose labor is worthless on the open market, are depicted pounding bones into meal so that they might remain just this side of starvation.[1] In short, I remain cynical when some commentators discover Mary Beth Whitehead as the anticapitalist Everywoman. If "surrogate" mothers were as well organized as the doctors who perform the much more expensive in vitro fertilization or as unionized baseball players they would earn a decent wage—say $100,000 instead of the ludicrously low $10,000—and opposition to surrogacy as emblematic of the evils of a free market in labor might be considered muted. (Though of course then the story might shift to emphasize the power of money to dissolve the very fabric of social decency, another nineteenth-century trope.)

I am, however, primarily interested in this case as the occasion for a return to naturalism. Feminism has been the most powerful denaturalizing theoretical force in my intellectual firmament and, more generally, a major influence in the academic and cultural affairs that concern me. I regard it as both true and liberating that "the idea that men and women are two mutually exclusive categories must arise out of something other than a nonexistent 'natural' opposition," and that "gender is a socially imposed division of the sexes."[2] A major strand of commentary on Baby M, however, rejects this tradition and instead insists that the category "mother" is natural, a given of the world outside culture. Phyllis Chesler, for example, in the major article of a special "Mothers" issue of *Ms.* (May 1988) argues that motherhood is a "fact," an ontologically different category than "fatherhood," which is an "idea." Thus, "in order for the *idea* [my emphasis] of fatherhood to triumph over the *fact* of motherhood," she says, "we had to see Bill as the 'birth father' and Mary Beth as the surrogate uterus." (Actually Chesler misstates the claims. Mary Beth has been, rightly or wrongly, called the "surrogate mother," not the "surrogate uterus." But since the point of the article seems to be that mother and uterus are more or less the same thing, this may be an intentional prevarication.)

I resist this view for obvious emotional reasons: it assumes that being the "factual" parent entails a stronger connection to the child that being the "ideational" parent. (This assumption is widespread. During my daughter Hannah's five-week stay in the preemie nursery her caretakers, in the "social comments" column of her chart, routinely recorded my wife's visits to her incubator as "mother in to bond," whereas my appearances were usually noted with the affectively neutral "father visited.") While I do not want to argue against the primacy of material connection directly, I do want to point out that it is not irrational to hold the opposite view and that, "in fact," the incorporeal quality of fatherhood has been the foundation of patriarchy's ideological edifice since the Greeks. In other words, simply stating that mothers have a greater material connection with the child is not to make an argument but to state a premise that historically has worked against Chesler's would-be conclusion. The Western philosophical tradition has generally valued idea over matter; manual labor for millennia was the great horizontal social divide. In other words, precisely because the mother's claim was "only" corporeal, because it was a matter of "fact," it was valued less.

I will recount some of the history of this discourse, but I also want to argue against its basic operating assumption: the unproblematic nature of fact especially in relation to such deeply cultural designations as mother or father and to the rights, emotions, or duties that are associated with them. The "facts" of motherhood—and of fatherhood for that matter—are not "given" but come into being as science progresses and as the adversaries in political struggles select what they need from the vast, ever-growing storehouses of knowledge. The idea that a child is of one's flesh and blood is very old, while its biological correlatives and their cultural importance depend on the available supplies of fact and on their interpretation.

But the reason that the facts of motherhood and fatherhood are not "given" has less to do with what is known or not known than with the fundamental gap, recognized by David Hume, between facts and their meaning. *Is* does not imply *ought,* and more generally no fact or set of facts taken together entails or excludes a moral right or commitment. Laws, customs, and precepts, sentiments, emotion, and the power of the imagination make biological facts assume cultural significance. An Algonquin chief, confronted by a Jesuit in the seventeenth century with the standard European argument against women's promiscuity (how else would you know that a child is yours?), replied that he found it puzzling that whites could apparently only love "their" children, that is, that only individual ownership entailed caring and affection.

Before proceeding I want to again warn my readers that some of my evidence and most of my passion arise from personal circumstance. I write as the father of a daughter to whom I am bound by the "facts" of a visceral love, not the molecular biology of reproduction. The fact of the matter is that from the instant the five-minute-old Hannah—a premature baby of 1,430 grams who was born by Caesarean section—grasped my finger (I know this was due to reflex and not affection) I felt immensely powerful, and before the event, inconceivably strong bonds with her. Perhaps if practioners of the various subspecialties of endocrinology had been present they might have measured surges of neurotransmitters and other hormones as strong as those that accompany parturition. But then what difference would that make—with what is one to feel if not with the body?

I also write as the would-be father, some sixteen months before Hannah came along, of a boy weighing something less than 800 grams who was aborted late one night—an induced stillbirth really—after twenty-four weeks of gestation because of a burst amniotic sac and the ensuing infection. I can recapture my sadness at his demise vividly and still regard the whole episode as one of the gloomiest of my life. Gail, my wife, was ambivalent about having the child—she was, she says, unprepared at age 40 for becoming pregnant the very first month at risk—and regards the abortion as a painful but not especially fraught episode that cleared the emotional ground to allow her to welcome Hannah's birth unequivocally.

Finally, I write as the male member of a family in which gender roles are topsy-turvy. Hannah early on announced that she would prefer being a daddy to being a mommy because mommies had to go to work—hers is a lawyer—while daddies only had to go to their study. (As she has grown older and observed my not silent suffering as I finished a book begun the year she was born, her views have been somewhat revised.) I am far guiltier of the stereotypical vices of motherhood—neurotic worry about Hannah's physical and mental well-being, unfounded premonitions of danger, excessive emotional demands, and general nudginess—than is Gail. In short, my experiences—ignoring for the moment a vast ethnographic and somewhat smaller historical literature—make me suspect of the naturalness of "mother" or "father" in any culturally meaningful sense.

The association of fatherhood with ideas and motherhood with facts is ancient; only its moral valences have been recently reversed by some feminists. The Marquis de Sade suggests that the "idea" of fatherhood—the notion that a child is "born of the father's blood" and only incidentally of a mother's body—means that it "owes filial tenderness to him alone, an assertion not without its appealing qualities."[3] Sade is the most rabid of antimaternalists, and his argument is made to induce a girl to sexually defile and humiliate her mother; but his relative valuation of fact and idea is standard. The "idea" of fatherhood gave, and displayed, the power of patriarchy for much of Western history since the Greeks.

Bolingbrooke in *Richard II* (1.3.69) addresses his father as

"Oh thou, the earthly author of my blood,
Whose youthful spirit, in me regenerate."

He is author and authority because, like the poet who has in his mind the design for the verses that subsequently appear, he has the conceit for the child in him. The physical act of writing, or of producing the child, matters little. Conceiving a child in this model is a man's sparking of an idea in the uterus, which contains, like a block of marble, a form waiting to be liberated. It is like writing on a piece of paper awaiting inscription. The "generation of things in Nature and the generation of things in Art take place in the same way," argued the great seventeenth-century physician William Harvey, who discovered the circulation of the blood. "Now the brain is the instrument of conception of the one . . . and of the other the uterus or egg."[4] And being the instrument is less elevated than being the author: "He," speaking of God, "was the author, thou the instrument," says King Henry in offering pardon to Warwick (*3 Henry VI*, 4.6.18).

But the idea of "father" as bound to his child in the way a poet is to verse, that is, its genitor, is much older than Shakespeare. It is, argues Freud, one of the cornerstones of culture; believing in fathers, like believing in the Hebrew God, reflects the power of abstract thought and hence of civilization itself.

The "Moses religion's" insistence that God cannot be seen—the graven image proscription—"means that a sensory perception was given second place to what may be called an abstract idea." This God represents "a triumph of intellectuality over sensuality [*Triumph der Geistigkeit über de Sinnlichkeit*], or strictly speaking, an instinctual renunciation." Freud briefs precisely the same case for fathers as for God in his analysis of Aeschylus' *Eumenides,* which follows immediately his discussion of the Second Commandment. Orestes denies that he has killed his mother by denying that being born of her entails special bonds or obligation. Apollo makes the defense's case: appearances notwithstanding, no man has a mother. "The mother is no parent of that which is called her child, but only nurse of the new-planted seed that grows." She is but "a stranger." The only true parent is "he who mounts."[5]

Here is the founding myth of the Father. "Paternity" [*Vaterschaft*], Freud concludes, "is a supposition," and like belief in the Jewish God it is "based on an inference, a premise," while "maternity" [*Mutterschaft*], like the old gods, is based on evidence of the senses alone. The invention of paternity, like that of a transcendent God, was thus also "a momentous step"; it likewise—Freud repeats the phrase but with a more decisive military emphasis—was "a conquest [*einen Sieg*] of intellectuality over sensuality." It too represented a victory of the more elevated, the more refined, the more spiritual over the less refined, the sensory, the material. It too is a world-historical "*Kulturfortschritt,*" a great cultural stride forward.

Similarly, the great medieval encyclopedist Isidore of Seville could, without embarrassment, make three different claims about the nature of seed—that only men had *sperma,* that only women had *sperma,* and that both had *sperma*—which would be mutually contradictory if they were about the body but perfectly compatible if they were instead corporeal illustrations of cultural truths purer and more fundamental than biological "fact." Isidore's entire work is predicated on the belief that the origin of words informs one about the pristine, uncorrupted, essential nature of their referents, of a reality beyond the corrupt senses, beyond facts.

In the first case Isidore is explaining consanguinity and, as one would expect in a society in which inheritance and legitimacy pass through the father, he is at pains to emphasize the exclusive origins of the seed in the father's blood, in the purest, frothiest, white part of that blood shaken from the body as the foam is beaten from the sea as it crashes on the rocks.[6] For a child to have a father *means* that it is "from one blood," the father's; and conversely to be a father *is* to produce the substance, semen, through which blood is passed on to one's successors. Generation seems to happen without woman at all and there is no hint that blood—"that by which man is animated, and is sustained, and lives," as Isidore tells us elsewhere—could in any fashion be transmitted other than through the male.[7] Now case two, illegitimate descent. This presents a quite different biology: the child under these circumstances is from the *body* of the mother alone; it is "spurious," he explains, because "the ancients called the female genitalia the *spurium*."[8] So, while the legitimate child is from the froth of the father, the illegitimate child seems to come solely from factual flesh, from the seed of the mother's genitals, as if the father did not exist. And finally, when Isidore is explaining why children resemble their progenitors and is not interested in motherhood or fatherhood he remarks pragmatically that "newborns resemble fathers, if the semen of the father is potent, and resemble mothers if the mothers' semen is potent." Both parents, in this account, have seeds, which engage in repeated combat for domination every time, and in each generation, a child is conceived.[9]

These three distinct and mutually exclusive arguments are a dramatic illustration that much of the debate about the nature of the seed and of the bodies that produce it was in fact not about bodies at all but rather about power, legitimacy, and the politics of fatherhood. They are in principle not resolvable by recourse to the senses. One might of course argue that "just so" stories like Isidore's or Aeschylus's are simply no longer tenable given what has been known since the nineteenth century about conception. Modern biology makes perfectly clear what "mother" and "father" are. But science is relevant only if these stories are understood as reductionistic, as claiming to be true because of biology, which is, rightly, not the sort of claim Isidore and Aeschylus are making. The facts they adduce to illustrate essentially cultural claims may no longer be acceptable, and we may persist in reading their cultural claims as based in a false biology. But the "fact" of women bearing children has never been in dispute and has nonetheless counted for relatively little historically in establishing their claims to recognition or authority over children or property.

Facts, as I suggested earlier, are but shifting sands for the construction of motherhood or fatherhood. They come and go and are ludicrously open to interpretation. Regnier de Graaf's discovery of the ovum in 1672 seemed to relegate the male/father to an unaccustomed and distinctly secondary role in reproduction. (Actually de Graaf discovered the follicle that bears his name but which he and others mistakenly took to be the egg. Karl Ernst von Baer in 1827 was the first to observe a mammalian egg, and an unfertilized human egg was not seen until 1930.)[10] The female after de Graaf could be imagined to provide the matter for the fetus in a preformed if not immediately recognized form, while the male "only serv'd to Actuate it." This, one contemporary observed, "derogates much from the dignity of the Male-Sex," which he thought was restored when "Mons. Leeuwenhoek by the Help of his Exquisite Microscope . . . detected Innumerable small *Animals* in the Masculine sperm, and by his Noble Discovery, at once removed that Difficulty."[11]

I hope by this egregious example to suggest that the form of the argument, and not just its factual premises, are flawed; both conclusions are silly. And the discovery, still accepted, that neither egg nor sperm contains a preformed human but that the fetus develops epigenetically according to plans acquired from both parents does not settle the question of the comparative claims of mother or father, just as the mistaken notions of the past did not entail judgments of their comparative dignities.

Interpretations, not facts, are at issue. The archbishop of Hartford announced in the *New York Times* on 26 August 1988 that he had quit the Democratic party because it supported abortion: "it is officially in favor of executing unborn babies whose only crime is that they temporarily occupy their mother's womb." No one would dispute that the "thing" in the mother's womb is, under some construction, an unborn baby. "Baby" is a common term for fetus as well as for a very young child, and the phrase "the baby is kicking again" to refer to an intrauterine action is generally acceptable; baby-as-fetus is indisputably only a temporary occupant. The archbishop's interpretation is objectionable because he elides the difference between "baby-in-the womb" and "baby-in-the world," between the womb and any other space an infant might occupy, and therefore between abortion and execution. At issue here is meaning, not nature.

David Hume makes manifest the chasm between the two. A beautiful fish, a wild animal, a spectacular landscape, or indeed "anything that neither belongs, nor is related to us," he says, inspires in us no pride or vanity or sense of obligation. We might with perfect reason fear a minor injury to ourselves and care almost nothing about the deaths of millions of distant strangers. The fault is not with the objects themselves but with their relationship to us. They are too detached and distant to arouse passion. Only, Hume argues, when these "external objects acquire any particular relation to ourselves, and are associated or connected with us," do they engage the emotions.[12] Owning the "external object" seems for Hume to be the most obvious way for this to happen, although ownership itself is, of course, an immensely elastic notion. A biological parent, uncle, clan, "family" can "own" a child in such a fashion as to love and cherish it. But more generally Hume is suggesting that moral concern and action are engendered not by the logic of the relationship between human beings but by the degree to which the emotional and imaginative connections that entail love or obligation have been forged.

The "fact" of motherhood is precisely the psychic labor that goes into making these connections, into appropriating the fetus and then child into a mother's moral and emotional economy. The "fact" of fatherhood is of a like order. If a labor theory of value gives parents rights to a child, that labor is of the heart, not the hand. (The heart, of course, does its work through the hand; we feel through the body. But I will let the point stand in its polemical nakedness.)

While I was working as a volunteer in an old people's home I was attracted to, and ultimately became rather good friends with, a gay woman who was its director of activities. At lunch one day—she had alerted me that she wanted to discuss "something" and not just, as we usually did, schmooz—she asked whether I would consider donating sperm should she and her longtime lover decide, as they were on the verge of doing, to have a child. I was for her a generally appropriate donor—Jewish, fit, with no history of genetic disorders in my family. She was asking me also, she said, because she liked me. It was the first, and remains the only, time I had been asked by anyone, much less someone I liked, so I was flattered and pleased.

I was also hesitant. My wife the lawyer raised serious legal difficulties with donating "owned" sperm, that is, sperm that is not given or sold for anonymous distribution. I would remain legally liable for child support for at least twenty-one years, not to speak of being generally entangled with the lives of a couple I liked but did not know well. (Anonymous sperm is alienated from its producer and loses its connection with him as if it were the jetsam and flotsam of the sea or an artisan's product in the marketplace. Semen, in other words, counts as one of these products of the body that can be alienated, like plasma and blood cells, and not like kidneys or eyes, whose marketing is forbidden.)

Legal issues however, did not weigh heavily with me. The attractive part of the proposition—that I was being asked because of who I was and therefore that I was to be a father and not just a donor—also weighed mightily against it. A thought experiment with unpleasant results presented itself. I immediately imagined this would-be child as a version of Hannah, imagined that I could see her only occasionally and for short periods of time, imagined that her parents would take her back to their native Israel and that I would never see her again. Potential conflicts with my friend about this baby were almost palpable on the beautiful sunny afternoon of our lunch. In short, I was much too cathexed with this imaginary child to ever give up the sperm to produce her.

I recognize now, and did at the time, that my response was excessive. My reveries of fatherhood sprang from a fetishistic attachment to one among millions of rapidly replenished microscopic organisms—men make on the order of 400 billion sperm in a lifetime—swimming in an abundant, nondescript saline fluid. All that I was really being asked to do was to "produce" some semen—a not unpleasant process—and to give it to my friend so that *a* very, very tiny sperm—actually only its 4 to 5 micrometers long and 2.5 to 3.5 micrometers wide (c. 1/10,000 to 1/20,000 of an inch) head—might contribute the strands of DNA wafting about in it to her egg. Since we humans apparently share 95 percent of our genetic material with chimpanzees, the sperm in question must share a still higher percentage of base pairs with those of my fellow humans. In short, my unique contribution to the proposed engagement, that which I did not share with billions of other men and monkeys, was infinitesimally small. I was making a mountain out of much, much, much less than a molehill and not very much more than a molecule.

But this is as it should be. For much of history the problem has been to make men take responsibility for their children. Prince and pauper as circumstances required could easily deny the paternity that nature did so little to make evident. The double standard of sexual morality served to insure that however widely they sowed their wild oats the fruits of their wives' wombs would be unambiguously theirs. In fact, until very recently paternity was impossible to prove and much effort went into developing histo-immunological assays that could establish the biological link between a specific man and child. The state, of course, has an interest in making some male, generally the "biological father," responsible for supporting "his" children. In short, a great deal of cultural work has gone into giving meaning to a small bit of matter. Ironically, now that tests make it possible to identify the father with about 100 percent accuracy, women—those who want children *without* a father—have considerable difficulty obtaining sperm free of filiation. History, social policy, imagination, and culture continue to encumber this cell with its haploid of chromosomes.

In 1978 Mary K., a gay woman living in Sonoma County, California, decided that she wanted to have a child, which she would "co-parent" with a close gay woman friend living nearby.[13] Mary wanted to find a sperm donor herself rather than use anonymous sperm for several reasons, which she later more or less clearly articulated. She did not want to make the repeated trips to Berkeley, the location of the nearest sperm bank; she did not want to use a physician in her community who might be able to acquire sperm anonymously because she felt that as a nurse she could not be assured of confidentiality; and—this would come to haunt her—she wanted some vestige of an individual human being to be associated with the sperm and with the hoped-for baby. She wanted a "father" of some ill-defined sort, and after a month or so of looking around and after interviewing three potential donors, she was introduced one January evening to a young gay man, Jhordan C., who seemed to fit her needs. He would become the "father" of her child, even though he did not have the red hair that she had originally sought in a donor.

Neither Jhordan or Mary thought very rigorously about what they expected from their relationship or just what his paternal rights and obligations would be. Neither sought legal counsel; they signed no contract or other written understanding and resolved only the most basic practical details of the matter: Jhordan, upon being notified that Mary was ovulating, would journey to her house, and "produce" sperm, which she would introduce into herself. It took six months before Mary conceived and each of his visits was apparently attended by commonplace social intercourse—some chitchat, tea, and other pleasantries.

After Mary conceived, she and Jhordan saw each other occasionally. She accepted his invitation to a small New Year's party at the home of one of his close friends. She testifies that he "reiterated" to her that "he wanted to be known as the father—and I told him I would let the child know who the biological father was—and that he wanted to travel with the child when the child was older." In all other respects she believed that they had an implicit understanding that she would be the child's guardian and primary parent; that Victoria T., Mary's friend, would be coparent; and that Jhordan would play effectively no role in the life of *her* child.

On the basis of Jhordan's own testimony, he did not know precisely what he meant by wanting "to be known as the father." The court-appointed psychologist described him as a young man of unsettled plans and interests. But Jhordan knew that he wanted somehow to be acknowledged. He was upset when Mary informed him, some months before the birth, that his name would not be on the birth certificate, and he became increasingly uneasy as he came to realize that he was being increasingly written out of the family drama that he had helped launch.

Mary admits that she too had been vague about what Jhordan's being her child's father meant to her and that he did have some grounds for his expectation that he would play some sort of paternal role. Language failed her when she tried to describe it:

I had thought about and I was considering whether or not I would tell Sean [not his real name] who the father was, but I didn't know if I would tell him as a father. Like he would know that Jhordan helped donate the sperm, but I did not know if he would ever know Jhordan—How do I say this? I didn't plan on Sean relating as a father. No.

The confusion of names and collapse of grammar here suggests precisely the underlying ambiguities of this case.

When Sean was born Mary felt increasingly threatened by Jhordan's insistence on seeing him, on displaying him to his family, on taking pictures to show friends and relatives, and in general on acting like a parent, a role that Mary had thought was reserved for herself and Victoria. Jhordan, on the other hand, told the psychologist who interviewed him to determine his fitness as a parent that when "he looked into Sean's eyes, he 'saw his whole family there.' " Whatever uncertainties he might have felt before vanished in the face of his imagined flesh and blood.

Mary finally refused to allow Jhordan to see the baby at all, and he eventually gave up trying. There matters might have rested had not, a year later, Mary applied for welfare. The state sued Jhordan for child support (it was after all his sperm) and he, of course, eagerly agreed to pay. Two years and two lawyers later he won visiting rights with Sean at the home of Mary's friend and coparent, Victoria. These privileges were subsequently expanded. From here on the story is like that of countless divorced couples: quarrels about visitation hours and pickup times, about where Sean would spend holidays and birthdays, about whether Jhordan allowed him to eat too much sugar, and about other of the many controversial niceties of child raising that divide parents in even the tightest of families. A court promulgated guidelines and issued orders; an uneasy peace settled over all the parties.

The trial judge in this case was a rather old-fashioned sort who did not seem terribly interested in the subtleties of law regarding the rights of sperm donors but believed that "blood is thicker than water" and that Sean both needed, and had "a right to," a father. Jhordan was the father and therefore ought, in the judge's view, to be given commensurate visitation rights.

Mary appealed.[14] The central question before the high court was how to interpret sections 7005(a) and (b) of the California Civil Code. These provide that if, under the supervision of a doctor, a married woman is inseminated by semen from a man who is not her husband, that man under certain circumstances is treated as if he were *not* the natural father while the husband is treated as if he were. Mary's lawyers argued that while their client's case did not quite fit under this statute, it was close enough, and that the only possible distinction was one of sexual orientation, which ought not to matter. Other California statutes provide that the law must not discriminate against unconventional parenting arrangements in adoption and other reproductive rights issues. If Mary had been married to someone and had acquired Jhordan's sperm in precisely the same circumstances—admittedly not meeting all the conditions of the statute—it would be ludicrous to suppose that the state would give him rights that infringed upon those of a husband. (A German court has held that a man has no claims on a child of a married woman even if he is acknowledged to be the "biological father." Today, as has been generally true for centuries, children born in wedlock are presumed to belong to the husband of the woman who bore them.)

Moreover, Mary's lawyers argued, section 7005(a)'s reference to semen given "to a licensed physician" was not intended to limit the law's application only to such cases but reflected simply a legislative directive to ensure proper health standards by recourse to a physician. Mary, because of her training as a nurse, was able to comply with this standard on her own. Her lawyers also cited another court case, which held—admittedly in different circumstances—that

> A child conceived through heterologous artificial insemination [i.e., with semen from a man other than the woman's husband] does not have a "natural father." . . . The anonymous donor of sperm can not be considered the "natural father," as he is no more responsible for the use made of his sperm than is a donor of blood or a kidney.

Echoes of Isidore of Seville. Jhordan might not have been anonymous but he was certainly a stranger to Mary.

His lawyers naturally argued for a stricter construal of section 7005 (a–b), and the appeals court sided with them. By not employing a physician, the court agreed, Mary had excluded herself from the law's protection. Moreover, the court viewed the case before it as being more like those in which artificial insemination occurred within the context of an established relationship and in which the sperm donor retained paternal rights than it was like cases of anonymous donation. Jhordan's lawyer cited a New Jersey Supreme Court case, for example, in which a man and a woman were dating and intended to marry. She wanted to bear his child but did not want to have premarital intercourse, so they resorted to artificial insemination. Three months into the pregnancy they broke up and she declared that she wanted nothing more to do with him and that she certainly would not allow him to visit their child. He sued for paternity and won.

Mary and Jhordan were obviously not as intimately involved as this couple, but, the court felt, neither were they the anonymous strangers envisaged by statute. Enough humanity remained in Jhordan's transaction with Mary to allow him to believe that his sperm, however introduced into Mary's body, retained some of him.

As this case and others like it suggest, the legal status of a sperm donor remains deeply problematic, and, advises a National Lawyers Guild Handbook, those "consulted by a lesbian considering artificial insemination must be extremely careful to explain the ramifications of the various choices available to their clients."[5] Usually a medically supervised sperm bank where the identity of the donor is unknown to the recipient is the most certain way to guarantee that the donor will not at some time in the future be construed as the father. Other possibilities include having a friend secure semen but keeping the source secret; using semen from multiple donors (not recommended because of possible immune reactions); using a known donor but having a physician as intermediary. Some lawyers recommend having the recipient pay the donor for his sperm and describing the transaction in an ordinary commercial contract of the sort with which the courts are familiar. And even if agreements between sperm donors and recipients are not predictably enforceable, lawyers suggest that the parties set down their understanding of their relationship as clearly as possible.

Any or all of these strategies might have stripped Jhordan's sperm of paternity, not just in the eyes of the law but more importantly in his heart, and might thus have saved Mary and her coparent their struggles with the parental claims of a near stranger. Mary was wrong to eschew a doctor's mediation or at least underestimated the hold that a very small bit of matter can, in the right circumstances, have on a man's imagination.

In designating a physician as middleman the legislature did not blindly medicalize an essentially social transaction but sought rather to appropriate one of modern medicine's least attractive features—its lack of humanity—for a socially useful end. Everyone knows, even politicians, that artificial insemination does not require a physician. Depaternalizing sperm might. A strange doctor in a lab coat working amidst white Formica furniture, high-tech instruments, officious nurses, and harried receptionists in a boxy office in a nondescript glass and steel building set in a parking lot may offer cold comfort to the sick and needy; he or she might, however, be perfect at taking the sparkle off sperm.

Had Jhordan donated sperm not at Mary's house, where he was offered tea and conversation, but at a clinic; had he never spoken to her after the inseminations began but only to the doctor's nurse, who would have whisked away the vial of fresh semen; had he never seen Mary pregnant or celebrated New Year's Eve with her, the fetish of the sperm might have been broken. The doctor as broker would have performed his or her priestly function, deblessed the sperm, and gotten rid of its "paternity." (This I imagine as the inversion of normal priestly work, providing extra emotional glue between the participants in weddings, funerals, and the like.) Similarly, selling sperm at a price fixed by contract—the lawyer or sperm bank owner as deblessing agent—would take off some of its paternal blush. Without such rites, a father's material claim in his child is small, but his imaginative claims can be as endless as a mother's. Great care must be taken to protect and not to squash them.

Because fatherhood is an "idea," it is not limited to men. In a recent case litigated in Alameda County, California (*Lofton v. Flouroy*), a woman was, rightly in my view, declared to be a child's father, if not its male parent. Ms. Lofton and Ms. Flouroy lived together and decided to have a child. Lofton's brother, Larry, donated the required sperm but expressed no interest in having any further role in the matter. Ms. Lofton introduced her brother's semen into Flouroy with a turkey baster, Flouroy became pregnant, and in due course a baby was born. The "birth mother" was listed on its birth certificate as "mother," and L. Lofton—Linda, not Larry, but who was to know?—was listed as "father."

Everything went well and the women treated the child as theirs, until, two years later, they split up. The mother kept the child, and there matters might have rested had not, as in the case of Mary and Jhordan, the state intervened. Flouroy applied for welfare benefits, that is, aid to dependent children, and when asked by the Family Support Bureau to identify the father she produced, in a moment of unabashed concreteness, the turkey baster. The bureau, not amused, did what it was meant to do and went after the "father" on the birth certificate—Linda, it was surprised to learn, not Larry. Like Jhordan she welcomed the opportunity to claim paternity, did not dispute the claim, and eagerly paid the judgment entered against her: child support, current and retroactive. She also demanded paternal visitation rights, which Ms. Flouroy resisted. Lofton then asked the court to compel mediation. It held that she was indeed a "psychological parent" and thus had standing to have her rights mediated. The other L. Lofton, Larry, makes no appearance in this drama.

Linda's claim is manifestly not biological or even material. That she borrowed her brother's sperm or owned the turkey baster is irrelevant. What matters is that, in the emotional economy of her relationship with her lover and their child, she was the father, whatever that means, and enjoyed the rights and bore the obligations of that status. She invested the required emotional and imaginative capital in the impregnation, gestation, and subsequent life to make the child in some measure hers.

I hasten to add that I do not regard biology in all circumstances as counting for nothing. Women have claims with respect to the baby within them simply by virtue of spatial relations and rights to bodily integrity. These are not the right to be or not to be a mother as against the right to be or not to be a father, nor the claims of a person as against those of a nonperson—the terms in which the abortion debate is usually put—but the right shared by all mentally competent adults to control and monitor corporeal boundaries, to maintain a body as theirs. Thus I would regard a court compelling a woman to bear a child against her will as a form of involuntary servitude however much its would-be father might wish for the child. And I would regard an enforced abortion as an even more egregious assault on her body. But this is not to acknowledge the "fact" of motherhood as much as the "fact" of flesh. History bears witness to the evils that ensue when the state abrogates a person's rights in her body.

The flesh does not make a mother's body an ahistorical font of motherhood and maternity. Anne Taylor Fleming, a writer who wants, but cannot herself have, a child and who finds surrogate motherhood morally unacceptable, "can not imagine" that "there are plenty of women now, the huge majority of surrogates who have, to hear them tell it, not suffered such a loss" as Mary Beth Whitehead's.[16] While her empathic instincts extend easily to Whitehead, she cannot, despite testimony to the contrary, conceive of a mother *not* feeling an instant and apparently unmediated bond to her child. Fleming cannot accept that feelings do not follow from flesh, so that "surrogate mothers" who feel otherwise than they supposedly should must suffer, like un-class-conscious workers, from false consciousness.

Ms.'s special "Mothers" issue, quite apart from Chesler's article, is striking by its very cover—an airbrushed, soft-toned picture of a 1950s young Ivory Soap woman, with straight blond hair of the sort that waves in shampoo commercials, holding a blue-eyed baby to her bare bosom and looking dreamily out of the frame of the picture—which would have been denounced by feminists as perpetuating an unacceptable stereotype of women had it appeared in *Family Circle* a decade ago. In 1988 it unashamedly represents the Mother in America's largest-selling feminist magazine.

What exactly are the facts of motherhood, and what of significance ought to follow from them? For advocates of Mrs. Whitehead's, like Phyllis Chesler, her egg and its genetic contents are not especially relevant. She shares with Bill, a.k.a. Dr. Stern, the provision of chromosomes. The critical fact is therefore her nine months of incubation, which would remain a fact even if the fertilized egg she was bringing to term were not hers. Her claim, it appears, rests on labor, on her physical intimacy with the child within her, and would be just as strong if a second woman sought a stake in the child on the basis of her contribution of half its chromosomes.

I am immensely sympathetic to this view, but not because of a fact of nature. Capitalist societies, as I suggested earlier, are not usually friendly to the notion that putting labor into a product entitles one to ownership or even to much credit. It is the rare company that gives its workers shares of stock. We associate a new production of *The Magic Flute* with David Hockney and not with those who sawed, hammered, and painted the sets; everyone knows that Walt Disney produced *Bambi,* but only the cognoscenti could name even one of the artists who actually made the pictures. Having the idea or the plan is what counts, which is why Judge Sokoloff told Dr. Stern that in getting Melissa he was only getting what was already his. (The judge should, of course, have said, "half his.")

I became so exercised by Baby M because Dr. Stern's claims have been reduced in some circles to his ownership of his sperm, which, as I said earlier, amounts to owning very little. This puts him—all fathers—at a distinct material disadvantage to Mrs. Whitehead—all women—who contribute so much more matter. But, this essay has suggested, his claims, like hers, arise from the intense and profound bonding with a child, unborn and born, that its biological kinship might spark in the moral and affective imagination, but that it does not entail.

The problem, of course, is that emotional capital does not accumulate steadily, visibly, and predictably as in a psychic payroll deduction plan. That is why, for example, it is unreasonable to demand of a woman specific performance on a surrogate mothering contract as if the baby were a piece of land or a work of art whose attributes would be well known to their vendor. A "surrogate mother," like a mother who offers to give up her baby for adoption to a stranger, must be allowed a reasonable time to change her mind and, if she does, in the case of a surrogacy arrangement, be prepared to argue for her rights against those of the father.

Each parent would bring to such a battle claims to have made another person emotionally part of themselves. "Facts" like bearing the child would obviously be significant evidence but would not be unimpeachable, would not be nature speaking unproblematically to culture. While we can continue to look forward to continuing conflict over the competing claims of parents, I suggest that we abandon the notion that biology—facts—will somehow provide the resolution. Neither, of course, will ideas alone in a world in which persons exist corporeally. The way out of the fact/idea dichotomy is to recognize its irrelevance in these matters. The "facts" of such socially powerful and significant categories as mother and father come into being only as culture imbues things, actions, and flesh with meaning. This is the process that demands our continued attention.

Notes

1. For an account of these industrial narratives see Catherine Gallagher, *The Industrial Reformation of English Fiction, 1832–1867* (Chicago: University of Chicago Press, 1985).

2. Gayle Rubin, "The Traffic in Women: Notes on the 'Political Economy' of Sex," in *Toward an Anthropology of Women,* ed., Rayna Reiter (New York: Monthly Review Press, 1975), 179–80.

3. Marquis de Sade, *Philosophy in the Bedroom* (New York: Grove Press, 1965), 106.

4. William Harvey, *Disputation Touching the Generation of Animals,* trans. Gweneth Whitteridge (Oxford: Oxford University Press, 1981), 182–83.

5. Sigmund Freud, *Moses and Monotheism* (1939), in *The Standard Edition of the Complete Psychoanalytical Works,* ed. James Strachey (London: Hogarth Press), 23:113–14; I have altered the translation slightly based on the standard German edition. Aeschylus, *The Eumenides,* trans. Richmond Lattimore, in *Greek Tragedies,* ed. David Greene and Lattimore, vol. 3 (Chicago: University of Chicago Press, 1960), 26–28.

6. Isidore, *Etimologias [Etymologiarum]* ed. and trans. with facing Latin text by J. O. Reta and M. A. Marcos (Madrid: Biblioteca de Autores Christianos, 1983), 6.4.

7. Ibid., 5.5.4. On blood, see 4.5.4.

8. Ibid., 9.5.24.

9. Ibid., 11.1.145.

10. See Thomas W. Laqueur, *Making Sex: Body and Gender from the Greeks to Freud* (Cambridge: Harvard University Press, 1990), for more extensive discussion of these points.

11. William Cowper, *The Anatomy of Humane Bodies* (1698), introduction, n.p.

12. David Hume, *A Treatise of Human Nature,* ed. L. A. Selby-Bigge (Oxford: Oxford University Press, 1965), 2.1.9, p. 303.

13. Civil case no. A-027810. I am grateful to Donna Hutchins, Esq., of San Francisco for making available the various depositions, briefs, and other court papers on which I base the following discussion.

14. *Jhordan C. v. Mary K.* (1986) 179 CA3d 386, 224 CR 530.

15. Roberta Achtenberg, ed., *Sexual Orientation and the Law* (New York: Clark, Boardman, 1989), section 1–70.

16. Anne Taylor Fleming, "Our Fascination with Baby M," *New York Times Magazine,* 29 March, 1987, 87. There were at the time of this article about one thousand known "surrogate mothers."

9

Thinking about Fathers

SARA RUDDICK

I am annoyed that we lack a history of fatherhood.

—Thomas W. Laqueur

For the first time in history . . . we are in a position to look around us at the Kingdom of the Fathers and take its measure.

—Adrienne Rich

Recent feminist literature abounds in disputes over the epistemological possibility and political consequences of making claims about "women." By contrast, there is a noticeable skittishness when "men" enter into feminist discussion. Women's studies students rush to rescue the few men in the room from attacks on their "masculinity," feminist teachers anxiously insist that only some men—usually ruling class, rich, white, "Western"—are intended by feminist talk of "men," and feminist writers cling to Great Male Thinkers and Presences (often white, "Western," rulers of their worlds, and rich). The very idea of "men" threatens intersex friendships, heterosexual relationships, political alliances, household arrangements, and race and class loyalties. Moreover, feminist women have to keep their jobs, advance their careers, take their sexual pleasures, engage in politics, and hold their families together in societies that are still male dominated and heterosexist.

Recently, however, the discomforting and oft-evaded "problem of men" has forced itself into feminist debate as a "problem of fathers." Most dramatically, feminists are struggling with a politics of birth. Some developing reproductive practices, notably "surrogate" mothering, increase the possibilities of male abuse. At the same time, a more open and efficient use of artificial insemination, combined with

This essay first appeared in *Conflicts in Feminism*, ed. Marianne Hirsch and Evelyn Fox Keller (New York: Routledge, 1990).

more flexible sexual mores and an insistent gay politics, allow women increasing control over the role of men in procreation and mothering. Women's procreative fears and powers are inseparable from their beliefs about the effect of father-men in children's and women's lives.

In the official story fathers are necessary ingredients both of childhood and of good-enough mothering. Daughters, as much as sons, long for the blessing of a protective, providing, just father. Heterosexual mothers willingly sacrifice ambition and pleasure in the hope of keeping even barely good-enough fathers—and their cash—in the house. This "wifely" choice is confirmed by an array of social critics who warn that "female-headed households" are symptomatic of—if not responsible for—misery and failure. Psychoanalysts weigh in with the claim that sons—and to a lesser extent daughters—must bond with a father against a powerful, engulfing mother; that children without a father are trapped within a preoedipal (precultural, almost prelinguistic) maternal dyad. Not surprisingly, even women who expect to mother alone or with other women often look for a male who is willing to become a "known and knowable" father.

But the official story cannot conceal the fact that, as Gertrude Stein remarked, "fathers are depressing." Barely known, scarcely knowable, the "absence" of fathers permeates feminist stories. Some fathers are literally lost or gone; others can be located but will not, except under rarely effective legal pressure, offer cash or services. Fathers who provide materially for their children as best they can rarely assume a full share of the emotional work and responsibility of child care. In developed countries, where the "double shift" has become notorious, cultural traditions and personal training undergird masculine entitlement. Fathers neither apologize nor worry if their jobs, hobbies, sports, fatigue, or personal ambition keep them from their children. By contrast, whatever their work, pleasures, or ambitions, mothers can (almost always) be counted on to take up the responsibilities of "parenting." In some feminist stories, even fathers who are determined to share parental responsibilities find themselves hindered by an entrenched, only partly conscious, gendered self-identity. According to this psychoanalytic tale, in societies where children are raised primarily by females, "men develop by contrast [with women] a self based more on a denial of relation and connection and on a more fixed and firmly split and repressed inner self-object world: 'the basic masculine sense of self is separate.' "[1] Hence the basically masculine son of a female mother will, as a father, unwittingly absent himself from his children in order to keep and defend the distance his sense of masculine/separateness requires.

If an absent father is depressingly disappointing, a present father can be dangerous to mothers and their children. The early childhood development that compels "masculine" men (and women) to keep a safe distance from others also requires them to control and, when necessary, to subjugate their children's disruptive, intrusive, unpredictable, needy wills. Hence the father with no time for the double shift may well have time enough to serve as a controlling judge of his children's lives. Whatever his personal tendencies, such a father's temptations toward excessive, judgmental control will be exacerbated by his sense that he is entitled to rule over women and children, a right accorded him by the sexual-social contract implicit in political understandings of (at least) Western-style democracies.[2]

A father who is authoritarian, capricious, intrusive, and controlling may nonetheless act kindly toward his children. Unfortunately, as feminist inquiry of the last decade has confirmed, many fathers are not kind. Children are vulnerable and provocative; parents are often exhausted, harassed, isolated, underhoused, and multiply unsupported. It is not surprising that many children suffer violence and neglect from desperate mothers and fathers. What is striking is the extent and variety of psychological, sexual, and physical battery suffered by women and children of all classes and social groups, often (though by no means always) at the hands of fathers, their mothers' male lovers, or male relatives.

If putative fathers are absent or perpetually disappearing and actual present fathers are controlling or abusive, who needs a father? What mother would want to live with one or wish one on her children? Even social theorists who bewail the toll of divorce and the immiseration of female-headed households recognize that while a good father is good for his children, a bad father is worse than none at all.[3] Most mothers do not choose and cannot afford to raise children alone. But in a state that provided for its children's basic needs, women could raise children together as lesbian coparents or as part of larger friendship circles or intergenerational households. Exceptional men who proved particularly responsible and responsive might be invited to contribute to maternal projects—that is, to donate, as other mothers do, their cash, labor, and love. But these donations would not be predictably connected to the donation of sperm nor would they confer upon the donating men any fatherly rights or privileges that mothering women did not enjoy.

Some feminists will descry utopian possibilities in the promise of such relatively father-free households and families. Secure in near-exclusively female enclaves that are governed by ideals of gender justice, women could undertake a politico-spiritual journey in which they (almost all) relinquished heterosexuality though not (necessarily) mothering, overcame their dependence on fathers and fears of fatherlessness, and claimed for themselves personal autonomy and collective political and cultural power. Their households and families could be seen as an aspect of, prelude to, preparation for, the more ambitious project of creating a "future that is female," a Herland in which men as well as women would live safely because women would govern.

Although this utopian vision is feminist, many feminists do not share the despairing (or imperious or oppressive?) judgment of fathers on which it appears to depend. Rather than attempting to free mothers from men, they (we) work to transform the institutions of fatherhood. Their (our) reasons are naive and familiar: many men, single and partnered, gay and heterosexual, prove themselves fully capable of responsible, responsive mothering; in a world short of love why do without them? Feminists cannot afford to distance themselves from the many heterosexually active women for whom heterosexual and birthing fantasies are intertwined and who want to share mothering with a sexual partner. Nor should feminists condescend to mothers, lesbian and heterosexual, who want their sons to want to care for children and to undertake protective and nurturant fatherlike relationships. Moreover, even in adverse social circumstances, mothering is often a deeply rewarding, life-structuring activity that tends to create in mothers distinctive capacities for responsibility, attentive care, and nonviolence. Men are roughly half of the world's people; it would be self-destructive as well as unjust to exclude them (or *any* social group) from a work that so often has such beneficial psychological and social effects. In any case, only a minority of women can afford a fatherless world. Under current U.S. economic conditions, increasing numbers of mothers are dependent on a (usually male) partner's wage as well as their own, and many are desperate for some measure of (usually his) economic support. And whatever their sexual persuasion, many women who have fought against oppression and tyranny find in their father-inclusive families a source of strength and resistance. Finally, there are the facts of bodily life, in particular the existence, the necessity of "the male body" that is represented in the fatherhood debate by the inconveniently necessary, unpredictably potent, increasingly traceable and manipulable male sperm.

For all these familiar reasons, many feminists, and I among them, envision a world where many more men are more capable of participating fully in the responsibilities and pleasures of mothering. But I have only to open a newspaper, read the testimony of women, listen to students, or walk into or (more frequently) remember the father-dominated homes of friends and colleagues to find myself fantasizing about a world without fathers. Because so many daughters, mothers, and wives have lived a sorry history of fatherhood, a feminist who works for gender-free, gender-full, mothering needs to imagine and justify her confidence in new ways of fathering. For this task, the words, as well as the work, of good and thoughtful fathers are indispensable.

Thomas Laqueur is a good father. Like many not-so-good fathers, he is bound powerfully by the "facts" of love for his child. Like the good fathers of fiction, he talks with his daughter, proudly repeats her remarks, and, we can assume, tells inventive, witty, and erudite tales in the traditionally paternal story hour. More importantly, Laqueur, unlike most fathers, assumes a full share of child tending in a household where, he tells us proudly, "gender roles are topsy-turvy" and, we assume, an easy fairness reigns. Although—or because—he never mentions money, it seems clear that Laqueur does not suffer from an often anguishing (and in cultural ideology a distinctly "fatherly") burden. He and his partner can support their child—she is a lawyer, he is a university teacher and writer with time left over to volunteer at an old people's home. It is understandable that a gay friend wants Laqueur to become the "known and knowable" sperm donor for her and her partner's child. Laqueur is utterly welcoming of his friend's enterprise and personally flattered. He refuses primarily because, to shorten his longer and complicated story, he would love the (her and his) child too much.

Yet this blessed and blessing, loving and liberal father is grumpy, and I, though convinced that he is a daughter's dream and wife's delight, find myself grumpy with him. He is annoyed that he lacks a history of fatherhood, that the story of "man-as-father" is not discernable in the patriarchal histories that treat of inheritance, "legitimacy," and public authority. I am annoyed that he lacks the history feminists have begun to create, a story of men as fathers that is inseparable from the economic and domestic powers—including the claims of inheritance, legitimacy, and authority—that "fathers" wield over women and their (women's and men's) children. While he worries about the "neoessentialist" claims of female birthgivers, I am struck by the shrinking significance of female birthgiving in the story such a good father tells.

Laqueur rightfully criticizes historians' acceptance of a nineteenth-century ideology that places men in public and women at home. Such a story cannot tell a father what it means to be a "new public man in private." But he says nothing about the women in father-ruled households of old. Feminists have pondered over the question of the degree of freedom and power enjoyed by women of different classes working in their own or other people's homes. But there is general agreement that the ideological construction of distinctive domestic power glosses over the very real, legal, psychosocial, physical, and too often abusive control that many men have exercised within the domain allegedly governed by women. But Laqueur, who is so evidently not tyrannical or abusive, is not much interested in the analysis of domestic power.

Nor, despite his proposing a labor theory of parenting, does Laqueur really attend to fathering as a kind of work. The distinctions he sometimes endorses between hand, heart, and brain are decidedly ill-suited for a work that is done with and amid bodies, provokes and requires distinctive kinds of thinking, and involves the passionate emotions of both parent and child. Laqueur initially distinguishes between heart and hand (while ignoring mind) in order to count fatherly emotion as a kind of work. He then needlessly protests his own paternal love. Feminists have never disputed the "fact" that many men—even some who are abusive—are bound by love to their children and make them "emotionally part of themselves." Indeed, father-love is often part of the father problem precisely because this "love"—in addition to binding children to damaging fathers—serves to establish fathers' claims to authority over children whether or not they have actually participated in the work of caring for them.

Indeed, Laqueur's distinctions can all too easily be bent to serve the purposes of "absent" and perhaps even damaging fathers (although this bending is clearly neither his intent nor his practice). As Laqueur amusingly relates in his tales of biological paternity, the totalizing dichotomies of the philosophers[4] associate masculinity, fatherhood, activity, and mind and set them against passive, female birthgiving. In the dichotomies I know best (for example, Plato, Augustine, and Hannah Arendt), "mind," and with it authority and power, is set sharply against emotion, domestic life, and bodily necessity. By breaking into the usual binary opposition Laqueur rescues emotion and—apparently—makes it the crucial, even defining element of parental labor. He rejects a conception of fatherhood as generative idea (opposed to the passive matter of maternity) but he does not make the even more helpful gesture of associating the work of mothering and fathering with distinctive kinds of thinking. And he explicitly identifies parental labor with "the heart *not* the hand" (italics added). Hence Laqueur effectively leaves fathers with emotions no one doubted they had, without the physical labor such emotions might rightly entail, but (at least in Laqueur's circles) with their minds intact but elsewhere. Most mothers are thus left not only with emotions everyone takes for granted but also with the physical labor that has been rightly thought to be theirs, and without the minds that no one thought they had anyway, unless, like fathers, they "go to [intellectual] work."

I am very sympathetic with Laqueur's labor theory of parenting. Indeed, I believe that if Laqueur reflected upon his *work* as a father he would quickly relinquish his ill-fitting and potentially harmful distinctions. But Laqueur is far less preoccupied with parenting than with procreation, and in particular with a father's reproductive acts and feelings. A labor theory of *parenting* loosens the ["essentialist"] conceptual connections between *birthgiving* and the very different work of child tending and thus provides a place of entrance for men and "adoptive" parents. But while a "labor theory" of parenting is gender inclusive, a labor theory of birthgiving, as Laqueur himself finally recognizes, must privilege the female who gestates and gives birth to a child. Any man or woman can assume the responsibilities and share in the pleasures of maternal work, whatever his or her relationship to the birthgivers of the children they tend. But the labor of the most emotion-ridden male progenitor*—no matter how anxiously,

---

*or the labor of a similarly emotional female egg donor, though donating eggs is a more complex and painful enterprise than donating sperm through sexual or artificial insemination.

joyously, tenderly, and responsibly he prepares for birthgiving and assists the birthgiver—cannot equal the labor of nine months' gestation and a body-encompassing, almost always painful birthgiving.

Suppose, however, we ignore, like some of Laqueur's predecessors, the active and complex physicality and the reflective consciousness that birthgiving requires. A man's or woman's *emotional* bonding with a fetus could then appear as the best kind of procreative work. Were he to adopt this conceptual construction of birthgiving as emotional labor, a man could compete with a female birthgiver for "best worker" and have a fighting chance of earning the prize. While he takes a proprietary interest in the child she carries, imagines dramas of fatherhood, dreams about his ancestors, and prepares to see "his whole family" in his baby's eyes, she, who may well have similar dreams and fantasies, also has other, often ambivalent emotional responses occasioned by the very physical activities and reflective consciousness that we have denied. She is sick, pulled out of shape, moves clumsily and worries about falling. She is tested and then makes conscious choices in response to those tests. She ponders over the effects of the simplest drug that might relieve a headache, often enough struggles against possibly damaging addictive habits, and frequently worries and then feels guilty about what she eats, drinks, or smokes. She is apprehensive of the pain she will almost surely suffer, yet (if she has the time and money) selects anesthetics and labor practices conducive to her infant's health. Typically, she expects to take on the greater share of the child tending on which parental visions ultimately depend; anxiously she devises strategies for getting the services she and her child will require and imagines ways in which she might maintain her job or pursue her career and still enjoy the friendships, projects, and pleasures of her prematernal adult life.

It is not surprising if a female birthgiver sometimes feels more invaded by than possessor of the baby she "carries." Despite the pain and struggle—and partly because of the excitement and pleasure that are also part of gestation and birth—many birthgivers report a nearly mystical connection with their newborn infant. But many other birthgivers feel that they have failed to "bond" with their child, a relationship that is romantically identified with welcoming, unambivalent love. While the experience of bonding is considered obligatory for female birthgivers, it may indeed come more easily to eager and financially confident fathers.

Suppose, however, that we take seriously a labor theory of birth-giving but insist on measuring "labor" by the variety of intellectual reflection, conscious choice, physical effort, *and* complex, ambivalent emotional experience and discipline that the work of birthgiving requires. Despite centuries of social construction designed to obscure the stories and "facts" of flesh, it is clear that female birthgivers perform by far the greatest part of birthing labor. Laqueur realizes this: "all fathers [are] at a distinct material disadvantage to . . . all women [birthgivers] who contribute so much more matter" and—he should have added—at least as much emotional "investment," intellectual reflection, and choice.

Turning to history and to current legal cases, Laqueur makes abundantly clear that the links between biological procreation and "mothering" or "fathering" are constructed and complex. Unlike many social constructionists before him, including many feminists, Laqueur does not intend to trivialize the experience of female birthgivers. He wants to include men, not to insult women; he is wittily critical of theorists who deny women's pro*creativity*. Nonetheless, he manages to contribute to reductive accounts of a birthgiver's myriad, emotionally laden, self-shaping, thought-provoking physical experiences. By focusing on legal cases and therefore (at least in the United States) creating an atmosphere in which conflict is irresoluble, he sets up a contest between female birthgivers and male progenitors. While the cases are meant only to underline the complexity of men's feelings (as well as the conventionality of connections between birthgiving and parenting), Laqueur tips the scales to the father by highlighting his emotional response to a genetic offspring and the birthgiver's insensitive or muddled reactions to him. Meanwhile, Laqueur ignores, though he never denies and probably takes for granted, the birthgiver's response to the fetal-infant life she carries and delivers.

More directly, Laqueur assimilates the hiring of women as birthgivers to the sexual exploitation of aspiring "starlets," the forced labor exchanges of the poor, employers' abuse of children's bodies, and "academic hiring fairs." "There are no new horrors here." Although Laqueur's concern for the sexual and economic exploitation of women, children, the desperately poor, and needy academics is admirable, it does not touch upon many women's specific, deeply felt rejection of the practices of surrogacy. At the end, Laqueur invokes a liberal theory of the right to "control and monitor corporeal boundaries," again with no specific reference to birthgiving or to the distinctive breakdown—or revisioning—of bodily boundary—as "fact" and "idea"—that birthgiving entails. Indeed, at his and my grumpiest moments, I felt that Laqueur, like many philosophers before him, was almost afraid—and anyhow failed—to look at, listen to, imagine his way into the social and intellectual complexities of the female birthgiving experience.

In rejecting easy, "essentialist," connections between birthgiving and parenting, and insisting that we attend to men's emotional and physical reproductive experience, Laqueur articulates crucial steps toward the necessary feminist enterprise of rethinking the social and metaphysical significance of birth. But for those feminists who wish to include fathers but recognize the necessity of transforming Fatherhood, the work—the emotional, intellectual, imaginative, and physical labor—of reconstruction is still to be done.

How then are feminists to think about fathers? I would begin as Laqueur does, not with birthgiving, but with the *work* of parenting. If we see or remember child tending accurately, we will be rid of distinctions, or more optimistically reimagine connections, between so-called physical, intellectual, and emotional activities.* We can also avoid the exclusive heterosexual coupledom in which parenting has been conceptually and ideologically mired. The *work* of child tending can be, and is being, undertaken by women and men, gay and straight, single, coupled, or in many kinds of social arrangements.

Unlike Laqueur, however, and like the feminists who envision a world without "fathers," I speak of "mothering" rather than "parenting" as the work in which child-tending men and women engage. This terminology acknowledges the "fact" that mothering has been—and still is—primarily the responsibility of women and that history has consequences. Also, by the slight if passing frisson of referring to men as mothers I hope to jar a listener into reflecting upon the distinctive rights and privileges of "fathers" and upon the heterosexist knot in which our ideas of mothering are tied. By contrast, the abstract notion of "parent" obscures the pervasive injustices suffered

---

*Focusing upon the *work* that child tending requires will prompt a more general metaphysical revision of the categories of mind, emotion, and "physical" labor. This revision is one of the philosophical rewards of attending to mothering as "work" or as a "practice."

by women-mothers and, more generally, the myriad father problems that vex and divide feminists.

In making the case for "mothering" as a gender-inclusive and therefore genderless activity, I have been struck by the resistance even of those men who fully engage in child tending. As a feminist I am aware of the dangers of "saming" (to borrow a useful phrase from Naomi Schor),[5] that is, denying the objectified other—in this case the male parent—"the right to [his] difference, submitting the other to the laws of [maternity]." But I do not understand what men fear to lose. Leaving aside penis, sperm, [phallus?,] and other "essentialist" and essentially unthreatened equipment, what makes a parent a "father"?

Consider Laqueur's gender-bending case of a lesbian parent separated from her birthgiving partner who is accorded the status of father, not because she inseminated her lover with her brother's sperm, but because she has invested the "emotional and imaginative capital," and, as it happens, the cash, "to make the child in some measure hers." Why don't these investments—most of which will have occurred after birth—make L. Lofton, as in my view they would make any man, in some measure a mother? Is L. Lofton called a "father" because she lives apart from her child, is therefore less a mother, but still an absent father? Does she, do we, grant rights to an absent *father,* when a similarly absent mother would be delinquent? If so, are we not conceptually embroiled in the very institutions of fatherhood we are trying to revision? Is L. Lofton a father because she was legally enjoined to contribute support? Despite the ideology of fatherly provision, countless mothers support their children, and absent, wage-earning mothers might be legally compelled to do so. Equally important, when fathering is identified with economic support in a way that mothering is not, and when men cannot consider themselves mothers, unemployed, impoverished young men cannot take themselves to be "parents."[6] Material support is not a distinctly *paternal* obligation but, on the contrary, is a fact of most women-mothers' lives and a necessary condition of any effective child care. To be sure, recognizing these facts of men's or women's mothering, unsustained by the myth of the Providing Father, requires both confronting the economic injustices women and poor men suffer and defining "child support" in terms of a *social* obligation to provide for children's needs. Troubles of transition aside, this is just the kind of change that talk of "mothering" is intended to abet.

Despite my refusal of the abstract "parent" and the different "father," I am as determined as Laqueur to disrupt the presumption that female birthgiving is either necessary or sufficient for good-enough mothering. I see all mothers, including women-mothers who have given birth, as "adoptive." A man or woman is a "mother," in my sense of the term, only if he or she acts upon a social commitment to nurture, protect, and train children. All mothering depends upon some woman's birthgiving, but there are many possible birth-respecting relationships between mothers and birthgivers. Finally, however, my account of "adoptive" maternal work and thinking comes no closer than Laqueur's labor theory of parenting to articulating a social, political, and metaphysical understanding of birth. It was only after several years of writing about potentially genderless mothering that I began to consider female birthgiving as an active, socially complex, chosen project.[7] Belatedly realizing that I had neglected (and feared) the female body, I insisted on birthgiving *women's* distinctive experiences and responsibilities. Determined to avoid reinscribing the "spurious" and "illegitimate" child of "single" or lesbian mothers, I construed the birthgiver and her infant(s) as a complex and complete couple, albeit economically, emotionally, and medically dependent upon others' help. Now, having read Laqueur's impassioned insistence on his participation in birthgiving, I realize that in my first attempts at reconceptualization I wrote male bodies out of birth. Laqueur reminds me that any account of birth that respects human bodily life should include male as well as female procreative acts and desires.

Ultimately it is men who will have to tell the story of male procreative feelings and acts. But mothers of both sexes might help to tell one version of the story by beginning at the beginning, attending to or remembering children's intense and elaborately imagined bodily lives and their own maternal engagement with children's bodies. Children's bodies, though phantastically interpreted, are irreducibly, "factually," given: whoever tends a child tends a particular bodily life. Mothers are meant to protect those bodies rather than assault or neglect them; they are meant to adorn, soothe, and feed, to applaud, delight, and caress. Children's bodies, like the bodies of adults, are sexual; the distinctive pleasures and curiosities of sexuality make their appearance not as an exception to but as an essential ingredient of childhood bodily life. To protect children's bodies means to protect rather than intrude upon, exploit, suppress, or unduly regiment children's desires and shifting sex/gender identities.

A welcoming response to bodily life is only an ideal, one that many mothers do not express or share. But when mothering is governed by this ideal, and when, as sometimes happens, mothers are fairly successful at enacting the ideal by which they are governed, a practice of welcoming and protecting bodies becomes part of children's heritage. When children have been protected and appreciated they have also been taught (at least implicitly) to protect—rather than to abuse or neglect—their own and each others' bodies. By the time "sperm" appears, along with excitements, nocturnal emissions, unpredictable erections, and other phenomena only males can speak of, there is a context in which young women and men can identify and protect young men's—as well as young women's—procreative capacities. To be sure, adolescents are dismally apt to abuse and endanger their own and others' bodies, flouting the protective circumstances on which they have depended. My point is that "sperm" and its/his adventures emerge within those practices, whether benign or punishing, protective or neglectful, that have constructed bodily life. If "bodies" are constructed as unpredictably developing beings that are meant to be enjoyed and protected, then it is more likely that male procreation—like female birthgiving—will be imagined as a chosen activity through which men create for themselves responsible, responsive ways and occasions for "donating sperm."

Still, the most benign sociopolitical context cannot make male procreation "equal" in physical, intellectual, or emotional labor to female birthgiving. As feminists have learned, the differences we deny come back to haunt us. Birthgiving is a complex, demanding, and sometimes self-transforming activity, and hitherto, as in the foreseeable future, only women can give birth. As Laqueur's history of procreative mythology (implicitly) documents, men have often written (and presumably acted) on behalf of men, inspired by the envy, fear, resentment, and guilt their "different" relationship to birth inspires. The task, as I see it, is to construct—really *construct,* socially, materially, and politically—birthgiving practices in which women and men can participate unequally but with realistic self-respect, mutual regard, and a commitment to the well-being of the children that they, or other mothers, will adopt.

This is of course utopian. As it is, young men's bodies are "thrown away"—neglected and assaulted, sacrificed to militarist endeavor, capitalist greed, and racist domination. In a society where male (as well as female) bodies are so abused, male sexuality and "sperm," and the absent and abusive fathers who embody them, have often proved to be the socially constructed enemy of women. In the midst of this unprotective, often cruel, society, a rough justice is arising. Women buy men's sperm but leave men out. A man's increasingly traceable sperm is used to bind him to economic relations he would not have chosen and often cannot sustain. Now, like a woman, a man can be made materially accountable for, yet socially alienated from, his sexual activities; he may therefore feel that, like a woman (though surely less painfully), he too is a victim of his procreative body.

Rough justice is an improvement upon the misogynist and male-dominated institutions in which women have had to give birth and undertake mothering. But the practices and rhetoric of rough justice *can* make a person grumpy. It is far more heartening to imagine feminist transformations that will prove protective of adult and child, male and female; far more gratifying to create the health care, nurseries, jobs, employment policies, and educational programs—the myriad social structures on which all good-enough mothering depends. Then women and men, whatever their personal couplings and connections, might join together in a collective commitment to nurture and cherish the procreative promise of their children.

Notes

1. Nancy Chodorow, *Feminism and Psychoanalytic Theory* (New Haven, Conn.: Yale University Press, 1989), 185.

2. See, for example, Carole Pateman, *The Sexual Contract* (Stanford, Calif.: Stanford University Press, 1988).

3. For example, Frank J. Furstenberg, Jr., reported this "finding" at a conference on adolescent pregnancy held at Stanford University, April 1989.

4. Feminists and poststructuralist critics have presented many versions of these dichotomies. The dichotomies are never so simple within the actual texts—including those of the authors I cite—as they are in feminist readings and deconstructions.

5. Naomi Schor, "This Essentialism Which Is Not One: Coming to Grips with Irigaray," *differences* 1, no. 2 (Summer 1989):38–58.

6. The lethal connections between poverty, racial injustice, and the capacity to be or to experience oneself as a father are among the most anguishing "facts of fatherhood" in the contemporary United States. See, for example, Marion Wright Edelman, *Families in Peril*

(Cambridge, Mass.: Harvard University Press, 1987), and William Julius Wilson, *The Truly Disadvantaged: The Inner City, the Underclass, and Public Policy* (Chicago: University of Chicago Press, 1987).

7. Throughout this section, I am drawing on my *Maternal Thinking: Toward a Politics of Peace* (Boston: Beacon Press, 1989).

10

The Fantasy of the Perfect Mother

NANCY CHODOROW AND SUSAN CONTRATTO

In the late 1960s and early 1970s, feminists raised initial questions
and developed a consensus of sorts about mothering. We pointed to
the pervasive pronatalism of our culture; argued for safe, available
abortions and birth control; criticized the health care system; and
advocated maternity and paternity benefits and leaves as well as accessible and subsidized parent- and community-controlled day care,
innovative work-time arrangements, shared parenting, and other
nontraditional child-rearing and household arrangements. These
consensual positions among feminists all centered on the argument
that women's lives should not be totally constrained by child care or
childbearing. Women should be free to choose not to bear children;
should have easy access to safe contraception and abortion; should
be able to continue their other work if mothers; and should have
available to them good day care. In contrast, recent feminist writing
on motherhood focuses more on the experience of mothering: If a
woman wants to be a mother, what is or should be her experience?
Given that parenting is necessary in any society, who should parent
and how should the parenting be done? Feminist writing now recognizes that many women, including many feminists, want to have children and experience mothering as a rich and complex endeavor.

The new feminist writing has turned to mothering even while insisting on women's right to choose not to mother or to do other
things in addition to mothering. Feminists often wish to speak to

© 1980 by Nancy Chodorow and Susan Contratto.
We are enormously indebted to Linda Gordon, Arlie Hochschild, Sara Ruddick, Judith Stacey, Catharine Stimpson, and Barrie Thorne for their very careful reading of an earlier version of this essay. We
also benefited greatly from discussions with Sherry Ortner and Norma Wikler. Although these people
did not always agree with our positions, their ideas aided our ongoing explorations of the issues we
examine. NIMH Training Grant MH 15 122–03 provided support for Susan Contratto during the writing of the essay. This essay appeared in the first edition of *Rethinking the Family*.

nonfeminist or antifeminist mothers about mothering without succumbing to heterosexism or promaternalism. The assumption that women have the right to mother, as well as not to mother, and the recognition that mothering, though it may be conflictual and oppressive, is also emotionally central and gratifying in some women's lives, has created a level of tension and ambivalence in recent writing that was missing in the earlier discussion.

This essay examines certain recurrent psychological themes in recent feminist writing on motherhood.[1] These themes include a sense that mothers are totally responsible for the outcomes of their mothering, even if their behavior is in turn shaped by male-dominant society. Belief in the all-powerful mother spawns a recurrent tendency to blame the mother on the one hand, and a fantasy of maternal perfectibility on the other. The writings also elaborate maternal sexuality or asexuality, aggression and omnipotence in the mother-child relationship, and the isolation of the mother-child dyad. This isolation provides the supercharged environment in which aggression and, to a lesser degree, sexuality become problematic, and the context in which a fantasy of the perfect mother can also be played out.

We point to, and are concerned with, two features of these understandings of motherhood. They have an unprocessed quality; it is as if notions that the personal is political have been interpreted to mean that almost primal fantasies constitute feminist politics or theory. Further, we think there is a striking continuity between these feminist treatments of motherhood and themes found in the culture at large, even among antifeminists. Feminists differ about the meaning of motherhood and women's mothering, but each of these themes finds its complement in nonfeminist or antifeminist writing. Both these features of the writings we discuss are problematic for feminist theory and politics.

The All-Powerful Mother: Blame and Idealization

Feminist writing on motherhood assumes an all-powerful mother who, because she is totally responsible for how her children turn out, is blamed for everything from her daughter's limitations to the crisis of human existence. Nancy Friday's *My Mother/My Self* exemplifies this genre at its most extreme.[2] The book's central argument is that mothers are noxious to daughters, and that a daughter's subsequent unhappiness and failings stem from this initial relationship. Friday follows the daughter through the life cycle and shows at each stage how mothers forcefully, intentionally, and often viciously constrain and control daughters, keep them from individuating, and, especially, deny daughters their sexuality and keep them from men.[3] Mothers make daughters in their image: As the mother, in becoming a mother, has denied her own sexuality, so she must deny sexuality to her daughter. Friday even seems to blame mothers for the act of toilet training their daughters.[4]

Even when Friday points to other causes of a daughter's problems, it is still the mother's fault: sexual information learned in school or from friends doesn't alter a mother's impact; women are ultimately responsible even for obstetrical atrocities performed by men in the interests of male power. Friday relates Seymour Fisher's finding that good female relationships with men depend on the belief that a daughter's father will not desert her, but then she asks, "But who put on the sexual brakes to begin with?"[5] Friday makes occasional disclaimers; for example, blaming mother is not taking responsibility for oneself.[6] But these disclaimers are buried in 460 pages of the opposite message. They are certainly not the message we remember from the book.

It is not clear whether Friday considers herself a feminist (though she certainly claims to be a woman's advocate and many see her as a feminist). In any event, she reflects in extreme form a widespread feminist position, one that also argues that mothers are the agents of their daughters' oppression and also pays lip service (or more) to the fact that mothers themselves are oppressed and are therefore not responsible. Judith Arcana's *Our Mothers' Daughters*,[7] for instance, written out of explicit feminist commitment and concern, gives us an account almost exactly like Friday's. The only difference from Friday is that Arcana claims that maternal behavior is a product of mothers' entrapment within patriarchy rather than a product of their evil intentions.

While Friday and Arcana condemn mothers for what they do to their daughters, Dorothy Dinnerstein in *The Mermaid and the Minotaur* discusses the disastrous impact of maternal caretaking on sons, daughters, and society as a whole.[8] Dinnerstein claims that, as a result of "mother-dominated infancy," adult men and women are "semi-human, monstrous"—grown-up children acting out a species-suicidal pathology.[9] In Dinnerstein's account the mother is an object of children's fury and desperation, and children will put up with and create anything to escape her evil influence: "The deepest root of our acquiescence to the maiming and mutual imprisonment of men and women lies in the monolithic fact of human childhood: under the arrangements that now prevail, a woman is the parental person who is every infant's first love, first witness, and first boss, the person who presides over the infant's first encounters with the natural surroundings and who exists for the infant as the first representative of the flesh."[10]

Dinnerstein's account, like Friday's and Arcana's, confuses infantile fantasy with the actuality of maternal behavior. Thus, even as Dinnerstein describes the infantile fantasies that emerge from female-dominated child care, she also asserts that mothers are in fact all-powerful, fearsome creatures. She emphasizes the *"absolute power"* of the *"mother's life-and-death control over helpless infancy: an intimately carnal control"* whose *"wrath is all-potent"* and whose *"intentionality is so formidable—so terrifying and . . . so alluring."*[11] This potency engages with the infant's totally helpless need and dependence; it humiliates, controls, and dominates as it seduces, succors, and saves. As a result, according to Dinnerstein, the mother (or whoever would care for the child) is inevitably the child's adversary.

Dinnerstein says that women's exclusive mothering affects the child's relationship to mother and father, attitudes toward the body, and adult erotic capacities. It shapes the later ambivalence toward nature and nature's resources, creates an unhealthy split between love and work, produces adults who parent differently according to sex, fosters particular kinds of destructive power and ensures patriarchal control of that power, and forms the nature of our history-making impulse.[12] In short, women's all-powerful mothering shapes the child's entire psychological, social, and political experience and is responsible for a species life that "is cancerous, out of control."[13]

The other side of blaming the mother is idealization of her and her possibilities: if only the mother wouldn't do what she is doing, she would be perfect. Friday's perfect mother is self-sacrificing and giving (though ultimately in the interest of her own deferred emotional rewards): "The truly loving mother is one whose interest and happiness is in seeing her daughter as a person, not just a possession. It is a process of being so generous and loving that she will forego some of her own pleasure and security to add to her daughter's development. If she does this in a genuine way, she really does end up with that Love Insurance Policy." "It is a noble role that mother must play here."[14] Friday, the new woman's advocate, sounds like the most traditional traditionalist.

Most feminist writing does not expect mothers to change on their own. As feminists locate blame, they also focus on the conditions—those of patriarchy—in which bad mothering takes place, in which mothers are victims and powerless in the perpetuation of evil. But this implies that if only we could remove these patriarchal constraints, mothering could be perfect. Arcana, in pointing to women who have broken out of the traditional mold, wants to turn these women into perfect mothers: "Such women may mother us all."[15]

These writings suggest not only that mothers can be perfect but also that the child's needs (e.g., those of the daughters in the books by Friday and Arcana) are necessarily legitimate and must be met. Such an implication persists in the most subtle and sophisticated feminist accounts. Jane Flax, for instance, offers an analysis of the psychodynamics of the mother-daughter relationship in which she writes of the difficulties of being a mother in a male-dominant society and of the psychological conflicts that setting generates.[16] She offers perceptive insights into the contradictory needs that emerge from being mothered by a woman. But her article still implies that mothers can be perfect and that the child's felt desires are absolute needs: "As a result of all these conflicts, it is more difficult for the mother to be as emotionally available as her infant daughter needs her to be."[17] The "needs" to which she refers are those of women patients talking about their mothers, and Flax accepts their accounts. She does not suggest that a child's "needs" might be unrealistic or unreasonable.

We find the idealization of maternal possibility not only in those accounts that blame the mother but also in another strain of feminist writing on motherhood, one that begins from identification with the mother rather than with the daughter. Adrienne Rich and Alice Rossi also premise their investigations of motherhood on the assumption that a maternal ideal or perfection could emerge with the overthrow of patriarchy.[18] Both discuss mothering as it has been affected by patriarchy and describe how patriarchy has controlled—as Rich observes, even killed—mothers and children. Mothers are not powerful, but powerless under patriarchy.

Rich provides a moving account of maternal love and concern and a vision of the potential power of women's maternal bodies, which could enable women to be intellectually, spiritually, and sexually transformative, and which could forge nurturant, sexual, and spiritual linkages among women:

> The repossession by women of our bodies will bring far more essential change to human society than the seizing of the means of production by workers. . . . We need to imagine a world in which every woman is the presiding genius of her own body. In such a world, women will truly create new life, bringing forth not only children (if and as we choose), but the visions and the thinking necessary to sustain, console and alter human existence—a new relationship to the universe. Sexuality, politics, intelligence, position, motherhood, work, community, intimacy will develop new meanings; thinking itself will be transformed. This is where we have to begin.[19]

Rossi, like Rich, turns to women's maternalism, but she focuses less on the global social and cultural implications of the freeing of motherhood from patriarchal technological constraints and more on the possibilities of the mothering experience. Rossi argues that women have a "biological edge" in parental capacities and implies that children will do best with their natural mothers if these mothers can reclaim their bodies and come in touch with their innate mothering potential, and if their experience can be removed from male-dominant social organization. Rossi stresses the natural and untutored quality of some of women's intuitive responses to infants and the potential interconnection of sexual and maternal gratification. All these qualities could be enhanced if their expression were not distorted or destroyed by doctor-centered obstetric management, by industrial threats to fetuses and pregnant women, by too close spacing of children, by women mothering according to a male life script (i.e., self-involved instead of nurturant). The return to a more natural mothering relationship would also sustain and further connections among women, the "women's culture" that the feminist movement has emphasized. Like Rich, Rossi implies that mothering could be wonderful if women could recognize and take pleasure in their procreative and maternal capacities and if these were not taken over by institutional constraints and alienated understandings of mothering.

Sexuality

Contradictory fantasies and expectations about maternity/mothering and sexuality also emerge in the new feminist literature. In *The Dialectic of Sex,* an influential early feminist book, Shulamith Firestone argued that biological sex is the basic social category and contradiction.[20] The reproductive difference between the sexes—that women bear children—leads to a sexual division of labor that is the root of all women's oppression by men, as well as oppressions of class and race. Since the fact of their biological childbearing capacities causes women's oppression, women must be freed from this biology. According to Firestone, the solution would be a technology that eliminates biological reproduction, untied to anyone's procreative body. This would end both biological and social motherhood.

In place of a male-dominant society based on women's biology and the biological family, Firestone envisions a society with total sexual liberation and a positively valued polymorphous perversity. By implication, freeing women from their reproductive biology leads to, and is a prerequisite of, sexual liberation. According to Firestone, pregnant bodies are ugly, and motherhood and sexuality are incompatible. In the new society, people would have individual freedom to move in and out of relationships, children could live where and with whom they want, and there would be no parental relationships as we know them. "Down with childhood" is the other side of "down with mothers." Firestone argues that the only alternative to the inequities of the family is no family at all, no long-term commitments of anyone to anyone; everyone must be an individual without ties. Thus, for Firestone, individualism goes along with a liberated sexuality, and both are inherently opposed to motherhood. For Nancy Friday, also, women's goal in life is to attain sexual individuality, which is the opposite of being a mother. Womanhood is nonmaternal (hetero)sexuality. Relationships between mother and daughter—and between women generally—are entirely negative. From early childhood, little girls try to do one another in. Sexual relationships with men offer the only positive direction, and the best thing a mother can do for her daughter is to promote her heterosexuality.

One strand of feminism, then, is represented by Shulamith Firestone, who would wipe out women's procreative capacities altogether, and by Nancy Friday, who poses a choice for women between exercising their procreative capacities and expressing their sexuality.

Both imply a radical split between sexuality and maternity and opt for sexuality, either in its polymorphous perverse or its genital heterosexual form.

We find an opposing strand in Rossi and Rich, who identify motherhood with sexuality and would locate one foundation of women's liberation and fulfillment in the repossession (in the broadest sense) of their maternal bodies. Rich and Rossi imply that patriarchal institutions have distorted a natural maternal essence and potential for the mother-child bond. Rossi points to the inherent sexual pleasures of the mothering experience, and Rich suggests a connection between the physical pleasures of the mother-infant (especially mother-daughter) relationship and sexual bonds between women.

Aggression and Death

If having a child makes a mother all-powerful or totally powerless, if women's maternal potential requires the desexing of women or enables fully embodied power, then the child who evokes this arrangement must also be all-powerful. The child's existence or potential existence can dominate the mother's. This leads to a fourth theme that emerges in recent feminist writing on motherhood, a theme that grows out of the writer's identification as a mother or potential mother: an almost primal aggression in the mother-child relationship, an aggression that goes from mother to child, from child to mother, from mother-as-child to her own mother. Cemented by maternal and infantile rage, motherhood becomes linked to destruction and death. Rich, for instance, introduces and concludes her account of mothering within patriarchy with the story of a depressed suburban housewife and mother who decapitated her two youngest children.

Feminist Studies, one of the major scholarly feminist journals, published a special issue, "Toward a Feminist Theory of Motherhood," on this theme.[21] With four exceptions, the issue is about motherhood, horror, and death. We read articles, poems, and autobiographical accounts about maternal death, children's deaths, the blood of childbirth, spontaneous abortions, stillbirths, the inability to conceive, childbirth as an experience of death, nineteenth-century obstetric torture techniques, unmothered monsters, child murder, and incest. Some of these articles, poems, and accounts are beautifully written, finely constructed, powerful, and persuasive. They illuminate women's fantasies and fears and guide us insightfully to themes and preoccupations we had not previously considered. Yet the whole obliterates the parts: we are left, not with memories of these individual creations, but with impressions of an inextricable linkage of motherhood, blood, gore, destruction, and death.

Rachel Blau DuPlessis, the issue editor, points out that the contributions of the issue, in stressing the intertwining of birth, life, and death, react to cultural images of the mother as idealized nurturer. DuPlessis points out that there is, as yet, no synthesis,[22] but she also does not seem to want to create one. On the contrary, polarities are writ large; an almost satanic imagery of blood, guts, and destruction and subjective expostulation substitutes for cultural idealization. There is little attempt to investigate reality in its complex subjective and objective breadth.

Kate Millett's book *The Basement: Meditations on a Human Sacrifice* further extends the linkage of motherhood, violence, and death.[23] The book is a true account of a woman, her seven children, and their torture-murder of a sixteen-year-old girl who was left in the woman's charge by her parents. Millet portrays the torturer-protagonist as society's victim: the squalor and poverty that surround her and her abandonment by men are not of her making. Therefore, her craziness is inevitable and understandable. Motherhood contributes to the violence she feels: she is supposed to be the "responsible" adult with her children, in a situation where she has little power, and she visits her rage and frustration on one of them. The victim-mother creates a victim-child.

Jane Lazarre's feminist and autobiographical book *The Mother Knot,* certainly less absolute and bleak than *The Basement,* also tells a story of maternal anger and victimization, and of the link between mother as victim and child as victim.[24] Lazarre sets out to tell the story of maternal ambivalence—the only "eternal and natural" feature of motherhood. Motherhood turns the woman's love relationship into the formal role pattern of Husband and Wife and brings her to the brink of madness. The protagonist's ambivalence is her profoundest reality. She desperately loves and resents her child, feels tenderness and rage at her husband. Hate and love, fury and overwhelming joy, remain unfused and unresolved, experienced only in their pure and alternating forms.[25]

In these accounts, a fantasied omnipotence, played out in the realm of aggression and anger, oscillates between mother and child. On the one hand we have an all-powerful mother and a powerless child. On the other hand we have the child who identifies with the all-powerful mother and whose very being casts its mother into the role of total victim or angel. Thus, in the *Feminist Studies* special issue, in Millett's story, and in Rich's account of the woman who murders her children, we find the notion that having a child is enough to kill a woman or make a woman into a murderer. Being a mother is a matter of life and death; having a child destroys the mother or the child. If antifeminists have tended more than feminists to blame the mother, feminists tend to blame the child, or the having of children.

Why? There is, of course, historical and psychological truth here. Women's lives change radically when they have children, and caring for children in our society is difficult. The institution of motherhood, as Rich shows, is indeed oppressive to mothers and to those who are not mothers. Moreover, millions of women have died in childbirth throughout history, often as a direct result of obstetrical interference. In the past, infant mortality was often as likely as infant survival. Even today, the United States ranks high in infant mortality rates when compared with other industrialized nations. Moreover, surviving a child, or experiencing one's infant's death, in an age when we expect orderly generational progression, is a tragedy that can leave a permanent scar.

And yet death and destruction are by no means the whole experience or institution of motherhood. Rich and Millett suggest that the continuity of violence from men to women and women to children accounts for the link of motherhood and death, and we feel this is partly correct. The *Feminist Studies* issue seems to suggest an even deeper, more inevitable link. The writer is the mother whose individuality and separateness are threatened by the child and whose fantasy therefore kills it; and she is the child who is both the destroyer of the mother and the object of destruction. In this rendition, mother and child seem caught in a fantasied exclusive and exclusionary dyad where aggression, frustration, and rage hold sway. These writers merge fantasies of maternal omnipotence into the totalizing quality of the experience of the mother-child relationship.

Maternal Isolation

Another assumption apparent in recent feminist literature is that mother and child are an isolated dyad. Mother and child are seen as both physically and psychologically apart from the world, existing within a magic (or cursed) circle. Sometimes, as in Millett's work, the isolation has a physical boundary to it. The woman's home is her castle, in which she is isolated and all-powerful in motherhood. The children's fathers have left her. Her neighbors, hearing the screams from her basement, choose to leave her alone; they say it is her right and responsibility to discipline her children, and besides, they do not want to get involved. Other adults—social workers, the school personnel, the minister—are also loath to tread on a mother's space.

More often, the isolation is psychological. Rich talks of the isolation that comes from responsibility, that of the single adult woman who, though physically surrounded by others, bears the total task of mothering. The successes, failures, and day-to-day burdens of child care are particularly hers. Lazarre chillingly describes the isolation of responsibility she faces (and creates), and she shows how that isolation helps lead to her desolation, rage, and destructiveness. Dinnerstein sees the isolation from the point of view of the child's development and describes how it magnifies the relation to the mother and creates in the child a desperate need to escape.

At the same time, some feminist writing wishes to maintain a form of isolated mother-child relationship but to make it unique and special in a positive way. The protagonist of *The Mother Knot* sets herself off from others and wishes to retreat into the perfect unit of infant and mother. Rich and Rossi wish conditions to change so that mothers receive the community support that would enable the specialness of the mothering relation to emerge.

In these accounts, this isolation, in which mother and child live in a unique and potent relationship, explains and even justifies the effects of mothering. It explains why mothers (even in their oppression by patriarchy) are so all-powerful in relation to their children, and why the mother-child relation is likely to be so bound up with powerful feelings. Mother and child are on a psychological desert island. Having only each other, each is continually impinging and intruding on the other, and there is no possibility of escape. As a result, the other becomes the object of aggressive fantasies and behaviors, and mothering becomes linked to extremist expectations about sexuality.

Cultural and Psychological Roots of Feminist Interpretations of Mothering

We have discussed four interrelated psychological themes that emerge from recent feminist work on mothering: (1) blaming and idealizing the mother, assuming that mothers are or can be all-powerful and perfect and that mothering either destroys the world or generates world perfection; (2) extreme expectations of maternal sexuality, asserting the incompatibility of motherhood and sexuality or romanticizing maternal sexuality; (3) a link between motherhood and aggression or death; and (4) an emphasis on the isolation of mother and child. All these themes share common characteristics: their continuity with dominant cultural understandings of mothering and their rootedness in unprocessed, infantile fantasies about mothers.

Our cultural understandings of mothering have a long history, but reached a peak in the nineteenth century. That century witnessed the growth of a sexual division of spheres that materially grounded mother-child isolation and bequeathed us a picture of the ideal mother who would guarantee both morally perfect children and a morally desirable world.[26] At a time when everyone's life was being affected by the frenzied growth of developing industrial capitalism, somehow mothers were seen as having total control and unlimited power in the creation of their children.

Post-Freudian psychology assumes the mother-child isolated unit that nineteenth-century industrial development produced and elaborates the notion that the early mother-infant relationship is central to later psychological development and to the psychological, emotional, and relational life of the child. As a result of this assumption, virtually all developmental research of the last thirty-five years has been directed to this early period. This focus has further reinforced and seemed to substantiate the popular view that the relationship of mother and infant has extraordinary significance. The assumption has also often led to a psychological determinism and reductionism that argues that what happens in the earliest mother-infant relationship determines the whole of history, society, and culture.[27]

Both nineteenth-century cultural ideology about motherhood and post-Freudian psychological theory blame mothers for any failings in their children and idealize possible maternal perfection. Blaming the mother, a major outcome of these theories and a major theme in feminist writings, has a long social history. David Levy's *Maternal Overprotection*, the Momism of Philip Wylie and Erik Erikson, literature on the schizophrenogenic mother, Joseph Rheingold's analysis of maternal aggression as the primary pathogenic influence on the child, Philip Slater's discussion of the oedipally titillating, overwhelming mother, and Christopher Lasch's account of the mother "impos[ing] her madness on everyone else," all suggest the terrible outcome of the omnipotent mother.[28] With the exception of Slater, they ignore any conditions that determine or foster maternal behavior in the first place and accept a completely deterministic view of child development.[29]

More recently, as women have entered the paid labor force and some have chosen not to become mothers, mothers have been blamed more for what is called "maternal deprivation" than for "maternal overprotection." Selma Fraiberg's *Every Child's Birthright: In Defense of Mothering* is a good example.[30] Describing herself as the child's advocate, Fraiberg has no sympathy for women who choose to work. Her message is clear: a good mother does not use regular substitute child care before the age of three.

Thus, feminists' tendency to blame the mother (the perspective of feminist-as-child) fits into cultural patterning. Feminists simply add on to this picture the notion that conditions other than the mother's incompetence or intentional malevolence create this maternal behavior. But feminists do not question the accuracy of this characterization of maternal behavior, nor its effects.

As we suggested, idealization and blaming the mother are two sides of the same belief in the all-powerful mother. In the nineteenth century, the bourgeois mother received moral training and guidance to enhance her motherly performance, guidance that, if followed, would lead children and the world to moral perfection. In contemporary child-rearing manuals, the good mother knows naturally how to mother if she will only follow her instincts,[31] or can be perfect if she will only stay home full-time,[32] or can provide proper stimulation and gentle teaching to her child.[33] Feminists take issue with the notion that a mother can be perfect in the here and now, given male dominance, lack of equality in marriage, and inadequate resources and support, but the fantasy of the perfect mother remains: if current limitations on mothers were eliminated, mothers would know naturally how to be good.

Blame and idealization of mothers have become our cultural ideology. This ideology, however, gains meaning from and is partially produced by infantile fantasies that are themselves the outcome of being mothered exclusively by one woman. If mothers have exclusive responsibility for infants who are totally dependent, then to the infant

they are the source of all good and evil.[34] Times of closeness, one-
ness, and joy are the quintessence of perfect understanding; times of
distress, frustration, discomfort, and too great separation are entirely
the mother's fault. For the infant, the mother is not someone with her
own life, wants, needs, history, other social relationships, work. She is
known only in her capacity as mother. Growing up means learning
that she, like other people in one's life, has and wants a life of her
own, and that loving her means recognizing her subjectivity and ap-
preciating her separateness. But people have trouble doing this and
continue, condoned and supported by the ideology about mothers
they subsequently learn, to experience mothers solely as people who
did or did not live up to their child's expectations. This experience
creates the quality of rage we find in "blame-the-mother" literature
and the unrealistic expectation that perfection would result if only a
mother would devote her life completely to her child and all imped-
iments to doing so were removed. Psyche and culture merge here and
reflexively create one another.

Originally, idealization of mothers is an infantile fantasy: no human being can be perfect. Thus, although the idealization of maternal
life found in both Rich's and Rossi's writing is more from the perspective of mothers, their accounts are also informed by some identification with the stance of the child, who *needs* certain things in
order to develop. One focus of Rossi's argument is the biological tie
of infant to mother. Rich also claims that the child has powerful,
strong feelings for the mother, "authentic" need—"a need vaster
than any single human being could satisfy, except by loving continuously, unconditionally, from dawn to dark, and often in the middle
of the night."[35] This need is evoked by the sense of uniqueness of the
mother, by her singularity. This leads us to ask: What will happen to
these "authentic" needs, and who will fulfill them? Does Rich think
these intense feelings will disappear in a non-male-dominant world?
Or are they inherent in mothering and, therefore, unavoidable? To
what degree are they a product of the institution of motherhood under patriarchy and the experience of mothering it generates? And
once there are "needs" and feelings like this, won't we start evaluating and idealizing mothers who do and do not meet them, and do and
do not feel them?[36]

Fantasy and cultural ideology also meet in themes about maternal
sexuality. An assumed incompatibility between sexuality and moth-

erhood is largely a product of our nineteenth-century heritage, and some women psychoanalysts have helped perpetuate this cultural and psychological belief. In *The Psychology of Women,* Helene Deutsch claims clinical and literary support for the view that there is a natural and desirable psychological split between motherliness and erotic feelings.[37] Therese Benedek suggests that "mature" (i.e., motherly) women are simply less sexual than "immature" women.[38]

Ambivalence about maternal bodies, especially around sexuality, is present in the experience of many women, both as mothers and as daughters/children or would-be mothers. The trend, ideologically and for individual women, has been to opt for asexual motherhood. Rossi and Rich argue strongly against the view that motherhood and sexuality are incompatible; other feminists, like Firestone and Friday, accept the traditional view of incompatibility yet, unlike the analysts, argue in favor of sexuality.[39]

The understandings of motherhood we have been describing are larger than life and seen only in extremes. For Dinnerstein, women's mothering generates conditions that threaten to destroy human existence. For DuPlessis, a feminist theory of motherhood must begin with the inextricable link of motherhood and death; motherhood, she says, relates to heaven and hell, and to speech and silence; the overcoming of the institution of motherhood will be the end of dualism. For Friday, we must choose to be sexual or maternal. For Firestone, we must either accept inequality or give up our reproductive biology.

Rage is an inevitable outcome of this extremism. Psychological theory and cultural ideology have focused on the harm that mothers can do to their children, and some feminists continue to focus on this harm. We magnify the impact of one individual, the mother, and when the child in us suffers the inevitable frustrations of living, we blame our mothers. *My Mother/My Self* has been extraordinarily popular. It speaks to the daughter in all women and tells them that their problems are not political, social, personal, or, heaven forbid, caused by men; their problems are caused solely by their mothers. We are all prone to mother-hating, for we live in a society that says that mothers can and should do all for their children. Moreover, we were all mothered, and our psyches retain the imprint of these origins.

Other feminists move beyond this position. They describe aggression done to women first by men and then by children, which leads to mothers' rageful fantasies and behaviors. Children's aggression in this model is expectation as much as actuality. Starting from the belief that "perfect" mothering is both centrally important and possible, if only a mother is totally devoted and attentive, as these feminists become mothers, or imagine being mothers, they fear the experience as all-consuming and come unconsciously and consciously to resent, fear, and feel devoured by their children. The outcome is the powerful aggressive feelings and behaviors and preoccupation with death we described above. The outcome also is to experience a total and overwhelming isolation of self with child.

Thus, we can see a progressive logic to feminist themes about motherhood, a logic that moves a woman from an identification as daughter or child to an identification as mother. Drawing from and reflecting a cultural ideology and infantile sense of infantile need and maternal responsibility for the outcomes of child rearing, feminists begin by identifying with the child and blaming the mother, or by expecting her to be more than perfect. Cultural ideology and fantasy can also lead to idealization of maternal life from the point of view of the mother, as in the writing of Rossi and Rich. More often, the belief in total infantile need and maternal responsibility, and identification with the angry child, lead to a maternal identification that is in its turn full of rage and fear, and a sense that the conditions of patriarchy totally oppress mothers and isolate them with their children.

Feminism and Mothering: Moving beyond a Politics of Primary Process

Where does this analysis lead us? In our identities as women, theoretically and programmatically, feminists need to move beyond the extremist assumptions and fantasies we have described. Insofar as we treat mothers as larger than life, omnipotent, all-powerful, or all-powerless, and motherhood as intimately connected to death, we deny mothers the complexity of their lives, their selfhood, their agency in creating from institutional context and experienced feelings. We deny them their place in a two-way relationship with their children, manifold relationships with the rest of the world; and we deny ourselves as mothers. But insofar as mothers are women, this involves a denial of all women as active subjects and a denial and split in our self-identities as children/daughters and people as well. This reflexively self-denying split of self from mother who is a fantasy partially accounts for the ambivalence and anger found in much of this writing.

As political beings, we must also question our involvement in child-centered assumptions about mothers. As individuals we can lament the past, wish we had gotten more than we had, wish we had been "better" mothered, and so forth. Although this stance may provide some temporary catharsis, it does not in itself help us to understand what we might do, personally or politically, in the present. We may think "our mothers" got us into this situation, but this knowledge alone can never tell us how to get out of it. Catharsis and rage may be a first step to political activity or working to change one's situation, but by themselves they lead nowhere. Rather, they trap us in our private psychical reality, and they dissipate energy.

In particular, feminists need to be especially self-conscious about the way they draw upon fantasy to inform theory and politics. Much of the feminist writing we have considered puts forth fantasy, or primary-process thinking as the whole of reality or as a self-evident basis for theory and politics.[40] Fantasies are obviously fundamental experiences, and we must take them into account in creating a feminism that speaks to women's lives, but they cannot in themselves constitute theory or justify political choices. We need to analyze and reflect upon them, to allow secondary-process thinking to mediate and interpret primary-process reality. Moreover, it is not enough simply to claim that a particular fantasy, feeling, or behavior is a product of patriarchy, or women's oppression, and that therefore it cannot be further evaluated.

A striking instance of the problem created by accepting fantasy as the self-evident basis of theory or politics—of believing that it is enough to know that a woman's feeling or behavior is a product of her oppression—is a peculiar preoccupation with and moral paralysis around acts of maternal violence in some of the accounts discussed. In the case of violence against women, feminists have been outraged. We have focused on the fact of this violence and have worked to protect women from the wife beater, rapist, and assaulter. We have been properly angered by research and policies whose goal is to understand the individual motivations and causes of this violence rather than to eliminate it and protect its victims. By contrast, when we read Rich on maternal violence, Millett on maternal torture-murder, and the rampant aggression conveyed in the *Feminist Studies* issue, we find that maternal violence is described but not opposed. These writings focus on the cause and motivation of maternal violence—"patriarchy"—to the exclusion of the fact of the violence.

The preoccupation with fantasies and their sources in oppression has embroiled us in violence, has allowed us to understand but not to condemn it, as we do in the case of violence against women. This preoccupation does not allow for the necessary political and moral argument that people, even within oppressive systems, can choose among a variety of actions; that although unreflected-upon feeling may determine action, it need not.

These accounts thus reflect the assumption that any act motivated by an internal emotional state, if that state reacts to women's oppression, is by definition political. Further, they lead to the conclusion that all acts motivated in this way are equally correct as political actions. But it is inadequate to imply that women's fantasies are automatically an extension of the personal that is political. Consider, for example, an abused wife who has murderous fantasies toward an abusive husband and kills him. We might call her act political, and we would in many circumstances defend her in the courts. But most of us would have preferred that she had left him and started a new life with the aid of a support group or shelter for battered wives. We would consider this a better individual and political strategy. That the personal is political, that we can understand motherhood as experience and institution, implies that fantasies and feelings inform but do not directly determine our thoughtful, analyzed political decisions and judgments. The feminist accounts of mothering we discussed do not take that step. They do not move beyond seeing personal experience (feeling) and political institution (patriarchy) as absolute.

Recent feminist writing on motherhood has moved us forward in many areas. Adrienne Rich has transformed our ability to locate the many facets of motherhood as institution and has written powerfully of the complexity of maternal feeling and experience. Other feminists have called attention to the constraints, if not horrors, of mothering in a male-dominant society that devalues mothering, a society in which many mothers have no economic, communal, familial, or medical resources. Dorothy Dinnerstein persuaded many feminists of the serious consequences of exclusively female mothering. The *Feminist Studies* special issue, Nancy Friday, and Jane Lazarre have all revealed how overwhelmed women may feel as mothers or as daughters of mothers. Rich, Rossi, and Lazarre have begun to articulate for us, sometimes in idealized ways (or ways that threaten to maintain the equation of woman and mother), what a nonpatriarchal motherhood or nurturance might be.

But all this writing has been limited in a particular way: feminist theories of motherhood have not been able to move further because, as we have suggested, they are trapped in the dominant cultural assumptions and fantasies about mothering, *which in turn* rest on fantasied and unexamined notions of child development. Feminists have analyzed assumptions and biases in various disciplines, and feminism early on led us to notice cultural assumptions about gender (e.g., about sexual orientation) in society. But feminists have been trying to build a theory of mothering without examining or noticing that a theory of mothering requires a theory of childhood and child development as well.

Instead of developing this theory, feminists have built their theories of mothering on the dominant cultural and psychological assumptions about childhood. Drawing on psychoanalysis, these assumptions include an idealization of early infancy, in which development is seen exclusively as a painful process. The baby is most peaceful in utero, and birth is the first trauma and fraught with inevitable anxiety. There is now a trend toward trying to take the edge off this experience by nonviolent birth. After initial bonding to a primary caretaker—a process both fragile and portentous—the infant begins the slow and often reluctant process of individuation, separation, and growth. Infantile rage, frustration, anxiety, loss, and fear spur emotional and cognitive development. Total dependency gives way to ambivalent independence, insatiable needs are grudgingly put aside when faced with reality, and impulses are tamed and controlled.

In this account children inevitably grow up with a residue of rage against those who frustrate their needs, even though they can grow up only if their needs are frustrated. In this model of development, mother and child are adversaries. The good mother helps the child grow up for his or her own good, and we expect and therefore allow children to be furious with their mothers for doing so. Rich's discussion of children's needs suggests such a model, as does Jane Flax's lack of differentiation between needs and wants. Dinnerstein's argument is based on the inevitable adversary relationship of parent and child. Her recommendation for shared parenting stems from her wish that the inevitable rage toward caretakers be shared between women and men.

A second set of assumptions in some feminist work draws from a simple role-learning theory of development. In the writings of Friday, Firestone, and Arcana we find the notion that children (daughters) are victims and recipients of pressures from their mothers in particular and from the culture in general. Mothers and the culture expect the repression of sexuality, feminine passivity and dependence, and docile role acceptance; and daughters passively conform to these expectations.

These models of child development seriously constrain feminist accounts of mothering. We would suggest that feminists draw upon and work to develop theories of child development that are interactive and that accord the infant and child agency and intentionality, rather than characterize it as a passive reactor to drives or environmental pressures. We need to build theories that recognize collaboration and compromise as well as conflict. We should look to theories that stress relational capacities and experiences instead of insatiable, insistent drives; to theories in which needs do not equal wants; in which separation is not equivalent to deprivation, and in which autonomy is different from abandonment; in which the child is thought to have some interest in growth and development. We need to separate what we take to be the infant's or child's subjective feelings from a more inclusive appraisal of the state of the infant or child. And we need theories that examine how the tie to primary caretakers develops and changes for both caretakers and child, and that examine the rewards of noninfantile modes of relating and cognizing. We must begin to look at times other than infancy in the developmental life span and relationships over time to people other than the mother to get a more accurate picture of what growing up is about.[41]

In the feminist writing we have discussed, there is an extraordinary current of energy and searching. To the extent that these accounts speak to shared feelings, they communicate with other women. The fantasy of the perfect mother, however, has led to the cultural oppression of women in the interest of a child whose needs are also fantasied. Although feminists did not invent this vision of motherhood and childhood, they have borrowed it. Feminist views of mothering, as mother and as daughter, have united infantile fantasies and a culturally child-centered perspective with a myth of maternal omnipotence, creating a totalistic, extreme, yet fragmented view of mothering and the mother-child relation in which both mother and child are paradoxically victim yet omnipotent. To begin to transform the relations of parenting and the relations of gender, to begin to transform women's lives, we must move beyond the myths and misconceptions embodied in the fantasy of the perfect mother.

Notes

1. The authors we discuss are all white and (broadly) professional/middle class. Thus they do not necessarily represent the whole feminist spectrum. We are focusing on certain dominant *themes* in several major feminist analyses of motherhood, but do not claim to discuss all aspects of those works or all feminist writing on motherhood. Although we are often critical of the work we discuss, we have also learned from and been moved by some of this writing.

2. Nancy Friday, *My Mother/My Self* (New York: Delacorte Press; 1977).

3. Ibid., 105.

4. Ibid., 133, 145.

5. Ibid., 147, 157.

6. Ibid., 83.

7. Judith Arcana, *Our Mother's Daughters* (Berkeley, Calif.: Shameless Hussy Press, 1979).

8. Dorothy Dinnerstein, *The Mermaid and the Minotaur* (New York: Harper & Row, 1976).

9. Ibid., 83, 85.

10. Ibid., 28.

11. Ibid., 161, 164.

12. Ibid., 81.

13. Ibid., 253. Nancy Chodorow's *The Reproduction of Mothering* (Berkeley and Los Angeles: University of California Press, 1978) has some important similarities with Dinnerstein's argument. Both books focus on the psychological meanings and consequences of women's mothering, and both argue that male and female parenting is essential for social change. Further, both take the stand that the conflicts typically found in relationships between adult men and women in our culture are grounded in the fact that both sexes are mothered by women. We are not considering Chodorow's argument here because we believe it is significantly different in ways that make it not relevant to our argument. Although Chodorow argues that women's mothering is perhaps the central feature in the reproduction of gender inequality, she also specifies the outcome of mothering in a way that leaves some autonomy to other aspects of cultural and social life. She does not take the

extremist, portentous position of Dinnerstein and, in fact, has been criticized unfavorably on that score. As part of our argument holds that extremism in the analysis of mothering hurts feminist understanding and politics, we are more comfortable with this less apocalyptic approach.

14. Friday, *My Mother/My Self*, 69, 113.

15. Arcana, *Our Mothers' Daughters*, 37.

16. Jane Flax, "The Conflict between Nurturance and Autonomy in Mother-Daugher Relationships and within Feminism," *Feminist Studies* 4, no. 2 (June 1978): 171–89.

17. Ibid., 175.

18. Adrienne Rich, *Of Woman Born: Motherhood as Experience and Institution* (New York: Norton, 1976); Alice S. Rossi, "Maternalism, Sexuality, and the New Feminism," in *Contemporary Sexual Behavior*, ed. Joseph Zubin and John Money (Baltimore: Johns Hopkins University Press, 1973); idem, 'A Biosocial Perspective on Parenting,' *Daedalus* 106, no. 2 (1977): 1–31; and idem, "Considering 'A Biosocial Perspective on Parenting': Reply by Alice Rossi," *Signs* 4, no. 4 (Summer 1979): 712–17. Rich has been lauded and idealized by many feminists, whereas Rossi, also a feminist, has been criticized for making antifeminist arguments. Rossi's work, put forth in several articles, is not nearly as theoretically complete or comprehensive as Rich's, but we cite them together because their accounts are remarkably similar in their fundamentals. Both decry the patriarchal alienation of women from their maternal bodies and mothering experiences; both link motherhood and sexuality (see below); both advocate compensatory training for men even while suggesting that women's maternal nature is in some way unique.

19. Rich, *Of Woman Born*, 292.

20. Shulamith Firestone, *The Dialectic of Sex* (New York: Morrow, 1970).

21. *Feminist Studies*, 4, no. 2, special issue, "Toward a Feminist Theory of Motherhood" (June 1978).

22. Rachel Blau DuPlessis, "Washing Blood," *Feminist Studies* 2 (June 1978): 1–12.

23. Kate Millett, *The Basement: Meditations on a Human Sacrifice* (New York: Simon & Schuster, 1979).

24. Jane Lazarre, *The Mother Knot* (New York: Dell, 1976).

25. Phyllis Chesler's *With Child: A Diary of Motherhood* (New York: Crowell, 1979) echoes many of these themes in a more straightforward autobiographical manner.

26. Ruth H. Bloch, "American Feminine Ideals in Transition: The Rise of the Moral Mother, 1785–1815," *Feminist Studies* 2 (June 1978): 100–126.

27. See, for instance, Dinnerstein, *Mermaid and the Minotaur;* Norman O. Brown, *Life against Death* (Middletown, Conn.: Wesleyan University Press, 1959); and Lloyd de Mause, ed., *The History of Childhood* (New York: Psychohistory Press, 1974).

28. David Levy, *Maternal Overprotection* (New York: Columbia University Press, 1943); Philip Wylie, *Generation of Vipers* (New York: Farrar, Rinehart, 1942); Erik Erikson, *Childhood and Society* (New York: Norton, 1950); Theodore Lidz, Stephen Fleck, and Alice R. Cornelison, *Schizophrenia and the Family* (New York: International Universities Press, 1965); Joseph C. Rheingold, *The Fear of Being a Woman: A Theory of Maternal Destructiveness* (New York: Grune & Stratton, 1964); Philip E. Slater, *The Pursuit of*

Loneliness (Boston: Beacon Press, 1970); Philip E. Slater, *Earthwalk* (New York: Bantam, 1974); and Christopher Lasch, *Haven in a Heartless World: The Family Besieged* (New York: Basic Books, 1977), 153.

29. For a more extended discussion of the issue of maternal blame in the psychological literature, see Susan Contratto Weisskopf, "Maternal Guilt and Mental Health Professionals: A Reconfirming Interaction," Michigan Occasional Paper, no. 5 (Ann Arbor: University of Michigan Women's Studies Program, 1978).

30. Selma Fraiberg, *Every Child's Birthright: In Defense of Mothering* (New York: Basic Books, 1977).

31. Benjamin Spock, *The Pocket Book of Baby and Child Care* (New York: Pocket Books, 1945, 1946, 1957, 1968); and D. W. Winnicott, *The Child, the Family, and the Outside World* (New York: Penguin Books, 1964).

32. Fraiberg, *Every Child's Birthright,* and T. Berry Brazelton, *Infants and Mothers: Differences in Development* (New York: Delacorte Press, 1969).

33. Frank Caplan, *The First Twelve Months of Life* (New York: Bantam Books, 1971); and Penelope Leach, *Your Baby and Child from Birth to Age Five* (New York: Knopf, 1978).

34. We are assuming in this argument that infants are at a stage of cognitive and ego development where they use concrete categories that are grossly affectively laden. With maturity, these categories become more elaborated, complicated, and subtle. See Jean Piaget, *The Construction of Reality in the Child* (New York: Basic Books, 1954); idem, *The Language and Thought of the Child* (New York: Humanities, 1959); W. R. D. Fairbairn, *An Object-Relations Theory of the Personality* (New York: Basic Books, 1952); Otto Kernberg, *Borderline Conditions and Pathological Narcissism* (New York: Jason Aronson, 1975); and idem, *Object Relations Theory and Clinical Psychoanalysis* (New York: Jason Aronson, 1976).

35. Rich, *Of Woman Born,* 4.

36. Rich's passionate, wide-ranging work has been the inspiration for much subsequent feminist writing on motherhood (see *Feminist Studies* special issue, June 1978, and *Frontiers* 3, special issue, "Mothers and Daughters" [Summer 1978]). We also see her work as a magnificent contribution. In some ways we feel that in criticizing it and expecting it to be even more perfect, we are reproducing the fantasy of the perfect mother. Nevertheless, we continue to think that it is problematic to look to the uniqueness and potential of women's maternal bodies and relationships, however broadly defined, for the perfectibility of women and society, and we are critical of theories of motherhood that begin from notions of need (see below).

37. Helen Deutsch, *The Psychology of Women,* vols. 1 and 2 (New York: Grune and Stratton, 1944, 1945).

38. Therese Benedek, Discussion of Sherfey's paper on female sexuality, *Journal of the American Psychoanalytic Association* 3 (1968): 424–48, and idem, "On the Psychobiology of Gender Identity," *Annual of Psychoanalysis* (New York: International Universities Press, 1976), 4:117–62.

39. See Susan (Contratto) Weisskopf, "Maternal Sexuality and Asexual Motherhood," *Signs* 5 (Summer 1980): 766–82, for a more detailed discussion of these issues. We suspect that infantile fantasies are also part of the root of notions of asexual motherhood.

40. Jessica Benjamin has suggested that we make this ideological and political work sound too easy. We do not mean to minimize the psychological processes involved in genuinely overcoming extreme feelings about mothers and mothering, the difficult struggle and growth involved in giving up infantile idealization and rage and learning to tolerate ambivalence. This process, Benjamin suggests, is something like forgiving and mourning one's should-be-perfect mother and one's should-have-been-perfect childhood. Our point here is that even if this difficult psychological work has not been accomplished, another struggle must go on: that against allowing these feelings to become the basis of theory or politics.

As we have argued, this lack of mediation or self-censorship, this putting forth of fantasy as final truth, is certainly not unique to feminist writing on motherhood. Writing and thinking about motherhood across the spectrum is rife with unexamined assumptions about maternal perfection, overwhelming rage, and so forth. We stress that such thinking is particularly problematic for feminists.

41. Psychoanalytic object relations theory stresses the relational affective development we have in mind. For feminist uses of this tradition, see Jessica Benjamin, "The Ends of Internalization: Adorno's Social Psychology," *Telos* 32 (Summer 1977): 42–64; idem, "Authority and the Family Revisited, or, a World without Fathers?" *New German Critique* 13 (Winter 1978): 35–57; Chodorow, *Reproduction of Mothering*, Chodorow, "Feminism and Difference: Gender, Relation, and Difference in Psychoanalytic Perspective," *Socialist Review* 46 (1979): 51–69; and Evelyn Fox Keller, "Gender and Science," *Psychoanalysis and Contemporary Thought* 1 (1978): 409–33. Cognitive developmental psychology in the Piagetian tradition gives the child agency in making something of its environment and an interest in development and change. For a feminist use of this tradition, see Carol Gilligan, "In a Different Voice: Women's Conceptions of the Self and of Morality," *Harvard Educational Review* 47 (November 1977): 481–517; idem, "Woman's Place in Man's Life Cycle," *Harvard Educational Review* 49 (Spring 1979): 431–46.

11

Black Women and Motherhood

PATRICIA HILL COLLINS

Just yesterday I stood for a few minutes at the top of the stairs leading to a white doctor's office in a white neighborhood. I watched one Black woman after another trudge to the corner, where she then waited to catch the bus home. These were Black women still cleaning somebody else's house or Black women still caring for somebody else's sick or elderly, before they came back to the frequently thankless chores of their own loneliness, their own families. And I felt angry and I felt ashamed. And I felt, once again, the kindling heat of my hope that we, the daughters of these Black women, will honor their sacrifice by giving them thanks. We will undertake, with pride, every transcendent dream of freedom made possible by the humility of their love.

—June Jordan[1]

June Jordan's words poignantly express the need for Black feminists to honor our mothers' sacrifice by developing an Afrocentric feminist analysis of Black motherhood. Until recently analyses of Black motherhood have largely been the province of men, both white and Black, and male assumptions about Black women as mothers have prevailed. Black mothers have been accused of failing to discipline their children, of emasculating their sons, of defeminizing their daughters, and of retarding their children's academic achievement.[2] Citing high rates of divorce, female-headed households, and out-of-wedlock births, white male scholars and their representatives claim that African-American mothers wield unnatural power in allegedly deteriorating family structures.[3] The African-American mothers observed by Jordan vanish from these accounts.

White feminist work on motherhood has failed to produce an effective critique of elite white male analyses of Black motherhood. Grounded in a white, middle-class women's standpoint, white feminist analyses have been profoundly affected by the limitations that

This essay first appeared in *Black Feminist Thought: Knowledge, Consciousness, and the Politics of Empowerment*, vol. 2 (Cambridge, Mass.: Unwin Hyman, 1990).

this angle of vision has on race.[4] While white feminists have effectively confronted white male analyses of their own experiences as mothers, they rarely challenge controlling images such as the mammy, the matriarch, and the welfare mother and therefore fail to include Black mothers "still cleaning somebody else's house or ... caring for somebody else's sick or elderly." As a result, white feminist theories have had limited utility for African-American women.[5]

In African-American communities the view has been quite different. As Barbara Christian contends, the "concept of motherhood is of central importance in the philosophy of both African and Afro-American peoples."[6] But in spite of its centrality, Black male scholars in particular typically glorify Black motherhood by refusing to acknowledge the issues faced by Black mothers who "came back to the frequently thankless chores of their own loneliness, their own families." By claiming that Black women are richly endowed with devotion, self-sacrifice, and unconditional love—the attributes associated with archetypal motherhood—Black men inadvertently foster a different controlling image for Black women, that of the "superstrong black mother."[7] In many African-American communities so much sanctification surrounds Black motherhood that "the idea that mothers should live lives of sacrifice has come to be seen as the norm."[8]

Far too many Black men who praise their own mothers feel less accountable to the mothers of their own children. They allow their wives and girlfriends to support the growing numbers of African-American children living in poverty.[9] Despite the alarming deterioration of economic and social supports for Black mothers, large numbers of young men encourage their unmarried teenaged girlfriends to give birth to children whose futures are at risk.[10] Even when they are aware of the poverty and struggles these women face, many Black men cannot get beyond the powerful controlling image of the superstrong Black mother in order to see the very real costs of mothering to African-American women. Michele Wallace describes the tenacity of this controlling image:

> I remember once I was watching a news show with a black male friend of mine who had a Ph.D. in psychology and was the director of an out-patient clinic. We were looking at some footage of a black woman.... She was in bed wrapped in blankets, her numerous small, poorly clothed children huddled around her. Her apartment

looked rat-infested, cramped, and dirty. She had not, she said, had
heat and hot water for days. My friend, a solid member of the middle class now but surely no stranger to poverty in his childhood, felt
obliged to comment . . . "That's a *strong* sister," as he bowed his
head in reverence.[11]

The absence of a fully articulated Afrocentric feminist standpoint
on motherhood is striking but not particularly surprising. While
Black women have produced insightful critiques of both white male
and white feminist analyses of motherhood,[12] we have paid far less
attention to Black male views. This silence partly reflects the self-
imposed restrictions that accompany African Americans' efforts to
present a united front to the dominant group. Part of Black women's
reluctance to challenge Black men's ideas in particular stems from the
vehement attacks sustained by those Black feminist scholars, such as
Michele Wallace, Alice Walker, and Ntozake Shange, who have been
perceived as critical of Black men.[13] But much of our silence ema-
nates from an unwillingness to criticize Black men's well-intentioned
efforts to defend and protect Black womanhood. Glorifying the
strong Black mother represents Black men's attempts to replace negative white male interpretations with positive Black male ones. But no
matter how sincere, externally defined definitions of Black womanhood—even those offered by sympathetic African-American men—
are bound to come with their own set of problems.

In the case of Black motherhood, the problems have been a stifling
of dialogue among African-American women and the perpetuation of
troublesome, controlling images, both negative and positive. As Renita Weems observes: "We have simply sat and nodded while others
talked about the magnificent women who bore and raised them and
who, along with God, made a way out of no way. . . . We paid to hear
them lecture about the invincible strength and genius of the Black
mother, knowing full well that the image can be as bogus as the one
of the happy slave."[14]

African-American women need an Afrocentric feminist analysis of
motherhood that debunks the image of "happy slave," whether the
white-male-created "matriarch" or the Black-male-perpetuated "superstrong Black mother." Some of the classic sociological and ethnographic work on African-American families gives a comprehensive
sense of how Black women mother.[15] This emphasis on Black

women's actions has recently been enriched by an outpouring of research on Black women's ideas by Black women scholars.[16] When coupled with the explorations of Black women's consciousness extant in Black women's autobiographies, fiction, and Black feminist literary criticism, these sources offer the rich conceptual terrain of a Black women's standpoint from which an Afrocentric feminist analysis of African-American motherhood can emerge.[17]

Exploring a Black Women's Standpoint on Mothering

The institution of Black motherhood consists of a series of constantly renegotiated relationships that African-American women experience with one another, with Black children, with the larger African-American community, and with themselves. These relationships occur in specific locations such as the individual households that make up African-American extended family networks, as well as in Black community institutions.[18] Moreover, just as Black women's work and family experiences varied during the transition from slavery to the post–World War II political economy, how Black women define, value, and shape Black motherhood as an institution shows comparable diversity.

Black motherhood as an institution is both dynamic and dialectical. An ongoing tension exists between efforts to mold the institution of Black motherhood to benefit systems of race, gender, and class oppression and efforts by African-American women to define and value our own experiences with motherhood. The controlling images of the mammy, the matriarch, and the welfare mother and the practices they justify are designed to oppress. In contrast, motherhood can serve as a site where Black women express and learn the power of self-definition, the importance of valuing and respecting ourselves, the necessity of self-reliance and independence, and a belief in Black women's empowerment. This tension leads to a continuum of responses. Some women view motherhood as a truly burdensome condition that stifles their creativity, exploits their labor, and makes them partners in their own oppression. Others see motherhood as providing a base for self-actualization, status in the Black community, and a catalyst for social activism. These alleged contradictions can exist side by side in African-American communities and families and even within individual women.

Embedded in these changing relationships are five enduring themes that characterize a Black women's standpoint on Black motherhood. For any given historical movement, the particular form that Black women's relationships with one another, children, community, and themselves actually take depends on how this dialectical relationship between the severity of oppression facing African-American women and our actions in resisting that oppression is expressed.

Bloodmothers, Othermothers, and Women-Centered Networks

In African-American communities, fluid and changing boundaries often distinguish biological mothers from other women who care for children. Biological mothers, or bloodmothers, are expected to care for their children. But African and African-American communities have also recognized that vesting one person with full responsibility for mothering a child may not be wise or possible. As a result, othermothers—women who assist bloodmothers by sharing mothering responsibilities—traditionally have been central to the institution of Black motherhood.[19]

The centrality of women in African-American extended families reflects both a continuation of West African cultural values and functional adaptations to race and gender oppression.[20] This centrality is not characterized by the absence of husbands and fathers. Men may be physically present and/or have well-defined and culturally significant roles in the extended family, and the kin unit may be woman-centered. Bebe Moore Campbell's parents separated when she was small. Even though she spent the school year in the North Philadelphia household maintained by her grandmother and mother, Campbell's father assumed an important role in her life. "My father took care of me," Campbell remembers. "Our separation didn't stunt me or condemn me to a lesser humanity. His absence never made me a fatherless child. I'm not fatherless now."[21] In woman-centered kin units such as Campbell's—whether a mother-child household unit, a married couple household, or a larger unit extending over several households—the centrality of mothers is not predicated on male powerlessness.[22]

Organized, resilient, women-centered networks of bloodmothers and othermothers are key in understanding this centrality. Grandmothers, sisters, aunts, or cousins act as othermothers by taking on child-care responsibilities for one another's children. When needed, temporary child-care arrangements can turn into long-term care or informal adoption.[23] Despite strong cultural norms encouraging women to become biological mothers, women who choose not to do so often receive recognition and status from othermother relationships that they establish with Black children.

In African-American communities these women-centered networks of community-based child care often extend beyond the boundaries of biologically related individuals and include "fictive kin."[24] The civil rights activist Ella Baker describes how informal adoption by othermothers functioned in the rural southern community of her childhood:

My aunt who had thirteen children of her own raised three more. She had become a midwife, and a child was born who was covered with sores. Nobody was particularly wanting the child, so she took the child and raised him . . . and another mother decided she didn't want to be bothered with two children. So my aunt took one and raised him . . . they were part of the family.[25]

Even when relationships are not between kin or fictive kin, African-American community norms traditionally were such that neighbors cared for one another's children. Sara Brooks, a southern domestic worker, describes the importance that the community-based child care a neighbor offered her daughter had for her: "She kept Vivian and she didn't charge me nothin either. You see, people used to look after each other, but now it's not that way. I reckon it's because we all was poor, and I guess they put theirself in the place of the person that they was helpin."[26] Brooks's experiences demonstrate how the African-American cultural value placed on cooperative child care traditionally found institutional support in the adverse conditions under which so many Black women mothered.

Othermothers are key not only in supporting children but also in helping bloodmothers who, for whatever reason, lack the preparation or desire for motherhood. In confronting racial oppression, maintaining community-based child care and respecting othermothers who assume child-care responsibilities serve a critical function in African-American communities. Children orphaned by sale or death of their parents under slavery, children conceived through rape, children of young mothers, children born into extreme poverty or to alcoholic or drug-addicted mothers, or children who for other reasons cannot remain with their bloodmothers have all been supported by othermothers, who, like Ella Baker's aunt, take in additional children even when they have enough of their own.

Young women are often carefully groomed at an early age to become othermothers. As a ten-year-old, civil rights activist Ella Baker learned to be an othermother by caring for the children of a widowed neighbor: "Mama would say, 'You must take the clothes to Mr. Powell's house, and give so-and-so a bath.' The children were running wild. . . . The kids . . . would take off across the field. We'd chase them down, and bring them back, and put 'em in the tub, and wash 'em off, and change clothes, and carry the dirty ones home, and wash them. Those kind of things were routine."[27]

Many Black men also value community-based child care but exercise these values to a lesser extent. Young Black men are taught how to care for children.[28] During slavery, for example, Black children under age ten experienced little division of labor. They were dressed alike and performed similar tasks. If the activities of work and play are any indication of the degree of gender role differentiation that existed among slave children, "then young girls probably grew up minimizing the difference between the sexes while learning far more about the differences between the races."[29] Differences among Black men and women in attitudes toward children may have more to do with male labor force patterns. As Ella Baker observes, "my father took care of people too, but . . . my father had to work."[30]

Historically, community-based child care and the relationships among bloodmothers and othermothers in women-centered networks have taken diverse institutional forms. In some polygynous West African societies, the children of the same father but different mothers referred to one another as brothers and sisters. While a strong bond existed between the biological mother and her child—one so strong that, among the Ashanti for example, "to show disrespect towards one's mother is tantamount to sacrilege"—children could be disciplined by any of their other "mothers."[31] Cross-culturally, the high status given to othermothers and the cooperative nature of child-care arrangements among bloodmothers and othermothers in Caribbean and other Black societies gives credence to the importance that people of African descent place on mothering.[32]

Although the political economy of slavery brought profound changes to enslaved Africans, cultural values concerning the importance of motherhood and the value of cooperative approaches to child care continued. While other women served as nurses and mid-wives, their most common occupation was caring for the children of parents who worked.[33] Informal adoption of orphaned children reinforced the importance of social motherhood in African-American communities.[34]

The relationship between bloodmothers and othermothers survived the transition from a slave economy to postemancipation southern rural agriculture. Children in southern rural communities were not solely the responsibility of their biological mothers. Aunts, grandmothers, and others who had time to supervise children served as othermothers.[35] The significant status women enjoyed in family networks and in African-American communities continued to be linked to their bloodmother and othermother activities.

The entire community structure of bloodmothers and othermothers is under assault in many inner-city neighborhoods, where the very fabric of African-American community life is being eroded by illegal drugs. But even in the most troubled communities, remnants of the othermother tradition endure. Bebe Moore Campbell's 1950s North Philadelphia neighborhood underwent some startling changes when crack cocaine flooded the streets in the 1980s. Increases in birth defects, child abuse, and parental neglect left many children without care. But some residents, such as Miss Nee, continue the othermother tradition. After raising her younger brothers and sisters and five children of her own, Miss Nee cares for three additional children whose families fell apart. Moreover, on any given night Miss Nee's house may be filled by up to a dozen children because she has a reputation for never turning away a needy child.

Traditionally, community-based child care certainly has been functional for African-American communities and for Black women. The Black feminist theorist Bell Hooks suggests that the relationships among bloodmothers and othermothers may have greater theoretical importance than currently recognized:

This form of parenting is revolutionary in this society because it takes place in opposition to the ideas that parents, especially mothers, should be the only childrearers. . . . This kind of shared responsibility for child care can happen in small community settings where people know and trust one another. It cannot happen in those settings if parents regard children as their "property," their possession.[36]

The resiliency of women-centered family networks illustrates how traditional cultural values—namely, the African origins of community-based child care—can help people cope with and resist oppression. By continuing community-based child care, African-American women challenge one fundamental assumption underlying the capitalist system itself: that children are "private property" and can be disposed of as such. Notions of property, child care, and gender differences in parenting styles are embedded in the institutional arrangements of any given political economy. Under the property model stemming from capitalist patriarchal families, parents may not literally assert that their children are pieces of property, but their parenting may reflect assumptions analogous to those they make in connection with property.[37] For example, the exclusive parental "right" to discipline children as parents see fit, even if discipline borders on abuse, parallels the widespread assumption that property owners may dispose of their property without consulting members of the larger community. By seeking the larger community as responsible for children and by giving othermothers and other nonparents "rights" in child rearing, African Americans challenge prevailing property relations. It is in this sense that traditional bloodmother/othermother relationships in women-centered networks are "revolutionary."

Mothers, Daughters, and Socialization for Survival

Black mothers of daughters face a troubling dilemma. On one hand, to ensure their daughters' physical survival, mothers must teach them to fit into systems of oppression. For example, as a young girl the Black activist Ann Moody questioned why she was paid so little for the domestic work she began at age nine, why Black women domestics were sexually harassed by their white male employers, why no one would explain the activities of the National Association for the Advancement of Colored People to her, and why whites had so much more than Blacks. But her mother refused to answer her questions and actually chastised her for questioning the system and stepping out of her "place."[38] Like Ann Moody, Black daughters learn to expect to work, to strive for an education so they can support themselves, and to anticipate carrying heavy responsibilities in their families and communities because these skills are essential to their own survival and that of those for whom they will eventually be responsible.[39] A New Yorker, Michele Wallace, recounts: "I can't remember when I first learned that my family expected me to work, to be able to take care of myself when I grew up. . . . It had been drilled into me that the best and only sure support was self-support."[40] Mothers also know that if their daughters uncritically accept the limited opportunities offered Black women, they become willing participants in their own subordination. Mothers may have ensured their daughters' physical survival, but at the high cost of their emotional destruction.

On the other hand, Black daughters with strong self-definitions and self-valuations who offer serious challenges to oppressive situations may not physically survive. When Ann Moody became active in the early 1960s in sit-ins and voter registration activities, her mother first begged her not to participate and then told her not to come home because she feared the whites in Moody's hometown would kill her. Despite the dangers, mothers routinely encourage Black daughters to develop skills to confront oppressive conditions. Learning that they will work and that education is a vehicle for advancement can also be seen as ways of enhancing positive self-definitions and self-valuations in Black girls. Emotional strength is essential, but not at the cost of physical survival.

The historian Elsa Barkley Brown captures this delicate balance Black mothers negotiate by pointing out that her mother's behavior demonstrated the "need to teach me to live my life one way and, at the same time, to provide all the tools I would need to live it quite differently."[41] Black daughters must learn how to survive in interlocking structures of race, class, and gender oppression while rejecting and transcending those same structures. In order to develop these skills in their daughters, mothers demonstrate varying combinations of behaviors devoted to ensuring their daughters' survival—such as providing them with basic necessities and protecting them in dangerous environments—to helping their daughters go further than mothers themselves were allowed to go.

This special vision of Black mothers may grow from the nature of work women have done to ensure Black children's survival. These work experiences have provided Black women with a unique angle of vision, a particular perspective on the world to be passed on to Black daughters. African and African-American women have long integrated economic self-reliance with mothering. In contrast to the cult of true womanhood, in which work is defined as being in opposition to and incompatible with motherhood, work for Black women has been an important and valued dimension of Afrocentric definitions of Black motherhood. Sara Brooks describes the powerful connections that economic self-reliance and mothering had in her childhood: "When I was about nine I was nursin my sister Sally—I'm about seven or eight years older than Sally. And when I would put her to sleep, instead of me goin somewhere and sit down and play, I'd get my little old hoe and get out there and work right in the field around the house."[42]

Mothers who are domestic workers or who work in proximity to whites may experience a unique relationship with the dominant group. For example, African-American women domestics are exposed to all the intimate details of the lives of their white employers. Working for whites offers domestic workers a view from the inside and exposes them to ideas and resources that might aid in their children's upward mobility. In some cases domestic workers form close, long-lasting relationships with their employers. But domestic workers also encounter some of the harshest exploitation confronting women of color. The work is low paid, has few benefits, and exposes women to the threat and reality of sexual harassment. Black domestics could see the dangers awaiting their daughters.

Willi Coleman's mother used a Saturday-night hair-combing ritual to impart a Black women's standpoint on domestic work to her daughters:

> Except for special occasions mama came home from work early on Saturdays. She spent six days a week mopping, waxing and dusting other women's houses and keeping out of reach of other women's husbands. Saturday nights were reserved for "taking care of them girls" hair and the telling of stories. Some of which included a recitation of what she had endured and how she had triumphed over "folks that were lower than dirt" and "no-good snakes in the grass." She combed, patted, twisted and talked, saying things which would have embarrassed or shamed her at other times.[43]

Bonnie Thornton Dill's study of the child-rearing goals of domestic workers illustrates how African-American women see their work as both contributing to their children's survival and instilling values that will encourage their children to reject their proscribed "place" as Blacks and strive for more. Providing a better chance for their children was a dominant theme among Black women. Domestic workers described themselves as "struggling to give their children the skills and training they did not have; and as praying that opportunities which had not been open to them would be open to their children."[44] But the women also realized that while they wanted to communicate the value of their work as part of the ethics of caring and personal accountability, the work itself was undesirable. Bebe Moore Campbell's grandmother and college-educated mother stressed the importance of education. Campbell remembers, "[they] wanted me to Be Somebody, to be the second generation to live out my life as far away from a mop and scrub brush and Miss Ann's floors as possible."[45]

Understanding this goal of balancing the need for the physical survival of their daughters with the vision of encouraging them to transcend the boundaries confronting them explains many apparent contradictions in Black mother-daughter relationships. Black mothers are often described as strong disciplinarians and overly protective; yet these same women manage to raise daughters who are self-reliant and assertive. To explain this apparent contradiction, Gloria Wade-Gayles suggests that Black mothers

> do not socialize their daughters to be "passive" or "irrational." Quite the contrary, they socialize their daughters to be independent, strong and self-confident. Black mothers are suffocatingly protective and domineering precisely because they are determined to mold their daughters into whole and self-actualizing persons in a society that devalues Black women.[46]

African-American mothers place a strong emphasis on protection, either by trying to shield their daughters as long as possible from the penalties attached to their race, class, and gender status or by teaching them skills of independence and self-reliance so that they will be able to protect themselves. Consider the following verse from a traditional blues song:

> *I ain't good lookin' and ain't got waist-long hair*
> *I say I ain't good lookin' and I ain't got waist-long hair*
> *But my mama gave me something that'll take me anywhere.*[47]

Unlike white women, symbolized by "good looks" and "waist-long hair," Black women have been denied male protection. Under such conditions it becomes essential that Black mothers teach their daughters skills that will "take them anywhere."

Black women's autobiographies and fiction can be read as texts revealing the multiple ways that African-American mothers aim to shield their daughters from the demands of being Black women in oppressive conditions. Michele Wallace describes her growing understanding of how her mother viewed raising Black daughters in Harlem: "My mother has since explained to me that since it was obvious her attempt to protect me was going to prove a failure, she was determined to make me realize that as a black girl in white America I was going to find it an uphill climb to keep myself together."[48] In discussing the mother-daughter relationship in Paule Marshall's *Brown Girl, Brownstones,* Rosalie Troester catalogues the ways mothers have aimed to protect their daughters and the impact this may have on relationships themselves:

> Black mothers, particularly those with strong ties to their community, sometimes build high banks around their young daughters, isolating them from the dangers of the larger world until they are old and strong enough to function as autonomous women. Often these dikes are religious, but sometimes they are built with education, family, or the restrictions of a close-knit and homogeneous community. . . . This isolation causes the currents between Black mothers and daughters to run deep and the relationship to be fraught with an emotional intensity often missing from the lives of women with more freedom.[49]

Michele Wallace's mother built banks around her headstrong adolescent daughter by institutionalizing her in a Catholic home for troubled girls. Wallace went willingly, believing, "I thought at the time that I would rather live in hell than be with my mother."[50] But years later Wallace's evaluation of her mother's decision changed: "Now that I know my mother better, I know that her sense of powerlessness made it all the more essential to her that she take radical action."[51]

African-American mothers try to protect their daughters from the dangers that lie ahead by offering them a sense of their own unique self-worth. Many contemporary Black women writers report the experience of being singled out, of being given a sense of specialness at an early age that encouraged them to develop their talents. My own mother marched me to the public library at age five, helped me get my first library card, and told me that I could do anything if I learned how to read. In discussing the works of Paule Marshall, Dorothy West, and Alice Walker, Mary Helen Washington observes that all three writers make special claims about the roles their mothers played in the development of their creativity: "The bond with their mothers is such a fundamental and powerful source that the term 'mothering the mind' might have been coined specifically to define their experiences as writers."[52]

Black women's efforts to provide a physical and psychic base for their children can affect mothering styles and the emotional intensity of Black mother-daughter relationships. As Gloria Wade-Gayles points out, "mothers in Black women's fiction are strong and devoted . . . they are rarely affectionate."[53] For example, in Toni Morrison's *Sula,* Eva Peace's husband ran off, leaving her with three small children and no money. Despite her feelings, "the demands of feeding her three children were so acute she had to postpone her anger for two years until she had both the time and energy for it."[54] Later in the novel Eva's daughter Hannah asks, "Mamma, did you ever love us?"[55] Eva angrily replies, "What you talkin' bout did I love you girl I stayed alive for you."[56] For far too many Black mothers, the demands of providing for children in interlocking systems of oppression are sometimes so demanding that they have neither the time nor the patience for affection. And yet most Black daughters love and admire their mothers and are convinced that their mothers truly love them.[57]

Black daughters raised by mothers grappling with hostile environments have to come to terms with their feelings about the difference between the idealized versions of maternal love extant in popular culture and the strict and often troubled mothers in their lives. For a daughter, growing up means developing a better understanding that even though she may desire more affection and greater freedom, her mother's physical care and protection are acts of maternal love. Ann Moody describes her growing awareness of the cost her mother paid as a domestic worker who was a single mother of three. Watching her mother sleep after the birth of another child, Moody remembers:

> For a long time I stood there looking at her. I didn't want to wake her up. I wanted to enjoy and preserve that calm, peaceful look on

her face, I wanted to think she would always be happy. . . . Adline and Junior were too young to feel the things I felt and know the things I knew about Mama. They couldn't remember when she and Daddy separated. They had never heard her cry at night as I had or worked and helped as I had done when we were starving.[58]

Moody initially sees her mother as a strict disciplinarian, a woman who tries to protect her daughter by withholding information. But as Moody matures and better understands the oppression in her community, her ideas change. On one occasion Moody left school early the day after a Black family had been brutally murdered by local whites. Moody's description of her mother's reaction reflects her deepening understanding: "When I walked in the house Mama didn't even ask me why I came home. She just looked at me. And for the first time I realized she understood what was going on within me or was trying to anyway."[59]

Another example of a daughter's efforts to understand her mother is offered in Renita Weems's account of coming to grips with maternal desertion. In the following passage Weems struggles with the difference between the stereotypical image of the superstrong Black mother and her own alcoholic mother's decision to leave her children: "My mother loved us. I must believe that. She worked all day in a department store bakery to buy shoes and school tablets, came home to curse out neighbors who wrongly accused her children of any impropriety (which in an apartment complex usually meant stealing), and kept her house cleaner than most sober women."[60] Weems concludes that her mother loved her because she provided for her to the best of her ability.

Othermothers often help to defuse the emotional intensity of relationships between bloodmothers and their daughters. In recounting how she dealt with the intensity of her relationship with her mother, Weems describes the women teachers, neighbors, friends, and othermothers she turned to—women who, she observes, "did not have the onus of providing for me, and so had the luxury of talking to me."[61] Cheryl West's household included her brother, her lesbian mother, and Jan, her mother's lover. Jan became an othermother to West: "Yellow-colored, rotund and short in stature, Jan was like a second mother. . . . Jan braided my hair in the morning, mother worked two jobs and tucked me in at night. Loving, gentle, and fastidious in the domestic arena, Jan could be a rigid disciplinarian. . . .

To the outside world . . . she was my 'aunt' who happened to live with us. But she was much more involved and nurturing than any of my 'real' aunts."[62]

June Jordan offers an eloquent analysis of one daughter's realization of the high personal cost African-American women can pay in providing an economic and emotional foundation for their children. In the following passage Jordan offers a powerful testament of how she came to see that her mother's work was an act of love:

As a child I noticed the sadness of my mother as she sat alone in the kitchen at night. . . . Her woman's work never won permanent victories of any kind. It never enlarged the universe of her imagination or her power to influence what happened beyond the front door of our house. Her woman's work never tickled her to laugh or shout or dance. But she did raise me to respect her way of offering love and to believe that hard work is often the irreducible factor for survival, not something to avoid. Her woman's work produced a reliable home base where I could pursue the privileges of books and music. Her woman's work invented the potential for a completely different kind of work for us, the next generation of Black women: huge, rewarding hard work demanded by the huge, new ambitions that her perfect confidence in us engendered.[63]

Community Othermothers and Political Activism

Black women's experiences as othermothers provide a foundation for Black women's political activism. Nurturing children in Black extended-family networks stimulates a more generalized ethic of caring and personal accountability among African-American women, who often feel accountable to all the Black community's children.

This notion of Black women as community othermothers for all Black children traditionally allowed African-American women to treat biologically unrelated children as if they were members of their own families. For example, sociologist Karen Fields describes how her grandmother, Mamie Garvin Fields, draws on her power as a community othermother when dealing with unfamiliar children: "She will say to a child on the street who looks up to no good, picking out a name at random, 'Aren't you Miz Pinckney's boy?' in that same reproving tone. If the reply is, 'No, *ma'am,* my mother is Miz Gadsden,' whatever threat there was dissipates."[64]

The use of family language in referring to members of the African-American community also illustrates this dimension of Black motherhood. In the following passage, Mamie Garvin Fields describes how she became active in surveying substandard housing conditions among African-Americans in Charleston. Note her explanation of why she uses family language:

> I was one of the volunteers they got to make a survey of the places where we were paying extortious rents for indescribable property. I said "we," although it wasn't Bob and me. We had our own home, and so did many of the Federated Women. Yet we still felt like it really was "we" living in those terrible places, and it was up to us to do something about them.[65]

Black women frequently describe Black children using family language. In recounting her increasingly successful efforts to teach a boy who had given other teachers problems, my daughter's kindergarten teacher stated, "You know how it can be—the majority of children in the learning disabled classes are *our children.* I know he didn't belong there, so I volunteered to take him." In their statements both women use family language to describe the ties that bind them as Black women to their responsibilities as members of an African-American community/family.

In explaining why the South Carolina Federation of Colored Women's Clubs founded a home for girls, Mrs. Fields observes, "We all could see that we had a responsibility for those girls: they were the daughters of our community coming up."[66] Mrs. Fields's activities as a community othermother on behalf of the "daughters" of her community represent an established tradition among educated Black women. Serving as othermothers to women in the Black community has a long history. A study of 108 of the first generation of Black club women found that three-quarters were married, three-quarters worked outside the home, but only one-fourth had children.[67] These women emphasized self-support for Black women, whether married or not, and realized that self-sufficient community othermothers were important. "Not all women are intended for mothers," declares an 1894 edition of the *Woman's Era.* "Some of us have not the temperament for family life. . . . Clubs will make women think seriously of their future lives, and not make girls think their only alternative is to marry."[68]

Black women writers also explore this theme of the African-American community othermother who nurtures the Black community. One of the earliest examples is found in Frances Ellen Watkins Harper's 1892 novel *Iola Leroy*. By rejecting an opportunity to marry a prestigious physician and dissociate herself from the Black community, nearly white Iola, the main character, chooses instead to serve the African-American community. Similarly, in Alice Walker's 1976 novel *Meridian* the main character rejects the controlling image of the "happy slave," the self-sacrificing Black mother, and chooses to become a community othermother. Giving up her biological child to the care of an othermother, Meridian gets an education, works in the civil rights movement, and eventually takes on responsibility for the children of a small southern town. She engages in a "quest that will take her beyond the society's narrow meaning of the word *mother* as a physical state and expand its meaning to those who create, nurture, and save life in social and psychological as well as physical terms."[69]

The sociologist Cheryl Gilkes suggests that community othermother relationships can be key in stimulating Black women's decisions to become community activists.[70] Gilkes asserts that many of the Black women community activists in her study became involved in community organizing in response to the needs of their own children and of those in their communities. The following comment is typical of how many of the Black women in Gilkes's study relate to Black children: "There were a lot of summer programs springing up for kids, but they were exclusive . . . and I found that most of *our kids* were excluded."[71] For many women what began as the daily expression of their obligations as community othermothers, as was the case for the kindergarten teacher, developed into full-fledged actions as community leaders.

This community othermother tradition also explains the "mothering the mind" relationships that can develop between Black women teachers and their Black women students. Unlike the traditional mentoring so widely reported in educational literature, this relationship goes far beyond that of providing students with either technical skills or a network of academic and professional contacts. Bell Hooks shares the special vision that teachers who see our work in community othermother terms can pass on to our students: "I understood from the teachers in those segregated schools that the work of any teacher committed to the full self-realization of students was necessarily and fundamentally radical, that ideas were not neutral, that to teach in a way that liberates, that expands consciousness, that awakens, is to challenge domination at its very core."[72] Like the mother-daughter relationship, this "mothering the mind" among Black women seeks to move toward the mutuality of a shared sisterhood that binds African-American women as community othermothers.

Community othermothers have made important contributions in building a different type of community in often hostile political and economic surroundings.[73] Community othermothers' actions demonstrate a clear rejection of separateness and individual interest as the basis of either community organization or individual self-actualization. Instead, the connectedness with others and common interest expressed by community othermothers models a very different value system, one whereby Afrocentric feminist ethics of caring and personal accountability move communities forward.

Motherhood as a Symbol of Power

Motherhood—whether bloodmother, othermother, or community othermother—can be invoked by African-American women as a symbol of power. Much of Black women's status in African-American communities stems not only from actions as mothers in Black family networks but from contributions as community othermothers.

Black women's involvement in fostering African-American community development forms the basis for community-based power. This is the type of power many African Americans have in mind when they describe the "strong Black women" they see around them in traditional African-American communities. Community othermothers work on behalf of the Black community by expressing ethics of caring and personal accountability that embrace conceptions of transformative power and mutuality.[74] Such power is transformative in that Black women's relationships with children and other vulnerable community members is not intended to dominate or control. Rather, its purpose is to bring people along, to—in the words of late nineteenth-century Black feminists—"uplift the race" so that vulnerable members of the community will be able to attain the self-reliance and independence essential for resistance.

When older African-American women invoke their power as community othermothers, the results can be quite striking. Karen Fields recounts a telling incident:

> One night . . . as Grandmother sat crocheting alone at about two in the morning, a young man walked into the living room carrying the portable TV from upstairs. She said, "Who are you looking for *this* time of night?" As Grandmother [described] the incident to me over the phone, I could hear a tone of voice that I know well. It said, "Nice boys don't do that." So I imagine the burglar heard his own mother or grandmother at that moment. He joined in the familial game just created: "Well, he told me that I could borrow it." "*Who* told you?" "John." "Um um, no *John* lives here. You got the wrong house."[75]

After this dialogue, the teenager turned around, went back upstairs, and returned the television.

In local African-American communities, community othermothers become identified as powerful figures through furthering the community's well-being. Sociologist Charles Johnson describes the behavior of an elderly Black woman at a church service in rural 1930s Alabama. Even though she was not on the program, the woman stood up to speak. The master of ceremonies rang for her to sit down, but she refused to do so claiming, "I am the mother of this church, and I will say what I please."[76] The master of ceremonies offered the following explanation to the congregation as to why he let the woman continue: "Brothers, I know you all honor Sister Moore. Course our time is short but she has acted as a mother to me. . . . Any time old folks get up I give way to them."[77]

The View from the Inside: The Personal Meaning of Mothering

Within African-American communities, women's innovative and practical approaches to mothering under oppressive conditions often bring power and recognition. But this situation should not obscure the costs of motherhood to many Black women. Black motherhood is fundamentally a contradictory institution. African-American communities value motherhood, but Black mothers' ability to cope with race, class, and gender oppression should not be confused with transcending those conditions. Black motherhood can be rewarding, but it can also extract high personal costs. The range of Black women's reactions to motherhood and the ambivalence that many Black women feel about mothering reflect motherhood's contradictory nature.

Certain dimensions of Black motherhood are clearly problematic. Coping with unwanted pregnancies and being unable to care for one's children is oppressive. Sara Brooks remembers, "I had babies one after another because I never knew how to avoid havin babies and I didn't ask nobody, so I didn't know nothin. . . . After I separated from my husband, I *still* didn't know nothin, so there come Vivian."[78] Brooks became pregnant again even though she was unmarried and had three children from a previous marriage whom she could not support. Brooks describes the strain placed on Black women who must mother under oppressive conditions: "I hated it. . . . I didn't want no other baby. I couldn't hardly take care of myself, and I had other kids I'da loved to have taken care of, and I couldn't do that."[79] Like Brooks, many Black women have children they really do not want. When combined with Black community values claiming that good Black women always want their children, ignorance about reproductive issues leaves many Black women with unplanned pregnancies and the long-term responsibilities of parenting.

Ann Moody's mother also did not celebrate her repeated pregnancies. Moody remembers her mother's feelings when her mother started "getting fat" and her boyfriend stopped coming by: "Again Mama started crying every night. . . . When I heard Mama crying at night, I felt so bad. She wouldn't cry until we were all in bed and she thought we were sleeping. Every night I would lie awake for hours listening to her sobbing quietly in her pillow. The bigger she got the more she cried, and I did too."[80] To her children, Moody's mother may have appeared to be the stereotypical strong Black mother, but Ann Moody was able to see the cost her mother paid for living with this controlling image.

Dealing with an unwanted pregnancy can have tragic consequences. All Sara Brooks could think about was "doing away with this baby." She self-medicated herself and almost died. But she was luckier than her mother. As Brooks recalls, "my momma, she got pregnant too close behind me—it was an unwanted pregnancy—and so she taken turpentine and she taken too much, I guess, and she died. She bled to death and died."[81] She was not alone. Prior to the 1973

Roe v. Wade U.S. Supreme Court decision that a woman's right to personal privacy gave her the right to decide whether or not to have an abortion, large numbers of women who died from illegal abortions were Black. In New York, for example, during the several years preceding the decriminalization of abortions, 80 percent of the deaths from illegal abortions involved Black and Puerto Rican women.[82]

Strong pronatalist values in African-American communities may stem in part from traditional Black values that vest adult status on women who become biological mothers. For many, becoming a biological mother is often seen as a significant first step toward womanhood. Annie Amiker, an elderly Black woman, describes the situation in the rural Mississippi of her childhood. When asked if there were many girls with out-of-wedlock children, she replied, "there was some but not many—not many because when you run upon a girl who had a child the other girls wouldn't have nothing to do with her ... she was counted as a grown person so she wasn't counted among the young people."[83] Joyce Ladner describes how this link between adult status and motherhood operates in low-income, urban communities: "If there was one common standard for becoming a woman that was accepted by the majority of the people in the community, it was the time when girls gave birth to their first child. This line of demarcation was extremely clear and separated the *girls* from the *women*."[84]

In spite of the high personal costs, Ann Moody's mother, Sara Brooks, and an overwhelming majority of unmarried Black adolescent mothers choose to keep their children.[85] Those women who give up their children can also pay high personal costs. In Alice Walker's *Meridian,* the fact that mothers cannot attend her prestigious Black women's college forces Meridian to choose between keeping her child and going to college. After relinquishing her child, Meridian suffers physiological and psychological illness. Although she knows that her son is better cared for by others, she feels "condemned, consigned to penitence for life," for she has committed the ultimate sin against Black motherhood. Knowing that she had parted with her baby when her enslaved maternal ancestors had done anything and everything to keep their children was almost too much for Meridian to bear.[86]

The pain of knowing what lies ahead for Black children while feeling powerless to protect them is another problematic dimension of Black mothering. Michele Wallace remembers, "I can understand why my mother felt desperate. No one else thought it would be particularly horrible if I got pregnant or got married before I had grown up, if I never completed college. I was a black girl."[87] Nineteen-year-old Harriet Jacobs, a slave mother, articulates the feelings of Black mothers who must raise their children in dangerous and impoverished environments: "When they told me my new-born babe was a girl, my heart was heavier than it had ever been before. Slavery is terrible for men; but it is far more terrible for women."[88] In a 1904 letter, a Black mother in the South wrote to a national magazine:

I dread to see my children grow. I know not their fate. Where the white girl has one temptation, mine will have many. Where the white boy has every opportunity and protection, mine will have few opportunities and no protection. It does not matter how good or wise my children may be, they are colored. When I have said that, all is said. Everything is forgiven in the South but color.[89]

Protecting Black children remains a primary concern of African-American mothers because Black children are at risk. Nearly 40 percent of all Black mothers receive no prenatal care in the first trimester of pregnancy. One in every eight Black infants has a low birth weight, a factor contributing to an infant mortality rate among Black babies that remains twice that for white infants. During the first year of life Black babies die from fires and burns at a rate 4.5 times greater than that of white infants. The number of cases of pediatric AIDS has doubled between 1986 and 1989, and more than 75 percent of children with AIDS are Black or Hispanic, more than half of them the offspring of intravenous drug users.[90] An anonymous mother expresses her concern for Black children:

I turn my eyes on the little children, and keep on praying that one of them will grow up at the right second, when the schoolteachers have time to say hello and give him the lessons he needs, and when they get rid of the building here and let us have a place you can breathe in and not get bitten all the time, and when the men can find work—because *they* can't have children, and so they have to drink or get on drugs to find some happy moments, and some hope about things.[91]

To this mother, even though her children are her hope, the conditions under which she must mother are intolerable.

Black mothers also pay the cost of giving up their own dreams of achieving full creative ability. Because many spend so much time feeding the physical needs of their children, as Alice Walker queries, "when . . . did my overworked mother have time to know or care about feeding the creative spirit?"[92] Much of that creativity goes into dimensions of Black culture that are relatively protected from the incursions of the dominant group. Many Black women blues singers, poets, and artists manage to incorporate their art into their daily responsibilities as bloodmothers and othermothers. But for far too many African-American women who are weighed down by the incessant responsibilities of mothering others, that creative spark never finds full expression.

Harriet Jacobs's autobiography gives a clear example of one mother's denial of her own self-actualization and illustrates the costs paid by Black mothers who assume the heavy responsibilities inherent in their bloodmother and othermother relationships. Jacobs desperately wanted to escape slavery but explains how having children created a particular dilemma:

> I could have made my escape alone; but it was more for my helpless children than for myself that I longed for freedom. Though the boon would have been precious to me, above all price, I would not have taken it at the expense of leaving them in slavery. Every trial I endured, every sacrifice I made for their sakes, drew them closer to my heart, and gave me fresh courage.[93]

Black mothers like those of Ann Moody and June Jordan and women like Harriet Jacobs and Sara Brooks are examples of women who gave up their freedom for the sake of their children. Community othermothers like Mamie Fields and Miss Nee pay a similar cost, not for the sakes of their own biological children but for the Black community's children.

Despite the obstacles and costs, motherhood remains a symbol of hope for many of even the poorest Black women. One anonymous mother describes how she feels about her children:

> To me, having a baby inside me is the only time I'm really alive. I know I can make something, do something, no matter what color

my skin is, and what names people call me. . . . You can see the little
one grow and get larger and start doing things, and you feel there
must be some hope, some chance that things will get better; because
there it is, right before you, a real, live, growing baby. . . . The baby
is a good sign, or at least he's *some* sign. If we didn't have that, what
would be the difference from death?[94]

Given the harshness of this mother's environment, her children offer
hope. They are all she has.

Mothering is an empowering experience for many African-
American women. Gwendolyn Brooks explores this issue of reproductive power in her 1953 novel *Maud Martha*. Maud Martha is
virtually silent until she gives birth to her daughter, when "pregnancy
and the birth of a child connect Maud to some power in herself, some
power to speak, to be heard, to articulate feelings."[95] Her child
serves as a catalyst for her movement into self-definition, self-
valuation, and eventual empowerment. Marita Golden describes a
similar experience that illustrates how the special relationship between mother and child can foster a changed definition of self and an
accompanying empowerment:

Now I belonged to me. No parents or husband claiming me. . . .
There was only my child who consumed and replenished me . . . my
son's love was unconditional and, as such, gave me more freedom
than any love I had known. . . . I at last accepted mama as my name.
Realized that it did not melt down any other designations. Discovered that it expanded them—and me.[96]

This special relationship that Black mothers have with their children
can also foster a creativity, a mothering of the mind and soul, for all
involved. It is this gift that Alice Walker alludes to when she notes,
"and so our mothers and grandmothers have, more often than not
anonymously, handed on the creative spark, the seed of the flower
they themselves never hoped to see."[97]

But what cannot be overlooked in work emphasizing mothers' influences on their children is how Black children affirm their mothers
and how important that affirmation can be in a society that deni-
grates Blackness and womanhood. In her essay "One Child of One's

Own," Alice Walker offers a vision of what African-American mother-child relationships can be:

> It is not my child who tells me: I have no femaleness white women must affirm. Not my child who says: I have no rights black men must respect. It is not my child who has purged my face from history and herstory, and left mystory just that, a mystery; my child loves my face and would have it on every page, if she could, as I have loved my own parents' faces above all others. . . . We are together, my child and I. Mother and child, yes, but *sisters* really, against whatever denies us all that we are.[98]

Notes

1. June Jordan, *On Call* (Boston: South End Press, 1985), 105.

2. Gloria Wade-Gayles, "She Who Is Black and Mother: On Sociology and Fiction, 1940–1970," in *The Black Woman,* ed. La Frances Rodgers-Rose (Beverly Hills, Calif.: Sage, 1980), 89–106.

3. Daniel Patrick Moynihan, *The Negro Family: The Case For National Action* (Washington, D.C.: GPO, 1965), and Maxine Baca Zinn, "Family, Race, and Poverty in the Eighties," in this volume.

4. Nancy Chodorow, "Family Structure and Feminine Personality," in *Woman, Culture, and Society,* ed. Michelle Zimbalist Rosaldo and Louise Lamphere (Stanford, Calif.: Stanford University Press, 1974), 43–66; idem, *The Reproduction of Mothering* (Berkeley and Los Angeles: University of California Press, 1978); Jane Flax, "The Conflict between Nurturance and Autonomy in Mother-Daughter Relationships and within Feminism," *Feminist Studies* 4, no. 2 (1978): 171–89; and Nancy Chodorow and Susan Contratto, "The Fantasy of the Perfect Mother," in this volume.

5. Gloria Joseph, "Black Mothers and Daughters: Traditional and New Perspectives," *Sage: A Scholarly Journal on Black Women* 1, no. 2 (1984): 17–21.

6. Barbara Christian, *Black Feminist Criticism: Perspective on Black Women Writers* (New York: Pergamon Press, 1985), 213.

7. Robert Staples, *The Black Woman in America* (Chicago: Nelson-Hall, 1973), and Daryl Dance, "Black Eve or Madonna? A Study of the Antithetical Views of the Mother in Black American Literature," in *Sturdy Black Bridges: Visions of Black Women in Literature,* ed. Roseann Bell, Bettye Parker, and Beverly Guy-Sheftall (Garden City, N.Y.: Anchor/Doubleday, 1979), 123–32.

8. Christian, *Black Feminist Criticism,* 234.

9. Franklin E. Frazier, *The Negro Family in the United States* (New York: Dryden Press, 1948); Linda Burnham, "Has Poverty Been Feminized in Black America?," *Black Scholar*

16, no. 2 (1985): 14–24; U.S. Department of Commerce, Bureau of the Census, *Money Income and Poverty Status of Families and Persons in the United States, 1985*, series P-60, no. 154 (Washington, D.C.: GPO, 1986); and idem, *Money Income of Households, Families, and Persons in the United States, 1987* series P-60, no. 162 (Washington, D.C.: GPO, 1989).

10. Joyce Ladner, *Tomorrow's Tomorrow: The Black Woman* (Garden City, N.Y.: Doubleday, 1971); Joyce Ladner and Ruby Morton Gourdine, "Intergenerational Teenage Motherhood: Some Preliminary Findings," *Sage* 1, no. 2 (1984): 22–24; and Margaret C. Simms, *The Choices That Young Black Women Make: Education, Employment, and Family Formation*, Working Paper no. 190 (Wellesley, Mass.: Center for Research on Women, Wellesley College, 1988).

11. Michele Wallace, *Black Macho and the Myth of the Superwoman* (New York: Dial Press, 1978), 108–9.

12. Mae King, "The Politics of Sexual Stereotypes," in *Black Scholar* 4, nos. 6–7 (1973): 12–23; Angela Y. Davis, *Women, Race, and Class* (New York: Random House, 1981); Cheryl Townsend Gilkes, "From Slavery to Social Welfare: Racism and the Control of Black Women," in *Class, Race, and Sex: The Dynamics of Control*, ed. Amy Swerdlow and Hanna Lessinger (Boston: G.K. Hall, 1983), 288–300; and Bell Hooks, *Ain't I a Woman: Black Women and Feminism* (Boston: South End Press, 1981).

13. Robert Staples, "The Myth of Black Macho: A Response to Angry Black Feminists," in *Black Scholar* 10, no. 6 (1979): 24–33.

14. Renita Weems, " 'Hush, Mama's Gotta Go Bye Bye': A Personal Narrative," *Sage* 1, no. 2 (1984): 27.

15. Melville J. Herskovits, *The Myth of the Negro Past* (Boston: Beacon Press, 1941; 1958); Virginia Meyer Young, "Family and Childhood in a Southern Negro Community," *American Anthropologist* 72, no. 32 (1970): 269–88; Ladner, *Tomorrow's Tomorrow*; Carol B. Stack, *All Our Kin: Strategies for Survival in a Black Community* (New York: Harper & Row, 1974); Joyce Aschenbrenner, *Lifelines: Black Families in Chicago* (Prospect Heights, Ill.: Waveland Press, 1975); Molly C. Dougherty, *Becoming a Woman in Rural Black Culture* (New York: Holt, Rinehart & Winston, 1978); and Bonnie Thornton Dill, " 'The Means to Put My Children Through': Child-Rearing Goals and Strategies among Black Female Domestic Servants," in *The Black Woman*, ed. Rodgers-Rose, 107–23.

16. Carrie Allen McCray, "The Black Woman and Family Roles," in *The Black Woman*, ed. Rodgers-Rose, 67–78; Gloria Joseph, "Black Mothers and Daughters: Their Roles and Functions in American Society," in *Common Differences*, ed. Gloria Joseph and Jill Lewis (Garden City, N.Y.: Anchor Books, 1981), 75–126; idem, "Black Mothers and Daughters: Traditional and New Perspectives"; Judith Rollins, *Between Women: Domestics and Their Employers* (Philadelphia: Temple University Press, 1985); Deborah Gray White, *Ar'n't I a Woman? Female Slaves in the Plantation South* (New York: Norton, 1985); *Sage* 1, no. 2, special issue, "Mothers and Daughters I" (1984); and *Sage* 4, no. 2, special issue, "Mothers and Daughters II" (1987).

17. Alice Walker, *In Search of Our Mothers' Gardens* (New York: Harcourt Brace Jovanovich, 1983); Mary Helen Washington, "I Sign My Mother's Name: Alice Walker, Dorothy West, and Paule Marshall," in *Mothering the Mind: Twelve Studies of Writers and their Silent Partners*, ed. Ruth Perry and Martine Watson Broronley (New York: Holmes & Meier, 1984), 143–63; and Christian, *Black Feminist Criticism*.

18. Elmer Martin and Joanne Mitchell Martin, *The Black Extended Family* (Chicago: University of Chicago Press, 1978), and Niara Sudarkasa, "Interpreting the African Heritage in Afro-American Family Organization," in *Black Families*, ed. Harriette Pipes McAdoo (Beverly Hills, Calif.: Sage, 1981), 37–53.

19. Rosalie Riegle Troester, "Turbulence and Tenderness: Mothers, Daughters, and 'Othermothers' in Paule Marshall's *Brown Girl, Brownstones*," *Sage* 1, no. 2 (1984): 13–16.

20. Nancy Tanner, "Matrifocality in Indonesia and Africa and among Black Americans," in *Woman, Culture, and Society*, ed. Rosaldo and Lamphere, 129–56; Stack, *All Our Kin*; Aschenbrenner, *Lifelines*; Martin and Martin, *The Black Extended Family*; Sudarsaka, "Interpreting the African Heritage in Afro-American Family Organization"; and Bernice Johnson Reagon, "African Diaspora Women: The Making of Cultural Workers," in *Women in Africa and the African Diaspora*, ed. Rosalyn Terborg-Penn, Sharon Harley, and Andrea Benton Rushing (Washington, D.C.: Howard University Press, 1987), 167–80.

21. Bebe Moore Campbell, *Sweet Summer: Growing Up with and without My Dad* (New York: Putnam, 1989), 271.

22. Tanner, "Matrifocality."

23. Stack, *All Our Kin*, and Herbert Gutman, *The Black Family in Slavery and Freedom, 1750–1925* (New York: Random House, 1976).

24. Stack, *All Our Kin*.

25. Ellen Cantarow, *Moving the Mountain: Women Working for Social Change* (Old Westbury, N.Y.: Feminist Press, 1980), 59.

26. Thordis Simonsen, ed., *You May Plow Here: The Narrative of Sara Brooks* (New York: Touchstone, 1986), 181.

27. Cantarow, *Moving the Mountain*.

28. Young, "Family and Childhood," and Diane K. Lewis, "The Black Family: Socialization and Sex Roles," *Phylon* 36, no. 3 (1975): 221–37.

29. White, *Ar'n't I a Woman?*, 94.

30. Cantarow, *Moving the Mountain*, 60.

31. Meyer Fortes, "Kinship and Marriage among the Ashanti," in *African Systems of Kinship and Marriage*, ed. A. R. Radcliffe-Brown and Daryll Forde (New York: Oxford University Press, 1950), 263.

32. Edith Clarke, *My Mother Who Fathered Me*, 2d ed. (London: Allen & Unwin, 1966); Demitri B. Shimkin, Edith M. Shimkin, and Dennis A. Frate, eds., *The Extended Family in Black Societies* (Chicago: Aldine, 1978); Niara Sudarsaka, "Female Employment and Family Organization in West Africa," in *The Black Woman Cross-Culturally*, ed. Filomina Chioma Steady (Cambridge, Mass.: Schenkman, 1981); and idem, "Interpreting the African Heritage in Afro-American Family Organization."

33. White, *Ar'n't I a Woman?*

34. Gutman, *The Black Family in Slavery and Freedom*.

35. Young, "Family and Childhood in a Southern Negro Community," 269–88, and Dougherty, *Becoming a Woman in Rural Black Culture*.

36. Bell Hooks, *From Margin to Center* (Boston: South End Press, 1984), 144.

37. Janet Farrell Smith, "Parenting as Property," in *Mothering: Essays in Feminist Theory,* ed. Joyce Trebilcot (Totawa, N.J.: Rowman & Allenheld, 1983), 199–212.

38. Ann Moody, *Coming of Age in Mississippi* (New York: Dell, 1968).

39. Ladner, *Tomorrow's Tomorrow,* and Joseph, "Black Mothers and Daughters: Their Roles and Functions in American Society."

40. Wallace, *Black Macho,* 89–90.

41. Elsa Barkley Brown, "African-American Women's Quilting: A Framework for Conceptualizing and Teaching African-American Women's History," *Signs* 14, no. 4 (1989): 929.

42. Simonsen, *You May Plow Here,* 86.

43. Willi Coleman, "Closets and Keepsakes," *Sage* 4, no. 2 (1987): 34.

44. Dill, " 'The Means to Put My Children Through,' " 110.

45. Campbell, *Sweet Summer,* 83.

46. Gloria Wade-Gayles, "She Who Is Black and Mother," 12.

47. Washington, "I Sign My Mother's Name," 144.

48. Wallace, *Black Macho,* 98.

49. Troester, "Turbulence and Tenderness," 13.

50. Wallace, *Black Macho,* 98.

51. Ibid.

52. Washington, "I Sign My Mother's Name," 144.

53. Wade-Gayles, "The Truths of Our Mothers' Lives: Mother-Daughter Relationships in Black Women's Fiction," *Sage* 1, no. 2 (1984): 10.

54. Toni Morrison, *Sula* (New York: Random House, 1974), 32.

55. Ibid., 67.

56. Ibid., 69.

57. Joseph, "Black Mothers and Daughters: Their Roles and Functions in American Society."

58. Moody, *Coming of Age in Mississippi,* 57.

59. Ibid., 136.

60. Weems, " 'Hush, Mama's Gotta Go Bye Bye,' " 26.

61. Ibid., 27.

62. Cheryl West, "Lesbian Daughter," *Sage* 4, no. 2 (1987): 43.

63. Jordan, *On Call,* 105.

64. Mamie Garvin Fields and Karen Fields, *Lemon Swamp and Other Places: A Carolina Memoir* (New York: Free Press, 1983), xvii.

65. Ibid., 195.

66. Ibid., 197.

67. Paula Giddings, *When and Where I Enter: The Impact of Black Women on Race and Sex in America* (New York: Morrow, 1984).

68. Ibid., 108.

69. Christian, *Black Feminist Criticism*, 242.

70. Cheryl Gilkes, " 'Holding Back the Ocean with a Broom': Black Women and Community Work," in *The Black Woman*, ed. Rodgers-Rose, 217–32; idem, "Successful Rebellious Professionals: The Black Women's Professional Identity and Community Commitment," *Psychology of Women Quarterly* 6, no. 3 (1982): 239–311; and idem, "Going Up for the Oppressed: The Career Mobility of Black Women Community Workers," *Journal of Social Issues* 39, no. 3 (1983): 115–39.

71. Gilkes, " 'Holding Back the Ocean with a Broom,' " 219.

72. Bell Hooks, *Talking Back: Thinking Feminist, Thinking Black* (Boston: South End Press, 1989), 50.

73. Reagon, "African Diaspora Women."

74. Eleanor H. Kuykendall, "Toward an Ethic of Nurturance: Luce Irigaray on Mothering and Power," in *Mothering*, ed. Treblicot, 263–74.

75. Fields and Fields, *Lemon Swap and Other Places*, xvii.

76. Charles S. Johnson, *Shadow of the Plantation* (Chicago: University of Chicago Press, 1934; 1979), 172.

77. Ibid., 173.

78. Simonsen, *You May Plow Here*, 174.

79. Ibid., 177.

80. Moody, *Coming of Age in Mississippi*, 46.

81. Simonsen, *You May Plow Here*, 160.

82. Davis, *Women, Race, and Class*.

83. Bettye J. Parker, "Mississippi Mothers: Roots," in *Sturdy Black Bridges*, ed. Bell, Parker, and Guy-Sheftall, 268.

84. Ladner, *Tomorrow's Tomorrow*, 212.

85. Simms, *The Choices That Young Black Women Make*.

86. Christian, *Black Feminist Criticism*.

87. Wallace, *Black Macho*, 98.

88. Harriet Jacobs, "The Perils of a Slave Woman's Life" (1860), in *Invented Lives: Narratives of Black Women, 1860–1960*, ed. Mary Helen Washington (Garden City, N.Y.: Anchor Books, 1987), 46.

89. Gerda Lerner, ed., *Black Women in White America: A Documentary History* (New York: Vintage Books, 1972), 158.

90. "Children of the Underclass," *Newsweek*, 11 September 1989, 27.

91. Lerner, *Black Women in White America*, 315.

92. Walker, *In Search of Our Mothers' Gardens*, 239.

93. Jacobs, "The Perils of a Slave Woman's Life," 59.

94. Lerner, *Black Women in White America*, 314.

95. Washington, *Invented Lives*, 395.

96. Marita Golden, *Migrations of the Heart* (New York: Ballantine, 1983), 240–41.

97. Walker, *In Search of Our Mothers' Gardens*, 240.

98. Alice Walker, "One Child of One's Own: A Meaningful Digression within the Work(s)," *Ms.*, August 1979, 75.

12

The Female World of Cards and Holidays: Women, Families, and the Work of Kinship

MICAELA DI LEONARDO

Why is it that the married women of America are supposed to write all the letters and send all the cards to their husbands' families? My old man is a much better writer than I am, yet he expects me to correspond with his whole family. If I asked him to correspond with mine, he would blow a gasket.

—Letter to Ann Landers

Women's place in man's life cycle has been that of nurturer, caretaker, and help-mate, the weaver of those networks of relationships on which she in turn relies.

—Carol Gilligan, *In a Different Voice*[1]

Feminist scholars in the past fifteen years have made great strides in formulating new understandings of the relations among gender, kinship, and the larger economy. As a result of this pioneering research, women are newly visible and audible, no longer submerged within their families. We see households as loci of political struggle, inseparable parts of the larger society and economy, rather than as havens from the heartless world of industrial capitalism.[2] And historical and cultural variations in kinship and family forms have become clearer with the maturation of feminist historical and social-scientific scholarship.

Two theoretical trends have been key to this reinterpretation of women's work and family domain. The first is the elevation to visibility of women's nonmarket activities—housework, child care, the servicing of men, and the care of the elderly—and the definition of all

Many thanks to Cynthia Costello, Rayna Rapp, Roberta Spalter-Roth, John Willoughby, and Barbara Gelpi, Susan Johnson, and Sylvia Yanagisako of *Signs* for their help with this article. I wish in particular to acknowledge the influence of Rayna Rapp's work on my ideas. Acknowledgement and gratitude to Carroll Smith-Rosenberg for my paraphrase of her title, "The Female World of Love and Ritual: Relations between Women in Nineteenth-Century America," *Signs* 1, no. 1 (Autumn 1975): 1–29.

This essay first appeared in *Signs: Journal of Women in Culture and Society* 12, no. 3 (1987).

these activities as *labor*, to be enumerated alongside and counted as part of overall social reproduction. The second theoretical trend is the nonpejorative focus on women's domestic or kin-centered networks. We now see them as the products of conscious strategy, as crucial to the functioning of kinship systems, as sources of women's autonomous power and possible primary sites of emotional fulfillment, and, at times, as the vehicles for actual survival and/or political resistance.[3]

Recently, however, a division has developed between feminist interpreters of the "labor" and the "network" perspectives on women's lives. Those who focus on women's work tend to envision women as sentient, goal-oriented actors, while those who concern themselves with women's ties to others tend to perceive women primarily in terms of nurturance, other-orientation—altruism. The most celebrated recent example of this division is the opposing testimony of historians Alice Kessler-Harris and Rosalind Rosenberg in the Equal Employment Opportunity Commission's sex discrimination case against Sears Roebuck and Company. Kessler-Harris argued that American women historically have actively sought higher-paying jobs and have been prevented from gaining them because of sex discrimination by employers. Rosenberg argued that American women in the nineteenth century created among themselves, through their domestic networks, a "women's culture" that emphasized the nurturance of children and others and the maintenance of family life and that discouraged women from competition over or heavy emotional investment in demanding, high-paid employment.[4]

I shall not here address this specific debate but, instead, shall consider its theoretical background and implications. I shall argue that we need to fuse, rather than to oppose, the domestic network and labor perspectives. In what follows, I introduce a new concept, the work of kinship, both to aid empirical feminist research on women, work, and family and to help advance feminist theory in this arena. I believe that the boundary-crossing nature of the concept helps to confound the self-interest/altruism dichotomy, forcing us from an either-or stance to a position that includes both perspectives. I hope in this way to contribute to a more critical feminist vision of women's lives and the meaning of family in the industrial West.

In my recent field research among Italian Americans in northern California, I found myself considering the relations between women's kinship and economic lives. As an anthropologist, I was concerned with people's kin lives beyond conventional American nuclear family or household boundaries. To this end, I collected individual and family life histories, asking about all kin and close friends and their activities. I was also very interested in women's labor. As I sat with women and listened to their accounts of their past and present lives, I began to realize that they were involved in three types of work: housework and child care, work in the labor market, and the work of kinship.[5]

By kin work I refer to the conception, maintenance, and ritual celebration of cross-household kin ties, including visits, letters, telephone calls, presents, and cards to kin; the organization of holiday gatherings; the creation and maintenance of quasi-kin relations; decisions to neglect or to intensify particular ties; the mental work of reflection about all these activities; and the creation and communication of altering images of family and kin vis-à-vis the images of others, both folk and mass media. Kin work is a key element that has been missing in the synthesis of the "household labor" and "domestic network" perspectives. In our emphasis on individual women's responsibilities within households and on the job, we reflect the common picture of households as nuclear units, tied perhaps to the larger social and economic system, but not to *each other.* We miss the point of telephone and soft drink advertising, of women's magazines' holiday issues, of commentators' confused nostalgia for the mythical American extended family: it is kinship contact *across households,* as much as women's work within them, that fulfills our cultural expectation of satisfying family life.

Maintaining these contacts, this sense of family, takes time, intention, and skill. We tend to think of human social and kin networks as the epiphenomena of production and reproduction: the social traces created by our material lives. Or, in the neoclassical tradition, we see them as part of leisure activities, outside an economic purview except insofar as they involve consumption behavior. But the creation and maintenance of kin and quasi-kin networks in advanced industrial societies is *work;* and, moreover, it is largely women's work.

The kin-work lens brought into focus new perspectives on my informants' family lives. First, life histories revealed that often the very existence of kin contact and holiday celebration depended on the presence of an adult woman in the household. When couples divorced or mothers died, the work of kinship was left undone; when women entered into sanctioned sexual or marital relationships with men in these situations, they reconstituted the men's kinship networks and organized gatherings and holiday celebrations. Middle-aged businessman Al Bertini, for example, recalled the death of his mother in his early adolescence: "I think that's probably one of the biggest losses in losing a family—yeah, I remember as a child when my Mom was alive . . . the holidays were treated with enthusiasm and love . . . after she died the attempt was there but it just didn't materialize." Later in life, when Al Bertini and his wife separated, his own and his son Jim's participation in extended-family contact decreased rapidly. But when Jim began a relationship with Jane Bateman, she and he moved in with Al, and Jim and Jane began to invite his kin over for holidays. Jane single-handedly planned and cooked the holiday feasts.

Kin work, then, is like housework and child care: men in the aggregate do not do it. It differs from these forms of labor in that it is harder for men to substitute hired labor to accomplish these tasks in the absence of kinswomen. Second, I found that women, as the workers in this arena, generally had much greater kin knowledge than did their husbands, often including more accurate and extensive knowledge of their husbands' families. This was true of both middle-aged and younger couples and surfaced as a phenomenon in my interviews in the form of humorous arguments and in wives' detailed additions to husbands' narratives. Nick Meraviglia, a middle-aged professional, discussed his Italian antecedents in the presence of his wife, Pina:

Nick: My grandfather was a very outspoken man, and it was reported he took off for the hills when he found out that Mussolini was in power.

Pina: And he was a very tall man; he used to have to bow his head to get inside doors.

Nick: No, that was my uncle.

Pina: Your grandfather too, I've heard your mother say.

Nick: My mother has a sister and a brother.

Pina: *Two* sisters!

Nick: You're right!

Pina: Maria and Angelina.

Women were also much more willing to discuss family feuds and crises and their own roles in them; men tended to repeat formulaic statements asserting family unity and respectability. (This was much less true for younger men.) Joe and Cetta Longhinotti's statements illustrate these tendencies. Joe responded to my question about kin relations: "We all get along. As a rule, relatives, you got nothing but trouble." Cetta, instead, discussed her relations with each of her grown children, their wives, her in-laws, and her own blood kin in detail. She did not hide the fact that relations were strained in several cases; she was eager to discuss the evolution of problems and to seek my opinions of her actions. Similarly, Pina Meraviglia told the following story of her fight with one of her brothers with hysterical laughter: "There was some biting and hair pulling and choking . . . it was terrible! I shouldn't even tell you." Nick, meanwhile, was concerned about maintaining an image of family unity and respectability.

Also, men waxed fluent while women were quite inarticulate in discussing their past and present occupations. When asked about their work lives, Joe Longhinotti and Nick Meraviglia, union baker and professional, respectively, gave detailed narratives of their work careers. Cetta Longhinotti and Pina Meraviglia, clerical and former clerical, respectively, offered only short descriptions focusing on factors of ambience, such as the "lovely things" sold by Cetta's firm.

These patterns are not repeated in the younger generation, especially among younger women, such as Jane Bateman, who have managed to acquire training and jobs with some prospect of mobility. These younger women, though, have *added* a professional and detailed interest in their jobs to a felt responsibility for the work of kinship.[6]

Although men rarely took on any kin-work tasks, family histories and accounts of contemporary life revealed that kinswomen often negotiated among themselves, alternating hosting, food-preparation, and gift-buying responsibilities—or sometimes ceding entire task clusters to one woman. Taking on or ceding tasks was clearly related to acquiring or divesting oneself of power within kin networks, but women varied in their interpretation of the meaning of this power. Cetta Longhinotti, for example, relied on the "family Christmas dinner" as a symbol of her central kinship role and was involved in painful negotiations with her daughter-in-law over the issue: "Last year she insisted—this is touchy. She doesn't want to spend the holiday dinner together. So last year we went there. But I still had my dinner the next day . . . I made a big dinner on Christmas Day, regardless of who's coming—candles on the table, the whole routine. I decorate the house myself too . . . well, I just feel that the time will come when maybe I won't feel like cooking a big dinner—she should take advantage of the fact that I feel like doing it now." Pina Meraviglia, in contrast, was saddened by the centripetal force of the developmental cycle but was unworried about the power dynamics involved in her negotiations with daughters- and mother-in-law over holiday celebrations.

Kin work is not just a matter of power among women but also of the mediation of power represented by household units.[7] Women often choose to minimize status claims in their kin work and to include numbers of households under the rubric of family. Cetta Longhinotti's sister Anna, for example, is married to a professional man whose parents have considerable economic resources, while Joe and Cetta have low incomes and no other well-off kin. Cetta and Anna remain close, talk on the phone several times a week, and assist their adult children, divided by distance and economic status, in remaining united as cousins.

Finally, women perceived housework, child care, market labor, the care of the elderly, and the work of kinship as competing responsibilities. Kin work was a unique category, however, because it was unlabeled and because women felt they could either cede some tasks to kinswomen and/or could cut them back severely. Women variously cited the pressures of market labor, the needs of the elderly, and their own desires for freedom and job enrichment as reasons for cutting back Christmas card lists, organized holiday gatherings, multifamily dinners, letters, visits, and phone calls. They expressed guilt and defensiveness about this cutback process and, particularly, about their failures to keep families close through constant contact and about their failures to create perfect holiday celebrations. Cetta Longhinotti, during the period when she was visiting her elderly mother every weekend in addition to working a full-time job, said of her grown children, "I'd have the whole gang here once a month, but I've been so busy that I haven't done that for about six months." And Pina Meraviglia lamented her insufficient work on family Christmases, "I wish I had really made it traditional . . . like my sister-in-law has special stories."

Kin work, then, takes place in an arena characterized simultaneously by cooperation and competition, by guilt and gratification. Like housework and child care, it is women's work, with the same lack of clear-cut agreement concerning its proper components: How often should sheets be changed? When should children be toilet trained? Should an aunt send a niece a birthday present? Unlike housework and child care, however, kin work, taking place across the boundaries of normative households, is as yet unlabeled and has no retinue of experts prescribing its correct forms. Neither home economists nor child psychologists have much to say about nieces' birthday presents. Kin work is thus more easily cut back without social interference. On the other hand, the results of kin work—frequent kin contact and feelings of intimacy—are the subject of considerable cultural manipulation as indicators of family happiness. Thus, women in general are subject to the guilt my informants expressed over cutting back kin-work activities.

Although many of my informants referred to the results of women's kin work—cross-household kin contacts and attendant ritual gatherings—as particularly Italian-American, I suggest that in fact this phenomenon is broadly characteristic of American kinship. We think of kin-work tasks such as the preparation of ritual feasts, responsibility for holiday card lists, and gift buying as extensions of women's domestic responsibilities for cooking, consumption, and nurturance. American men in general do not take on these tasks any more than they do housework and child care—and probably less, as these tasks have not yet been the subject of intense public debate. And my informants' gender breakdown in relative articulateness on kinship and workplace themes reflects the still-prevalent occupational segregation—most women cannot find jobs that provide enough pay, status, or promotion possibilities to make them worth focusing on—as well as women's perceived power within kinship networks. The common recognition of that power is reflected in Selma Greenberg's book on nonsexist child rearing. Greenberg calls mothers "press agents" who sponsor relations between their own children and other relatives; she advises a mother whose relatives treat her disrespectfully to deny those kin access to her children.[8]

Kin work is a salient concept in other parts of the developed world as well. Larissa Adler Lomnitz and Marisol Pérez Lizaur have found that "centralizing women" are responsible for these tasks and for communicating "family ideology" among upper-class families in Mexico City. Matthews Hamabata, in his study of upper-class families in Japan, has found that women's kin work involves key financial transactions. Sylvia Junko Yanagisako discovered that, among rural Japanese migrants to the United States, the maintenance of kin networks was assigned to women as the migrants adopted the American ideology of the independent nuclear family household. Maila Stivens notes that urban Australian housewives' kin ties and kin ideology "transcend women's isolation in domestic units."[9]

This is not to say that cultural conceptions of appropriate kin work do not vary, even within the United States. Carol B. Stack documents institutionalized fictive kinship and concomitant reciprocity networks among impoverished Black American women. Women in populations characterized by intense feelings of ethnic identity may feel bound to emphasize particular occasions—Saint Patrick's or Columbus Day—with organized family feasts. These constructs may be mediated by religious affiliation, as in the differing emphases on Friday or Sunday family dinners among Jews and Christians. Thus the personnel involved and the amount and kind of labor considered necessary for the satisfactory performance of particular kin-work tasks are likely to be culturally constructed.[10] But while the kin and quasi-kin universes and the ritual calendar may vary among women according to race or ethnicity, their general responsibility for maintaining kin links and ritual observances does not.

As kin work is not an ethnic or racial phenomenon, neither is it linked only to one social class. Some commentators on American family life still reflect the influence of work done in England in the 1950s and 1960s (by Elizabeth Bott and by Peter Willmott and Michael Young) in their assumption that working-class families are close and extended, while the middle class substitutes friends (or anomie) for family. Others reflect the prevalent family pessimism in their presumption that neither working- nor middle-class families have extended kin contact.[11] Insofar as kin contact depends on residential proximity, the larger economy's shifts will influence particular groups' experiences. Factory workers, close to kin or not, are likely to disperse when plants shut down or relocate. Small businesspeople or independent professionals may, however, remain resident in particular areas—and thus maintain proximity to kin—for generations, while professional employees of large firms relocate at their firms' behest. This pattern obtained among my informants.

In any event, cross-household kin contact can be and is effected at long distance through letters, cards, phone calls, and holiday and vacation visits. The form and functions of contact, however, vary according to economic resources. Stack and Brett Williams offer rich accounts of kin networks among poor Blacks and migrant Chicano farmworkers functioning to provide emotional support, labor, commodity, and cash exchange—a funeral visit, help with laundry, the gift of a dress or piece of furniture.[12] Far different in degree are exchanges such as the loan of a vacation home, a multifamily boating trip, or the provision of free professional services—examples from the kin networks of my wealthier informants. The point is that households, as labor- and income-pooling units, whatever their relative wealth, are somewhat porous in relation to others with whose members they share kin or quasi-kin ties. We do not really know how class differences operate in this realm; it is possible that they do so largely in terms of ideology. It may be, as David Schneider and Raymond T. Smith suggest, that the affluent and the very poor are more open in recognizing necessary economic ties to kin than are those who identify themselves as middle class.[13]

Recognizing that kin work is gender rather than class based allows us to see women's kin networks among all groups, not just among working-class and impoverished women in industrialized societies. This recognition in turn clarifies our understanding of the privileges and limits of women's varying access to economic resources. Affluent women can "buy out" of housework, child care—and even some kin-work responsibilities. But they, like all women, are ultimately responsible, and subject to both guilt and blame, as the administrators of home, children, and kin network. Even the wealthiest women must negotiate the timing and venue of holidays and other family rituals with their kinswomen. It may be that kin work is the core women's work category in which all women cooperate, while women's perceptions of the appropriateness of cooperation for housework, child care, and the care of the elderly varies by race, class, region, and generation.

But kin work is not necessarily an appropriate category of labor, much less gendered labor, in all societies. In many small-scale societies, kinship is the major organizing principle of all social life, and all contacts are by definition kin contacts.[14] One cannot, therefore, speak of labor that does not involve kin. In the United States, kin work as a separable category of gendered labor perhaps arose historically in concert with the ideological and material constructs of the moral mother/cult of domesticity and the privatized family during the course of industrialization in the eighteenth and nineteenth centuries. These phenomena are connected to the increase in the ubiquity of productive occupations *for men* that are not organized through kinship. This includes the demise of the family farm with the capitalization of agriculture and rural-urban migration; the decline of family recruitment in factories as firms grew, ended child labor, and began to assert bureaucratized forms of control; the decline of artisanal labor and of small entrepreneurial enterprises as large firms took greater and greater shares of the commodity market; the decline of the family firm as corporations—and their managerial work forces— grew beyond the capacities of individual families to provision them; and, finally, the rise of civil service bureaucracies and public pressure against nepotism.[15]

As men increasingly worked alongside non-kin, and as the ideology of separate spheres was increasingly accepted, perhaps the responsibility for kin maintenance, like that for child rearing, became gender-focused. Mary Ryan points out that "built into the updated family economy . . . was a new measure of voluntarism." This voluntarism, though, "perceived as the shift from patriarchal authority to domestic affection," also signaled the rise of women's moral responsibility for family life. Just as the "idea of fatherhood itself seemed almost to wither away" so did male involvement in the responsibility for kindred lapse.[16]

With postbellum economic growth and geographic movement, women's new kin burden involved increasing amounts of time and labor. The ubiquity of lengthy visits and of frequent letter writing among nineteenth-century women attests to this. And for visitors and for those who were residentially proximate, the continuing commonalities of women's domestic labor allowed for kinds of work sharing—nursing, child keeping, cooking, cleaning—that men, with their increasingly differentiated and controlled activities, probably could not maintain. This is not to say that some kin-related male productive work did not continue; my own data, for instance, show kin involvement among small businessmen in the present. It is, instead, to suggest a general trend in material life and a cultural shift that influenced even those whose productive and kin lives remained commingled. Yanagisako has distinguished between the realms of domestic and public kinship in order to draw attention to anthropology's relatively "thin descriptions" of the domestic (female) domain. Using her typology, we might say that kin work as gendered labor comes into existence within the domestic domain with the relative erasure of the domain of public, male kinship.[17]

Whether or not this proposed historical model bears up under further research, the question remains, Why do women do kin work? However material factors may shape activities, they do not determine how individuals may perceive them. And in considering issues of motivation, of intention, of the cultural construction of kin work, we return to the altruism versus self-interest dichotomy in recent feminist theory. Consider the epigraphs to this article. Are women kin workers the nurturant weavers of the Gilligan quotation, or victims, like the fed-up woman who writes to complain to Ann Landers? That is, are we to see kin work as yet another example of "women's culture" that takes the care of others as its primary desideratum? Or are we to see kin work as another way in which men, the economy, and the state extract labor from women without a fair return? And how do women themselves see their kin work and its place in their lives?

As I have indicated above, I believe that it is the creation of the self-interest/altruism dichotomy that is itself the problem here. My women informants, like most American women, accepted their primary responsibility for housework and the care of dependent children. Despite two major waves of feminist activism in this century, the gendering of certain categories of unpaid labor is still largely unaltered. These work responsibilities clearly interfere with some women's labor-force commitments at certain life-cycle stages; but, more important, women are simply discriminated against in the labor market and rarely are able to achieve wage and status parity with men of the same age, race, class, and educational background.[18]

Thus for my women informants, as for most American women, the domestic domain is not only an arena in which much unpaid labor must be undertaken but also a realm in which one may attempt to gain human satisfactions—and power—not available in the labor market. Anthropologists Jane Collier and Louise Lamphere have written compellingly on the ways in which varying kinship and economic structures may shape women's competition or cooperation with one another in domestic domains.[19] Feminists considering Western women and families have looked at the issue of power primarily in terms of husband-wife relations or psychological relations between parents and children. If we adopt Collier and Lamphere's broader canvas, though, we see that kin work is not only women's labor from which men and children benefit but also labor that women undertake in order to create obligations in men and children and to gain power over one another. Thus Cetta Longhinotti's struggle with her daughter-in-law over the venue of Christmas dinner is not just about a competition over altruism, it is also about the creation of future obligations. And thus Cetta's and Anna's sponsorship of their children's friendship with each other is both an act of nurturance and a cooperative means of gaining power over those children.

Although this was not a clear-cut distinction, those of my informants who were more explicitly antifeminist tended to be most invested in kin work. Given the overwhelming historical shift toward greater autonomy for younger generations and the withering of children's financial and labor obligations to their parents, this investment was in most cases tragically doomed. Cetta Longhinotti, for example, had repaid her own mother's devotion with extensive home nursing during the mother's last years. Given Cetta's general failure to direct her adult children in work, marital choice, religious worship, or even frequency of visits, she is unlikely to receive such care from them when she is older.

The kin-work lens thus reveals the close relations between altruism and self-interest in women's actions. As economists Nancy Folbre and Heidi Hartmann point out, we have inherited a Western intellectual tradition that both dichotomizes the domestic and public domains and associates them on exclusive axes such that we find it difficult to see self-interest in the home and altruism in the workplace.[20] But why, in fact, have women fought for better jobs if not, in part, to support their children? These dichotomies are procrustean beds that warp our understanding of women's lives both at home and at work. "Altruism" and "self-interest" are cultural constructions that are not necessarily mutually exclusive, and we forget this to our peril.

The concept of kin work helps to bring into focus a heretofore unacknowledged array of tasks that is culturally assigned to women in industrialized societies. At the same time, this concept, embodying notions of both love and work and crossing the boundaries of households, helps us to reflect on current feminist debates on women's work, family, and community. We newly see both the interrelations of these phenomena and women's roles in creating and maintaining those interrelations. Revealing the actual labor embodied in what we culturally conceive as love and considering the political uses of this labor helps to deconstruct the self-interest/altruism dichotomy and to connect more closely women's domestic and labor-force lives.

The true value of the concept, however, remains to be tested through further historical and contemporary research on gender, kinship, and labor. We need to assess the suggestion that gendered kin work emerges in concert with the capitalist development process; to probe the historical record for women's and men's varying and changing conceptions of it; and to research the current range of its cultural constructions and material realities. We know that household boundaries are more porous than we had thought—but they are undoubtedly differentially porous, and this is what we need to specify. We need, in particular, to assess the relations of changing labor processes, residential patterns, and the use of technology to changing kin work.

Altering the values attached to this particular set of women's tasks will be as difficult as are the housework, child-care, and occupational-segregation struggles. But just as feminist research in these latter areas is complementary and cumulative, so researching kin work should help us to piece together the home, work, and public-life landscape—to see the female world of cards and holidays as it is constructed and lived within the changing political economy. How female that world is to remain, and what it would look like if it were not sex-segregated, are questions we cannot yet answer.

Notes

1. Ann Landers letter printed in *Washington Post*, 15 April, 1983; Carol Gilligan, *In a Different Voice: Psychological Theory and Women's Development* (Cambridge, Mass.: Harvard University Press, 1982), 17.

2. Heidi I. Hartmann, "The Family as the Locus of Gender, Class, and Political Struggle: The Example of Housework," *Signs* 6, no. 3 (Spring 1981): 366–94, and Christopher Lasch, *Haven in a Heartless World: The Family Besieged* (New York: Basic Books, 1977).

3. Representative examples of the first trend include Joann Vanek, "Time Spent on Housework," *Scientific American* 231 (November 1974): 116–20; Ruth Schwartz Cowan, "A Case Study of Technological and Social Change: The Washing Machine and the Working Wife," in *Clio's Consciousness Raised*, ed. Mary Hartmann and Lois Banner (New York: Harper & Row, 1974), 245–53; Ann Oakley, *Women's Work: The Housewife, Past and Present* (New York: Vintage Books, 1974); Hartmann, "The Family"; and Susan Strasser,

Never Done: A History of American Housework (New York: Pantheon Books, 1982). Key contributions to the second trend include Louise Lamphere, "Strategies, Cooperation, and Conflict among Women in Domestic Groups," in *Women, Culture, and Society,* ed. Michelle Zimbalist Rosaldo and Louise Lamphere (Stanford, Calif.: Stanford University Press, 1974), 97–112; Mina Davis Caulfield, "Imperialism, the Family, and the Cultures of Resistance," *Socialist Revolution* 20 (October 1974): 67–85; Carroll Smith-Rosenberg, "The Female World of Love and Ritual: Relations between Women in Nineteenth-Century America," *Signs* 1, no. 1 (Autumn 1975): 1–29; Sylvia Junko Yanagisako, "Women-Centered Kin Networks and Urban Bilateral Kinship," *American Ethnologist* 4, no. 2 (1977): 207–26; Jane Humphries, "The Working Class Family, Women's Liberation and Class Struggle: The Case of Nineteenth Century British History," *Review of Radical Political Economics* 9 (Fall 1977): 25–41; Blanche Weisen Cook, "Female Support Networks and Political Activism: Lillian Wald, Crystal Eastman, Emma Goldman," in *A Heritage of Her Own,* ed. Nancy F. Cott and Elizabeth H. Pleck (New York: Simon & Schuster, 1979); Temma Kaplan, "Female Consciousness and Collective Action: The Case of Barcelona, 1910–1918," *Signs* 7, no. 3 (Spring 1982): 545–66.

4. On this debate, see Jon Weiner, "Women's History on Trial," *Nation* 241, no. 6 (7 September, 1985): 161, 176, 178–80; Karen J. Winkler, "Two Scholars' Conflict in Sears Sex-Bias Case Sets Off War in Women's History," *Chronicle of Higher Education* (5 February 1986), 1, 8; Rosalind Rosenberg, "What Harms Women in the Workplace," *New York Times,* 27 February 1986; Alice Kessler-Harris, "Equal Employment Opportunity Commission vs. Sears Roebuck and Company: A Personal Account," *Radical History Review* 35 (April 1986): 57–79.

5. Portions of the following analysis are reported in Micaela di Leonardo, *The Varieties of Ethnic Experience: Kinship, Class, and Gender among California Italian-Americans* (Ithaca, N.Y.: Cornell University Press, 1984), chap. 6.

6. Clearly, many women do, in fact, discuss their paid labor with willingness and clarity. The point here is that there are opposing gender tendencies in an identical interview situation, tendencies that are explicable in terms of both the material realities and current cultural constructions of gender.

7. Papanek has rightly focused on women's unacknowledged family status production, but what is conceived of as "family" shifts and varies (Hanna Papanek, "Family Status Production: The 'Work' and 'Non-Work' of Women," *Signs* 4, no. 4 [Summer 1979]: 775–81).

8. Selma Greenberg, *Right from the Start: A Guide to Nonsexist Child Rearing* (Boston: Houghton Mifflin, 1978), 147. Another example of indirect support for kin work's gendered existence is a recent study of university math students, which found that a major reason for women's failure to pursue careers in mathematics was the pressure of family involvement. Compare David Maines et al., *Social Processes of Sex Differentiation in Mathematics* (Washington, D.C.: National Institute of Education, 1981).

9. Larissa Adler Lomnitz and Marisol Pérez Lizaur, "The History of a Mexican Urban Family," *Journal of Family History* 3, no. 4 (1978): 392–409, esp. 398; Matthews Hamabata, *Crested Kimono: Power and Love in the Japanese Business Family* (Ithaca, N.Y.: Cornell University Press, 1990); Sylvia Junko Yanagisako, "Two Processes of Change in Japanese-American Kinship," *Journal of Anthropological Research* 31 (1975): 196–224; Maila Stivens, "Women and Their Kin: Kin, Class, and Solidarity in a Middle-Class Suburb of Sydney, Australia," in *Women United, Women Divided,* ed. Patricia Caplan and Janet M. Bujra (Bloomington: Indiana University Press, 1979), 157–84.

10. Carol B. Stack, *All Our Kin: Strategies for Survival in a Black Community* (New York: Harper & Row, 1974). These cultural constructions may, however, vary within ethnic/racial populations as well.

11. Elizabeth Bott, *Family and Social Network*, 2d ed. (New York: Free Press, 1971); Michael Young and Peter Willmott, *Family and Kinship in East London* (London: Routledge & Kegan Paul, 1957); and idem, *Family and Class in a London Suburb* (London: Routledge & Kegan Paul, 1960). Classic studies that presume this class difference are Herbert Gans, *The Urban Villagers: Group and Class in the Life of Italian-Americans* (New York: Free Press, 1962), and Mirra Komarovsky, *Blue-Collar Marriage* (New York: Random House, 1962). A recent example is Ilene Philipson, "Heterosexual Antagonism and the Politics of Mothering," *Socialist Review* 12, no. 6 (November–December 1982): 55–77. Edward Shorter, *The Making of the Modern Family* (New York: Basic Books, 1975), epitomizes the pessimism of the "family sentiments" school. See also Mary Lyndon Shanley, "The History of the Family in Modern England: Review Essay," *Signs* 4, no. 4 (Summer 1979): 740–50.

12. Stack, *All Our Kin*, and Brett Williams, "The Trip Takes Us: Chicano Migrants to the Prairie" (Ph.D. diss., University of Illinois at Urbana-Champaign, 1975).

13. David Schneider and Raymond T. Smith, *Class Differences and Sex Roles in American Kinship and Family Structure* (Englewood Cliffs, N.J.: Prentice-Hall, 1973), esp. 27.

14. See Nelson Graburn, ed., *Readings in Kinship and Social Structure* (New York: Harper & Row, 1971), esp. 3–4.

15. The moral mother/cult of domesticity is analyzed in Barbara Welter, "The Cult of True Womanhood, 1820–1860," *American Quarterly* 18, no. 2 (Summer 1966): 151–74; Nancy Cott, *The Bonds of Womanhood: "Women's Sphere" in New England, 1780–1835* (New Haven, Conn.: Yale University Press, 1977); and Ruth Bloch, "American Feminine Ideals in Transition: The Rise of the Moral Mother, 1785–1815," *Feminist Studies* 4, no. 2 (June 1978): 101–26. The description of the general political-economic shift in the United States is based on Harry Braverman, *Labor and Monopoly Capital: The Degradation of Work in the Twentieth Century* (New York: Monthly Review Press, 1974); Peter Dobkin Hall, "Family Structure and Economic Organization: Massachusetts Merchants, 1700–1850," in *Family and Kin in Urban Communities, 1700–1950*, ed. Tamara K. Hareven (New York: New Viewpoints, 1977), 38–61; Michael Anderson, "Family, Household, and the Industrial Revolution," in *The American Family in Social-Historical Perspective*, ed. Michael Gordon (New York: St. Martin's Press, 1978), 38–50; Tamara K. Hareven, *Amoskeag: Life and Work in an American Factory City* (New York: Pantheon Books, 1978); Richard Edwards, *Contested Terrain: The Transformation of the Workplace in the Twentieth Century* (New York: Basic Books, 1979); Mary Ryan, *The Cradle of the Middle Class: The Family in Oneida County, New York, 1790–1865* (Cambridge: Cambridge University Press, 1981); and Alice Kessler-Harris, *Out to Work: A History of Wage-Earning Women in the United States* (New York: Oxford University Press, 1982).

16. Ryan, *Cradle of the Middle Class*, 231–32.

17. Sylvia Junko Yanagisako, "Family and Household: The Analysis of Domestic Groups," *Annual Review of Anthropology* 8 (1979): 161–205.

18. See Donald J. Treiman and Heidi I. Hartmann, eds., *Women, Work, and Wages: Equal Pay for Jobs of Equal Value* (Washington, D.C.: National Academy Press, 1981).

19. Lamphere, "Strategies, Cooperation, and Conflict"; Jane Fishburne Collier, "Women in Politics," in *Women, Culture, and Society*, ed. Rosaldo and Lamphere, 89–96.

20. Nancy Folbre and Heidi I. Hartmann, "The Rhetoric of Self-Interest: Selfishness, Altruism, and Gender in Economic Theory," in *The Consequences of Economic Rhetoric*, ed. Arjo Klamer and Donald McCloskey (New York: Cambridge University Press, 1989).

13

Family Violence, Feminism, and Social Control

L I N D A   G O R D O N

In studying the history of family violence, I found myself also confronting the issue of social control, incarnated in the charitable "friendly visitors" and later professional child protection workers who composed the case records I was reading. At first I experienced these social control agents as intruding themselves unwanted into my research. My study was based on the records of Boston "child-saving" agencies, in which the oppressions of class, culture, and gender were immediately evident. The "clients" were mainly poor, Catholic, female immigrants. (It was not that women were responsible for most of the family violence but that they were more often involved with agencies, for reasons we shall see below.) The social workers were exclusively well educated and male and overwhelmingly white Anglo-Saxon Protestants (WASPs). These workers, authors of case records, were often disdainful, ignorant, and obtuse—at best, paternalistic—toward their clients.

Yet, ironically, these very biases created a useful discipline, showing that it was impossible to study family violence as an objective problem. Attempts at social control were part of the original definition and construction of family violence as a social issue. The very concept of family violence is a product of conflict and negotiation be-

Because this paper distills material I have been musing on throughout my work on my book about family violence (*Heroes of Their Own Lives: The Politics and History of Family Violence* [New York: Viking Press, 1988]), my intellectual debts are vast. Several friends took the time to read and help me with versions of this essay, including Ros Baxandall, Sara Bershtel, Susan Stanford Friedman, Allen Hunter, Judith Leavitt, Ann Stoler, Susan Schechter, Pauline Terrelonge, and Barrie Thorne; I am extremely grateful. Elizabeth Pleck took time out from her own book on the history of family violence to give me the benefit of her detailed critique. I had help in doing this research from Anne Doyle Kenney, Paul O'Keefe, and Jan Lambertz in particular. Discussions with Ellen Bassuk, Wini Breines, Caroline Bynum, Elizabeth Ewen, Stuart Ewen, Marilyn Chapin Massey, and Eve Kosofsky Sedgwick helped me clarify my thoughts. This essay first appeared in *Feminist Studies* 12, no. 3 (Fall 1986).

tween people troubled by domestic violence and social control agents attempting to change their supposedly unruly and deviant behavior.

In this essay I want to argue not a defense of social control but a critique of its critiques and some thoughts about a better, feminist, framework. I would like to make my argument as it came to me, through studying child abuse and neglect. Nine years ago, when I began to study the history of family violence, I assumed I would be focusing largely on wife beating because that was the target of the contemporary feminist activism that had drawn my attention to the problem. I was surprised, however, to find that violence against children represented a more complex challenge to the task of envisioning feminist family policy and a feminist theory of social control.

Social Control

Many historians of women and the family have inherited a critical view of social control, as an aspect of domination and the source of decline in family and individual autonomy. In situating ourselves with respect to this tradition, it may be useful to trace very briefly the history of the concept. "Social control" is a phrase usually attributed to the sociologist E. A. Ross. He used the phrase as the title of a collection of his essays in 1901, referring to the widest range of influence and regulation societies imposed upon individuals.[1] Building on a Hobbesian view of human individuals as naturally in conflict, Ross saw "social control" as inevitable. Moving beyond liberal individualism, however, he argued for social control in a more specific, American Progressive sense. Ross advocated the active, deliberate, expert guidance of human life not only as the source of human progress but also as the best replacement for older, familial, and communitarian forms of control, which he believed were disappearing in modern society.

Agencies attempting to control family violence are preeminent examples of the kind of expert social control institutions that were endorsed by Ross and other Progressive reformers. These agencies— the most typical were the Societies for the Prevention of Cruelty to Children (SPCCs)—were established in the 1870s in a decade of acute international alarm about child abuse. They began as punitive and moralistic "charitable" endeavors, characteristic of nineteenth-century elite moral-purity reforms. These societies blamed the problem of family violence on the depravity, immorality, and drunkenness of individuals, which they often traced to the innate inferiority of the immigrants who constituted the great bulk of their targets. By the early twentieth century the SPCCs took on a more ambitious task, hoping not merely to cure family pathology but also to reform family life and child raising. Describing the change slightly differently, in the nineteenth century, child protection agents saw themselves as paralegal, punishing specific offenses, protecting children from specific dangers; in the early twentieth century, they tried to supervise and direct the family lives of those considered deviant.

The view that intervention into the family has increased, and has become a characteristic feature of modern society, is now often associated with Talcott Parsons's writings of the late 1940s and 1950s. Parsons proposed the "transfer of functions" thesis, the notion that professionals had taken over many family functions (for example, education, child care, therapy, and medical care). Parsons's was a liberal, optimistic view; he thought this professionalization a step forward, leaving the family free to devote more of its time and energy to affective relations. There was already a contrasting, far more pessimistic, interpretation, emanating from the Frankfurt school of German Marxists, who condemned the decline of family autonomy and even attributed to it, in part, the horrors of totalitarianism.

The latter tradition, critical of social control, has conditioned most of the historical writings about social control agencies and influences. Much of the earlier work in this mid-twentieth-century revival of women's history adopted this perspective on social control, substituting gender for class or national categories in the analysis of women's subordination. In the field of child saving in particular, the most influential historical work has adopted this perspective.[2] These critiques usually distinguished an "us" and a "them," oppressed and oppressor, in a dichotomous relation. They were usually functionalist: they tended to assume or argue that the social control practices in question served (were functional for) the material interests of a dominant group and hindered (were dysfunctional to) the interests of the subordinate. More recently, some women's historians have integrated class and gender into this model, arguing that the growth of the state in the last 150 years has increased individual rights for prosperous women but has only subjected poor women to ever greater control.[3] Alternatively, women's historians represent social control as half of a

bargain in which material benefits—welfare benefits, for example—
are given to those controlled in exchange for the surrender of power
or autonomy.[4]

The development of women's history in the last decade has begun
to correct some of the oversimplifications of this "anti–social control" school of analysis. A revival of what might be called the Beard-
ian tradition (after Mary Beard) recognizes women's activity—in this
case, in constructing modern forms of social control.[5] Historians of
social work or other social control institutions, however, have not
participated in the rethinking of the paradigm of elite domination
and plebian victimization.[6]

The critique of the domination exercised by social work and human services bureaucracies and professionals is not wrong, but its in-
completeness allows for some serious distortion. My own views
derive from a study of the history of family violence and its social
control in Boston from 1880 to 1960, using both the quantitative and
qualitative analysis of case records from three leading child-saving
agencies.[7] Looking at these records from the perspective of children
and their primary caretakers (and abusers), women, reveals the impoverishment of the anti–social control perspective sketched above
and its inadequacy to the task of conceptualizing who is controlled
and who is controlling in these family conflicts. A case history may
suggest some of the complexities that have influenced my thinking.

In 1910 a Syrian family in Boston's South End, here called the
Kashys, came to the attention of the Massachusetts Society for the
Prevention of Cruelty to Children (MSPCC) because of the abuse of
the mother's thirteen-year-old girl.[8] Mr. Kashy had just died of ap-
pendicitis. The family, like so many immigrants, had moved back and
forth between Syria and the United States several times; two other
children had been left in Syria with their paternal grandparents. In
this country, in addition to the central "victim," whom I shall call
Fatima, there was a six-year-old boy and a three-year-old girl, and
Mrs. Kashy was pregnant. The complainant was the father's sister,
and indeed all the paternal relatives were hostile to Mrs. Kashy. The
MSPCC investigation substantiated their allegations: Mrs. Kashy hit
Fatima with a stick and with chairs, bit her ear, kept her from school,
and overworked her, expecting her to do all the housework and to
care for the younger children. When Fatima fell ill, her mother refused to let her go to the hospital. The hostility of the paternal

relatives, however, focused not only on the mother's treatment of Fatima but mainly on her custody rights. It was their position that custody should have fallen to them after Mr. Kashy's death, arguing that "in Syria a woman's right to the care of her chn [abbreviations in original] or the control of property is not recognized." In Syrian tradition, the paternal grandfather had rights to the children, and he had delegated this control to his son, the children's paternal uncle.

The paternal kin, then, had expected Mrs. Kashy to bow to their rights; certainly her difficult economic and social situation would make it understandable if she had. The complainant, the father's sister, was Mrs. Kashy's landlady and was thus in a position to make her life very difficult. Mrs. Kashy lived with her three children in one attic room without water; she had to go to the ground level and carry water up to her apartment. The relatives offered her no help after her bereavement, and Mrs. Kashy was desperate; she was trying to earn a living by continuing her husband's peddling. She needed Fatima to keep the house and care for the children.

When Mrs. Kashy resisted their custody claims, the paternal relatives called in as mediator a Syrian community leader, publisher of the *New Syria,* a Boston Arabic-language newspaper. Ultimately the case went to court, however, and here the relatives lost, as their custody traditions conflicted with the new preference in the United States for women's custody. Fatima's wishes were of no help to the agency in sorting out this conflict, because throughout the struggle she was ambivalent: sometimes she begged to be kept away from her mother, yet when away, she begged to be returned to her mother. Ultimately, Mrs. Kashy won custody but no material help in supporting her children by herself. As in so many child abuse cases, it was the victim who was punished: Fatima was sent to the Gwynne Home, where—at least so her relatives believed—she was treated abusively.

If the story had stopped there one might be tempted to see Mrs. Kashy as relatively blameless, driven perhaps to episodes of harshness and temper by her difficult lot. But thirteen years later, in 1923, a "school visitor" took the second daughter, now sixteen, to the MSPCC to complain of abuse by her mother and by her older, now married, sister Fatima. In the elapsed years, this second daughter had been sent back to Syria; perhaps Mrs. Kashy had had to give up her efforts to support her children. Returning to the United States eighteen months previously, the girl had arrived to find that her mother intended to marry her involuntarily to a boarder. The daughter displayed blood on her shirt which she said came from her mother's beatings. Interviewed by an MSPCC agent, Mrs. Kashy was now openly hostile and defiant, saying that she would beat her daughter as she liked.

In its very complexity, the Kashy case exemplifies certain generalizations central to my argument. One is that it is often difficult to identify a unique victim. It should not be surprising that the oppressed Mrs. Kashy was angry and violent, but feminist rhetoric about family violence has often avoided this complexity. Mrs. Kashy was the victim of her isolation, widowhood, single motherhood, and patriarchal, hostile in-laws; she also exploited and abused her daughter. Indeed, Mrs. Kashy's attitude to Fatima was patriarchal: she believed that children should serve parents and not vice versa. This aspect of patriarchal tradition served Mrs. Kashy. But, in other respects, the general interests of the oppressed group—here the Syrian immigrants—as expressed by its male, petit bourgeois leadership, were more inimical to Mrs. Kashy's (and other women's) aspirations and "rights" than those of the elite agency, the MSPCC. Furthermore, one can reasonably surmise that the daughters were also actors in this drama, resisting their mother's expectations as well as those of the male-dominated community, as New World ideas of children's rights coincided with aspirations entirely their own. None of the existing social control critiques can adequately conceptualize the complex struggles in the Kashy family, nor can they propose nonoppressive ways for Fatima's "rights" to be protected.

Feminism and Child Abuse

Feminist theory in general and women's history in particular have moved only slowly beyond the "victimization" paradigm that dominated the rebirth of feminist scholarship. The obstacles to perceiving and describing women's own power have been particularly great in issues relating to social policy and to family violence, because of the legacy of victim blaming. Defending women against male violence is so urgent that we fear women's loss of status as deserving, political "victims" if we acknowledge women's own aggressions. These complexities are at their greatest in the situation of mothers, because they are simultaneously victims and victimizers, dependent and depended on, weak and powerful.

If feminist theory needs a new view of social control, thinking about child abuse virtually demands it. Child abuse cases reveal suffering that is incontrovertible, unnecessary, and remediable. However severe the biases of the social workers attempting to "save" the children and reform their parents—and I will have more to say about this later—one could not advocate a policy of inaction in regard to children chained to beds, left in filthy diapers for days, turned out in the cold. Children, unlike women, lack even the potential for social and economic independence. A beneficial social policy could at least partly address the problem of wife beating by empowering women to leave abusive situations, enabling them to live in comfort and dignity without men, and encouraging them to espouse high standards in their expectations of treatment by others. It is not clear how one could empower children in analogous ways. If children are to have "rights" then some adults must be appointed and accepted, by other adults, to define and defend them.

Women, who do most of the labor of child care and have the strongest emotional bonds to children, have fought for and largely won rights to child custody over the last 150 years. Yet women are often the abusers and neglecters of children. Indeed, child abuse becomes the more interesting and challenging to feminists because in it we meet women's rage and abuses of power. Furthermore, child abuse is a gendered phenomenon, related to the oppression of women, whether women or men are the culprits, because it reflects the sexual division of the labor of reproduction. Because men spend, on the whole, so much less time with children than do women, what is remarkable is not that women are violent toward children but that men are responsible for nearly half of the child abuse. But women are always implicated, because even when men are the culprits, women are usually the primary caretakers who have been, by definition, unable to protect the children. When protective organizations remove children or undertake supervision of their caretakers, women often suffer greatly, for their maternal work, trying as it may be, is usually the most pleasurable part of their lives.

Yet in the last two decades of intense publicity and scholarship about child abuse, the feminist contribution has been negligible. This silence is the more striking in contrast to the legacy of the first wave of feminism, particularly in the period 1880 to 1930, in which the women's rights movement was tightly connected to child welfare reform campaigns. By contrast, the second wave of feminism, a movement heavily influenced by younger and childless women, has spent relatively little energy on children's issues. Feminist scholars have studied the social organization of mothering in theory but not the actual experiences of child raising, and the movement as a whole has not significantly influenced child welfare debates or policies. When such issues emerge publicly, feminists too often assume that women's and children's interests always coincide. The facts of child abuse and neglect challenge this assumption, as does the necessity sometimes of severing maternal custody in order to protect children.

Protecting Children

Child abuse was "discovered" as a social problem in the 1870s. Surely many children had been ill treated by parents before this, but new social conditions created an increased sensitivity to the treatment of children and, possibly, actually worsened children's lot. Conditions of labor and family life under industrial capitalism may have made poverty, stress, and parental anger bear more heavily on children. The child abuse alarm also reflected growing class and cultural differences in beliefs about how children *should* be raised. The anti-cruelty-to-children movement grew out of an anti-corporal-punishment campaign, and both reflected a uniquely professional-class view that children could be disciplined by reason and with mildness. The SPCCs also grew from widespread fears among more privileged people about violence and "depravity" among the urban poor; in the United States these fears were exacerbated by the fact that these poor were largely immigrants and Catholics, threatening the WASP domination of city culture and government.

On one level, my study of the case records of Boston child-saving agencies corroborated the anti–social control critique: the work of the agencies did represent oppressive intervention into working-class families. The MSPCC attempted to enforce culturally specific norms of proper parenting that were not only alien to the cultural legacy of their "clients" but also flew in the face of many of the economic necessities of the clients' lives. Thus, MSPCC agents prosecuted cases in which cruelty to children was caused, in their view, by children's labor: girls doing housework and child care, often staying home from school because their parents required it; girls and boys working in shops, peddling on the streets; boys working for organ grinders and lying about their ages to enlist in the navy. Before World War I the enemies of the truant officers were usually parents, not children. To immigrants from peasant backgrounds it seemed irrational and blasphemous that adult women should work while able-bodied children remained idle. Similarly, the MSPCC was opposed to the common immigrant practice of leaving children unattended and allowing them to play and wander in the streets. Both violated the MSPCC's norm of domesticity for women and children; proper middle-class children in those days did not—at least not in the cities—play outside on their own.

The child savers were attempting to impose a new, middle-class urban style of mothering and fathering. Mothers were supposed to be tender and gentle and above all, to protect their children from immoral influences; the child savers considered yelling, rude language, or sexually explicit talk to be forms of cruelty to children. Fathers were to provide models of emotional containment, to be relatively uninvolved with children; their failure to provide adequate economic support was often interpreted as a character flaw, no matter what the evidence of widespread, structural unemployment.

MSPCC agents in practice and in rhetoric expressed disdain for immigrant cultures. They hated the garlic and olive oil smells of Italian cooking and considered this food unhealthy (overstimulating, aphrodisiac). The agents were unable to distinguish alcoholics and heavy drinkers from moderate wine and beer drinkers, and they believed that women who took spirits were degenerate and unfit as mothers. They associated many of these forms of depravity with Catholicism. Agents were also convinced of the subnormal intelligence of most non-WASP and especially non-English-speaking clients; indeed, the agents' comments and expectations in this early period were similar to social workers' views of Black clients in the mid-twentieth century. These child welfare specialists were particularly befuddled by and disapproving of non-nuclear childraising patterns: children raised by grandmothers, complex households composed of children from several different marriages (or, worse, out-of-wedlock relationships), children sent temporarily to other households.

The peasant backgrounds of so many of the "hyphenated" Americans created a situation in which ethnic bias could not easily be separated from class bias. Class misunderstanding, moreover, took a form specific to urban capitalism: a failure to grasp the actual economic and physical circumstances of this immigrant proletariat and subproletariat. Unemployment was not yet understood to be a structural characteristic of industrial capitalism. Disease, overcrowding, crime, and—above all—dependence were also not understood to be part of the system, but rather were seen as personal failings.

This line of criticism, however, only partially uncovers the significance of child protection. Another dimension and a great deal more complexity are revealed by considering the feminist aspect of the movement. Much of the child welfare reform energy of the nineteenth century came from women and was organized by the "woman movement."[9] The campaign against corporal punishment, from which the anti–child abuse movement grew, depended on a critique of violence rooted in feminist thought and in women's reform activity. Women's reform influence, the "sentimentalizing" of the Calvinist traditions,[10] was largely responsible for the softening of child-raising norms. The delegitimation of corporal punishment, noticeable among the prosperous classes by midcentury, was associated with exclusive female responsibility for child raising, with women's victories in child custody cases, even with women's criticisms of traditionally paternal discipline.[11]

Feminist thinking exerted an important influence on the agencies' original formulations of the problem of family violence. Most MSPCC spokesmen (and those who represented the agency in public were men) viewed men as aggressors and women and children, jointly, as blameless victims. However simplistic, this was a feminist attitude. It was also, of course, saturated with class and cultural elitism: these "brutal" and "depraved" men were of a different class and ethnicity than the MSPCC agents, and the language of victimization applied to women and children was also one of condescension. Nevertheless, despite the definition of the "crime" as cruelty to children, MSPCC agents soon included wife beating in their agenda of reform.

Even more fundamentally, the very undertaking of child protection was a challenge to patriarchal relations. A pause to look at my definition of patriarchy is necessary here. In the 1970s a new definition of that term came into use, first proposed by Kate Millett but quickly adopted by the U.S. feminist movement: patriarchy became a synonym for male supremacy, for "sexism." I use the term in its earlier, historical, and more specific sense, referring to a family form in which fathers had control over all other family members—children, women, and servants. This concept of a patriarchal family is an abstraction, postulating common features among family forms that differed widely across geography and time. If there was a common material base supporting this patriarchal family norm (a question requiring a great deal more study before it can be answered decisively), it was an economic system in which the family was the unit of production. Most of the MSPCC's early clients came from peasant societies in which this kind of family economy prevailed. In these families, fathers maintained control not only over property and tools but also, above all, over the labor power of family members. Historical patriarchy defined a set of parent-child relations as much as it did relations between the sexes, for children rarely had opportunities for economic independence except by inheriting the family property, trade, or craft. In some ways mothers, too, benefited from patriarchal parent-child relations. Their authority over daughters and young sons was important when they lacked other kinds of authority and independence, and in old age they gained respect, help, and consideration from younger kinfolk.

The claim of an organization such as an SPCC to speak on behalf of children's rights, its claim to the license to intervene in parental treatment of children, was an attack on patriarchal power. At the same time, the new sensibility about children's rights and the concern about child abuse were symptoms of a weakening of patriarchal family expectations and realities that had already taken place, particularly during the eighteenth and early nineteenth centuries in the United States. In this weakening, father-child relations had changed more than husband-wife relations. Children had, for example, gained the power to arrange their own betrothals and marriages and to embark on wage work independent of their fathers' occupations (of course, children's options remained determined by class and cultural privileges or the lack of them, inherited from fathers). In contrast, however, wage labor and long-distance mobility often made women, on balance, more dependent on husbands for sustenance and less able to deploy kinfolk and neighbors to defend their interests against husbands.

Early child protection work did not, of course, envision a general liberation of children from arbitrary parental control or from the responsibility of filial obedience. On the contrary, the SPCCs aimed as much to reinforce a failing parental/paternal authority as to limit it. Indeed, the SPCC spokesmen often criticized excessive physical violence against children as a symptom of inadequate parental authority. Assaults on children were provoked by children's insubordination; in the interpretation of nineteenth-century child protectors, this showed that parental weakness, children's disobedience, and child abuse were mutually reinforcing. Furthermore, by the turn of the century, the SPCCs discovered that the majority of their cases concerned neglect, not assault, and neglect exemplified to them the problems created by the withdrawal, albeit not always conscious or deliberate, of parental supervision and authority (among the poor who formed the agency clientele there were many fathers who deserted and many more who were inadequate providers). Many neglect and abuse cases ended with *children* being punished, sent to reform schools on stubborn-child charges.

In sum, the SPCCs sought to reconstruct the family along lines that altered the old patriarchy, already economically unviable, and to replace it with a modern version of male supremacy. The SPCCs' rhetoric about children's rights did not extend to a parallel articulation of women's rights; their condemnation of wife beating did not include endorsement of the kind of marriage later called "companionate," implying equality between wife and husband. Their new family and child-raising norms included the conviction that children's respect for parents needed to be inculcated ideologically, moralistically, and psychologically because it no longer rested on an economic dependence lasting beyond childhood. Fathers, now as wage laborers rather than as slaves, artisans, peasants, or entrepreneurs, were to have single-handed responsibility for economic support of their families; women and children should not contribute to the family economy, at least not monetarily. Children instead should spend their time in learning cognitive lessons from professional teachers, psychological and moral lessons from the full-time attention of a mother. In turn, women should devote themselves to mothering and domesticity.

Feminism, Mothering, and Industrial Capitalism

This child-raising program points to a larger irony—that the "modernization" of male domination, its adaptation to new economic and social conditions, was partly a result of the influence of the first wave

of feminism. These first "feminists" rarely advocated full equality between women and men and never promoted the abolition of traditional gender relations or the sexual division of labor. Allowing for
differences of emphasis, the program just defined constituted a feminist as well as a liberal family reform program in the 1870s. Indeed,
organized feminism *was* in part such a liberal reform program, a program to adapt the family and the civil society to the new economic
conditions of industrial capitalism, for consciously or not, feminists
felt that these new conditions provided greater possibilities for the
freedom and empowerment of women.

To recapitulate, child protection work was an integral part of the
feminist as well as the bourgeois program for modernizing the family.
Child saving had gender as well as class and ethnic content, but in
none of these aspects did it simply or homogeneously represent the
interests of a dominant group (or even of the composite group of
WASP elite women, that hypothetical stratum on which it is fashionable to blame the limitations of feminist activity). The antipatriar-
chalism of the child protection agencies was an unstable product of
several conflicting interests. Understanding this illuminates the influence of feminism on the development of a capitalist industrial culture
even as feminists criticized the new privileges it bestowed on men and
its degradation of women's traditional work. The relation of feminism to capitalism and industrialism is usually argued in dichotomous and reductionist fashion: either feminism is the expression of
bourgeois woman's aspirations, an ultimate individualism that tears
apart the remaining noninstrumental bonds in a capitalist society, or
feminism is inherently anticapitalist, deepening and extending the critique of domination to show its penetration even of personal life and
the allegedly "natural." Although there is a little truth in both versions, at least one central aspect of feminism's significance for capitalism has been omitted in these formulations—its role in redefining
family norms and particularly norms of mothering.

Changes in the conditions of motherhood in an industrializing society were an important part of the experiences that drew women to
the postbellum feminist movement. For most women, and particularly for urban poor women, motherhood became more difficult in
wage labor conditions. Mothers were more isolated from support
networks of kin, and mothering furthered that isolation, often requiring that women remain out of public space. The potential dangers

from which children needed protection multiplied, and the increasing cultural demands for a "psychological parenting" increased the potential for maternal "failure."[12] These changes affected women of all classes, while at the same time motherhood remained the central identity for women of all classes. Childbirth and child raising, the most universal parts of female experience, were the common referents—the metaphoric base of political language—by which feminist ideas were communicated.

As industrial capitalism changed the conditions of motherhood, so women began to redefine motherhood in ways that would influence the entire culture. They "used" motherhood simultaneously to increase their own status, to promote greater social expenditure on children, and to loosen their dependence on men, just as capitalists "used" motherhood as a form of unpaid labor. The working-class and even sub-working-class women of the child abuse case records drew "feminist" conclusions—that is, they diagnosed their problems in terms of male supremacy—in their efforts to improve their own conditions of mothering. In their experiences, men's greater power (economic and social), in combination with men's lesser sense of responsibility toward children, kept them from being as good at mothering as they wanted. They responded by trying to rid themselves of those forms of male domination that impinged most directly on their identity and work as mothers and on children's needs as they interpreted those needs.

But if child protection work may have represented *all* mothers' demands, it made *some* mothers—poor urban mothers—extremely vulnerable by calling into question the quality of their mothering, already made more problematic by urban wage labor living conditions, and by threatening them with the loss of their children. Poor women had less privacy and therefore less impunity in their deviance from the new child-raising norms, but their poverty often led them to ask for help from relief agencies, therefore calling themselves to the attention of the child-saving networks. Yet poor women did not by any means figure only on the victim side, for they were also often enthusiastic about defending children's "rights" and correcting cruel or neglectful parents. Furthermore, they used an eclectic variety of arguments and devices to defend their control of their children. At times they mobilized liberal premises and rhetoric to escape from patriarchal households and to defend their custody rights; they were quick to learn the right language of the New World in which to criticize their husbands and relatives and to manipulate social workers to side with them against patriarchal controls of other family members. Yet at other times they called upon traditional relations when community and kinfolk could help them retain control or defend children. Poor women often denounced the "intervention" of outside social control agencies like the SPCCs but only when it suited them, and at other times they eagerly used and asked such agencies for help.

Let me offer another case history to illustrate this opportunistic and resourceful approach to social control agencies. An Italian immigrant family, which I will call the Amatos, were "clients" of the MSPCC from 1910 to 1916.[13] They had five young children from the current marriage, and Mrs. Amato had three from a previous marriage, two of them still in Italy and one daughter in Boston. Mrs. Amato kept that daughter at home to do housework and look after the younger children while she earned money doing piece rate sewing at home. This got the family in trouble with a truant officer, and they were also accused, in court, of lying to Associated Charities (a consortium of private relief agencies), saying that the father had deserted them when he was in fact living at home. Furthermore, once while left alone, probably in the charge of a sibling, one of the younger children fell out of a window and had to be hospitalized. This incident provoked agency suspicions that the mother was negligent.

Despite her awareness of these suspicions against her, Mrs. Amato sought help from many different organizations, starting with those of the Italian immigrant community and then reaching out to elite social work agencies, reporting that her husband was a drunkard, a gambler, a nonsupporter, and a wife beater. The MSPCC agents as first doubted her claims because Mr. Amato impressed them as a "good and sober man," and they blamed the neglect of the children on his wife's incompetence in managing the wages he gave her. The MSPCC ultimately became convinced of Mrs. Amato's story because of her repeated appearance with severe bruises and the corroboration of the husband's father, who was intimately involved in the family troubles and took responsibility for attempting to control his son. Once the father came to the house and gave his son "a warning and a couple of slaps," after which he improved for a while. Another time the father extracted from him a pledge not to beat his wife for two years!

Mrs. Amato wanted none of this. She begged the MSPCC agent to help her get a divorce; later she claimed that she had not dared take this step because her husband's relatives threatened to beat her if she tried it. Then Mrs. Amato's daughter (from her previous marriage) took action, coming independently to the MSPCC to bring an agent to the house to help her mother. As a result of this complaint, Mr. Amato was convicted of assault once and sentenced to six months. During that time Mrs. Amato survived by "a little work and . . . Italian friends have helped her." Her husband returned, more violent than before: he went at her with an ax, beat the children so much on the head that their "eyes wabbled [sic]" permanently, and supported his family so poorly that the children went out begging. This case closed, like so many, without a resolution.

The Amatos' case will not support the usual anti–social control interpretation of the relation between oppressed clients and social agencies. There was no unity among the client family and none among the professional intervenors. Furthermore, the intervenors were often dragged into the case and by individuals with conflicting points of view. Mrs. Amato and Mrs. Kashy were not atypical in their attempts to use "social control" agencies in their own interests. Clients frequently initiated agency intervention; even in family violence cases, where the stakes were high—losing one's children—the majority of complaints in this study came from parents or close relatives who believed that their own standards of child raising were being violated.[14]

In their sparring with social work agencies, clients did not usually or collectively win because the professionals had more resources. Usually no one decisively "won." Considering these cases collectively, professional social work overrode working-class or poor people's interests, but in specific cases the professionals did not always formulate definite goals, let alone achieve them. Indeed, the bewilderment of the social workers (something usually overlooked because most scholarship about social work is based on policy statements, not on actual case records) frequently enabled the clients to go some distance toward achieving their own goals.

The social control experience was not a simple two-sided trade-off in which the client sacrificed autonomy and control in return for some material help. Rather, the clients helped shape the nature of the social control itself. Formulating these criticisms about the inadequacy of simple anti–social control explanations in some analytic order, I would make four general points.

First, the condemnation of agency intervention into the family, and the condemnation of social control itself as something automatically evil, usually assumes that there can be, and once was, an autonomous family. On the contrary, no family relations have been immune from social regulation.[15] Certainly the forms of social control I examine here are qualitatively and quantitatively different, based on regulation from "outside," by those without a legitimate claim to caring about local, individual values and traditions. Contrasting the experience of social control to a hypothetical era of autonomy, however, distorts both traditional and modern forms of social regulation.

The tendency to consider social control as unprecedented, invasive regulation is not only an academic mistake. It grew from nineteenth-century emotional and political responses to social change. Family autonomy became a symbol of patriarchy only in its era of decline (as in 1980s New Right rhetoric). Family "autonomy" was an oppositional concept in the nineteenth century, expressing a liberal ideal of home as a private and caring space in contrast to the public realm of increasingly instrumental relations. This symbolic cluster surrounding the family contained both critical and legitimating responses to industrial capitalist society. But as urban society created more individual opportunities for women, the defense of family autonomy came to stand against women's autonomy in a conservative opposition to women's demands for individual freedoms. (The concept of family autonomy today, as it is manipulated in political discourse, mainly has the latter function, suggesting that women's individual rights to autonomous citizenship will make the family more vulnerable to outside intervention.) The Amatos' pattern, a more patriarchal pattern, of turning to relatives, friends, and, when they could not help, Italian-American organizations (no doubt the closest analogue to a "community" in the New World), was not adequate to the urban problems they now encountered. Even the violent and defensive Mr. Amato did not question the right of his father, relatives, and friends to intervene forcibly, and Mrs. Amato did not appear shocked that her husband's relatives tried, perhaps successfully, to hold her forcibly in her marriage. Family autonomy was not an expectation of the Amatos.

Second, the social control explanation sees the flow of initiative going in only one direction: from top to bottom, from professionals to clients, from elite to subordinate. The power of this interpretation of social work comes from the large proportion of truth it holds and also from the influence of scholars of poor people's movements who have denounced elite attempts to blame "the victims." The case records show, however, that clients were not passive but rather active negotiators in a complex bargaining. Textbooks of casework recognize the intense interactions and relationships that develop between social worker and client. In the social work version of concern with countertransference, textbooks often attempt to accustom the social worker to examining her or his participation in that relationship.[16] This sense of mutuality, power struggle, and intersubjectivity, however, has not penetrated historical accounts of social work/social control encounters.

Third, critics of social control often fail to recognize the active role of agency clients because they conceive of the family as a homogeneous unit. There is an intellectual reification here that expresses itself in sentence structure, particularly in academic language: "The family is in decline," "threats to the family," "the family responds to industrialization." Shorthand expressions attributing behavior to an aggregate such as the family would be harmless except that they often express particular cultural norms about what "the family" is and does, and they mask intrafamily differences and conflicts of interest. Usually "the family" becomes a representation of the interests of the family head, if it is a man, carrying an assumption that all family members share his interests. (Families without a married male head, such as single-parent or grandparent-headed families are, in the common usage, broken, deformed, or incomplete families, and thus do not qualify for these assumptions regarding family unity.) Among the clients in family violence cases, outrage over the intervention into the family was frequently anger over a territorial violation, a challenge to male authority; expressed differently, it was a reaction to the exposure to others of intrafamily conflict and of the family head's lack of control. Indeed, the interventions actually *were* more substantive, more invasive, when their purpose was to change the status quo than if they had been designed to reinforce it. The effect of social workers' involvement was often to change existing family power relations, usually in the interest of the weaker family members.

Social work interventions were often invited by family members; the inviters, however, were usually the weaker members of a family power structure, women and children. These invitations were made despite the fact, well known to clients, that women and children usually had the most to lose (despite fathers' frequent outrage at their loss of face) from MSPCC intervention, because by far the most common outcome of agency action was not prosecution and jail sentences but the removal of children, an action fathers dreaded less than mothers. In the immigrant working-class neighborhoods of Boston the MSPCC became known as "the Cruelty," eloquently suggesting poor people's recognition and fear of its power. But these fears did not stop poor people from initiating contact with the organization. After the MSPCC had been in operation ten years, 60 percent of the complaints of known origin (excluding anonymous accusations) came from family members, the overwhelming majority of these from women, with children following second. These request for help came not only from victims but also from mothers distressed that they were not able to raise their children according to their own standards of good parenting. Women also maneuvered to bring child welfare agencies into family struggles on their sides. There was no Society for the Prevention of Cruelty to Women, but in fact women like Mrs. Amato were trying to turn the SPCC into just that. A frequent tactic of beaten, deserted, or unsupported wives was to report their husbands as child abusers; even when investigations found no evidence of child abuse, social workers came into their homes offering, at best, help in getting other things women wanted—such as support payments, separation and maintenance agreements, relief—and, at least, moral support to the women and condemnation of the men.[17]

A fourth problem is that simple social control explanations often imply that the clients' problems are only figments of social workers' biases. One culture's neglect may be another culture's norm, and in such cultural clashes, one group usually has more power than the other. In many immigrant families, for example, five-year-olds were expected to care for babies and toddlers; to middle-class reformers, five-year-olds left alone were neglected, and their infant charges deserted. Social control critiques are right to call attention to the power of experts not only to "treat" social deviance but also to define problems in the first place. But the power of labeling, the representation of poor people's behavior by experts whose status is defined through their critique of the problematic behavior of others, coexists with real family oppressions. In one case an immigrant father, who sexually molested his thirteen-year-old daughter, told a social worker that that was the way it was done in the old country. He was not only lying but also trying to manipulate a social worker, perhaps one he had recognized as guilt-ridden over her privileged role, using his own fictitious cultural relativism. His daughter's victimization by incest was not the result of oppression by professionals.

Feminism and Liberalism

The overall problem with virtually all existing critiques of social control is that they remain liberal and have in particular neglected what feminists have shown to be the limits of liberalism. Liberalism is commonly conceived as a political and economic theory without social content. In fact, liberal political and economic theory rests on assumptions about the sexual division of labor and on notions of citizens as heads of families.[18] The currently dominant left-wing tradition of anti–social control critique, that of the Frankfurt school, merely restates these assumptions, identifying the sphere of the "private" as somehow natural, productive of strong egos and inner direction, in contrast to the sphere of the public as invasive, productive of conformity and passivity. If we reject the social premises of liberalism (and of Marx), that gender and the sexual division of labor are natural, then we can hardly maintain the premise that familial forms of social control are inherently benign and public forms are malignant.

Certainly class relations and domination are involved in social control. Child protection work developed and still functions in class society, and the critique of bureaucracies and professionalism has shown the inevitable deformation of attempts to "help" in a society of inequality, where only a few have the power to define what social order should be. But this critique of certain kinds of domination often serves to mask other kinds, particularly those between women and men and between adults and children. And it has predominantly been a critique that emphasizes domination as opposed to conflict.

Social work and, more generally, aspects of the welfare state have a unique bearing on gender conflicts. Women's subordination in the family, and their struggle against it, not only affected the construction of the welfare state but also the operations of social control bureaucracies. In fact, social control agencies such as the MSPCC—and, more often, individual social workers—did sometimes help poor and working-class people. They aided the weaker against the stronger, and not merely by rendering clients passive. Social work interventions rarely changed assailants' behavior, but they had a greater impact on

victims. Ironically, the MSPCC thereby contributed more to help battered women, defined as outside its jurisdiction, than it did abused
children. Industrial capitalist society gave women some opportunity
to leave abusive men, because they could earn their own livings. In
these circumstances, even a tiny bit of material help, a mere hint as to
how to "work" the relief agencies, could turn these women's aspirations for autonomy into reality. Women could sometimes get this help
despite class and ethnic prejudices against them. Italian-American
women might reap this benefit even from social workers who held
derogatory views of Italians; single mothers might be able to get help
in establishing independent households despite charity workers' suspicions of the immorality of their intentions. Just as in diplomacy the
enemy of one's enemy may be ipso facto a friend, in these domestic
dramas the enemy of one's oppressor could be an ally.

These immigrant clients—victims of racism, sexism, and poverty,
perhaps occasional beneficiaries of child welfare work—were also
part of the creation of modern child welfare standards and institutions. The welfare state was not a bargain in which the poor got material help by giving up control. The control itself was invented and
structured out of these interactions. Because many of the MSPCC's
early "interventions" were in fact invitations by family members, the
latter were in some ways teaching the agents what were appropriate
and enforceable standards of child care. A more institutional example is the mothers' pension legislation developed in most of the United
States between 1910 and 1920. As I have argued elsewhere, the feminist reformers who campaigned for that reform were influenced by
the unending demands of single mothers, abounding in the records of
child neglect, for support in raising their children without the benefit
of men's wages.[19]

The entire Progressive era's child welfare reform package, the social program of the women's rights movement, and the reforms that
accumulated to form the "welfare state" need to be reconceived as
not only a campaign spearheaded by elites. They resulted also from a
powerful if unsteady pressure for economic and domestic power from
poor and working-class women. For them, social work agencies were
a resource in their struggle to change the terms of their continuing,
traditional social control, which included but was not limited to the
familial. The issues involved in an anti–family violence campaign
were fundamental to poor women: the right to immunity from phys-

ical attack at home, the power to protect their children from abuse, the right to keep their children—not merely the legal right to custody but the actual power to support their children—and the power to provide a standard of care for those children that met their own standards and aspirations. That family violence became a social problem at all, that charities and professional agencies were drawn into attempts to control it, were as much a product of the demands of those at the bottom as of those at the top.

Still, if these family and child welfare agencies contributed to women's options, they had a constricting impact too. I do not wish to discard the cumulative insights offered by many critiques of social control. The discrimination and victim blaming women encountered from professionals was considerable, the more so because they were proffered by those defined as "helping." Loss of control was an *experience,* articulated in many different ways by its victims, including those in these same case records. Often the main beneficiaries of professionals' intervention hated them most, because in wrestling with them one rarely gets what one really wants but rather another interpretation of one's needs. An accurate view of the meanings of this "outside" intervention into the family must maintain in its analysis, as the women clients did in their strategic decisions, awareness of a tension between various forms of social control and the variety of factors that might contribute to improvements in personal life. This is a contradiction that women particularly face, and there is no easy resolution of it. There is no returning to an old or newly romanticized "community control" when the remnants of community rest on a patriarchal power structure hostile to women's aspirations. A feminist critique of social control must contain and wrestle with, not seek to eradicate, this tension.

Notes

1. E. A. Ross, *Social Control* (New York, 1901).

2. A few examples follow: Anthony M. Platt, *The Child Savers: The Invention of Delinquency* (Chicago: University of Chicago Press, 1969); Barbara Ehrenreich and Deirdre English, *For Her Own Good: One Hundred and Fifty Years of the Experts' Advice to Women* (Garden City, N.Y.: Anchor/Doubleday, 1978); Christopher Lasch, *Haven in a Heartless World: The Family Besieged* (New York: Basic Books, 1977); idem, *The Culture of Narcissism: American Life in an Age of Diminishing Expectations* (New York: Norton, 1979);

Jacques Donzelot, *The Policing of Families*, trans. Hurley (New York: Pantheon Books, 1979); Barbara M. Brenzel, *Daughters of the State: A Social Portrait of the First Reform School for Girls in North America, 1856–1905* (Cambridge, Mass.: MIT Press, 1983); Stuart Ewen, *Captains of Consciousness: Advertising and the Social Roots of the Consumer Culture* (New York: McGraw-Hill, 1976); Daniel T. Rodgers, *The Work Ethic in Industrial America, 1850–1920* (Chicago: University of Chicago Press, 1974); and Nigel Parton, *The Politics of Child Abuse* (New York: St. Martin's Press, 1985).

3. Eileen Boris and Peter Bardaglio, "The Transformation of Patriarchy: The Historic Role of the State," in *Families, Politics, and Public Policy: A Feminist Dialogue on Women and the State*, ed. Irene Diamond (New York: Longman, 1983), 70–93; Judith Areen, "Intervention between Parent and Child: A Reappraisal of the State's Role in Child Neglect and Abuse Cases," *Georgetown Law Journal* 63 (March 1975): 899–902; Mason P. Thomas, Jr., "Child Abuse and Neglect, pt. 1: Historical Overview, Legal Matrix, and Social Perspectives," *North Carolina Law Review* 50 (February 1972): 299–303.

4. John H. Ehrenreich, *The Altruistic Imagination: A History of Social Work and Social Policy in the United States* (Ithaca, N.Y.: Cornell University Press, 1985).

5. Alice Kessler-Harris, *Out to Work: A History of Wage-Earning Women in the United States* (New York: Oxford University Press, 1982), esp. chap. 7; Gwendolyn Wright, *Moralism and the Modern Home: Domestic Architecture and Cultural Conflict in Chicago, 1873–1913* (Chicago: University of Chicago Press, 1980); Kathryn Sklar, "Hull House As a Community of Women in the 1890s," *Signs* 10 (Summer 1985); Susan Ware, *Beyond Suffrage: Women in the New Deal* (Cambridge, Mass.: Harvard University Press, 1981).

6. Exceptions include Michael C. Grossberg, "Law and the Family in Nineteenth-Century America" (Ph.D. diss., Brandeis University, 1979), and Boris and Bardaglio, "The Transformation of Patriarchy."

7. The agencies were the Boston Children's Service Association, the Massachusetts Society for the Prevention of Cruelty to Children, and the Judge Baker Guidance Center. A random sample of cases from every tenth year was coded and analyzed. A summary of the methodology and a sampling of findings can be found in my "Single Mothers and Child Neglect, 1880–1920," *American Quarterly* 37 (Summer 1985): 173–92.

8. Case code no. 2044.

9. In Boston the MSPCC was called into being largely by Kate Gannett Wells, a moral reformer, along with other members of the New England Women's Club and the Moral Education Association. These women were united as much by class as by gender unity. Wells, for example, was an antisuffragist, yet in her club work she cooperated with suffrage militants such as Lucy Stone and Harriet Robinson, for they considered themselves all members of a larger, loosely defined but nonetheless coherent community of prosperous, respectable women reformers. This unity of class and gender purpose *was* organized feminism at this time. See New England Women's Club Papers, Schlesinger Library; MSPCC Correspondence Files, University of Massachusetts/Boston Archives, folder 1; Arthur Mann, *Yankee Reformers in the Urban Age* (Cambridge, Mass.: Harvard University Press, 1954), 208.

10. Ann Douglas, *The Feminization of American Culture* (New York: Knopf, 1977).

11. For examples of the growing anti-corporal-punishment campaign, see Lyman Cobb, *The Evil Tendencies of Corporal Punishment as a Means of Moral Discipline in Families and School* (New York, 1847); Mrs. C. A. Hopkinson, *Hints for the Nursery* (Boston,

1863); Mary Blake, *Twenty-Six Hours a Day* (Boston: D. Lothrop, 1883); Bolton Hall, "Education by Assault and Battery," *Arena* 39 (June 1908): 466–67. For historical commentary, see H. Ray Hiner, "Children's Rights, Corporal Punishment, and Child Abuse: Changing American Attitudes, 1870–1920," *Bulletin of the Menninger Clinic* 43, no. 3 (1979): 233–48; Carl F. Kaestle, "Social Change, Discipline, and the Common School in Early Nineteenth-Century America," *Journal of Interdisciplinary History* 9 (Summer 1978): 1–17; Myra C. Glenn, "The Naval Reform Campaign against Flogging: A Case Study in Changing Attitudes toward Corporal Punishment, 1830–1850," *American Quarterly* 35 (Fall 1963): 408–25; Robert Elno McGlone, "Suffer the Children: The Emergence of Modern Middle-Class Family Life in America, 1820–1870" (Ph.D. diss., University of California at Los Angeles, 1971).

12. Nancy Chodorow and Susan Contratto, "The Fantasy of the Perfect Mother," in this volume; Joseph Goldstein, Anna Freud, and Albert J. Solnit, *Beyond the Best Interests of the Child* (New York: Free Press, 1973); and idem, *Before the Best Interests of the Child* (New York: Free Press, 1979).

13. Case code no. 2042.

14. To this argument it could be responded that it is difficult to define what would be a parent's "own" standards of child rearing. In heterogeneous urban situations, child-rearing patterns change rather quickly, and new patterns become normative. Certainly the child welfare agencies were part of a "modernization" (in the United States called Americanization) effort, attempting to present new family norms as objectively right. However, in the poor neighborhoods, poverty, crowding, and the structure of housing allowed very little privacy, and the largely immigrant clients resisted these attempts and retained autonomous family patterns, often for several generations. Moreover, my own clinical and research experience suggests that even "anomic" parents, or mothers, to be precise, tend to have extremely firm convictions about right and wrong child-rearing methods.

15. Nancy Cott, for example, has identified some of the processes of community involvement in family life in eighteenth-century Massachusetts, in her "Eighteenth-Century Family and Social Life Revealed in Massachusetts Divorce Records," *Journal of Social History* 10 (Fall 1976): 20–43; Ann Whitehead has described the informal regulation of marital relations that occurred in pub conversations in her "Sexual Antagonism in Herefordshire," in *Dependence and Exploitation in Work and Marriage*, ed. Diana Leonard Barker and Sheila Allen (London: Longman, 1976), 169–203.

16. For example, see William Jordan, *The Social Worker in Family Situations* (London: Routledge & Kegan Paul, 1972); James W. Green, *Cultural Awareness in the Human Services* (Englewood Cliffs, N.J.: Prentice-Hall, 1982); and Alfred Kadushin, *Child Welfare Services* (New York: Macmillan, 1980), chap. 13.

17. Indeed, so widespread were these attempts to enmesh social workers in intrafamily feuds that they were responsible for a high proportion of the many unfounded complaints the MSPCC always met. Rejected men, then as now, often fought for the custody of children they did not really want as a means of hurting their wives. One way of doing this was to bring complaints against their wives of cruel treatment of children, or the men charged wives with child neglect when their main desire was to force the women to live with them again. Embittered, deserted wives might arrange to have their husbands caught with other women.

18. Zillah Eisenstein, *The Radical Future of Liberal Feminism* (New York: Longman, 1981); Joan B. Landes, "Hegel's Conception of the Family" (125–44), and Mary Lyndon

Shanley, "Marriage Contract and Social Contract in Seventeenth-Century English Political Thought" (80–95), both in *The Family in Political Thought*, ed. Jean Bethke Elshtain (Amherst: University of Massachusetts Press, 1982).

19. See my "Single Mothers and Child Neglect."

14

Why Men Resist

WILLIAM J. GOODE

Although few if any men in the United States remain entirely un-touched by the women's movement, to most men what is happening seems to be "out there" and has little direct effect on their own roles. Indeed, since the mass media constantly inform both men and women that the movement toward equality has ended, they are confirmed in that tendency. To most men, the movement often seems to be a dia-logue mainly among women, conferences of women about women, a mixture of just or exaggerated complaints and shrill and foolish de-mands to which men need not even respond, except now and then. When men see that a woman resents a common male act of conde-scension, such as making fun of women in sports or management, most males are sometimes still as surprised as corporation heads are when they are told to stop polluting a river.

Men are correct in this perception if one focuses on the short run only. It is not often that social behavior so deeply rooted in tradition alters rapidly. Over the longer run, they are not likely to be correct, and indeed I believe they are vaguely uneasy when they consider their present situation. Unlike numerous popular commentators, I do not think we are now witnessing a return to the old ways, a politically reactionary trend, and I do not think the contemporary attack on male privilege will ultimately fail.

The worldwide demand for equality is voiced not only by women. Many groups have pressed for it, with more persistence, strength, and success over the past generations than in any prior epoch of world history. It has also been pressed by more kinds of people than ever before: ethnic and racial groups; castes; subnational groups such as the Scots, Basques, or Azerbaijani; classes; colonies; and

An earlier version of this essay first appeared in the journal *Dissent* and was reprinted in the first edition of *Rethinking the Family.*

political regimes. Even the Russians have recently joined in this great swell. The profoundly moving ideal of equality will ultimately prevail, in some measure, where the structural bases for traditional dominance are weakened. The ancient bases for male dominance are no longer as secure as they once were, and male resistance to these pressures will weaken.

Males will stubbornly resist but reluctantly adjust, because women will continue to want more equality than they now enjoy and will be unhappy if they do not get it; because men on average will prefer that the women they care about be happy; because a majority of either sex will not find an adequate substitute for the other sex; and because neither will be able to build an alternative social system alone. When dominant classes or groups cannot rig the system as much in their favor as they once did, they will work within it just the same; to revise an old adage, if that is the only roulette wheel in town, they will play it even if it is honest and fair.

For many women, the very title of my essay is an exercise in banality, for there is no puzzle. To analyze the peculiar thoughtways of men seems unnecessary, since ultimately their resistance is that of dominant groups throughout history: they enjoy an exploitive position that yields them an unearned profit in money, power, and prestige. Why should they give it up?

That answer contains, of course, some part of the truth, but we shall move more effectively toward equality only if we grasp much more of the truth than that bitter view reveals. If it were completely true, then the great power of men would have made all societies male-vanity cultures, in which women are kept behind blank walls and forced to work at productive tasks only with their sisters, while men laze away their hours in parasitic pleasure. In fact, one can observe that the position of women varies a good deal by class, by society, and over time, and no one has succeeded in proving that those variations are only the result of men's exploitation.

Indeed, there are inherent socioeconomic contradictions in any attempt by males to create a fully exploitative set of material advantages for all males. Moreover, there are inherent emotional contradictions in any effort to achieve full domination in that intimate sphere.

As to the first contradiction, women—and men, too, in the same situation—who are powerless, slavish, and ignorant are most easily exploitable, and thus there are always some male pressures to place them in that position. Unfortunately, such women (or men) do not yield much surplus product. In fact, they do not produce much at all. Women who are freer and are more in command of productive skills, as in hunting and gathering societies and increasingly in modern industrial ones, produce far more, but they are also more resistant to exploitation or domination. Without understanding that powerful relationship, men have moved throughout history toward one or the other of these great choices, with their built-in disadvantages and advantages.

As to emotional ties, men would like to be lords of their castle and to be loved absolutely—if successful, this is the cheapest exploitative system—but in real life this is less likely to happen unless one loves in return. In that case what happens is what happens in real life: men care about the joys and sorrows of the women to whom they are attached. Mutual caring reduces the degree to which men are willing to exploit their wives, mothers, and sisters. More interesting, their caring also takes the form of wanting to prevent other men from exploiting these women when they are in the outside world. That is, men as individuals know that they are to be trusted, and so should have great power, but other men cannot be trusted, and therefore the laws should restrain such fellows.

These large sets of contrary tensions have some effect on even those contemporary men who do not believe that the present relations between men and women are unjust. Both sets, moreover, support the present trend toward greater equality. In short, men do resist, but these and other tensions prevent them from resisting as fully as they might otherwise, and not so much as a cynical interpretation of their private attitudes would expect. On the other hand, they do resist somewhat more strenuously than we should predict from their public assertion in favor of, for example, equal pay, or slogans like "liberty and justice for all."

Why is that resistance so strenuous? My attempt here to answer that question is necessarily limited. Even to present the latest data on the supposed psychological traits of males would require more space than is available here. I shall try to avoid the temptation of simply describing men's reactions to the women's movement, although I do plan to inform you of men's attitudes toward some aspects of equality. I shall try to avoid defending men, except to the extent that explaining them may be a defense. And, as is already obvious, I shall not assert that we are on the brink of a profound, sudden change in sex-role allocations in the direction of equality, for we must never underestimate the cunning or the staying power of those in charge. Finally, because we are all observers of men, it is unlikely that I can bring forward many findings that are entirely unknown to you. At best, I can suggest some fruitful, perhaps new, ways of looking at male roles. Within these limitations, I shall focus on the following themes:

1. As against the rather narrow definition of men's roles to be found in the current literature on the topic, I want to remind you of a much wider range of traditionally approved roles in this and other cultures.

2. As against the conspiracy theory of the oppression of women, I shall suggest a modest "sociology of the dominant group" to interpret men's behavior and thinking about male roles and thus offer some robust hypotheses about why they resist.

3. I shall point to two central areas of role behavior, occupations and domestic tasks, where change seems glacial at present and men's resistance strong.

4. As against those who feel that if utopia does not arrive with the next full moon, we should all despair, I shall point to some processes now occurring that are different from any in recorded history and that will continue to press toward more fundamental changes in men's social positions and roles in this as well as other countries of the world.

The Range of Sex Roles

Let me begin by reminding you of the standard sociological view about the allocation of sex roles. First, although it is agreed that we can, with only small error, divide the population into males and females, the biological differences between the two that might affect the distribution of sex roles—which sex is supposed to do which social tasks, which should have which rights—are much too small to determine the large differences in sex-role allocation within any given society or to explain the curious doctrines that serve to uphold it. Second, even if some differences would give an advantage to men (or women) in some tasks or achievements, the overlap in talent is so great that a large minority of women (or men)—perhaps even a majority—could do any task as well as could members of the other sex. Third, the biological differences are too fixed in anatomy and physiology to account for the wide diversity of sex-role allocation we observe when we compare different societies over time and cultures.

Consequently, most of the sex-role allocation must be explained by how we rear children, by the sexual division of labor, by the cultural definitions of what is appropriate to the sexes, and by the social pressures we put on the two sexes to keep each in its place. Since human beings created these role assignments, they can also change them. On the other hand, these roles afford large advantages to men (e.g., opportunity, range of choices, mobility, payoffs for what is accomplished, cultivation of skills, authority, and prestige) in this and every other society we know. Consequently, men are likely to resist large alterations in roles. They will do so even though they understand that in exchange for their privileges, they have to pay high costs in morbidity, mortality, and failure.[1] As a consequence of this fact about men's position, it can be supposed that they will resist unless their ability to rig the system in their favor is somehow reduced. It is my belief that this capacity is in fact being undermined somewhat, though not at a rapid rate.

A first glance at descriptions of the male role, especially as described in the literature on mass media, social stereotypes, family roles, and personality attributes, suggests that the male role is definite, narrow, and agreed upon. Males, we are told, are pressed into a specific mold. For example, "the male role prescribes that men be active, aggressive, competitive, . . . while the female role prescribes that women should be nurturant, warm, altruistic . . . and the like."[2] The male role requires the suppression of emotion: "the male role, as personally and socially defined, requires men to appear tough, objective, striving, achieving, unsentimental. . . . If he weeps, if he shows weakness, he will likely be viewed as unmanly." Or: "Men are programmed to be strong and 'aggressive.'"[3] Those statements were published some time ago, but the flood of books since then has only elaborated that description.

We are so accustomed to reading such descriptions that we almost believe them, unless we stop to ask, first, how many men do we actually know who carry out these social prescriptions (i.e., how many are emotionally anesthetized, aggressive, physically tough and daring, unwilling or unable to give nurturance to a child)? Second, and this is the test of a social role, do they lose their membership cards in the male fraternity if they fail in these respects? If socialization and social pressures are so all-powerful, where are all the John Wayne types in our society? Or, to ask a more searching question, how seriously should we take such sex-role prescriptions if so few men live up to them? The recent creation of male groups chanting around a campfire, searching for the lost primitive hunter within each bosom, suggests that our generation can not even play the role anymore without a great deal of coaching.

The key fact is not that many men do not live up to such prescriptions; that is obvious. They never did. Rather, many other qualities and performances have always been viewed as acceptable or admirable, and this is true even among boys, who are often thought to be strong supporters of sex stereotypes. The macho boy is admired, but so is the one who edits the school newspaper, who draws cartoons, or who is simply a warm friend. There are at least a handful of ways of being an admired professor. Indeed, a common feminist complaint against the present system is that women are much more narrowly confined in the ways they are permitted to be professors, or members of any occupation.

But we can go further. A much more profound observation is that oppressed groups are *typically* given narrow ranges of social roles, while dominant groups afford their members a far wider set of behavior patterns, each qualitatively different but each still accepted or esteemed in varying degrees. One of the privileges granted, or simply assumed, by ruling groups, is that they can indulge in a variety of eccentricities while still demanding and getting a fair measure of authority or prestige. Consider in this connection, to cite only one spectacular example, the crotchets and quirks cultivated by the English upper classes over the centuries.

Moreover, if we enlarge our vision to encompass other times and places, the range becomes even greater. We are not surprised to observe Latin American men embrace one another, Arab or Indian boys walk together hand in hand, or seminary students being gentle. The male role prescriptions that commonly appear in the literature do not describe correctly the male ideal in Jewish culture, which embodies a love of music, learning, and literature; an avoidance of physical violence; an acceptance of tears and sentiment, nurturance, and a sensitivity to others' feelings. In the South that I knew half a century ago, young rural boys were expected to nurture their younger siblings, and male-male relations were ideally expected to be tender, supporting, and expressed occasionally by embraces. Among my own kin, some fathers then kissed their school-age sons; among Greek Americans in New York City, that practice continues many decades later. Or, to consider England once more, let us remember the admired men of Elizabethan England. True enough, one ideal was the violent, daring Sir Francis Drake and the brawling poet Ben Jonson. But men also expressed themselves in kissing and embracing, writing love poems to one another, donning decorative (not to say gaudy and flamboyant) clothing, and studying flowers as well as the fiery heavens.

I assert, then, that men manage to be in charge of things in all societies but that their very control permits them to create a wide range of ideal male roles, with the consequence that large numbers of men, not just a few, can locate rewarding positions in the social structure. Thereby, too, they considerably narrow the options left for feminine sex roles. Feminists especially resent the narrowness of the feminine role in informal interaction, where they feel they are dealt with only as women, however this may be softened by personal warmth or affection.

We can recognize that general relationship in a widespread male view, echoed over the centuries, that males are people, individuals, while women are lumped together as an aggregate. Or, in more modern language: women have specific roles, a delimited number of parts to play, but men cannot be described so simply.

Nor is that peculiar male view contradicted by the complaint, again found in all major civilizations, that women are mysterious, unpredictable, moved by forces outside men's understanding, and not controllable. Even that master of psychodynamics Sigmund Freud expressed his bewilderment by asking, "What do women want?" Men have found their women difficult to understand for a simple reason: they have continued to try to think of them as a set of roles (above all else, mothers and wives), but in fact women do not fit these roles, neither now nor in the past. Some women were great fighting machines, not compliant; some were competitive and aggressive, not nurturant; many were incompetent or reluctant mothers. They have been queens and astronomers, moralists and nurturers, leaders of religious orders as well as corporations, and so on.

At any point, men could observe that women were ignoring or breaking out of their social molds, and men experienced that discrepancy as puzzling. However, it is only recently that many have faced the blunt fact that there is no feminine riddle at all: women are as complex as men are, and will always escape the confinements of any narrow set of roles.

The Sociology of Superordinates

That set of relationships is only part of the complex male view, and I want to continue with my sketch of the main elements in what may be called the "sociology of superordinates." That is, I believe there are some general principles or regularities to be found in the relationships between superordinates—here, the sex-class called males—and subordinates, in this instance women. Those regularities do not justify, but they do explain in some degree, the modern resistance of men to their social situation.[4] Here are some of them:

1. The observations made by either men or women about members of the other sex are limited and somewhat biased by what they are most interested in and by their lack of opportunity to observe behind the scenes of each others' lives.[5] However, far less of what men do is determined by women; what men do affects women much more. As a consequence, men are often simply less motivated to observe carefully many aspects of women's behavior and activity because women's behavior does not affect as much what men propose to do. By contrast, almost everything men do will affect what women *have* to do, and thus women are motivated to observe men's behavior as keenly as they can.

2. Since any given cohort of men know they did not create the system that gives them their advantages, they reject any charges that they conspired to dominate women.

3. Since men, like other dominants or superordinates, take for granted the system that gives them their status, they are not aware of how much the social structure, from attitude patterns to laws, pervasively yields small, cumulative, and eventually large advantages in most competitions. As a consequence, they assume that their greater accomplishments are actually the result of inborn superiority. Dominants are never satisfied with their rule unless they can also justify it.

4. As a corollary to this male view, when men weigh their situation, they are more aware of the burdens and responsibilities they bear than of their unearned advantages.

5. Superiors, and thus men, do not easily notice the talents or accomplishments of subordinates, and men have not in the past seen
much wisdom in giving women more opportunities for growth, for
women, in their view, are not capable of much anyway, especially in
the areas of men's special skills. As is obvious, this is a self-validating
process. Thus, few women have embarrassed men in the past by becoming superior in those areas. When they did, their superiority was
seen, and is often still seen, as an odd exception. As a consequence,
men see their superior position as a just one.

6. Men view even small losses of deference, advantages, or opportunities as large threats and losses. Their own gains, or their maintenance of old advantages, are not noticed as much.[6]

Although the male view is similar to that of superordinates generally, as the foregoing principles suggest, one cannot simply equate the
two. The structural position of males is different from that of superordinate groups, classes, ethnic populations, or castes. Males are,
first, not a group, but a social segment or a statistical aggregate
within the society. They share much of a common destiny, but they
share few if any group or collective goals (within small groups they
may be buddies, but not with all males). Second, males share with
certain women whatever gain or loss they experience as members of
high or low castes, ethnic groups, or classes. For example, women in
a ruling stratum share with their men a high social rank, deference
from the lower orders, and so on; men in a lowly Indian caste share
that rank with their women, too. In modern societies, men and
women in the same family are on a more or less equal basis with respect to "inheritance, educational opportunity (at least undergraduate), personal consumption of goods, most rights before the law, and
the love and responsibility of their children."[7] They are not fully
equal, to be sure, but much more equal than are members of very different castes or social classes.

Moreover, from the male view, women also enjoy certain exemp-
tions: "freedom from military conscription, whole or partial exemp-
tion from certain kinds of heavy work, preferential courtesies of
various kinds." Indeed, men have generally believed, on the whole,
that their own lot is the more difficult one.[8]

It is possible, however, that feminist cries of indignation have
touched their hearts, and those of women too, in recent years. Without giving a breakdown by gender, Gallup announced "a remarkable
shift of opinion" in 1989: almost half those polled asserted that men

"have a better life" than women, compared with only 32 percent in 1975. Almost certainly many women have been convinced, since nearly two-thirds of younger women felt that way.[9] Fifty-nine percent of a 1990 *Times Mirror* sample of women aged eighteen to twenty-four agreed, but so did 65 percent of the men.

As the student of polls will recognize, however, that shift has many sources. The judgment, of course, is about all men, whether single, married, or divorced, and includes all aspects of life. In a society in which people seem to be moving toward less personal long-term investments in the collectivity of the family, men are better able to reap the benefits of abandoning costly family obligations—and thus may be seen as "having a better life." I continue to be certain, however, that most men with families still believe that their lot is harder than that of most women.

Most important as a structural fact that prevents men from cunningly exploiting their superordinate status is that they do not live in communities, neighborhoods, or families set apart from women. Of course, some other social categories are not sequestered either, such as alcoholics, former mental patients, or the physically handicapped; but these are, as Goffman points out, "scattered somewhat haphazardly through the social structure." That is not so for men; like their women, they are allocated to households in a nonrandom way, for "law and custom allow only one to a household, but strongly encourage the presence of that one."[10]

A consequence of this important structural arrangement is that men and women are separated from their own sex by having a stake in the organization that gives each a set of different roles, or a different emphasis to similar roles. Women especially come to have a vested interest in the social unit that at the same time imposes inequalities on them. This coalition between the two individuals makes it difficult for members of one sex to join with large numbers of their own sex for purposes of defense against exploitation. This applies equally to men and women.

One neat consequence may be seen in the hundreds of family law provisions created over the centuries that seem to run at cross-purposes. Some gave more freedom to women in order to protect them from predatory or exploitative males (i.e., in a man's view, other men), and some took freedom away from women and put it in the hands of supposedly good and kindly men (i.e., himself). Or, in more recent times, the growing efforts of some fathers to press their daughters toward career competence so they will not be helpless when abandoned by their future husbands, against those same fathers' efforts to keep their daughters docile and dutiful toward their protecting fathers.

You will note that male views are not contradictory in such instances, even though their actions may be. In coalition with their women, they oppose the exploitative efforts of outside men; within the family unit, however, they see little need for such protections against themselves, for they are sure of their own goodheartedness and wisdom.

That men see themselves as bound in a coalition with their families and thus with their daughters and wives is the cause of much common male resistance to the women's movement, even while the same men feel anger at the unfair treatment their wives and daughters have experienced from other men. The failure of many women to understand that complex male view has led to much misunderstanding.

Responses of Superordinates to Rebellion

Because of similarities in their position and views, superordinates are likely to respond to rebellion in many common ways.[11] One of these is surprise. To be sure, contemporary men are not as startled as the men of the 1960s and 1970s, for then they were confronted by a sudden, large social movement. Even now, however, most men are startled at times when a woman friend is annoyed by a "trivial" denial of respect for her as a person. Most men simply do not remain steadily aware of the depth of resentment that many women have harbored, though sometimes, of course, it comes as a surprise to many women, too.

Second, men are also hurt, for they feel vaguely betrayed. They discover, or begin to suspect, that the previously contented or pleasant facade their women presented to them was false, that perhaps they were even manipulated to believe in that presentation of self. Because males view themselves as giving protection against anyone exploiting or hurting their women, they respond with anger to the hostility they encounter, to the discovery that they were deceived, and to the charge they have selfishly used the dominant position they feel they have rightfully earned.

A deeper, more complex source of male anger requires a few additional comments, for it relates to a central male role, that of job holder and breadwinner. Most men, but especially most men outside the privileged stratum of professionals and managers, see their job as not yielding much intrinsic satisfaction, not being fun in itself, but they pride themselves on the hard work and personal sacrifice they make as breadwinners. In the male view, men make a gift of all this to their wives and children.[12]

Now they are told that it was not a gift, and they have not earned any special deference for it. In fact, their wives earned what they received, and indeed nothing is owing. If the work was a sacrifice, they are told, so were all the services, comforts, and self-deprivations women provided. Whatever the justice of either claim, clearly if people think they are giving or sacrificing much to make gifts to someone over a period of time, and then they learn he or she feels the gifts were completely deserved, since the countergifts are asserted to have been as great and no gratitude or special debt was incurred, they are likely to be hurt or angry.[13]

I am reasonably certain about the processes I have just described. Let me go a step further and speculate that the male resentment is the greater because many fathers had already come to suspect that their children, especially in adolescence, were indifferent to those sacrifices, as well as to the values that justified them.[14] Sennett and Cobb made that observation in the 1970s, and I believe that paternal feeling of injustice is even stronger today. Thus, when women too begin to assert that men's gifts are not worth as much as men thought, the worth of the male is further denied.

Some Areas of Change and Nonchange

Although I have not heard specific complaints about it, I believe that the most important change in men's position, as they experience it, is a loss of centrality, a decline in the extent to which they are the center of attention. In our time, other superordinates have also suffered this loss: colonial rulers, monarchs and nobles, and U.S. whites both northern and southern, to name a few.

Boys and grown men have always taken for granted that what they were doing was more important than what the other sex was doing;

the action was where they were. Their women accepted that definition (though I am equally sure that older women in traditional societies everywhere have laughed, railed, and shaken their heads at the
childishness of men, too). Men occupied center stage, and women's
attention was focused on them. Although that position is at times
perilous, open to failure, it is also desirable, even at times heady.

Men are still there, of course, and will be there throughout our lifetime. Nevertheless, some changes are perceptible. The center of attention shifts to women more now than in the past. I believe that this
shift troubles men far more, and creates more of their resistance, than
the women's demand for equal opportunity and pay in employment.

The change is especially observable in informal relations, and men
who were involved with women in the liberation movement experienced it more often than other men did. Women find each other more
interesting than in the past, and focus more on what each other is
doing, for they are in fact doing more interesting things. Even when
they are not, their work occupies more of their attention, whether
they are professionals or factory workers. Being without a man for a
while does not seem to be so bereft a state as it once was. I also believe that this change affects men more now than at the time of the
suffragist movement, not only because more women now participate
in it but also because men were then more solidary and could rely on
more all-male organizations and clubs. Now they are more dependent on women for solace and intimacy, for typically they have fewer
close friends than women do.

As a side issue, let me note that the loss of centrality has its coun-
terpart among feminist women too, and its subtlety should be noted.
Such women now reject a certain type of traditional centrality they
used to experience, because its costs are too great. Most women
know the experience of being the center of attention: when they enter
a male group, even now, conversation changes in tone and subject.
They are likely to be the focus of comments, many of them pleasurable: affectionate teasing, compliments, warmth. However, these
comments put women into a special mold, the stereotyped female.
Their serious comments are less welcomed or applauded, or their
ideas are more likely to be treated as amusing. Their sexuality is emphasized. Now, after all these years of education about gender,
women are more likely to experience that kind of centrality as less

pleasant—in fact, it seems condescending—and they avoid it when they can. In turn, many men feel awkward in this new situation, for sometimes their repertory of social graces is now called boorish.

Although I have noted men's feelings of hurt and anger, I want to emphasize that I believe no backlash of any consequence has been occurring, and no trend toward more reactionary male attitudes exists. Briefly, there is a continuing attitude change on the part of both men and women, in favor of more equality. The frequent expressions of male objection, sometimes loosely called "backlash" in the popular press, can be attributed to two main sources: (1) the discovery, by some men (and women) who once paid lip service to the principle of equality, that they do not approve of its concrete application; and (2) active resistance by men and women who simply never approved of equality anyway and who have now begun to oppose it openly because it can no longer be seen as a trivial threat.

If the term is used to refer simply to any adverse reaction to the forward movement of women toward equality, then surely that is nothing new, and it would not be easy to claim the present adverse reaction is *more* intense than in the days when feminists were derided publicly as mere "bra-burners." This is not, of course, a denial of the setbacks and slowdowns of the 1980s.[15] I am merely asserting that little of it should be dignified by the term "backlash."

Some analysts would argue that the contemporary backlash has generated much political support for Reagan and Bush in their efforts to turn the clock back. However, in that context the notion should be recognized as having a concealed political goal: It asserts that "women have gone too far"—beyond equality, on into preference or privilege—and therefore people have been sensibly trying to reverse those excesses. Both presidents have been successful in making "redneckism" or anti-intellectualism respectable, and they have smiled on policies that aimed at putting women back in "their place." In turn, their policies have been given a patina of apparent scholarship through reports emanating from well-endowed conservative and right-wing think tanks. Nevertheless, general public opinion has not moved backward to join those groups.

It is not possible to summarize here all the various changes in public opinion about sex roles over the past generation, simply because pollsters have often failed to chart them, especially in the earlier years. Sometimes they did not capture certain social trends because

they did not consistently ask the same questions in successive decades. One unfortunate result is that one of the most fiercely debated
events of that period, the resurgence of the women's liberation movement that began in the 1960s, is not salient in the polls until rather
late in the 1970s.[16]

The single finding that seems solid is that the data show no backward or regressive trend in men's attitudes about women's progress
toward equality. The most often repeated question is not a profound
one: whether a respondent would vote for a qualified woman for
president. Favorable answers rose from about one-fourth of the men
in 1937 to two-thirds in 1971, and to 89 percent among men and
women combined in 1990. Another repeated question is whether a
married woman should work if she has a husband able to support
her, and here the answers of men and women combined rose from
18 percent in 1936 to 62 percent in 1975, and to 82 percent in 1990.
In contrast to these large changes, a sizeable majority favored equal
pay, in principle at least, as early as 1942, and later data report
no decrease.

In 1953, 21 percent of men said it made no difference whether
they worked for a man or woman, and that figure rose slightly to
32 percent in 1975.[17] By 1989, it had risen a bit more, to 41 percent.
Indeed, by that time, women were more inclined to prefer a man as
boss (54 percent) than men were (43 percent). Even by 1978 polls
showed that a large majority of the nation, both men and women,
was in favor of the enforcement of laws forbidding job discrimination
against women or discrimination in education; and most agreed that
more women should be elected to public office.[18] A plurality of only
about 40 percent had held such favorable opinions in 1970. On such
issues, men and women do not differ by much, while men's attitudes
in many polls have been somewhat more favorable toward equality.
Divisions of opinion are sharper along other lines: the young are in
favor more than the old, the more educated more favorable than
the less educated, city dwellers more than rural people, Blacks more
than whites.

Whatever the differences, clearly no substantial amount of male
backlash has appeared. A *Times Mirror* poll of 1990 reported that
nearly three-fourths of the men agreed or strongly agreed "with the
goals of the women's movement."[19] Through men's eyes, at least the
principle of equality seems more acceptable than in the past. Their

resistance is not set against that abstract idea—modest progress, to be sure, but progress nonetheless.

Domestic Duties and Jobs

So far, the opinion data give some small cause for optimism. Nevertheless, all announcements of the imminent arrival of utopias are premature. Although men's approval of more equality for women has risen, the record in two major areas of men's roles—the spheres of home and occupation—gives some reason for optimism, but little for rejoicing. Here we can be brief, for though voluminous and complex data exist, the main conclusions can easily be summarized.[20] Changes have occurred, but they are not great if we consider the society as a whole and focus on changes in behavior. In short, men have gained great credit (in conformity with their higher ranking) for a few modest steps toward equality.

Let us consider first the domestic role of men. The many complex studies done during the past decade have at least shown how difficult it is to pin down the causes of the present division of labor in the home. Thus, a simple summary is not adequate, but I note some salient findings here.

Women who work full-time have reduced the hours they spend on household tasks—in some studies, by almost half, while the reduction is substantial even if only routine tasks are included.[21] Husbands do not do much more housework if their wives are employed full time; nevertheless, over time men have increased their contribution (especially in child care), although the increase must be measured by a few minutes per day. White men and men with high incomes are least likely to increase their contribution. About half of both husbands and wives believe they ought to share equally; four-fifths think this of child care.[22] This represents a substantial change among wives, since until the end of the 1970s only about one-fourth of wives stated that they thought their husbands should work more, while the vanguard of opinion was led by the young, the educated, and African Americans.[23]

I have sometimes suggested that men generally decide that if they must contribute more equally to housework, then they begin to feel the seduction of doing it in a quicker, more slovenly fashion. One study of a highly educated sample suggests this relationship: both spouses at least express more satisfaction when the division is equal, but the two want different things. The man wants to spend only a few hours in household work, while the woman wants the traditional chores (laundry, shopping, cooking) to be shared.[24] In the United States, as in other counties, men are quicker to express support for equality in that sphere than actually to practice it. They may be wise in doing so, for that is surely less costly, at least for the present.

Of course, there are some differences. If a child two years or younger is in the house, the father does more, especially in child care. Better-educated husbands do a bit more, and so do younger husbands. But the indisputable fact is that men's domestic contribution does not change much whether or not they work, and whether or not their wives work.

With reference to the second large area of men's roles, holding jobs, we observe two further general principles of the relations between superordinates and those at lesser ranks. One is that men do not, in general, feel threatened by competition from women if they believe that the competition is fair and that women do not have an inside track. (To be sure, against overwhelming evidence, many do believe women enjoy that preference, while many whites believe that Blacks also have the inside track.) Men still feel that they are superior and will do better if given the chance. Since no society has actually tried the radical notion of genuinely fair competition, they have little reason to fear as yet. Except in a few occupations, they have lost very little ground. Women's position (by some measures) did improve during the 1970s, but changed very little in the 1980s.[25]

The second general principle of superordination noted here is that those who hold advantaged positions in the social structure (men, in this case) can perceive or observe that they are being flooded by people they consider their inferiors—women, Blacks, or the lower classes—while the massive statistical fact is that only a few such people are rising by much. There are several causes of this seeming paradox.

First, the new arrivals are more visible, by being different from those who have held the jobs up to this time. The second cause is our perception of relative numbers. Since there are far fewer positions at higher job levels, only a few new arrivals constitute a fair-size minority of the total at that level. Third, the mass media emphasize the hiring of women in jobs that seem not to be traditional for them, for that is considered news. Men's structural position, then, causes them to perceive radical change here even when little has taken place, and they resist it.

Nevertheless, the general conclusion does not change much. There is progress, but it is not at all clear-cut. After all, as long as the entrance of a few women into good jobs is news, the reality is less rosy than one might hope. Here are a few details:

—The number of businesses owned by women increased by 63 percent between 1982 and 1987.[26]

—The percentage of physicians who were women rose to 20 percent by 1988, an increase of two-thirds from 1980.

—Women made almost no inroads into the skilled crafts.

—Women made up almost one-half of all bakers, but nearly all simply put the dough through the final process in retail stores.

—As buyers and as administrators or managers in education, auditing, personnel, and training, women occupied about one-half of the jobs by 1988. However, they made up only about 3 percent of the top executives in large U.S. companies by 1991, almost no change from 1980. In general, their earnings in this group of managerial jobs were about two-thirds of male salaries.[27]

—As bus drivers and bartenders, women had almost half of the jobs.

—Over the decade, women's salaries rose; instead of making two-thirds of men's wages, they were making 72 percent.

The strongest variable that determines the lower wages of women is occupational segregation by sex, and that changed very little in the 1980s.[28] The blunt fact is that women have been able to enter a given occupation easily only if men no longer defend that territory. Or, more dramatically, the common pattern of "feminization" in most occupations is simple: They are rising on an elevator in a crumbling building. The job itself is being downgraded. They get better wages than other women, perhaps, but lower wages than men once made in those occupations.

Although the mass figures are correct, we need not discount all our daily observation either. We do see women entering formerly masculine jobs, from garbage collecting to corporate management. That helps undermine sex stereotypes and thereby becomes a force against inequality. Although occupational segregation continues to be strong, it did decline in most professions (e.g., engineering, dentistry, science, law, medicine). That is, the percentage of women in those professions did rise. Generally they doubled or trebled in the period 1970–88.[29] Of course, the absolute percentages of women in such professions remain modest (4–22 percent), because in occupations where almost everyone was once male, it is not possible to recruit, train, and hire enough women to achieve equality within even a generation. Still, the trend seems clear.

A secondary effect of these increasing numbers should be noted. Percentages are important, but so are absolute numbers. When women lawyers increase from about seven thousand to more than a hundred thousand, they become a much larger social force, even though they still form no more than about 22 percent of the total occupation. When women medical students, while remaining a minority in their classes, increase in number so that they can form committees, petition administrators, or give solidarity to one another against any traditional masculine badgering and disesteem, they greatly increase their influence on discriminatory attitudes and behavior. That is, as their rise in numbers permits the formation of real groups in any occupation, their power mounts faster (except at the very start) than the numbers or the percentages. Thus, changes occur even when the percentage of the occupation made up of women is not really large.

Bases of Present Changes

Most large-scale, objective measures of men's roles show little change over the past decade, but men do feel now and then that their position is in question, and their security somewhat fragile. I believe they are right, for they sense a set of forces that lie deeper and are more powerful than the day-to-day negotiation and renegotiation of advantage among individual husbands and wives, fathers and children, or bosses and those who work for them. Men are troubled by this new situation.

The conditions we live in are different from those of any earlier civilization, and they give less support to men's claims of superiority than perhaps any other historical era. When these conditions weaken that support, men can rely only on previous tradition, on power, or on their attempts to socialize their children to shore up their faltering advantages. Such rhetoric is not likely to be successful against the new objective conditions and the claims of aggrieved women. Thus, men are correct when they feel they are losing some of their privileges, even if many continue to smile at the rhetoric of the women's liberation movement.

The new conditions can be listed concretely, but I shall also give you a theoretical formulation of the process. Concretely, because of the increased use of various mechanical gadgets and devices, fewer tasks require much strength. As to those that still require strength, most men cannot do them either. Women can now do more household tasks that men once felt only they could do, and still more tasks are done by repair specialists called in to do them. With the development of modern warfare, there are few if any important combat activities that only men can do. Even now, their "auxiliary" tasks take them in and around battle zones as a matter of course. Women are much better educated than before.

With each passing year, psychological and sociological research reduces the areas in which men are reported to excel over women and discloses far more overlap in talents, so that even when males still seem to have an advantage, it is but slight. It is also becoming more widely understood that the top posts in government and business are not best filled by the stereotypical aggressive male but by the people, male or female, who are sensitive to others' needs, adept at obtaining cooperation, and skilled in social relations. Indeed, had male management in a number of U.S. industries followed that truth over the past decade, their failure to meet Japanese competition would surely have been less. Finally, in one sphere after another, the number of women who try to achieve rises, and so does the number who succeed.

Although the pressure of new laws has its direct effect on these conditions, the laws themselves arise from an awareness of the foregoing forces. Phrased in more theoretical terms, the underlying shift is toward the decreasing marginal utility of males, and this I suspect is the main source of men's resistance to women's liberation. That is, fewer people believe that what the male does is indispensable, is nonsubstitutable, or adds such a special value to any endeavor that it justifies his extra "price" or reward. In past wars, for example, males enjoyed a very high value not only because it was felt that they could do the job better than women but also because they might well make the key or marginal difference between being conquered and remaining free. In many societies, their marginal utility came from their contribution of animal protein through hunting. As revolutionary heroes, explorers, hunters, warriors, and daring capitalist entrepreneurs, men felt, and doubtless their women did too, that their contribution was beyond anything women could do. Without question, this would not be true of all men, but it would have been true of men as a distinct group. Men thereby earned extra privileges of rank, authority, and creature services.

It is not then as individuals, as persons, that males will be deemed less worthy in the future or their contributions less needed. Rather, they will be seen as having no claims to extra rewards solely because they are members of the male sex-class. This is part of a still broader trend of our generation, which will also increasingly deny that being white or upper-class produces a marginally superior result and thus justifies extra privileges.

The relations of individuals are subject to continuous renegotiation as people try to gain or keep advantages or cast off burdens. They fail or succeed in part because one or the other person has special resources or deficits that are unique to that individual. Over the long run, however, the outcome of those negotiations depends on the deeper social forces I have been describing, which ultimately determine which qualities or performances are more or less valued.

Men now perceive that they may be losing some of their advantages and that more aspects of their social roles are subject to public challenge and renegotiation than in the past. They resist these changes, and we can suppose they will continue to do so. In all such changes, there are gains and losses. Commonly, when people at lower social ranks gain freedom, those at higher ranks lose some power or centrality. When those at the lower ranks also lose some protection, some support, those at the higher ranks lose some of the burden of responsibility. It is also true that the care or help given by any dominant group in the past was never as much as their members believed, and their loss in political power or economic rule was never as great as they feared.

On the other hand, I know of no instance when a group or social stratum gained its freedom or moved toward more respect and then its members decided that they did not want it. Therefore, although men will not joyfully give up their rank, in spite of its burdens, neither will women decide that they would like to get back the older feminine privileges, accompanied by the lack of respect and material rewards that went with those courtesies.

I believe that men perceive their roles as being under threat in a world that is different from any in the past. No society has yet come even close to equality between the sexes, but the modern social forces described here did not exist before, either. At the most cautious, we must concede that the conditions favoring a trend toward more equality are more favorable than at any previous time in history. If we have little reason to conclude that equality is at hand, let us at least rejoice that we are still marching in the right direction.

Notes

1. Herbert Goldberg, *The Hazards of Being Male* (New York: Nash, 1976), and Patricia C. Sexton, *The Feminized Male: Classrooms, White Collars, and the Decline of Manliness* (New York: Random House, 1969). On the recognition of disadvantages, see J. S. Chafetz, *Masculine/Feminine or Human?* (Itasca, Ill.: Peacock, 1974), 56 ff.

2. Joseph H. Pleck, "The Psychology of Sex Roles: Traditional and New Views," in *Women and Men: Changing Roles, Relationships, and Perceptions*, ed. Libby A. Cater and Anne F. Scott (New York: Aspen Institute for Humanistic Studies, 1976), 182. Pleck has carried out the most extensive research on male roles, and I am indebted to him for special help in this inquiry.

3. Sidney M. Jourard, "Some Lethal Aspects of the Male Role," in *Men and Masculinity*, ed. Joseph H. Pleck and Jack Sawyer (Englewood Cliffs, N.J.: Prentice-Hall, 1974), 22, and Irving London, "Frigidity, Sensitivity, and Sexual Roles," in *Men and Masculinity*, ed. Pleck and Sawyer, 42. See also the summary of such traits in I. K. Braverman et al., "Sex-Role Stereotypes: A Current Appraisal," in *Women and Achievement*, ed. Martha T. S. Mednick, S. S. Tangri, and Lois W. Hoffman (New York: Wiley, 1974), 32–47.

4. Robert Bierstedt's "The Sociology of the Majority," in his *Power and Progress* (New York: McGraw-Hill, 1974), 199–220, does not state these principles, but I was led to them by thinking about his analysis.

5. Robert K. Merton, in "The Perspectives of Insiders and Outsiders," in his *The Sociology of Science* (Chicago: University of Chicago Press, 1973), 99–136, has analyzed this view in some detail.

6. This general pattern is noted at various points in my monograph *The Celebration of Heroes: Prestige as a Social Control System* (Berkeley and Los Angeles: University of California Press, 1979).

7. Erving Goffman, "The Arrangement between the Sexes," *Theory and Society* 4 (1977): 307.

8. Hazel Erskine, "The Polls: Women's Roles," *Public Opinion Quarterly* 35 (Summer 1971).

9. Linda DeStefano and Diane Colasanto, Gallup Organization press release, 5 February 1989. For the *Times Mirror* sample, see Times Mirror Center for the People and the Press, press release, September 1990, 5.

10. Goffman, "Arrangement between the Sexes," 308.

11. A simple analysis of these responses is presented in William J. Goode, *Principles of Sociology* (New York: McGraw-Hill, 1977), 359 ff.

12. See Joseph H. Pleck, "The Power of Men," in *Women and Men: The Consequences of Power*, ed. Dana V. Hiller and R. Sheets (Cincinnati: Office of Women's Studies, University of Cincinnati, 1977), 20. See also Colin Bell and Howard Newby, "Husbands and Wives: The Dynamic of the Deferential Dialectic," in *Dependence and Exploitation in Work and Marriage*, ed. Diana L. Barker and Sheila Allen (London: Longman, 1976), 162–63, as well as Richard Sennett and Jonathan Cobb, *The Hidden Injuries of Class* (New York: Vintage Books, 1973), 125. On the satisfaction of work, see Daniel Yankelovich, "The Meaning of Work," in *The Worker and the Job*, ed. Jerome Rosow (Englewood Cliffs, N.J.: Prentice-Hall, 1974), 19–49. Men now recognize that they cannot easily use this rhetoric in family arguments, but I suspect they still believe it.

13. Whatever other sacrifices women want from men, until recently a large majority did not believe men should do more housework. On this matter, see Joseph H. Pleck, *Working Wives, Working Husbands* (Newbury Park, Calif.: Sage, 1985). In the mid-1970s only about one-fourth of wives agreed with such a proposal.

14. Sennett and Cobb, *Hidden Injuries of Class*, 125.

15. Susan Faludi, *Backlash: The Undeclared War against American Women* (New York: Crown, 1991), also documents in some detail many of the different efforts made during the 1980s to put women "back in their place," but little of what Faludi describes is truly "backlash." Leaving aside the innocents whom she attacks, most of these efforts were carried out by people who never thought women should have left "their" place to begin with.

16. To date, the most complete published summary for that period is that by Erskine ("The Polls," 275–91). From the late 1970s onward, however, the documentation is much fuller.

17. Stephanie Greene, "Attitudes toward Working Women Have 'a Long Way to Go,' " Gallup Opinion Poll, March 1976, 33. A wide variety of related questions are to be found in *Public Opinion Quarterly* 53 (1989): 265–76.

18. Harris Survey, 16 February 1978; see also Harris Survey, 11 December 1975.

19. Time Mirror Center for the People and the Press, press release, September 1990, 10.

20. By now, the research data on household tasks are voluminous, their conclusions complex, and by the time they are published they may be somewhat dated. For comparisons with other countries, see Jonathan Gershuny and John P. Robinson, "Historical Changes in the Household Division of Labor," *Demography* 25 (1988): 537–52. See also Linda Thompson and Alexis J. Walker, "Gender in Families: Women and Men in Marriage, Work, and Parenthood," *Journal of Marriage and the Family* 51 (1989): 845–71; Mary H. Benin and Joan Agostinelli, "Husbands' and Wives' Satisfaction with the Division of Labor," *Journal of Marriage and the Family* 50 (1988): 349–61; and Beth A. Shelton, "The Distribution of Household Tasks," *Journal of Family Issues* 11 (1990): 115–35. Joseph Pleck was a leader in these studies during the 1970s and 1980s.

21. Shelton, "Distribution of Household Tasks," table 2, p. 124; Gershuny and Robinson, "Historical Changes," 550.

22. Thompson and Walker, "Gender in Families," 857.

23. Arland Thornton and Deborah S. Freedman, "Changes in the Sex Role Attitudes of Women, 1962–1977," *American Sociological Review* 44 (1979): 833.

24. Benin and Agostinelli, "Husbands' and Wives' Satisfaction," 360.

25. For an excellent analysis of the many complex processes involved in these changes, see Barbara F. Reskin and Patricia A. Roos, *Job Queues, Gender Queues* (Philadelphia: Temple University Press, 1990).

26. U.S. Department of Commerce, Bureau of the Census, *Statistical Abstract of the United States, 1991* (Washington, D.C.: GPO, 1992).

27. These and other related data were published in *U.S. News and World Report,* 17 June 1991, from a study of the "glass ceiling" conducted for the Department of Labor but not officially issued.

28. Reskin and Roos, *Job Queues, Gender Queues,* tables I.7, I.8. See especially the case studies of changes in occupational segregation in ibid., part 2. In the usual case of "desegregation," women move into men's jobs (bartending, in-store baking, bus driving, banking) when those jobs are downgraded, usually technologically, so that the wages no longer attract men. Most of the expansion of women's jobs has occurred in "female" jobs, service jobs at lower levels.

29. Ibid., 19. On the earlier period, see also Victor R. Fuchs, "A Note on Sex Segregation in Professional Occupations," *Explorations in Economic Research* 2, no. 1 (Winter 1975): 105–11.

Index